Eating Disorders
SOURCEBOOK

Fourth Edition

Fourth Edition

Eating Disorders

SOURCEBOOK

*Basic Consumer Health Information about
Anorexia Nervosa, Bulimia Nervosa, Binge Eating Disorder,
Orthorexia, and Other Eating Disorders and Related
Concerns, Such as Compulsive Exercise, Female Athlete
Triad, and Body Dysmorphic Disorder, including Details
about Risk Factors, Warning Signs, Media Influence,
Adverse Health Effects, Methods of Prevention,
Treatment Options, and the Recovery Process*

*Along with Suggestions for Maintaining a Healthy Weight,
Improving Self-Esteem, and Promoting a Positive Body
Image, a Glossary of Related Terms, and a Directory of
Resources for More Information*

OMNIGRAPHICS

615 Griswold, Ste. 901, Detroit, MI 48226

Bibliographic Note

Because this page cannot legibly accommodate all the copyright notices, the Bibliographic Note portion of the Preface constitutes an extension of the copyright notice.

* * *

Omnigraphics, Inc.

Editorial Services provided by Omnigraphics, Inc.,
a division of Relevant Information, LLC

Keith Jones, *Managing Editor*

* * *

Library of Congress Cataloging-in-Publication Data

Names: Omnigraphics, Inc., issuing body.

Eating disorders sourcebook: basic consumer health information about anorexia nervosa, bulimia nervosa, binge eating disorder, and other eating disorders and related concerns, such as compulsive exercise, female athlete triad, and body dysmorphic disorder, including details about risk factors, warning signs, adverse health effects, methods of prevention, treatment options, and the recovery process; along with suggestions for maintaining a healthy weight, improving self-esteem, and promoting a positive body image, a glossary of related terms, and a directory of resources for more information.

Description: Fourth edition. | Detroit, MI: Omnigraphics, Inc., [2016] | Series: Health reference series | Includes bibliographical references and index.

Identifiers: LCCN 2016001175 (print) | LCCN 2016001747 (ebook) | ISBN 9780780814660 (hardcover: alk. paper) | ISBN 9780780814653 (ebook) Subjects: LCSH: Eating disorders. | Consumer education.

Classification: LCC RC552.E18 E287 2016 (print) | LCC RC552.E18 (ebook) | DDC 616.85/26--dc23

Table of Contents

Part II: Risk Factors for Eating Disorders

Part III: Causes of Eating Disorders

Part VI: Preventing Eating Disorders and Achieving a Healthy Weight

Preface

About This Book

According to the National Eating Disorders Association, 20 million women and 10 million men in the United States suffer from a clinically significant eating disorder at some time in their life. Suicide, depression, and severe anxiety are common, and eating disorders can lead to major medical complications, including electrolyte imbalance, cognitive impairment, osteoporosis, infertility, or even death. Furthermore, although eating disorders can be successfully treated—even to complete remission—estimates suggest that only one in ten people with an eating disorder receives treatment.

Eating Disorders Sourcebook, Fourth Edition, provides basic consumer health information about anorexia nervosa, bulimia nervosa, binge eating disorder, and other eating disorders and related concerns, such as female athlete triad, the abuse of laxatives and diet pills, and rumination disorder. It explains the factors that put people at risk for developing eating disorders, and it discusses their adverse health affects and the methods used to prevent, diagnose, and treat them. Tips for determining a healthy weight and promoting self-esteem and a positive body image are also included, along with guidelines for safe weight loss and exercise, and a glossary of terms related to eating disorders, and a list of resources for further information.

How to Use This Book

This book is divided into parts and chapters. Parts focus on broad areas of interest. Chapters are devoted to single topics within a part.

Part I: What Are Eating Disorders? defines eating disorders and explains how they differ from disordered and normal eating patterns. It describes the most common types of eating disorders, as well as other related disorders that often accompany them, such as body dysmorphic disorder and compulsive exercising. The part also examines popular eating disorder myths.

Part II: Risk Factors for Eating Disorders discusses the potential risk factors for eating disorders, and the specific populations most at risk for eating disorders. It also describes other problems that frequently co-occur with eating disorders.

Part III: Causes of Eating Disorders explains what is known about the biological factors and genetic predispositions that may lead to the development of certain eating disorders. Environmental factors that can cause eating disorders are described, as well as the effect of the media in distorting body image and encouraging these disorders.

Part IV: Medical Complications of Eating Disorders provides information about the adverse—and sometimes fatal—physical health effects of eating disorders, including infertility, oral health problems, and osteoporosis.

Part V: Recognizing and Treating Eating Disorders describes the physiological and behavioral warning signs of an eating disorder and provides suggestions for confronting a person with an eating disorder. It explains the treatment process, from determining the level of care needed to choosing a treatment facility. It also details the different treatment options available, including medications, psychotherapeutic approaches, and insurance coverage for such treatments. Issues common to the recovery process such as overcoming negative thoughts and preventing relapse are also discussed.

Part VI: Preventing Eating Disorders and Achieving a Healthy Weight offers guidelines for the prevention of eating disorders, including tips for promoting self-esteem and a positive body image. It explains how people can determine a medically optimal weight for themselves and offers suggestions for safe weight gain, loss, and maintenance. Nutrition guidelines and suggestions for exercising safely are also included.

Part VII: Additional Help and Information includes a glossary of terms related to eating disorders and a directory of resources for additional help and support.

Bibliographic Note

This volume contains documents and excerpts from the following U.S. government agencies and publications: Centers for Disease Control and Prevention (CDC); Federal Trade Commission (FTC); Genetic and Rare Diseases Information Center (GARD); Genetics Home Reference (GHR); Military Health System (MHS); National Heart, Lung, and Blood Institute (NHLBI); National Institute of Arthritis and Musculoskeletal and Skin Diseases (NIAMS); National Institute of Child Health and Human Development (NICHD); National Institute of Diabetes and Digestive and Kidney Diseases (NIDDK); National Institute of Mental Health (NIMH); National Institute of Neurological Disorders and Stroke (NINDS); National Institute on Aging (NIA); National Institutes of Health (NIH); Office of Dietary Supplements (ODS); Office of Disease Prevention and Health Promotion (ODPHP); Office on Women's Health (OWH); Substance Abuse and Mental Health Services Administration (SAMHSA); U.S. Food and Drug Administration (FDA); U.S. Department of Agriculture (USDA); U.S. Department of Health and Human Services (HHS); U.S. Department of Veterans Affairs (VA); and WhiteHouse.gov.

In addition, this volume contains copyrighted documents from the following organizations and publications: Eating Disorders Victoria; National Eating Disorders Association; and The Nemours Foundation.

It may also contain original material produced by Omnigraphics, Inc. and reviewed by medical consultants.

About the Health Reference Series

The *Health Reference Series* is designed to provide basic medical information for patients, families, caregivers, and the general public. Each volume takes a particular topic and provides comprehensive coverage. This is especially important for people who may be dealing with a newly diagnosed disease or a chronic disorder in themselves or in a family member. People looking for preventive guidance, information about disease warning signs, medical statistics, and risk factors for health problems will also find answers to their questions in the *Health Reference Series*. The *Series*, however, is not intended to serve as a tool for diagnosing illness, in prescribing treatments, or as a substitute for the physician/patient relationship. All people concerned about medical symptoms or the possibility of disease are encouraged to seek professional care from an appropriate health care provider.

A Note about Spelling and Style

Health Reference Series editors use *Stedman's Medical Dictionary* as an authority for questions related to the spelling of medical terms and the *Chicago Manual of Style* for questions related to grammatical structures, punctuation, and other editorial concerns. Consistent adherence is not always possible, however, because the individual volumes within the *Series* include many documents from a wide variety of different producers, and the editor's primary goal is to present material from each source as accurately as is possible. This sometimes means that information in different chapters or sections may follow other guidelines and alternate spelling authorities.

Medical Review

Omnigraphics contracts with a team of qualified, senior medical professionals who serve as medical consultants for the *Health Reference Series*. As necessary, medical consultants review reprinted and originally written material for currency and accuracy. Citations including the phrase, "Reviewed (month, year)" indicate material reviewed by this team. Medical consultation services are provided to the *Health Reference Series* editors by:

Dr. Vijayalakshmi, MBBS, DGO, MD
Dr. Senthil Selvan, MBBS, DCH, MD
Dr. K. Sivanandham, MBBS, DCH, MS (Research), PhD

Our Advisory Board

We would like to thank the following board members for providing initial guidance on the development of this series:

- Dr. Lynda Baker, Associate Professor of Library and Information Science, Wayne State University, Detroit, MI

- Nancy Bulgarelli, William Beaumont Hospital Library, Royal Oak, MI

- Karen Imarisio, Bloomfield Township Public Library, Bloomfield Township, MI

- Karen Morgan, Mardigian Library, University of Michigan-Dearborn, Dearborn, MI

- Rosemary Orlando, St. Clair Shores Public Library, St. Clair Shores, MI

Health Reference Series *Update Policy*

The inaugural book in the *Health Reference Series* was the first edition of *Cancer Sourcebook* published in 1989. Since then, the *Series* has been enthusiastically received by librarians and in the medical community. In order to maintain the standard of providing high-quality health information for the layperson the editorial staff at Omnigraphics felt it was necessary to implement a policy of updating volumes when warranted.

Medical researchers have been making tremendous strides, and it is the purpose of the *Health Reference Series* to stay current with the most recent advances. Each decision to update a volume is made on an individual basis. Some of the considerations include how much new information is available and the feedback we receive from people who use the books. If there is a topic you would like to see added to the update list, or an area of medical concern you feel has not been adequately addressed, please write to:

Managing Editor
Health Reference Series
Omnigraphics, Inc.
615 Griswold, Ste. 901
Detroit, MI 48226

Part One

What Are Eating Disorders?

Chapter 1

Eating Disorders: An Overview

Chapter Contents

Section 1.1

What Is an Eating Disorder?

This section contains text excerpted from the following sources:
Text beginning with the heading "What Is an Eating Disorder?" is
excerpted from "Eating Disorders Awareness," U.S. Department
of Veterans Affairs (VA), March 7, 2013; Text under the heading
"Spotlight on Eating Disorders" is excerpted from "Director's Blog:
Spotlight on Eating Disorders," National Institute of Mental Health
(NIMH), February 24, 2012. Reviewed March 2016; Text under
the heading "Key Messages on Eating Disorders" is excerpted from
"Eating Disorders," National Institute of Mental Health (NIMH),
July 23, 2011. Reviewed March 2016.

What Is an Eating Disorder?

About 20 million women and 10 million men suffer from an eating
disorder at some point in their life. An eating disorder is an abnormal disturbance of eating habits that interferes with one's life. It
may involve restricting food consumption, or it may include eating
extremely large amounts of food.

A person with an eating disorder may have started out just eating
smaller or larger amounts of food, but at some point, the urge to eat
less or more spiraled out of control. Severe distress or concern about
body weight or shape may also signal an eating disorder. Common
eating disorders include anorexia nervosa, bulimia nervosa, and binge
eating disorder. If left untreated, eating disorders can create health
concerns and become life threatening.

Causes of Eating Disorder

Eating disorders affect all demographics of people. Although they
are thought to be commonly associated with women and young teens,
eating disorders are also prevalent in men and into adulthood. There
is not one conclusive cause of eating disorders; however, factors that
influence eating disorders include:

- Genetics: Eating disorders commonly run in families

- Individuals suffering from posttraumatic stress disorder (PTSD) or Military Sexual Trauma
- Lack of coping skills
- Individuals with morbid obesity
- Those who suffer from substance or alcohol abuse
- Feelings of lack of control in life

Everyone responds differently to stressful situations in their lives. Some people are emotional eaters, while others experience trouble eating when they are upset. Sufferers from eating disorders are 4 times more common to suffer from alcohol and other substance abuse disorders. If these issues go untreated, they could result in serious health problems.

Four Main Categories of Eating Disorders

1. **Anorexia nervosa**—Anorexia nervosa is characterized by extreme thinness and an intense fear of gaining weight. Symptoms include thinning of bones, brittle hair, low blood pressure and chronic fatigue.

2. **Bulimia nervosa**—This involves the consumption of large amounts of food in one setting, and then compensating for the excessive food intake though laxatives, vomiting, fasting or excessive exercise.

3. **Binge eating disorders**—This is characterized by eating large amounts of food in a short time period. The individuals usually feels out of control and as though they cannot stop eating.

4. **Eating disorder not otherwise specified (EDNOS)**—This is a classification for eating disorders that do not meet the criteria of anorexia nervosa or bulimia nervosa; however, it involves a combination of multiple symptoms of eating disorders. It is the most common diagnosis of eating disorder among individuals seeking treatment.

Spotlight on Eating Disorders

What is the most fatal mental disorder? The answer, which may surprise you, is anorexia nervosa. It has an estimated mortality rate of around 10 percent. What is the cause of this high rate of mortality? The answer is complicated. While many young women and men with this disorder die from starvation and metabolic collapse, others die of suicide, which is much more common in women with anorexia than most other mental disorders.

The last week of February is National Eating Disorders Awareness Week. Eating disorders include anorexia nervosa, bulimia nervosa, and binge eating disorder. We often hear about the epidemic of obesity and the health consequences of overeating, but the perils of anorexia and bulimia are less recognized. Here are some little known facts about eating disorders, all gleaned from research funded by National Institute of Mental Health (NIMH).

First, the demographics of eating disorders may be changing. The National Co-Morbidity Study-Replication, an NIMH-funded population-based epidemiologic study, struggled with estimating the prevalence of eating disorders because the researchers found that many respondents were reluctant to admit to these syndromes during a structured interview. Nevertheless, the study reported that these disorders are more common in women. The lifetime rate for anorexia nervosa among women was estimated at 0.9 percent compared to 0.3 percent among men. The lifetime rate among women for bulimia nervosa was 0.5 percent compared to 0.1 percent among men. And the lifetime rate among women for binge eating disorder was 3.5 compared to 2 percent among men. Almost certainly, these numbers are under-estimates. In addition, contrary to the traditional stereotype that eating disorders mostly affect white upper middle class females, the ethnic makeup of those contending with eating disorders may be changing.

Second, the treatments for eating disorders are changing. Traditionally, anorexia in adolescents has been viewed as a "family systems" problem requiring a "parentectomy"—exclusion of the parents or caregivers from the teen's treatment plan. But research at the Maudsley Hospital in London, which was replicated in the United States, has shown that outcomes appear much better if parents are empowered and included, rather than excluded, from the treatment. In fact, a carefully controlled trial evaluating the effectiveness of a family-based treatment approach found 50 percent of participants continued to experience full remission one year after the end of therapy. Whether this same approach will work for older patients is not clear, but research is currently underway that incorporates families in the treatment of adults with anorexia. The proof of principle is important: family involvement can be critical for recovery.

It is encouraging to have new and effective treatments, but families report that a teenager who has received insurance coverage for intensive care for a metabolic crisis could not get coverage for the underlying eating disorder. While the dynamic duo of mental health parity and health reform may lead to a solution, coverage of treatment for eating disorders will ultimately differ by state. That is all the more reason to remember—at least one week of the year—that eating disorders are serious, sometimes fatal, disorders.

Key Messages on Eating Disorders

- Eating disorders do not discriminate, they affect males and females, young and old.

- You can't tell by someone's size whether they have an eating disorder.

- Families do not cause eating disorders—they can be patient's best allies in treatment.

- Both genetic and environmental factors influence eating disorders.

- Eating disorders are serious biologically-influenced mental illnesses, not passing fads.

- Complete recovery is possible.

Section 1.2

The Main Categories of Eating Disorders

What Is Anorexia Nervosa?

Anorexia nervosa, often called anorexia, is a very dangerous eating disorder. In fact, it is more deadly than any other mental health condition.

Someone with anorexia often thinks about food and limits what they eat very strictly. They may feel like they are getting control over their life by controlling their eating. But the truth is that the disease is in control.

Eating disorders can start at any age, but they usually start during the teen years. Females are more likely to get eating disorders than males.

Signs and Symptoms of Anorexia Nervosa

- A low body weight for their height

- A strong fear of gaining weight

- Thoughts that they are fat even when they are very thin

- A lot of weight loss

- Excessive exercising, like making exercise more important than many other things

- Being very careful to eat only certain foods and other extreme dieting habits

- Absent or missing menstrual periods (at least three menstrual periods in a row, if she started having periods)

Other symptoms and medical complications may develop over time, including:

- Thinning of the bones (osteopenia or osteoporosis)
- Brittle hair and nails
- Dry and yellowish skin
- Growth of fine hair all over the body (lanugo)
- Mild anemia, muscle wasting, and weakness
- Severe constipation
- Low blood pressure, or slowed breathing and pulse
- Damage to the structure and function of the heart
- Brain damage
- Multi-organ failure
- Drop in internal body temperature, causing a person to feel cold all the time
- Lethargy, sluggishness, or feeling tired all the time
- Infertility

Anorexia can cause a lot of serious problems, including weak bones, infections, seizures, and heart trouble. If you think you or someone you know may have anorexia, talk to an adult you trust.

What Is Bulimia Nervosa?

Bulimia nervosa, usually called bulimia, has two main parts. These are binge eating and purging, which is trying to make up for the binging.

Binge eating is eating an unusually large amount of food in a short time. During a binge, a person may eat really fast even though they aren't even hungry. Someone with bulimia usually feels they can't control the binging, and may feel really embarrassed about it.

Trying to make up for the binging can take different forms. Some examples include the following:

- Purging, which means trying to get rid of the food. This could include:
  - Making yourself throw up
  - Taking laxatives (pills or liquids that cause a bowel movement)
- Exercising a lot
- Eating very little or not at all
- Taking pills to urinate (pee) often to lose weight

Because of these behaviors, people with bulimia may not be overweight. But they often worry about what they weigh and how their body looks. Usually, bulimic behavior is done secretly because it is often accompanied by feelings of disgust or shame. The binge eating and purging cycle can happen anywhere from several times a week to many times a day.

Bulimia can cause serious health problems, including damage to your throat, teeth, stomach, and heart.

Symptoms include:

- Swollen salivary glands in the neck and jaw area
- Worn tooth enamel, and increasingly sensitive and decaying teeth as a result of exposure to stomach acid
- Acid reflux disorder and other gastrointestinal problems
- Intestinal distress and irritation from laxative abuse
- Severe dehydration from purging of fluids
- Electrolyte imbalance—too low or too high levels of sodium, calcium, potassium, and other minerals that can lead to a heart attack or stroke

What Is Binge Eating Disorder?

A person with binge eating disorder eats an unusually large amount of food in a short time and feels out of control during the binges. For example, the person may eat an entire bag of cookies and a whole pizza in one short sitting.

A binge eater may feel like they can't stop overeating. That's why binge eating disorder is also sometimes called compulsive overeating. Everybody overeats sometimes, but a binge eater does it often, like once a week or more.

People with binge eating disorder also may do the following:

- Eat more quickly than usual during binges
- Eat until they are uncomfortably full
- Eat when they are not at all hungry
- Eat alone because of embarrassment
- Feel disgusted, depressed, or guilty after binging

Binge eaters are often overweight or obese, because they don't do some of the things people with bulimia or anorexia do, like throw up food or diet very strictly. Binge eating can cause a lot of health problems, including conditions that come from gaining too much weight, such as diabetes and heart disease.

Other Eating Disorders

The most recent version of the *Diagnostic and Statistical Manual of Mental Disorders* (DSM-5) has made several changes to the categorization of eating disorders. The category that was known as Eating Disorder Not Otherwise Specified (EDNOS), has been removed, and there are two new categories; Other Specified Feeding or Eating Disorder (OSFED) and Unspecified Feeding or Eating Disorder (UFED). These new categories are intended to more appropriately recognize and categorize conditions that do not more accurately fit into anorexia nervosa, bulimia nervosa, binge eating disorder, or the other eating and feeding disorders.

It is important to note that these new categories are not an indication of a less severe eating disorder, simply a different constellation of symptoms. Another significant change is the inclusion of some types of "Feeding Disorders" that were previously listed in other chapters of the DSM, and now listed together with eating disorders.

Other Specified Feeding or Eating Disorder (OSFED)

According to the DSM-5 criteria, to be diagnosed as having OSFED a person must present with a feeding or eating behaviours that cause clinically significant distress and impairment in areas of functioning, but do not meet the full criteria for any of the other feeding and eating disorders.

A diagnosis might then be allocated that specifies a specific reason why the presentation does not meet the specifics of another disorder (e.g., bulimia nervosa—low frequency). The following are further examples for OSFED:

- **Atypical Anorexia Nervosa:** All criteria are met, except despite significant weight loss, the individual's weight is within or above the normal range.

- **Binge Eating Disorder** (of low frequency and/or limited duration): All of the criteria for BED are met, except at a lower frequency and/or for less than three months.

- **Bulimia Nervosa** (of low frequency and/or limited duration): All of the criteria for bulimia nervosa are met, except that the binge eating and inappropriate compensatory behaviour occurs at a lower frequency and/or for less than three months.

- **Purging Disorder:** Recurrent purging behaviour to influence weight or shape in the absence of binge eating

- **Night Eating Syndrome:** Recurrent episodes of night eating. Eating after awakening from sleep, or by excessive food consumption after the evening meal. The behavior is not better explained by environmental influences or social norms. The behavior causes significant distress/impairment. The behavior is not better explained by another mental health disorder (e.g., BED).

Unspecified Feeding or Eating Disorder (UFED)

According to the DSM-5 criteria this category applies to where behaviours cause clinically significant distress/impairment of functioning, but do not meet the full criteria of any of the "Feeding or Eating Disorder" criteria. This category may be used by clinicians where a clinician chooses not to specify why criteria are not met, including presentations where there may be insufficient information to make a more specific diagnosis (e.g., in emergency room settings)

Avoidant / Restrictive Food Intake Disorder (ARFID)

Avoidant/restrictive food intake disorder (ARFID) is a new term that some people think just means "picky eating," but a number of other eating issues can also cause it. People with ARFID don't have anorexia or bulimia, but they still struggle with eating and as a result don't eat enough to keep a healthy body weight.

Types of eating problems that might be considered ARFID include:

- difficulty digesting certain foods

- avoiding certain colors or textures of food

- eating only very small portions

- having no appetite

- being afraid to eat after a frightening episode of choking or vomiting

Because they don't get enough nutrition in their diet, people with ARFID lose weight, or, if they're younger kids, they may not gain weight or grow as expected. Many people with ARFID need supplements each day to get the right amount of nutrition and calories.

People with ARFID also might have issues in their day-to-day lives, at school, or with their friends because of their eating problems. For example, they might avoid going out to eat or eating lunch at school, or it might take so long to eat that they're late for school or don't have time to do their homework.

Some people with ARFID may go on to develop another eating disorder, such as anorexia or bulimia.

Section 1.3

Common Eating Disorder Myths

This section includes text excerpted from "9 Eating Disorders Myths Busted," National Institute of Mental Health (NIMH), February 27, 2014.

Myth #1: You Can Tell by Looking at Someone

You can tell by looking at someone whether they have an eating disorder. This is a myth that you have to bust. Eating disorders come in all shapes and sizes. In fact, with the new *Diagnostic and Statistical Manual of Mental Disorders* (DSM-5), you can be at normal or overweight and still get a diagnosis of atypical anorexia nervosa if you have lost a lot of weight. Similarly, you don't have to be overweight or obese to have binge eating disorder. It can happen anywhere along the body mass index (BMI) spectrum.

Myth #2: Families Are to Blame

One of the biggest myths about eating disorders—and our families have suffered from this myth—is that families are to blame. What is known in eating disorders is that families are often the best allies in treatment—they don't cause the disorders, but allies in recovery.

Myth #3: Eating Disorders Are a Choice

So here's another huge myth—that eating disorders are a choice. This is perhaps the most damaging one that patients have had to deal with. When patients go to the emergency room, they get triaged really far down the priority list because the physician thinks that somehow they chose to have a ruptured esophagus or they chose to have electrolyte imbalance. We're going to bust it now. One of the reasons that this myth has really stuck with anorexia nervosa, perhaps more than other psychiatric disorders, is due to the tyranny of face validity.

People see this all the time in People magazine. They see the Calvin Klein ads, they see Twiggy back in the sixties, or they see the models, and they may make an association between the cultural thin ideal and what they imagine to be anorexia nervosa. What they don't see is the difference between these two pictures. This would never be on the front of People magazine because that has nothing to do with the cultural thin ideal. If you ask patients if something like People magazine or models was what put them on the path to develop anorexia nervosa, the vast majority of them say no. There might have been a role in the very beginning that made them think "I'm going to go on that first diet." But the minute they go on that first diet, their anomalous biology kicks in and anorexia nervosa just sends them down a path that they have no control over. So eating disorders are illnesses not choices.

Myth #4: Eating Disorders Are the Province of White Upper-Middle Class Teenage Girls

Another myth—that eating disorders are somehow the province of white upper middle class teenage girls. Another one that's got to go. The number of middle age women that come to clinics and say that they went to their physician and were told by their physician that they can't have an eating disorder because that's only for teenagers. Or the number of guys that show up and have the courage to say, "I think I'm suffering from this women's illness," and then their physician puts them through a huge battery of tests because you can't have a teenage girl's illness. That's the kind of things people are still running into out there. Running into out there that needs to get into medical education to change people's perceptions about who is affected by these disorders.

Eating disorders absolutely do not care about your race, your ethnicity, your sex, your socioeconomic status. They cut across all of those lines. And so, one needs to be vigilant and aware for everyone who might be at risk for these disorders. So these are the official U.S. epidemiological statistics. So anorexia nervosa, about one percent in females, about three percent in males. Bulimia, about 1.5 percent in females, 0.5 percent in males. Binge eating disorder is the most common eating disorder, afflicting about 3.5 percent of females and two percent of males. And this is just binge eating behavior. So binge eating just as a behavior occurs in about five percent of females and four percent of males. That all translates to about 14 million Americans—and that number is probably an under-estimate. And it goes up when you include sub threshold conditions.

This is just a little bit about men. In a study in 1800 men in the northwestern United States, about 26 percent reported overeating, 20 percent talked about losing control, which is the hallmark feature of binge eating. Eight percent binge ate every week, 1.5 percent purged, and three percent used laxatives. The only complicated thing in assessing bulimia and binge eating disorders in men is that men don't particularly like to say that they feel out-of-control. It's just not something that flows naturally off their tongues. So questions were asked backwards sometimes and say things simply like, "do you ever feel like once you start eating you just can't just stop?" It's a lot easier for them to say yes to than actually asking the out-of-control question.

Here are some realities. This is a really interesting work about African-Americans and eating disorders. There's some suggestion that African-American women might be slightly protected against the development of anorexia, but there are higher rates of binge eating disorder in the African-American population. There's a second layer of shame about talking about eating disorders in various racial and ethnic groups, especially if it doesn't jibe with what the belief is about how you "should" feel about your body.

There is also a higher prevalence of binge eating disorder and bulimia nervosa in Latina women than in Caucasian women, but underutilization is a huge problem. So there is much less use of healthcare than the prevalence would suggest. Many Latinas report feeling caught between two standards of beauty, leaving them either not feeling beautiful in either culture or feeling beautiful in one, but not the other. They feel as if they are on the precipice of judgment, caught between American pop culture and the values and cultural traditions of their families.

The LGBT community. This myth that if you have an eating disorder and you're a guy, of course you're gay because only gay men get eating disorders. Not the case at all. The prevalence of eating disorders is somewhat higher in gay than in straight men, but it's not known if that's just because they're more comfortable disclosing that they have an eating disorder or seeking healthcare for it. There's no difference in prevalence between lesbian and straight women, and the myth that only gay men get eating disorders keep men from seeking treatment.

And then there's the age myth. An online survey of over 1800 women, ages 50 and over was conducted, just trying to find out what they're thinking about their body image and what kind of disordered eating behaviors they're exhibiting. Eight percent purging in the last five years. So remember, this is women 50 and older—3.5 percent binge eating.

Myth #5: Eating Disorders Are Benign

Another myth that needs to be busted is that eating disorders are somehow trivial or benign. They're not. Looking at suicide attempts in Sweden across a variety of eating disorders phenotypes, the suicide attempt rate of population who have no eating disorders is under 2%. But, anorexia nervosa restricting subtype accounts to a little less than 8%, anorexia binge-purge subtype a little over 13%, people who had both anorexia and bulimia at some point in their life a little over 17%. And these are all significant. Bulimia accounts for 13%. Binge eating disorder—a little less than 14% and purging disorder—a little less than 11%. So, we're seeing high suicide risk in individuals with eating disorders.

Myth #6: Genes Are Destiny

So the other thing to be careful about though is this sense that somehow genes are destiny. Because, environment and genes are

16

definitely not destiny. Hereditability for any of these disorders is not 100 percent. If environment didn't matter, heritability would be 100 percent. It's not. There's always somewhere between 40 and 60 percent of variance that's unaccounted for, and that's when we have to start looking at the environment—gene-environment interaction epigenetic factors. So for eating disorders, the environment can have both positive and negative influences. In terms of negative influences, environment can increase risk.

Some of the things to know about:

1. Sports with an appearance or weight focus (Ski jumping—nasty. Ski jumping has completely changed how they do their sport to decrease the number of people who develop anorexia nervosa.)

2. Dieting—the number one thing that people talk about as the first step toward developing eating disorders is "going on a diet." One wouldn't want obesity interventions to create more eating disorders and that's why weight stigma and obesity stigma is such a concern.

3. Modeling—being obsessed with looks.

So many people with eating disorders have teasing or bullying histories—and not necessarily just about their physical appearance or their weight. But teasing is one of these nonspecific risk factors that that many people have in their histories.

But environment can also have positive influences. Some of the things that may decrease risk for the development of eating disorders:

1. Models for healthy eating—making sure that you really do model healthy eating, non-emotional eating, and making sure that your family is a place where healthy eating occurs.

2. Being able to separate body-esteem from self-esteem. The first thing people usually say about kids is what they look like. If someone gives your child a compliment about especially her physical appearance, make sure you parrot right away with something like "Oh yeah, and she's also really great at playing the flute" or "She got an A in Chemistry" or something like that so your child is hearing more than just physical appearance–based compliments.

3. Role models for body respect.

4. Family involvement.

5. Supportive peers who value who you are, not just how you look.

6. But also letting parents know that they can't control everything. You can have all the stuff in place and your child might still develop an eating disorder.

Myth #7: Eating Disorders Are for Life

So the seventh myth is that eating disorders are for life. And this gets a little complicated because some people do prefer, and this is a patient preference, to say that they are in recovery, sort of forever, to keep them vigilant about slipping or relapsing again. And it's really important to validate and respect that patient preference. But eating disorders are not for life—so eating disorders are treatable. Recovery can and does occur every age. For anorexia nervosa, nutritional rehabilitation and weight restoration are essential but only the first step in treatment. Whether your intervention is through family-based therapy or through in-patient re-feeding, the single most important thing to do is to get weight back on a patient first because their brains aren't working. You could do a lot of psychotherapy and get nowhere—you're just spinning your wheels in the mud because their brains simply aren't working.

There is the danger of that first diet. The reason it's dangerous is that we all respond to negative energy balance or not eating enough food—being hungry—differently. Most of us when we're hungry find a really aversive experience. You might get more irritable, you might get a headache, you start foraging and looking around for food, you might have difficulty making decisions because you're so hungry you don't know what to eat—it is not pleasant.

People who have or who are vulnerable to developing anorexia nervosa: when they go on that first diet, they find it calming. So at baseline they're very dysphoric and anxious and miserable. And it's the food deprivation that calms them. And so throughout their life, what they have to be really careful of is when they go through periods of stress again, falling back into that restriction trap because it gives them—it's like a drug, it's like a calming drug and that's their high risk for relapse. Figuring out the neurobiology of what makes food restriction reinforcing for them is a gold mine when it comes to understanding anorexia nervosa.

Cognitive behavioral therapy works well for bulimia nervosa and for binge eating disorder. No medications have been shown to be effective in the treatment of anorexia nervosa—the only medication approved by U.S. Food and Drug Administration (FDA) is fluoxetine or Prozac for bulimia nervosa. No other meds for any of the eating disorders. Medication can and does play a role in the treatment of bulimia and binge eating disorder but short term. It doesn't lead to long-term effects from what researchers know so far. Psychotherapy does seem to give people the tools to be able to keep their behavior under control in the long run. And finally, individuals with eating disorders can thrive after recovery.

Chapter 2

Normal Eating, Disordered Eating, and Eating Disorders

Chapter Contents

21

Section 2.1

What Are Normal Eating, Disordered Eating, and Eating Disorders?

"Normal Eating, Disordered Eating, and Eating Disorders,"
© 2016 Omnigraphics, Inc. Reviewed March 2016.

To be diagnosed with an eating disorder, an individual must meet the clinical definitions listed in the American Psychiatric Association's *Diagnostic and Statistical Manual of Mental Disorders* for anorexia nervosa, bulimia nervosa, binge eating disorder, or eating disorder not otherwise specified (EDNOS). Although only a small fraction of the U.S. population meets the diagnostic criteria for one of these conditions, research suggests that an estimated 50 percent of Americans demonstrate unhealthy or disordered eating patterns.

Experts point to a cultural obsession with weight, body shape, and diet as a primary factor in the prevalence of disordered eating. In comparing themselves to the unattainable ideals of thinness and fitness that are promoted in the media, many Americans develop a negative body image and an unhealthy relationship with food. Countless people follow extremely restrictive diets, feel ashamed or guilty about eating, exercise obsessively, or resort to harmful practices like bingeing and purging in an effort to lose weight. Although these are signs of a disordered relationship with food, many people view such behavior as normal, common, or even healthy. As a result, they never seek help for the problem and put both their physical and emotional health at risk.

Normal Eating

Although there is no medical definition of "normal" eating, experts generally agree on the basic characteristics of a healthy relationship with food. People who exhibit normal eating patterns eat when they are hungry and stop eating when they feel satisfied and comfortably full. Although they usually make food selections with proper nutrition in mind, they do not deny themselves foods they enjoy. Rather than considering certain foods "bad" or "off limits," they allow themselves to eat everything in moderation without judgment. They enjoy eating and do not feel guilty, ashamed, or embarrassed about satisfying their appetites. They focus on health and well-being and do not let concerns about food or weight interfere with their lives.

Yet the American media and popular culture routinely promote ideas that contradict these healthy eating principles. People are applauded for restricting their food intake and encouraged to follow fad diets and extreme fitness regimens in an effort to change their body proportions. These cultural influences contribute to disordered eating and eating disorders.

Disordered Eating vs. Eating Disorders

An eating disorder is a form of mental illness in which an individual uses food and eating as a means of coping with a complex range of emotional and psychological issues. Although a person with disordered eating may engage in some of the same behaviors as someone with an eating disorder—such as restricting food intake, binge eating, self-induced vomiting, or abusing diet pills or laxatives—they typically do so less often or to a lesser extent. While the symptoms may not be as extreme, however, disordered eating can still cause health problems, and it also increases the risk of developing an eating disorder or other types of psychiatric issues.

Disordered eating is characterized by an unhealthy or abnormal relationship with food. People with disordered eating are likely to think about food obsessively and worry about every bite they consume. Eating too much or eating "bad" foods makes them feel terribly guilty and ashamed. They may respond by punishing themselves, restricting food even more severely, or exercising excessively in order to burn off the calories. They are likely to count calories and deny themselves certain foods or entire food groups, even if they experience cravings. They tend to be rigid and inflexible about food, and they may feel anxious about eating in restaurants, trying new foods, or attending social events where food is served because they cannot control what they consume. They often evaluate their self-worth based on their body shape, weight, and success in controlling what they eat.

Preventing and Managing Disordered Eating

Although disordered eating is quite common, it is not considered normal or healthy and can be self-destructive. Disordered eating may turn into an eating disorder that requires medical treatment if it affects an individual's daily functioning. Worrying about food and eating may take up so much time and attention that it affects a person's concentration, ability to focus, and performance at school or on the job. Disordered eating may also cause a person to avoid socializing because they worry about consuming forbidden foods or disrupting an exercise routine. Finally, disordered eating may require treatment if a person's relationship to food becomes a source of anxiety or a way to cope with the problems and stresses of everyday life.

A mental health professional can help people distinguish between disordered eating and eating disorders and determine whether they need treatment. Therapy can help people understand the complex relationships between food and self-image and establish healthier eating and exercise patterns. Some other tips to help prevent or manage disordered eating include avoiding restrictive fad diets, incorporating all foods in moderation, focusing on health rather than weight, limiting use of the scale, maintaining a positive and nonjudgmental attitude toward one's body, and setting healthy limits on exercise.

References

1. Gottlieb, Carrie. "Disordered Eating or Eating Disorder: What's the Difference?" Psychology Today, February 23, 2014.

2. Klein, Sarah. "14 Habits of People with a Healthy Relationship to Food," Huffington Post, April 17, 2014.

3. Narins, Elizabeth. "25 Signs You Have a Terrible Relationship with Food," Cosmopolitan, May 4, 2015.

4. Tartakovsky, Margarita. "What Is Normal Eating?" PsychCentral, August 26, 2009.

Section 2.2

Emotional Eating

This section includes excerpts from "Overcoming
Stress Eating," Military Health System (MHS), October
19, 2015; text from "Emotional Eating," © 1995–2016. The
Nemours Foundation/KidsHealth®. Reprinted with permission;
and text from "Emotions and Your Weight," U.S. Department
of Veterans Affairs (VA), November 27, 2013.

What Is Emotional Eating?

Emotional eating is when people use food as a way to deal with feelings instead of to satisfy hunger. We've all been there, finishing a whole bag of chips out of boredom or downing cookie after cookie while cramming for a big test. But when done a lot—especially without realizing it—emotional eating can affect weight, health, and overall well-being.

Not many of us make the connection between eating and our feelings. But understanding what drives emotional eating can help people take steps to change it.

One of the biggest myths about emotional eating is that it's prompted by negative feelings. Yes, people often turn to food when they're stressed out, lonely, sad, anxious, or bored. But emotional eating can be linked to positive feelings too, like the romance of sharing dessert on Valentine's Day or the celebration of a holiday feast.

Sometimes emotional eating is tied to major life events, like a death or a divorce. More often, though, it's the countless little daily stresses that cause someone to seek comfort or distraction in food.

Emotional eating patterns can be learned: A child who is given candy after a big achievement may grow up using candy as a reward for a job well done. A kid who is given cookies as a way to stop crying may learn to link cookies with comfort.

It's not easy to "unlearn" patterns of emotional eating. But it is possible. And it starts with an awareness of what's going on.

"Comfort" Foods

We all have our own comfort foods. Interestingly, they may vary according to moods and gender. One study found that happy people seem to want to eat things like pizza, while sad people prefer ice cream and cookies. Bored people crave salty, crunchy things, like chips. Researchers also found that guys seem to prefer hot, homemade comfort meals, like steaks and casseroles. Girls go for chocolate and ice cream.

This brings up a curious question: Does no one take comfort in carrots and celery sticks? Researchers are looking into that, too. What they're finding is that high-fat foods, like ice cream, may activate certain chemicals in the body that create a sense of contentment and fulfillment. This almost addictive quality may actually make you reach for these foods again when feeling upset.

Physical Hunger vs. Emotional Hunger

We're all emotional eaters to some extent (who hasn't suddenly found room for dessert after a filling dinner?). But for some people, emotional eating can be a real problem, causing serious weight gain or cycles of binging and purging.

The trouble with emotional eating (aside from the health issues) is that once the pleasure of eating is gone, the feelings that cause it remain. And you often may feel worse about eating the amount or type of food you did. That's why it helps to know the differences between physical hunger and emotional hunger.

Next time you reach for a snack, check in and see which type of hunger is driving it.

Table 2.1. Physical Hunger vs. Emotional Hunger

Physical Hunger	Emotional Hunger
Tends to come on gradually and can be postponed	Feels sudden and urgent
Can be satisfied with any number of foods	Causes very specific cravings(say, for pizza or ice cream)
Once full, you're likely to stop eating	you tend to eat more than you normally would
Doesn't cause feeling of guilt	Can cause guilt afterwards

Questions to Ask Yourself

You can also ask yourself these questions about your eating:

- Have I been eating larger portions than usual?

- Do I eat at unusual times?

- Do I feel a loss of control around food?

- Am I anxious over something, like school, a social situation, or an event where my abilities might be tested?

- Has there been a big event in my life that I'm having trouble dealing with?

- Am I overweight, or has there recently been a big jump in my weight?

- Do other people in my family use food to soothe their feelings too?

- If you answered yes to many of these questions, then it's possible that eating has become a coping mechanism instead of a way to fuel your body.

Breaking the Cycle

Managing emotional eating means finding other ways to deal with the situations and feelings that make someone turn to food.

For example, do you come home from school each day and automatically head to the kitchen? Stop and ask yourself, "Am I really hungry?" Is your stomach growling? Are you having difficulty concentrating or feeling irritable? If these signs point to hunger, choose something light and healthy to take the edge off until dinner.

Not really hungry? If the post-school food foraging has just become part of your routine, think about why.

Tips to Try

1. **Explore why you're eating and find a replacement activity.**

   For example:

   - If you're bored or lonely, call or text a friend or family member.

- If you're stressed out, try a yoga routine. Or listen to some feel-good tunes and let off some steam by jogging in place, doing jumping jacks, or dancing around your room until the urge to eat passes.

- If you're tired, rethink your bedtime routine. Tiredness can feel a lot like hunger, and food won't help if sleepless nights are causing daytime fatigue.

- If you're eating to procrastinate, open those books and get that homework over with. You'll feel better afterwards (honestly!).

2. **Write down the emotions that trigger your eating.** One of the best ways to keep track is with a mood and food journal. Write down what you ate, how much, and how you felt as you ate (e.g., bored, happy, worried, sad, mad) and whether you were really hungry or just eating for comfort.

   Through journaling, you'll start to see patterns emerging between what you feel and what you eat. You'll be able to use this information to make better choices (like choosing to clear your head with a walk around the block instead of a bag of Doritos).

3. **Pause and "take 5" before you reach for food.** Too often, we rush through the day without really checking in with ourselves. We're so stressed, overscheduled, and plugged-in that we lose out on time to reflect.

Instead of eating when you get in the door, take a few minutes to transition from one part of your day to another. Go over the things that happened that day. Acknowledge how they made you feel: Happy? Grateful? Excited? Angry? Worried? Jealous? Left out?

Getting Help

Even when we understand what's going on, many of us still need help breaking the cycle of emotional eating. It's not easy—especially when emotional eating has already led to weight and self-esteem issues. So don't go it alone when you don't have to.

Take advantage of expert help. Counselors and therapists can help you deal with your feelings. Nutritionists can help you identify your eating patterns and get you on track with a better diet. Fitness experts can get your body's feel-good chemicals firing through exercise instead of food.

If you're worried about your eating, talk to your doctor. He or she can make sure you reach your weight-loss goals safely and put you in touch with professionals who can put you on a path to a new, healthier relationship with food.

Chapter 3

Binge Eating Disorder

What Is Binge Eating Disorder?

Binge eating means eating a large amount of food in a short period of time. Most of us may overeat during a special occasion, like a holiday. But people who have this disorder binge eat on a regular basis and feel a lack of control over their eating.

A binge eater often:

- Eats 5,000–15,000 calories in one sitting

- Often snacks, in addition to eating three meals a day

- Overeats throughout the day

Binge eating may occur on its own or with another eating disorder, such as bulimia. People who have bulimia nervosa also binge eat on a regular basis. However, they try to make up for the binge eating by using unhealthy behaviors, such as vomiting, using laxatives

This chapter contains text excerpted from the following sources: Text beginning with the heading "What Is Binge Eating Disorder?" is excerpted from National Institute of Diabetes and Digestive and Kidney Diseases (NIDDK), December 2012. Reviewed March 2016; Text under the heading "Loss of Control (LOC) Eating" is excerpted from "Management and Outcomes of Binge Eating Disorder," Agency for Healthcare Research and Quality (AHRQ), December 9, 2015; Text under the heading "Study Links Attention Disorder and a Form of Binge Eating Syndrome" is excerpted from "ADHD Tied to Higher Risk of Eating Disorder in Kids and Teens," U.S. Department of Health and Human Services (HHS), May 1, 2015.

or diuretics (water pills), fasting, and/or doing too much exercise. Unlike bulimia nervosa, periods of binge eating are not followed by compensatory behaviors like purging, excessive exercise, or fasting. As a result, people with binge eating disorder often are overweight or obese. Obesity is usually defined as having a body mass index (BMI) of 30 or greater. The BMI is a measure of your weight in relation to your height.

People with binge eating disorder are usually very upset by their binge eating and may experience stress, trouble sleeping, and depression. Binge eating disorder may lead to weight gain and to related health problems, such as heart disease and diabetes. They also experience guilt, shame, and distress about their binge eating, which can lead to more binge eating.

Most people who binge eat try to hide their problem. Often they become so good at hiding it that even close friends and family members may not know that their loved one binge eats.

Binge eating disorder can be successfully treated. If you think that you or someone close to you may have binge eating disorder, share your concerns with a healthcare provider. He or she can connect you to helpful sources of care.

How Common Is Binge Eating Disorder?

Binge eating disorder is the most common eating disorder in the United States. Among adults, about 3.5 percent of women and 2 percent of men are estimated to have binge eating disorder. About 1.6 percent of adolescents may also be affected.

Among women, binge eating disorder is most common in early adulthood, while among men it is most common in midlife. Binge eating disorder affects blacks as often as whites, but it is not known how often it affects people in other racial and ethnic groups.

People with obesity are at a higher risk for developing the disorder than people of normal weight. Although most people with obesity do not have binge eating disorder, about 2 in 3 people who have the disorder are obese. People of normal weight can also have binge eating disorder.

How Do I Know If I Have Binge Eating Disorder?

People who have binge eating disorder

- eat a large amount of food in a short period of time (for example, within 2 hours).

- feel a lack of control over their eating. For example, they may feel that they cannot stop eating or control what or how much they are eating.

People who have binge eating disorder may also

- eat much more quickly than usual
- eat until uncomfortably full
- eat large amounts of food even when not really hungry
- eat alone
- feel disgusted, depressed, or guilty after overeating

What Causes Binge Eating Disorder?

No one knows for sure what causes binge eating disorder. Like other eating disorders, binge eating disorder may result from a mix of genetic, psychological, emotional, social, and other factors. Binge eating disorder has been linked to depression and anxiety.

Researchers are looking at the following factors that may affect binge eating:

- **Depression.** As many as half of all people with binge eating disorder are depressed or have been depressed in the past.

- **Dieting.** Some people binge after skipping meals, not eating enough food each day, or avoiding certain kinds of food.

- **Coping skills.** Studies suggest that people with binge eating may have trouble handling some of their emotions. Many people who are binge eaters say that being angry, sad, bored, worried, or stressed can cause them to binge eat.

- **Biology.** Researchers are looking into how brain chemicals and metabolism (the way the body uses calories) affect binge eating disorder. Research also suggests that genes may be involved in binge eating, since the disorder often occurs in several members of the same family. Neuroimaging, or pictures of the brain, may also lead to a better understanding of binge eating disorder.

- **Painful childhood experiences**—such as family problems and critical comments about shape, weight, or eating—may also make some people more likely to develop the disorder.

Although binge eating is related to dieting, it is not clear if dieting causes binge eating disorder. Among some people, trying to diet in unhealthy ways—such as by skipping meals, not eating enough food each day, or avoiding certain kinds of food—may lead to binge eating. Studies suggest that changes to eating habits that are made as part of obesity treatment are not harmful to people with binge eating disorder and may promote weight loss.

What Are the Health Risks of Binge Eating Disorder?

People with binge eating disorder are usually very upset by their binge eating and may become depressed. They may also miss school, social activities, or work to binge eat. In addition, binge eating disorder may lead to weight gain and to health problems related to obesity.

Excess weight may increase the risk for many health problems, including

- type 2 diabetes
- high blood pressure
- heart disease and strokes
- certain types of cancer
- sleep apnea (pauses in breathing during sleep)
- osteoarthritis (a disease where the joints wear down, causing stiffness and pain)
- fatty liver disease
- kidney disease
- irregular periods and infertility in women
- pregnancy problems, such as high blood sugar during pregnancy, high blood pressure, and increased risk for cesarean delivery (C-section)

Obese people with binge eating disorder often have other mental health conditions, including:

- anxiety
- depression
- personality disorders

Research suggests that people with binge eating disorder report more health problems, stress, trouble sleeping, and suicidal thoughts than do people without an eating disorder. Other problems that may result from binge eating disorder could include digestive problems, headaches, joint pains, menstrual problems, and muscle pains.

Should People with Binge Eating Disorder Try to Lose Weight?

Many people with binge eating disorder have excess weight and related health problems. Losing weight may help prevent or reduce some of these problems. However, binge eating may make it difficult to lose weight and keep it off. People with binge eating disorder who are obese may benefit from a weight-loss program that also offers treatment for eating disorders. However, some people with binge eating disorder may do just as well in a standard weight-loss program as people who do not binge eat.

Diagnostic Criteria for Binge Eating Disorder

In May 2013, the American Psychiatric Association (APA) recognized binge eating disorder (BED) as a distinct eating disorder in the *Diagnostic and Statistical Manual of Mental Disorders*, 5th Edition (DSM-5). Previously (in the DSM-IV), BED had been designated as a provisional diagnosis.

Table 3.1 presents the DSM-IV and DSM-5 diagnostic criteria for BED. In the shift from provisional to formal diagnosis for BED, APA experts changed the criterion for frequency of BED from twice per week to once per week and the duration criterion from 6 months to 3 months, in line with those for bulimia nervosa.

Table 3.1. DSM-IV and DSM-5 Diagnostic Criteria for Binge Eating Disorder

Criteria Set and Severity Grading	Specific Definitions for Each Criterion
Criterion 1	Recurrent episodes of binge eating. An episode of binge eating is characterized by both of the following: 1. Eating, in a discrete period of time (e.g., within any 2-hour period), an amount of food that is definitely larger than most people would eat in a similar period of time under similar circumstances 2. The sense of lack of control over eating during the episode (e.g., a feeling that one cannot stop eating or control what or how much one is eating)

Table 3.1. Continued

Criteria Set and Severity Grading	Specific Definitions for Each Criterion
Criterion 2	Binge eating episodes are associated with 3 or more of the following: 1. Eating much more rapidly than normal 2. Eating until feeling uncomfortably full 3. Eating large amounts of food when not feeling physically hungry 4. Eating alone because of being embarrassed by how much one is eating 5. Feeling disgusted with oneself, depressed, or very guilty after overeating
Criterion 3	Marked distress regarding binge eating is present.
Criterion 4	The binge eating occurs, on average— 1. At least 2 days a week for 6 months (DSM-IV frequency and duration criteria) 2. At least 1 day a week for 3 months (DSM-5 frequency and duration criteria)
Criterion 5	The binge eating is not associated with the regular use of inappropriate compensatory behavior (e.g., purging, fasting, excessive exercise) and does not occur exclusively during the course of anorexia nervosa or bulimia nervosa.
Severity Grading	DSM-IV does not include a BED severity grading scale. Applicable to DSM-5 only, BED severity is graded as follows: • Mild: 1 to 3 episodes per week • Moderate: 4 to 7 episodes per week • Severe: 8 to 13 episodes per week • Extreme: 14 or more episodes per week

BED = binge eating disorder; DSM = Diagnostic and Statistical Manual of Mental Disorders

How Is Binge Eating Disorder Treated?

People with binge eating disorder should get help from a specialist in eating disorders, such as a psychiatrist or a psychologist. Treatment may include the use of behavior change therapy, counseling on eating patterns, and/or drugs. The goal is to change the thoughts and beliefs that lead to binge eating and promote healthy eating and physical activity habits.

In addition to treatment from specialists, self-help books and DVDs have been found to help some people control their binge eating. Support groups may also be a good source of encouragement, hope, and advice on coping with the disorder.

If you have any symptoms of binge eating disorder, talk to your healthcare provider about the type of help that may be best for you. Ask for a referral to a specialist or a support group in your area.

The good news is that most people do well in treatment and can overcome binge eating.

Loss of Control (LOC) Eating

A sense of loss of control (LOC) during binge episodes is a core feature of binge eating disorder (BED). The term "LOC eating" is used to describe these episodes, but it is also used more broadly to describe binge-like eating behavior accompanied by a sense of LOC that occurs across a wide spectrum of individuals. That spectrum includes, among others, individuals who exhibit some features of BED but do not meet full diagnostic criteria for the disorder (i.e., subthreshold BED) and individuals with other eating disorders (bulimia nervosa, anorexia nervosa binge eating/ purge subtype).

The spectrum of those described as exhibiting LOC eating also includes individuals for whom diagnosis of threshold BED is challenging for unique reasons, such as post-bariatric surgery patients and children. Bariatric surgery significantly reduces the stomach size and capacity, effectively rendering it physically impossible for a patient to meet BED criterion 1.1 (Table 3.1; i.e., to consume a definitely large amount of food). In the bariatric surgery literature, LOC eating is used not only to describe binge-like behavior that falls short of meeting criterion 1.1, but also to describe eating behavior that is contraindicated based on meal size and meal content. Children, especially young children, may not meet BED criterion 1.1 because their parents or others limit the quantity of food they consume or because they are unable to provide accurate quantification of the amount they eat. For the purposes of review, LOC eating treatment and outcomes are limited to post-bariatric surgery patients and children, and do not include individuals in other groups who may meet subclinical diagnosis of BED.

Study Links Attention Disorder and a Form of Binge Eating Syndrome

The eating disorder is called loss of control eating syndrome (LOC-ES). As the name implies, people with this disorder sometimes can't stop eating, even if they want to, according to the researchers from the Johns Hopkins Children's Center in Baltimore.

Their study included 79 children between the ages of 8 and 14. The kids were assessed for attention deficit hyperactivity disorder (ADHD) and the eating disorder. Those with ADHD were 12 times more likely to have the eating disorder than those without ADHD, the study revealed.

Among overweight and obese children, those with LOC-ES were seven times more likely to have ADHD than those without the eating disorder. Also, children who scored higher on tests of impulsivity were more likely to have the eating disorder, whether or not they had ADHD, according to the study. Children with both ADHD and LOC-ES may have a more severe form of ADHD marked by more impulsive behavior that shows up strongly in their eating habits. Or it may be that children with both ADHD and LOC-ES have a shared underlying risk factor, such as a genetic predisposition to impulsivity.

Further research is needed to learn more about the connection between the two disorders, but doctors should screen for both ADHD and eating disorders. The findings underscore the need for developing new treatment strategies that could help target disinhibited eating in kids who have both ADHD and LOC-ES.

Chapter 4

Anorexia Nervosa

What Is Anorexia Nervosa?

A person with anorexia nervosa, often called anorexia, has an intense fear of gaining weight. Someone with anorexia thinks about food a lot and limits the food she or he eats, even though she or he is too thin. Anorexia is more than just a problem with food. It's a way of using food or starving oneself to feel more in control of life and to ease tension, anger, and anxiety. Most people with anorexia are female. An anorexic:

- Has a low body weight for her or his height
- Resists keeping a normal body weight
- Has an intense fear of gaining weight
- Thinks she or he is fat even when very thin
- Misses 3 menstrual periods in a row (for girls/women who have started having their periods)

Who Becomes Anorexic?

While anorexia mostly affects girls and women (85–95 percent of anorexics are female), it can also affect boys and men. It was once thought that women of color were shielded from eating disorders by

This chapter includes text excerpted from "Anorexia Nervosa Fact Sheet," Office on Women's Health (OWH), July 16, 2012. Reviewed March 2016.

their cultures, which tend to be more accepting of different body sizes. It is not known for sure whether African American, Latina, Asian/ Pacific Islander, and American Indian and Alaska Native people develop eating disorders because American culture values thin people. People with different cultural backgrounds may develop eating disorders because it's hard to adapt to a new culture (a theory called "culture clash"). The stress of trying to live in two different cultures may cause some minorities to develop their eating disorders.

What Causes Anorexia?

There is no single known cause of anorexia. Eating disorders are real, treatable medical illnesses with causes in both the body and the mind. Some of these things may play a part:

- **Culture.** Women in the United States are under constant pressure to fit a certain ideal of beauty. Seeing images of flawless, thin females everywhere makes it hard for women to feel good about their bodies. More and more, women are also feeling pressure to have a perfect body.

- **Families.** If you have a mother or sister with anorexia, you are more likely to develop the disorder. Parents who think looks are important, diet themselves, or criticize their children's bodies are more likely to have a child with anorexia.

- **Life changes or stressful events.** Traumatic events (like rape) as well as stressful things (like starting a new job), can lead to the onset of anorexia.

- **Personality traits.** Someone with anorexia may not like her or himself, hate the way she or he looks, or feel hopeless. She or he often sets hard-to-reach goals for her or himself and tries to be perfect in every way.

- **Biology.** Genes, hormones, and chemicals in the brain may be factors in developing anorexia.

What Are Signs of Anorexia?

Someone with anorexia may look very thin. She or he may use extreme measures to lose weight by:

- Making her or himself throw up
- Taking pills to urinate or have a bowel movement

- Taking diet pills
- Not eating or eating very little
- Exercising a lot, even in bad weather or when hurt or tired
- Weighing food and counting calories
- Eating very small amounts of only certain foods
- Moving food around the plate instead of eating it

Someone with anorexia may also have a distorted body image, shown by thinking she or he is fat, wearing baggy clothes, weighing her or himself many times a day, and fearing weight gain.

Anorexia can also cause someone to not act like her or himself. She or he may talk about weight and food all the time, not eat in front of others, be moody or sad, or not want to go out with friends. People with anorexia may also have other psychiatric and physical illnesses, including:

- Depression
- Anxiety
- Obsessive behavior
- Substance abuse
- Issues with the heart and/or brain
- Problems with physical development

What Happens to Your Body with Anorexia?

With anorexia, your body doesn't get the energy from foods that it needs, so it slows down. Look at the picture to find out how anorexia affects your health.

Can Someone with Anorexia Get Better?

Yes. Someone with anorexia can get better. A healthcare team of doctors, nutritionists, and therapists will help the patient get better. They will:

- Help bring the person back to a normal weight
- Treat any psychological issues related to anorexia
- Help the person get rid of any actions or thoughts that cause the eating disorder

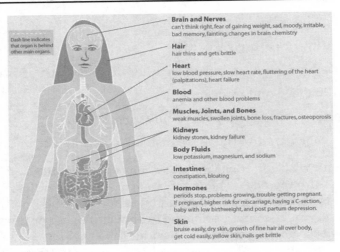

Figure 4.1. *Anorexia affecting body parts*

These three steps will prevent "relapse" (relapse means to get sick again, after feeling well for a while).

Some research suggests that the use of medicines—such as antidepressants, antipsychotics, or mood stabilizers—may sometimes work for anorexic patients. It is thought that these medicines help the mood and anxiety symptoms that often co-exist with anorexia.

Other recent studies, however, suggest that antidepressants may not stop some patients with anorexia from relapsing. Also, no medicine has shown to work 100 percent of the time during the important first step of restoring a patient to healthy weight. So, it is not clear if and how medications can help anorexic patients get better, but research is still happening.

Some forms of psychotherapy can help make the psychological reasons for anorexia better. **Psychotherapy** is sometimes known as "talk therapy." It uses different ways of communicating to change a patient's thoughts or behavior. This kind of therapy can be useful for treating eating disorders in young patients who have not had anorexia for a long time.

Individual counseling can help someone with anorexia. If the patient is young, counseling may involve the whole family. Support groups may also be a part of treatment. In support groups, patients and families meet and share what they've been through.

Some researchers point out that prescribing medicines and using psychotherapy designed just for anorexic patients works better at treating anorexia than just psychotherapy alone. Whether or not a treatment works, though, depends on the person involved and his or her situation. Unfortunately, no one kind of psychotherapy always works for treating adults with anorexia.

Is It Safe for Young People to Take Antidepressants for Anorexia?

It may be safe for young people to be treated with antidepressants. However, drug companies who make antidepressants are required to post a "black box" warning label on the medication. A "black box" warning is the most serious type of warning on prescription drugs.

It may be possible that antidepressants make children, adolescents, and young adults more likely to think about suicide or commit suicide.

The latest information from the

U.S. Food and Drug Administration (FDA)—including what drugs are included in this warning and things to look for—can be found on their website at www.fda.gov.

What Is Outpatient Care for Anorexia Treatment and How Is It Different from Inpatient Care?

With outpatient care, the patient receives treatment through visits with members of their healthcare team. Often this means going to a doctor's office. Outpatients usually live at home.

Some patients may need "partial hospitalization." This means that the person goes to the hospital during the day for treatment, but sleeps at home at night.

Sometimes, the patient goes to a hospital and stays there for treatment. This is called inpatient care. After leaving the hospital, the patient continues to get help from their healthcare team and becomes an outpatient.

Can Women Who Had Anorexia in the Past Still Get Pregnant?

It depends. When a woman has "active anorexia," meaning she currently has anorexia, she does not get her period and usually does not ovulate. This makes it hard to get pregnant. Women who have recovered from anorexia and are at a healthy weight have a better chance of getting pregnant. If you're having a hard time getting pregnant, see your doctor.

Can Anorexia Hurt a Baby When the Mother Is Pregnant?

Yes. Women who have anorexia while they are pregnant are more likely to lose the baby. If a woman with anorexia doesn't lose the baby, she is more likely to

- have the baby early
- deliver by C-section
- deliver a baby with a lower birthweight or
- have depression after the baby is born

What Should I Do If I Think Someone I Know Has Anorexia?

If someone you know is showing signs of anorexia, you may be able to help.

1. **Set a time to talk.** Set aside a time to talk privately with your friend. Make sure you talk in a quiet place where you won't be distracted.

2. **Tell your friend about your concerns.** Be honest. Tell your friend about your worries about her or his not eating or over exercising. Tell your friend you are concerned and that you think these things may be a sign of a problem that needs professional help.

3. **Ask your friend to talk to a professional.** Your friend can talk to a counselor or doctor who knows about eating issues. Offer to help your friend find a counselor or doctor and make an appointment, and offer to go with her or him to the appointment.

4. **Avoid conflicts.** If your friend won't admit that she or he has a problem, don't push. Be sure to tell your friend you are always there to listen if she or he wants to talk.

5. **Don't place shame, blame, or guilt on your friend.** Don't say, "You just need to eat." Instead, say things like, "I'm concerned about you because you won't eat breakfast or lunch." Or, "It makes me afraid to hear you throwing up."

6. **Don't give simple solutions.** Don't say, "If you'd just stop, then things would be fine!"

7. **Let your friend know that you will always be there no matter what.**

Chapter 5

Bulimia Nervosa

What Is Bulimia?

Bulimia nervosa, often called bulimia, is a type of eating disorder. Bulimia is an illness in which a person binges on food or has regular episodes of overeating and feels a loss of control. The person then uses different methods—such as vomiting or abusing laxatives—to prevent weight gain. Also, bulimics might exercise a lot, eat very little or not at all, or take pills to pass urine often to prevent weight gain.

Many (but not all) people with bulimia also have anorexia nervosa. Unlike anorexia, people with bulimia can fall within the normal range for their age and weight. But like people with anorexia, bulimics:

- Fear gaining weight
- Want desperately to lose weight
- Are very unhappy with their body size and shape

Who Becomes Bulimic?

Many people think that eating disorders affect only young, upper-class white females. It is true that most bulimics are women (around 85–90 percent). But bulimia affects people from all walks of life, including males, women of color, and even older women. It is not known for

This chapter includes text excerpted from "Bulimia Nervosa Fact Sheet," Office on Women's Health (OWH), July 16, 2012. Reviewed March 2016.

45

sure whether African American, Latina, Asian/Pacific Islander, and American Indian and Alaska Native people develop eating disorders because American culture values thin people. People with different cultural backgrounds may develop eating disorders because it's hard to adapt to a new culture (a theory called "culture clash"). The stress of trying to live in two different cultures may cause some minorities to develop their eating disorders.

What Causes Bulimia?

Bulimia is more than just a problem with food. A binge can be triggered by dieting, stress, or uncomfortable emotions, such as anger or sadness. Purging and other actions to prevent weight gain are ways for people with bulimia to feel more in control of their lives and ease stress and anxiety. There is no single known cause of bulimia, but there are some factors that may play a part.

- **Culture.** Women in the United States are under constant pressure to fit a certain ideal of beauty. Seeing images of flawless, thin females everywhere makes it hard for women to feel good about their bodies.

- **Families.** If you have a mother or sister with bulimia, you are more likely to also have bulimia. Parents who think looks are important, diet themselves, or criticize their children's bodies are more likely to have a child with bulimia.

- **Life changes or stressful events.** Traumatic events (like rape), as well as stressful things (like starting a new job), can lead to bulimia.

- **Personality traits.** A person with bulimia may not like herself, hate the way she looks, or feel hopeless. She may be very moody, have problems expressing anger, or have a hard time controlling impulsive behaviors.

- **Biology.** Genes, hormones, and chemicals in the brain may be factors in developing bulimia.

What Are Signs and Symptoms of Bulimia?

A person with bulimia may be thin, overweight, or have a normal weight. Also, bulimic behavior, such as throwing up, is often done in private because the person with bulimia feels shame or disgust. This makes it hard to know if someone has bulimia. But there are warning signs to look out for. Someone with bulimia may use extreme measures to lose weight by:

- Using diet pills, or taking pills to urinate or have a bowel movement
- Going to the bathroom all the time after eating (to throw up)
- Exercising a lot, even in bad weather or when hurt or tired

Someone with bulimia may show signs of throwing up, such as:

- Swollen cheeks or jaw area
- Calluses or scrapes on the knuckles (if using fingers to induce vomiting)
- Teeth that look clear
- Broken blood vessels in the eyes

Symptoms include:

- Chronically inflamed and sore throat
- Swollen salivary glands in the neck and jaw area
- Worn tooth enamel and increasingly sensitive and decaying teeth as a result of exposure to stomach acid
- Acid reflux disorder and other gastrointestinal problems
- Intestinal distress and irritation from laxative abuse
- Severe dehydration from purging of fluids
- Electrolyte imbalance (too low or too high levels of sodium, calcium, potassium and other minerals) which can lead to stroke or heart attack

People with bulimia often have other mental health conditions, including:

- Depression
- Anxiety
- Substance abuse problems
- May not want to go out with friends

Someone with bulimia may also have a distorted body image, shown by thinking she or he is fat, hating her or his body, and fearing weight gain.

People with bulimia are often at a normal weight, but they may see themselves as being overweight. Because the person's weight is often normal, other people may not notice this eating disorder.

What Happens to Someone Who Has Bulimia?

Bulimia can be very harmful to the body. Look at the picture to find out how bulimia affects your health.

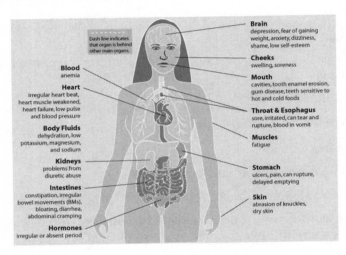

Figure 5.1. *Bulimia affecting body parts*

Can Someone with Bulimia Get Better?

Yes. Someone with bulimia can get better. A healthcare team of doctors, nutritionists, and therapists will help the patient recover. They will help the person learn healthy eating patterns and cope with their thoughts and feelings. Treatment for bulimia uses a combination of options. Whether or not the treatment works depends on the patient.

To stop a person from binging and purging, a doctor may recommend the patient:

- Receive nutritional advice and psychotherapy, especially cognitive behavioral therapy (CBT)

- Be prescribed medicine

CBT is a form of psychotherapy that focuses on the important role of thinking in how we feel and what we do. CBT that has been tailored to treat bulimia has shown to be effective in changing binging and purging behavior, and eating attitudes. Therapy for a person with bulimia may be one-on-one with a therapist or group-based.

Some antidepressants, such as fluoxetine (Prozac), which is the only medication approved by the U.S. Food and Drug Administration (FDA) for treating bulimia, may help patients who also have depression and/or anxiety. It also appears to help reduce binge eating and purging behavior, reduces the chance of relapse, and improves eating attitudes.

Is It Safe for Young People to Take Antidepressants for Bulimia?

It may be safe for young people to be treated with antidepressants. However, drug companies who make antidepressants are required to post a "black box" warning label on the medication. A "black box" warning is the most serious type of warning on prescription medicines.

It may be possible that antidepressants make children, adolescents, and young adults more likely to think about suicide or commit suicide.

The latest information from the U.S. Food and Drug Administration (FDA)—including what drugs are included in this warning and things to look for—can be found on their website at www.fda.gov.

- It may be safe for young people to be treated with antidepressants. However, drug companies who make antidepressants are required to post a "black box" warning label on the medication. A "black box" warning is the most serious type of warning on prescription medicines.

It may be possible that antidepressants make children, adolescents, and young adults more likely to think about suicide or commit suicide.

Can Women Who Had Bulimia in the past Still Get Pregnant?

Active bulimia can cause a woman to miss her period sometimes. Or, she may never get her period. If this happens, she usually does not ovulate. This makes it hard to get pregnant. Women who have recovered from bulimia have a better chance of getting pregnant once their monthly cycle is normal. If you're having a hard time getting pregnant, see your doctor.

How Does Bulimia Affect Pregnancy?

If a woman with active bulimia gets pregnant, these problems may result:

- Miscarriage
- High blood pressure in the mother
- Baby isn't born alive
- Baby tries to come out with feet or bottom first
- Birth by C-section
- Baby is born early
- Low birth weight
- Birth defects, such as blindness or mental retardation
- Problems breastfeeding
- Depression in the mother after the baby is born
- Diabetes in the mother during pregnancy

If a woman takes laxatives or diuretics during pregnancy, her baby could be harmed. These things take away nutrients and fluids from a woman before they are able to feed and nourish the baby. It is possible they may lead to birth defects as well, particularly if they are used regularly.

What Should I Do If I Think Someone I Know Has Bulimia?

If someone you know is showing signs of bulimia, you may be able to help.

1. **Set a time to talk.** Set aside a time to talk privately with your friend. Make sure you talk in a quiet place where you won't be distracted.

2. **Tell your friend about your concerns.** Be honest. Tell your friend about your worries about his or her eating or exercising habits. Tell your friend you are concerned and that you think these things may be a sign of a problem that needs professional help.

3. **Ask your friend to talk to a professional.** Your friend can talk to a counselor or doctor who knows about eating

issues. Offer to help your friend find a counselor or doctor and make an appointment, and offer to go with him or her to the appointment.

4. **Avoid conflicts.** If your friend won't admit that he or she has a problem, don't push. Be sure to tell your friend you are always there to listen if he or she wants to talk.

5. **Don't place shame, blame, or guilt on your friend.** Don't say, "You just need to eat." Instead, say things like, "I'm concerned about you because you won't eat breakfast or lunch." Or, "It makes me afraid to hear you throwing up."

6. **Don't give simple solutions.** Don't say, "If you'd just stop, then things would be fine!"

7. **Let your friend know that you will always be there no matter what.**

Chapter 6

Orthorexia

What Is Orthorexia Nervosa?

Orthorexia nervosa, often called orthorexia, is a form of disordered eating that is characterized by an extreme obsession with consuming only foods that are perceived to be healthy or pure. Although orthorexia is not listed as an eating disorder in the American Psychiatric Association's *Diagnostic and Statistical Manual of Mental Disorders*, the condition is widely recognized by healthcare professionals and shares many traits with eating disorders. Orthorexia was first described in 1996 by Dr. Steven Bratman, who coined the name from the Greek words meaning "correct diet."

As part of their fixation with eating only healthy foods, people with orthorexia carefully avoid foods that they consider to be unwholesome or harmful. They typically establish strict rules to determine which foods they will eat and which foods they will avoid. For instance, they may eliminate entire food groups, such as fats or carbohydrates, or they may refuse to eat any food that contains artificial ingredients or additives. For many people with orthorexia, the need to plan meals and restrict food choices prevents them from attending social events or eating at restaurants because they cannot control the menu. They may also feel superior to people who do not follow a strict diet and who consume foods they reject as unhealthy.

Orthorexia resembles anorexia and bulimia because all of these conditions involve an obsession with controlling food intake. People with these eating disorders often experience severe anxiety surrounding meal planning and food consumption, and they may evaluate their self-worth based on their success in restricting their diet. Orthorexia differs from anorexia and bulimia, however, because people with orthorexia are primarily concerned with the quality of the food they consume, rather than the quantity. In addition, the main goal of their dietary limitations is typically to feel clean, pure, and healthy rather than to lose weight.

Signs of Orthorexia

Doctors, nutritionists, and public health agencies all emphasize the benefits of eating healthy foods. In addition, the media promotes an endless array of fad diets that recommend limiting food choices or even eliminating food groups as a path to better health. As a result, it can be difficult to sort through all the contradictory dietary advice and determine the point at which an interest in healthy eating becomes disordered eating. Orthorexia occurs when people take healthy eating to such an extreme point that it actually compromises their health or well-being. Some of the common warning signs of orthorexia include the following:

- Strictly limiting food choices, including eliminating entire food groups, in an effort to achieve a "perfect" diet;

- Spending extreme amounts of time and money planning meals and preparing "healthy" foods;

- Experiencing severe anxiety regarding meal planning or food preparation;

- Avoiding social events where food is served for fear of being unable to comply with a strict diet;

- Feeling fulfilled or virtuous when self-imposed rules for eating "healthy" are followed successfully;

- Feeling guilty or embarrassed when unable to adhere to strict dietary standards;

- Viewing others negatively if they lack the self-control to avoid "unhealthy" foods.

Treatment for Orthorexia

The behaviors associated with orthorexia extend beyond reasonable efforts to eat well and maintain a healthy lifestyle. As the condition progresses, such extreme dietary restrictions can take a toll on a person's physical, emotional, and mental health. In fact, some of the potential negative health effects are similar to those seen in people with anorexia or bulimia, such as malnutrition, loss of bone density, heart or kidney problems, social isolation, and emotional instability.

People with orthorexia may benefit from working with a team of eating disorder specialists, including physicians, psychiatrists, therapists, and nutritionists. Professional treatment can help people with orthorexia identify and address the underlying issues that may contribute to the condition and develop dietary practices that support overall health.

References

1.   Ekern, Jacquelyn. "Orthorexia, Excessive Exercise, and Nutrition." Eating Disorder Hope, January 31, 2014.

2.   Ekern, Jacquelyn and Karges, Crystal. "How to Recognize Orthorexia?" Eating Disorder Hope, May 17, 2014.

Chapter 7

Diet Pill, Diuretic, Ipecac, and Laxative Abuse

Common Purging Methods

While maintaining a healthy weight is a positive goal, sometimes people become so focused on losing weight that they resort to unproven and dangerous weight-loss methods that can lead to serious health problems. Those with eating disorders like bulimia, for instance, may use various methods of purging—such as self-induced vomiting, consuming ipecac syrup, or abusing laxatives or diuretics—in an effort to rid the body of the calories they consume. Although the idea behind purging is to force food to leave the body before the calories have been absorbed, it is not an effective weight loss strategy. The body absorbs nutrients very quickly, and mainly fluids are expelled through vomiting or use of laxatives and diuretics. Purging is also extremely dangerous and can cause many serious, long-term, and potentially fatal health complications. Some of the common purging methods employed by people with eating disorders include:

Diet Pills

Diet pills or appetite suppressants are another form of medication that can be abused by people with eating disorders. Many of these substances stimulate the central nervous system and have the potential to be addictive. Since they are considered supplements rather than food or drugs, they are poorly regulated and may contain harmful ingredients. Excessive use of diet pills can cause nausea, headaches, anxiety, irritability, insomnia, dizziness, diarrhea, skin rashes, elevated blood pressure, and heart complications.

Diuretic Abuse

Diuretics are medications that are used to eliminate water from the body. When used as directed, they can be helpful for people who have high blood pressure or a severe form of swelling called edema. People with eating disorders sometimes misuse diuretics in the belief that they promote weight loss. In reality, however, any weight lost occurs due to a loss of water. Not only will the water weight return as soon as the person consumes fluids, long-term abuse of diuretics may actually cause weight gain as the body chronically retains water to offset the effects of the medication. The health risks associated with diuretic abuse include dehydration, electrolyte imbalance, low blood pressure, fainting, irregular heartbeat, kidney damage, and death.

Ipecac Syrup

Syrup of ipecac is a liquid medication that induces vomiting. It can be helpful in emergency medical situations when a person swallows something that is poisonous or toxic. Taking ipecac syrup immediately afterward may enable the person to expel the poison by vomiting before it is absorbed into the bloodstream. But some people with eating disorders abuse ipecac syrup by using it to purge after eating. When overused or abused, ipecac syrup can be extremely harmful or even deadly. In addition to the problems associated with repeated vomiting, ipecac abuse can cause muscle weakness, difficulty breathing, seizures, internal bleeding, chest pain, and heart complications.

Laxatives

Laxatives are medications that can help relieve constipation by loosening stool and triggering the large intestine to produce bowel movements. Although laxatives can be helpful when used as directed, they are also commonly abused by people with eating disorders such as bulimia. People who abuse laxatives take them after overeating in an effort to empty the food out of their digestive system before their body can absorb the calories. Laxatives do not help people lose weight, however, because most calories and fat are absorbed before food reaches the large intestine. Instead, laxatives mainly cause the body to lose water, minerals, and electrolytes. Any weight that is lost is typically regained as soon as the person drinks fluids. Misusing laxatives can cause a number of serious health problems, including:

- severe dehydration, with symptoms including weakness, confusion, and accelerated heart rate;
- electrolyte imbalance and loss of important minerals such as magnesium, potassium, and sodium;
- nausea, stomach pain, bowel problems, stretching or infection of the intestines, and an increased risk of colon cancer;
- damage to kidneys and other organs;
- heart attack.

Self-Induced Vomiting

Many people with eating disorders force themselves to vomit after eating in an effort to absorb fewer calories and lose weight. In people with bulimia, purging through self-induced vomiting often follows overeating or binge eating. The process of digestion begins as soon as food enters the mouth, however, so vomiting does not prevent the absorption of all the calories consumed. In addition, forced vomiting is associated with a wide range of dangerous health issues, such as:

- dental problems from teeth coming into contact with stomach acid, including stained teeth, sensitivity to temperature, and erosion of tooth enamel;
- hardened skin or scarring on the back of the hand, known as Russell's sign, from inserting the fingers into the back of the throat to induce vomiting;
- swelling, tearing, or other damage to the esophagus (the tube that transports food from the mouth to the stomach);
- dehydration and loss of minerals and electrolytes;
- irregular heartbeat and heart failure.

Resisting the Urge to Purge

To avoid the health hazards associated with misuse of diet pills, diuretics, ipecac syrup, laxatives, and other medications, people should seek support from an organization or treatment center that focuses on eating disorders. Specialized programs and professional assistance from doctors, therapists, and nutritionists can help people stop abusing these products and recover their physical and mental health. Additional strategies for resisting the urge to purge include throwing away any laxatives, diet pills, or related products in the home; staying well hydrated and avoiding caffeine and alcohol; eating a fiber-rich diet to promote intestinal health; and exercising—especially in the morning—to stimulate digestive function.

References

1. Bano, Musarrat. "Dangerous Methods of Weight Loss," May 27, 2014.

2. "Laxative Abuse: A Common Practice among Bulimics," Casa Palmera, September 19, 2012.

3. "Purging," Kelty Eating Disorders, n.d.

Chapter 8

Female Athlete Triad

Eating vs. Being Active

Sports and exercise are part of a balanced, healthy lifestyle. People who play sports are healthier; get better grades; are less likely to experience depression; and use alcohol, cigarettes, and drugs less frequently than people who aren't athletes. But for some girls, not balancing the needs of their bodies and their sports can have major consequences.

Some girls who play sports or exercise intensely are at risk for a problem called female athlete triad. Female athlete triad is a combination of three conditions: disordered eating, amenorrhea, and osteoporosis. A female athlete can have one, two, or all three parts of the triad.

This chapter contains text excerpted from the following sources: Text under the heading "Female Athlete Triad" is excerpted from "Female Athlete Triad," © 1995–2016. The Nemours Foundation/KidsHealth®. Reprinted with permission; Text under the heading "Signs of Not Eating Enough and Eating Disorders" is excerpted from "Do You Exercise a Lot?" Office on Women's Health (OWH), March 27, 2015; Text under the heading "Are You at Risk for Female Athlete Triad?" is excerpted from "Are You at Risk for Female Athlete Triad?" Military Health System (MHS), October 27, 2015; Text under the heading "Amenorrheic Women and the Female Athlete Triad" is excerpted from "Calcium," Office of Dietary Supplements (ODS), November 21, 2013.

Triad Factor #1: Disordered Eating

Most girls with female athlete triad try to lose weight as a way to improve their athletic performance. The disordered eating that accompanies female athlete triad can range from not eating enough calories to keep up with energy demands to avoiding certain types of food the athlete thinks are "bad" (such as foods containing fat) to serious eating disorders like anorexia nervosa or bulimia nervosa.

Triad Factor #2: Amenorrhea

Exercising intensely and not eating enough calories can lead to decreases in the hormones that help regulate the menstrual cycle. As a result, a girl's periods may become irregular or stop altogether. Of course, it's normal for teens to occasionally miss periods, especially in the first year. A missed period does not automatically mean female athlete triad. It could mean something else is going on, like pregnancy or a medical condition. If you are having sex and miss your period, talk to your doctor.

Some girls who participate intensively in sports may never even get their first period because they've been training so hard. Others may have had periods, but once they increase their training and change their eating habits, their periods may stop.

Triad Factor #3: Osteoporosis

Estrogen is lower in girls with female athlete triad. Low estrogen levels and poor nutrition, especially low calcium intake, can lead to osteoporosis, the third aspect of the triad. Osteoporosis is a weakening of the bones due to the loss of bone density and improper bone formation. This condition can ruin a female athlete's career because it may lead to stress fractures and other injuries.

Usually, the teen years are a time when girls should be building up their bone mass to their highest levels—called peak bone mass. Not getting enough calcium now can also have a lasting effect on how strong a woman's bones are later in life.

Are You at Risk for Female Athlete Triad?

In female athletes and active women in the military, low bone-mineral density, menstrual irregularities, certain dietary patterns, and a history of prior stress fractures are associated with an increased risk of future stress fractures.

Female service members can be at risk for developing the Triad if they don't get enough calories (underfueling) and if training is too intense. But you can prevent it easily by focusing on your overall health and nutrition rather than your weight and by following these tips:

- Eat when you're hungry and include a variety of nutrient-rich foods such as lean sources of protein—lean fish, poultry, beans, nuts, and low-fat dairy products—along with whole grains, fruits, and vegetables. Skipping meals and snacks or severely restricting your food intake will keep you from getting enough calories and other important nutrients such as protein, vitamins, and minerals.

- Eat a recovery snack that consists of carbs and protein after your workout. Carbs are your body's primary fuel source to keep you energized, and you need protein to build and repair your muscles.

- Talk to a registered dietitian for an individual nutrition plan. A registered dietitian who specializes in sports nutrition can help you choose the best foods and the right amounts to optimize your performance.

Amenorrheic Women and the Female Athlete Triad

Amenorrhea, the condition in which menstrual periods stop or fail to initiate in women of childbearing age, results from reduced circulating estrogen levels that, in turn, have a negative effect on calcium balance. Amenorrheic women with anorexia nervosa have decreased calcium absorption and higher urinary calcium excretion rates, as well as a lower rate of bone formation than healthy women. The "female athlete triad" also called as Athletic Performance and Energy Deficit (This means you have a "deficit," or lack, of the energy your body needs to stay healthy.) refers to the combination of disordered eating, amenorrhea, and osteoporosis. Exercise-induced amenorrhea generally results in decreased bone mass. Such women should be advised to consume adequate amounts of calcium and vitamin D. Supplements of these nutrients have been shown to reduce the risk of stress fractures in female Navy recruits during basic training.

Chapter 9

Pica and Rumination Disorder

Chapter Contents

Section 9.1

Pica

This section contains text excerpted from the following sources:
Text beginning the heading "Pica" is excerpted from © 1995–2016.
"Pica," © 1995–2016. The Nemours Foundation/KidsHealth®.
Reprinted with permission; Text under the heading "Can It Be
Prevented?" is excerpted from "Pica Behavior and Contaminated
Soil," Centers for Disease Control and Prevention (CDC),
February 22, 2011. Reviewed March 2016.

Many young kids put nonfood items in their mouths at one time or
another. They're naturally curious about their environment and might,
for instance, eat some dirt out of the sandbox.

Kids with pica, however, go beyond this innocent exploration of
their surroundings. Between 10 percent and 30 percent of kids ages
of 1 to 6 years have the eating disorder pica, which is characterized
by persistent and compulsive cravings (lasting 1 month or longer) to
eat nonfood items.

About Pica

The word pica comes from the Latin word for magpie, a bird known
for its large and indiscriminate appetite.

Pica behavior is the craving to eat nonfood items, such as dirt, paint
chips, and clay. Some children, especially preschool children, exhibit
pica behavior. Soil ingestion is the consumption of soil resulting from
various behaviors including, but not limited to, mouthing objects or
dirty hands, eating dropped food, and intentionally consuming soil.
All children (and even adults) ingest small amounts of soil daily from
these behaviors. The distinguishing factor for soil-pica is the recurrent
ingestion of unusually high amounts of soil either intentionally by
eating dirt or unintentionally from excessive mouthing behavior or
eating dropped food. While the typical child might ingest 1/8 teaspoon
soil daily, children with soil-pica behavior ingest about a teaspoon or
more of soil daily.

Pica and specifically soil-pica is a public health issue that has gotten little attention because people do not realize that it can lead to

significant exposure to chemicals. However, soil ingestion has already been shown to be a significant risk factor for increased blood lead levels (BLL) and for exposure to soil-transmitted parasites. Up to 20% of preschool children have soil-pica behavior, which parents may not notice since their preschool children may play unattended in the safety of their back yards.

In addition, pica behavior has also been observed in adults, and in particular pregnant women. In many cases of adult pica, the practice has cultural significance or is the result of craving during pregnancy. In some cases, the craving is due to a nutritional deficiency, such as iron-deficiency anemia.

Pica is most common in people with developmental disabilities, including autism and mental retardation. Pica also may surface in children who've had a brain injury affecting their development, as well as people with epilepsy.

An example of an element that may be found in soil is arsenic. Inorganic arsenic doesn't degrade and binds to soil particles at the surface. Historically, repeated applications of arsenic-containing pesticides and herbicides may have increased arsenic levels in top soil to very high concentrations and can be a potential problem for children with soil-pica behavior. Pesticides containing arsenic are no longer commercially available. However, in many cases, soils were treated decades ago, yet the arsenic remains at the surface increasing the risk of contact from children's play activities. If soil ingestion is suspected among children, it is important to know

1. the amount of soil ingested,

2. the frequency of ingestion, and

3. the type of material ingested.

People with pica frequently crave and consume nonfood items such as:

- dirt
- clay
- paint chips
- plaster
- chalk
- cornstarch
- laundry starch

- baking soda
- coffee grounds
- cigarette ashes
- burnt match heads
- cigarette butts
- feces
- ice

- glue
- hair
- buttons
- paper
- sand
- toothpaste
- soap

Pica is an eating disorder that can result in serious health problems, such as lead poisoning and iron-deficiency anemia.

Who's at Risk?

Groups at risk of soil-pica behavior include children aged 6 years and younger as well as individuals of any age who are developmentally delayed. Soil-pica behavior is highest in 1- and 2-year-old children and declines as the children grow older.

Signs of Pica

Warning signs that a child may have pica include:

- repetitive consumption of nonfood items, despite efforts to restrict it, for a period of at least 1 month or longer
- the behavior is considered inappropriate for your child's age or developmental stage (older than 18 to 24 months)
- the behavior is not part of a cultural, ethnic, or religious practice

Why Do Some People Eat Nonfood Items?

The specific causes of pica are unknown, but certain conditions and situations can increase a person's risk:

- **nutritional deficiencies**, such as iron or zinc, that may trigger specific cravings (however, the nonfood items craved usually don't supply the minerals lacking in the person's body)
- **dieting**—people who diet may attempt to ease hunger by eating nonfood substances to get a feeling of fullness
- **malnutrition**, especially in underdeveloped countries, where people with pica most commonly eat soil or clay
- **cultural factors**—in families, religions, or groups in which eating nonfood substances is a learned practice

- **parental neglect**, lack of supervision, or food deprivation— often seen in children living in poverty

- **developmental problems,** such as mental retardation, autism, other developmental disabilities, or brain abnormalities

- **mental health conditions**, such as obsessive-compulsive disorder (OCD) and schizophrenia

- **pregnancy**, but it's been suggested that pica during pregnancy occurs more frequently in women who exhibited similar practices during their childhood or before pregnancy or who have a history of pica in their family

Eating earth substances such as clay or dirt is a form of pica known as geophagia, which can cause iron deficiency. One theory to explain **geophagia** is that in some cultures, eating clay or dirt may help relieve nausea (and therefore, morning sickness), control diarrhea, increase salivation, remove toxins, and alter odor or taste perception.

Some people claim to enjoy the taste and texture of dirt or clay or other non-food item, and eat it as part of a daily habit (much like smoking is a daily routine for others). Pica may also be a behavioral response to stress.

Another explanation is that pica is a cultural feature of certain religious rituals, folk medicine, and magical beliefs. For example, some people in various cultures believe that eating dirt will help them incorporate magical spirits into their bodies.

None of these theories, though, explains every form of pica. A doctor must treat each case individually to try to understand what's causing the condition.

When to Call the Doctor?

If your child is at risk for pica, talk to your doctor. If your child has consumed a harmful substance, seek medical care immediately. If you think your child has ingested something poisonous, call Poison Control at 800-222-1222.

A child who continues to consume nonfood items may be at risk for serious health problems, including:

- lead poisoning (from eating lead-based paint chips or dirt contaminated with lead)

- constipation or diarrhea (from consuming indigestible substances like hair, cloth, etc.)

- intestinal obstruction or perforation (from eating objects that could block or injure the intestines)

- dental injury (from eating hard substances that could harm the teeth)

- parasitic and other infections (from eating dirt, feces, or other infected substances)

Medical emergencies and death can occur if the craved substance is toxic or contaminated with lead or mercury, or if the item forms an indigestible mass blocking the intestines. Pica involving lead-containing substances during pregnancy may be associated with an increase in both maternal and fetal lead levels.

What Will the Doctor Do?

Your doctor will play an important role in helping you manage and prevent pica-related behaviors, educating you on teaching your child about acceptable and unacceptable food substances. The doctor will also work with you on ways to restrict the nonfood items your child craves (i.e., using child-safety locks and high shelving, and keeping household chemicals and medications out of reach).

Some kids require behavioral intervention and families may need to work with a psychologist or other mental health professional.

Medication may also be prescribed if pica is associated with significant behavioral problems not responding to behavioral treatments.

Your doctor may check for anemia or other nutritional deficiencies, if indicated. A child who has ingested a potentially harmful substance, such as lead, will be screened for lead and other toxic substances and might undergo stool testing for parasites. In some cases, X-rays or other imaging may be helpful to identify what was eaten or to look for bowel problems, such as an obstruction.

Fortunately, pica usually improves as kids get older. But for individuals with developmental or mental health concerns, pica may continue to be a problem. Ongoing treatment and maintaining a safe environment are key to manage this condition.

Can It Be Prevented?

Parents and guardians must be responsible for closely monitoring young children and persons who have developmental delays to ensure that soil is not ingested. Additionally, proper hand-washing techniques must be employed after being outside and before eating to ensure that contaminants and parasites in soil do not pose any further threats through hand-to-mouth contact.

Section 9.2

Rumination Disorder

This section includes text excerpted from "Rumination Disorder," Genetic and Rare Diseases Information Center (GARD), April 23, 2015.

Overview of Rumination Disorder

Rumination disorder is the backward flow of recently eaten food from the stomach to the mouth. The food is then re-chewed and swallowed or spat out. A non-purposeful contraction of stomach muscles is involved in rumination. It may be initially triggered by a viral illness, emotional distress, or physical injury. In many cases, no underlying trigger is identified. Behavioral therapy is the mainstay of treatment.

What Are the Signs and Symptoms of Rumination Disorder?

Signs and symptoms of rumination disorder includes the backward flow of recently eaten food from the stomach to the mouth. This typically occurs immediately to 15 to 30 minutes after eating. Rumination often occurs without retching or gagging. Rumination may be proceeded by a feeling of pressure, the need to belch, nausea, or discomfort. Some people with rumination disorder experience bloating, heartburn, diarrhea, constipation, abdominal pain, headaches, dizziness, or sleeping difficulties. Complications of severe disorder include weight loss, malnutrition, and electrolyte imbalance.

What Causes Rumination Disorder?

Rumination disorder may occur following a viral illness, emotional stress, or physical injury. It is theorized that while the initial stressor

71

improves, an altered sensation in the abdomen persist. This ultimately results in the relaxation of the muscle at the bottom of the esophagus. To relieve this discomfort people with rumination disorder use abdominal wall muscles to expel and regurgitate foods. As a result of the relief of symptoms, the person repeats the same response when the discomfort returns. Overtime the person unconsciously adopts this learned behavior.

Some cases of rumination disorder occur without a precipitating event or illness. Other people with the disorder describe also having ingestion, which may serve as a trigger. Studies have shown that some people with rumination disorder also have depression, anxiety, or a eating disorder. These conditions may likewise play a role in rumination disorder. Conditions like depression and anxiety are known to be more common in people with other functional gastrointestinal conditions as well, for example irritable bowel syndrome.

How Is Rumination Disorder Diagnosed?

Diagnosis can be made by a clinical evaluation of the person's signs and symptoms and history. The following diagnostic criteria is used to aid in diagnosis. These criteria must be met for the last 3 months, with symptoms beginning at least 6 months prior to diagnosis:

- Repeated regurgitation and rechewing or expulsion of food that

  - Begins soon after eating

  - Does not occur during sleep

  - Does not respond to standard treatment for GERD

- No retching

- Symptoms are not explained by inflammatory, anatomic, metabolic, or neoplastic processes

These criteria help distinguish rumination syndrome from other disorders of the GI tract, such as gastroparesis and achalasia where vomiting occurs hours after eating, gastroesophageal reflux where symptoms occur at night, and cyclic vomiting syndrome where the symptoms are chronic/persistent.

Antroduodenal manometry can assist in making and confirming the diagnosis. Antroduodenal manometry involves putting a catheter through the nose into the stomach and small bowel to measure pressure changes.

How Might Rumination Disorder Be Treated?

The mainstay treatment of rumination disorder is behavioral therapy. This may involve habitat reversal strategies, relaxation, diaphrag-
matic breathing, and biofeedback. These types of therapies can often
be administered by a gastroenterologist. Other professionals, such
as nurse practitioners, psychologists, massage therapists, and recre-
ational therapists may also be involved in care. Ensuring adequate
nutrition is essential and treatment will also involve managing other
symptoms, such as anxiety, nausea and stomach discomfort (which
may involve anti-depressive agents or SSRIs).

If behavioral therapy is unsuccessful, treatment with baclofen may
be considered. There is limited data regarding optimal treatment of
rumination disorder, but success with baclofen has been reported.

Chapter 10

Disorders Often Accompanying Eating Disorders

Chapter Contents

Section 10.1

Body Dysmorphic Disorder

This section includes text excerpted from "Cognitive-Behavioral Therapy and Supportive Psychotherapy for Body Dysmorphic Disorder," National Institute of Neurological Disorders and Stroke (NINDS), October 18, 2015.

Body dysmorphic disorder (BDD) is a severe, often chronic, and common disorder consisting of distressing or impairing preoccupation with perceived defects in one's physical appearance. Individuals with BDD have very poor psychosocial functioning and high rates of hospitalization and suicidality. Because BDD differs in important ways from other disorders, psychotherapies for other disorders are not adequate for BDD. Despite BDD's severity, there is no adequately tested psychosocial treatment (psychotherapy) of any type for this disorder.

Symptoms of BDD

- Being preoccupied with minor or imaginary physical flaws, usually of the skin, hair, and nose, such as acne, scarring, facial lines, marks, pale skin, thinning hair, excessive body hair, large nose, or crooked nose.

- Having a lot of anxiety and stress about the perceived flaw and spending a lot of time focusing on it, such as frequently picking at skin, excessively checking appearance in a mirror, hiding the imperfection, comparing appearance with others, excessively grooming, seeking reassurance from others about how they look, and getting cosmetic surgery.

Getting cosmetic surgery can make BDD worse. They are often not happy with the outcome of the surgery. If they are, they may start to focus attention on another body area and become preoccupied trying to fix the new "defect." In this case, some patients with BDD become angry at the surgeon for making their appearance worse and may even become violent towards the surgeon.

Treatment for BDD

- **Medications.** Serotonin reuptake inhibitors or SSRIs are antidepressants that decrease the obsessive and compulsive behaviors.

- **Cognitive behavioral therapy.** This is a type of therapy with several steps:

  - The therapist asks the person to enter social situations without covering up their "defect."

  - The therapist helps them stop doing the compulsive behaviors to check the defect or cover it up. This may include removing mirrors, covering skin areas that the person picks, or not using make-up.

  - The therapist helps the individual change their false beliefs about their appearance.

Section 10.2

Compulsive Exercise

About Compulsive Exercise

Compulsive exercise (also called obligatory exercise and anorexia athletica) is best defined by an exercise addict's frame of mind: He or she no longer chooses to exercise but feels compelled to do so and struggles with guilt and anxiety if he or she doesn't work out. Injury, illness, an outing with friends, bad weather—none of these will deter those who compulsively exercise. In a sense, exercising takes over a compulsive exerciser's life because he or she plans life around it.

Of course, it's nearly impossible to draw a clear line dividing a healthy amount of exercise from too much. The government's 2005 dietary guidelines, published by the U.S. Department of Agriculture (USDA) and the U.S. Department of Health and Human Services (HHS), recommend at least 60 minutes of physical activity for kids and teens on most—if not all—days of the week.

Experts say that repeatedly exercising beyond the requirements for good health is an indicator of compulsive behavior, but because different amounts of exercise are appropriate for different people, this definition covers a range of activity levels. However, several workouts a day, every day, is overdoing it for almost anyone.

Much like with eating disorders, many people who engage in compulsive exercise do so to feel more in control of their lives, and the majority of them are female. They often define their self-worth through their athletic performance and try to deal with emotions like anger or depression by pushing their bodies to the limit. In sticking to a rigorous workout schedule, they seek a sense of power to help them cope with low self-esteem.

Although compulsive exercising doesn't have to accompany an eating disorder, the two often go hand in hand. In anorexia nervosa, the excessive workouts usually begin as a means to control weight and become more and more extreme. As the rate of activity increases, the amount the person eats might decrease. Someone with bulimia also may use exercise as a way to compensate for binge eating.

Compulsive exercise behavior can grow out of student athletes' demanding practice schedules and their quest to excel. Pressure, both external (from coaches, peers, or parents) and internal, can drive an athlete to go too far to be the best. He or she ends up believing that just one more workout will make the difference between first and second place then keeps adding more workouts.

Eventually, compulsive exercising can breed other compulsive behavior, from strict dieting to obsessive thoughts about perceived flaws. Exercise addicts may keep detailed journals about their exercise schedules and obsess about improving themselves. Unfortunately, these behaviors often compound each other, trapping the person in a downward spiral of negative thinking and low self-esteem.

Why Is Exercising Too Much a Bad Thing?

We all know that regular exercise is an important part of a healthy lifestyle. But few people realize that too much can cause physical and psychological harm:

- Excessive exercise can damage tendons, ligaments, bones, cartilage, and joints, and when minor injuries aren't allowed to heal, they often result in long-term damage. Instead of building muscle, too much exercise actually destroys muscle mass, especially if the body isn't getting enough nutrition, forcing it to break down muscle for energy.

- Girls who exercise compulsively may disrupt the balance of hormones in their bodies. This can change their menstrual cycles (some girls lose their periods altogether, a condition known as amenorrhea) and increase the risk of premature bone loss (osteoporosis). And of course, working their bodies so hard leads to exhaustion and constant fatigue.

- An even more serious risk is the stress that excessive exercise can place on the heart, particularly when someone is also engaging in unhealthy weight loss behaviors such as restricting intake, vomiting, and using diet pills or supplements. In extreme cases, the combination of anorexia and compulsive exercise can be fatal.

- Psychologically, exercise addicts are often plagued by anxiety and depression. They may have a negative image of themselves and feel worthless. Their social and academic lives may suffer as they withdraw from friends and family to fixate on exercise. Even if they want to succeed in school or in relationships, working out always comes first, so they end up skipping homework or missing out on time spent with friends.

Warning Signs

Someone may be exercising compulsively if he or she:

- won't skip a workout, even if tired, sick, or injured
- doesn't enjoy exercise sessions, but feels obligated to do them
- seems anxious or guilty when missing even one workout
- does miss one workout and exercises twice as long the next time
- is constantly preoccupied with his or her weight and exercise routine
- doesn't like to sit still or relax because of worry that not enough calories are being burnt

- has lost a significant amount of weight

- exercises more after eating more

- skips seeing friends, gives up activities, and abandons responsibilities to make more time for exercise

- seems to base self-worth on the number of workouts completed and the effort put into training

- is never satisfied with his or her own physical achievements

It's important, too, to recognize the types of athletes who are more prone to compulsive exercise because their sports place a particular emphasis on being thin. Ice skaters, gymnasts, wrestlers, and dancers can feel even more pressure than most athletes to keep their weight down and their body toned. Runners also frequently fall into a cycle of obsessive workouts.

Getting Professional Help

If you recognize some of the warning signs of compulsive exercise in your child, call your doctor to discuss your concerns. After evaluating your child, the doctor may recommend medical treatment and/or other therapy.

Because compulsive exercise is so often linked to an eating disorder, a community agency that focuses on treating these disorders might be able to offer advice or referrals. Extreme cases may require hospitalization to get a child's weight back up to a safe range.

Treating a compulsion to exercise is never a quick-fix process—it may take several months or even years. But with time and effort, kids can get back on the road to good health. Therapy can help improve self-esteem and body image, as well as teach them how to deal with emotions. Sessions with a nutritionist can help develop healthy eating habits. Once they know what to watch out for, kids will be better equipped to steer clear of unsafe exercise and eating patterns.

Ways to Help at Home

Parents can do a lot to help a child overcome a compulsion to exercise:

- Involve kids in preparing nutritious meals.

- Combine activity and fun by going for a hike or a bike ride together as a family.

- Be a good body-image role model. In other words, don't fixate on your own physical flaws, as that just teaches kids that it's normal to dislike what they see in the mirror.

- Never criticize another family member's weight or body shape, even if you're just kidding around. Such remarks might seem harmless, but they can leave a lasting impression on kids or teens struggling to define and accept themselves.

- Examine whether you're putting too much pressure on your kids to excel, particularly in a sport (because some teens turn to exercise to cope with pressure). Take a look at where kids might be feeling too much pressure. Help them put it in perspective and find other ways to cope.

Most important, just be there with constant support. Point out all of your child's great qualities that have nothing to do with working out—small daily doses of encouragement and praise can help improve self-esteem.

If you teach kids to be proud of the challenges they've faced and not just the first-place ribbons they've won, they will likely be much happier and healthier kids now and in the long run.

Part Two

Risk Factors for Eating Disorders

Chapter 11

Factors that Increase Risk for Eating Disorders

Risk Factors

Eating disorders do not have a single, identifiable cause. There are psychological, biological and social risk factors which may increase the likelihood of an eating disorder developing, as well as behaviours and traits which can be changed (such as dieting, poor self-esteem, perfectionism). Eating disorders can occur across all ages, socio-economic groups and genders. Some potential risk factors for the development of an eating disorder include:

Psychological Factors

- Low self-esteem

- Feelings of inadequacy

- Depression or anxiety

- A belief that love from family and friends is dependent on high achievement

- Difficulty expressing emotions and feelings, particularly negative emotions such as anger, sadness, anxiety or fear

This chapter includes text excerpted from "Risk Factors," © 2016 Eating Disorders Victoria. For more information, visit www.eatingdisorders.org.au. Reprinted with permission.

- Ineffective coping strategies

- Perfectionism

- Fear or avoidance of conflict

- Competitiveness

- Impulsive or obsessive behaviours

- Highly concerned with the opinions of others, often with a need to please

- Prone to extremes, such as 'black and white' thinking

Social Factors

- Cultural value placed on thinness as an inextricable part of beauty

- Current cultural emphasis on the goal to strive for a 'perfect' body

- Valuing of people according to outward appearance and not inner qualities

- Media and popular culture's unrealistic portrayal of people's shapes and bodies

- Pressure to achieve and succeed

- Professions with an emphasis on body shape and size (eg. dancers, models, athletes)

Biological Factors

- Scientists are currently researching possible biochemical and biological factors and their role in the development of eating disorders. Research has indicated that in some people with eating disorders there is an imbalance of certain chemicals in the brain

- Adolescence and the associated physical, hormonal and neural changes

- Genetic or familial factors, for example a person who is exposed to a parent or sibling with an eating disorder is at a higher risk of developing an eating disorder themselves. While no conclusive outcome has been reached, research has provided evidence that in some cases this is due to genetic predisposition rather than learned behaviour

External Factors

- Life events, particularly those involving major changes (eg. loss of a family member or friend, the divorce or separation of parents, moving schools or jobs)

- Dieting

- Peer pressure

- Inability to effectively deal with stress

- Personal or family history of obesity, depression, substance abuse or eating disorders

- Troubled personal or family relationships

- Sexual or physical abuse

- History of teasing or bullying, particularly when based on weight or shape

Some of the other risk factors include:

Dieting

Dieting is the number one risk factor in the development of an eating disorder.

Recent research shows that women who diet severely are eighteen times more likely to develop an eating disorder. Women who diet moderately are five times more likely to develop an eating disorder.

The strict, restrictive and often unsustainable nature of many diets can lead to over-compensatory behaviours, fluctuating weight and many related psychological effects such as feelings of guilt over 'lack of self-control', low self-esteem and obsessive thoughts and behaviours surrounding food. In addition, people who diet frequently are more likely to experience depression.

Many dieting behaviours can be damaging to physical and psychological health. Fluctuating weight is common for most people who diet frequently, as most people re-gain all the weight they have lost after a diet. Weight loss or weight gain may lead to long-term physical side effects.

As well as the physical effects, dieting can be damaging to people's emotional and psychological health, for example, people who diet frequently are more likely to experience depression.

Body Image

What is body image?

Body image refers to how a person perceives, thinks and feels about their body and appearance.

These thoughts and feelings can be positive, negative, or a combination of both. A person's body image can change over time, and can be strongly influenced by what a person reads, sees and hears.

People's psychological perceptions of their bodies are not always accurate, and this can affect what they see. For example, some people may believe their body is larger or fatter than it actually is, or become fixated on a particular body part and start to see it as being very unattractive. When people feel dissatisfied about their body, this can affect their behaviour; for example, someone who thinks they are overweight may choose not to exercise in public.

Healthy body image

A healthy body image means being content with your body and the way you look. People with a positive body image usually have greater self-esteem, better self-acceptance and a healthier lifestyle. When you are free from worrying about your body image, you have more time and freedom to spend on positive activities such as developing friendships and enjoying your talents and hobbies.

Body image dissatisfaction

Negative body image usually involves a difference between how someone thinks they should look, and how they actually look. People are influenced by family, friends, their peers and mass media. Body image dissatisfaction is not just about size and weight; it can also be about skin color, ethnic diversity, disabilities and strength or fitness.

Anyone can be affected by negative body image—men, women, children, teenagers and adults. However studies show that young people are particularly affected. Adolescence is usually when negative body image begins, but without a conscious effort to change, people can be affected by body image dissatisfaction well into adulthood.

What causes negative body image?

The pressure to conform to a particular "look" comes from many different sources in today's society. The messages given by the media, people's family, friends and peers can all have a negative effect. It can also be unhelpful to be around people who are overly concerned about their body image and engage in weight loss dieting and talking about their body in a negative way.

There are certain personal characteristics that can contribute to someone's susceptibility to developing negative body image. These can include: perfectionism, "black and white" thinking, low self-esteem, as well as a person's age, gender, sexual orientation and culture.

It's important to remember that much of your physical appearance cannot be changed. Your height, muscle composition and bone structure are all determined by your genes.

How can you improve your body image?

Media literacy

We are all faced with a constant barrage of images from the media (TV, magazines, the Internet and advertisements). These images are often unrealistic and unattainable, and send the strong message that females should be thin, and men should be muscular and buff. Our society places a lot of emphasis on external appearances, which has the tendency to make us feel inadequate and also gives us a distorted view of what we should look like.

Become media literate–question the messages and images you are viewing. Are you being sold something? Are the images you are viewing unrealistic and unattainable? Have they been digitally altered? Do you feel bad about yourself after seeing them? If so, be careful about allowing yourself to be manipulated.

Be kind to yourself

Instead of criticizing yourself and focusing on what you don't like about yourself, try focusing on what you do like. Avoid seeing yourself as a collection of separate body parts, and try to see yourself as a whole person. Focus on all the great things your body does for you.

Positive thinking

If you find yourself criticizing yourself or engaging in negative self-talk, catch yourself and stop. Give yourself a pat on the back when you've done something well, and treat yourself as you would treat a friend.

Avoid critiquing other people's bodies

Stop yourself from making unkind comments about other people's appearances. Not only are such comments potentially hurtful, they reinforce the importance of adhering to unrealistic beauty ideals to anyone listening.

Look after yourself

Take the time to look after yourself and spend time doing what makes you happy. Having hobbies, taking time to relax, and engaging in self-care are all extremely important. Rather than setting goals around weight loss, focus your goals on being healthy and happy.

Self-Esteem

Self-esteem and body image are closely related risk factors in the development of an eating disorder.

Self-esteem represents a person's perception of their internal and external faculties as a whole—an all-inclusive sense of self-worth.

Body image, on the other hand, is the perception of a person's physical appearance. Low self-esteem is a central theme in the development of an eating disorder, and it often manifests as a critical voice which creates and feeds perceptions of poor body image. Low self-esteem naturally leads to negative perceptions of one's physical appearance. A person's distorted body image is reconciled only when internal issues with low self-esteem are corrected.

Self-esteem determines how a person lives—how they talk, handle relationships, choose career paths and create lifestyles. Low self-esteem is a major risk factor in the development of an eating disorder, so an important preventative measure is to consciously enhance and rebuild self-esteem. While for some, it may seem like a long and arduous path in retraining the mind, building and improving upon self-esteem is a choice which is available to everybody and worth making.

Tips for Improving Self-Esteem

Below are some general tips for improving self-esteem. Whether you apply these as a preventative measure for low self-esteem, as self care practices in the midst of an eating disorder, or as an exercise in maintaining a healthy level of self-esteem, these tips have something to benefit everybody.

- Ensure you are providing your body and mind with the basic necessities for healthy living. Get enough rest. Eat a balanced diet containing foods with plenty of nutrients for living. Exercise for the simple joy of moving and feeling alive.

- Spend more time with people who encourage you, and less time with people who discourage you.

- Take a strong commitment and a conscious effort to succeed in building your own self-esteem.

- The next time you make a mistake, be forgiving of yourself.

- Celebrate your achievements, no matter how small or large. recognize the good choices you make and congratulate yourself on your successes.

- Stand and walk with good posture.

- Do things you enjoy and know you're worth it. Make the time to do the things that make you feel relaxed, calm and happy. Whether it's reading a book, going for a hike, seeing a movie or getting a massage, ensure these activities are a priority for you, especially at times when you are feeling low or sensitive.

- Redefine "selfish." Learn to love yourself and to take care of your needs effectively. You can get your needs met and still have love in your life.

- Take responsibility for your life and your wellbeing and stop taking responsibility for other people's lives. It's great to help people, but they are still responsible for their own situations and actions.

- As you make new choices, set out goals and strategies for improving the way you think and live.

- Treat yourself with deliberate acts of kindness.

Perfectionism

Perfectionism goes beyond setting personal goals and doing your best. People with perfectionist traits set extremely high standards that are unrealistic, and feel distressed when they fail to meet these impossible standards.

Often people set such high standards for themselves to manage low self-esteem or a sense of worthlessness. They mistakenly believe that if they can meet these high standards, they will have a sense of control and be "worthwhile" and "successful." They may strive for perfection in their academic or work performance, morality, relationships, cleanliness and order, or dieting, exercise, body weight or shape. It is common for people with perfectionist traits to think in an "all-or-nothing" way where anything other than perfection is seen as failure.

Perfectionism is a common personality trait in people with an eating disorder, who may feel the need to maintain complete control over their weight. Early intervention is key, so if a person with perfectionist tendencies becomes aware of the development of disordered eating behaviours such as rigidity or guilt surrounding eating patterns, it is important to seek help immediately.

- Some ideas to help conquer perfectionism

- Identify the high standards you hold yourself to. What would be a more realistic standard?

- Next, identify the behaviours you use to reach your standards. How can you let go and change your actions?

- Be willing to take risks, and be gentle with yourself when a risk results in failure.

- Try not to be competitive with your thinking or behaviour, and avoid thinking in black and white extremes.

- Accept there's no such thing as a life completely free from sadness or anxiety.

- Practice compassion for yourself and others.

- Try to replace negative thinking patterns with positive thoughts.

- Accept that as a human being you have limitations and will make mistakes, but you still have intrinsic self-worth.

- Try to laugh at yourself and your mistakes—as hard as it may seem!

Chapter 12

Eating Disorders in Youth and Young Adults

Chapter Contents

Section 12.1

Eating Disorders in Children

This section includes text excerpted from "Eating Disorders and Children," © 2016 Eating Disorders Victoria. For more information, visit www.eatingdisorders.org.au. Reprinted with permission.

Although it is most common for eating disorders to develop during adolescence, young children can also be affected.

Eating disorders are particularly dangerous in young children, as they can escalate quickly as well as permanently stunt growth and development. They can be difficult to diagnose as children's body weight and nutrition requirements vary as they experience growth spurts. Eating disorders are not the same as fussiness, picky eating or eating difficulties that are linked to other issues such as autism spectrum disorder.

With so many mixed messages about what to eat, how to exercise, the "obesity crisis," celebrity culture and social media, many children are feeling confused and pressured. Up to 80% of United States 10 year old girls have already been on a diet.

Research suggests 20–25 percent of children affected by eating disorders are boys and there also may be a link between childhood obesity and the development of an eating disorder as an adolescent or adult.

Regardless of age, eating disorders are about underlying emotions, not food. Changes in behaviour with food could signal that a child is experiencing emotional, social or developmental issues such as depression, teasing, bullying or abuse. Often the eating disorder develops as a way for a child to feel in control over what's happening in their life.

Preventative Measures

Children are influenced by parents and teachers, who play an important role in modelling healthy and balanced attitudes towards food, exercise and body image.

Some important guidelines for parents and teachers include:

- Try not to label foods as 'good' or 'bad' as this may lead to feelings of guilt and shame when 'bad' foods are eaten

- Avoid using food as bribes, punishment or rewards

- Avoid promoting unrealistic or perfectionist ideals in terms of your child's behaviour, grades and achievements, and instead encourage self-acceptance

- Encourage children to celebrate diversity, and not place too much value on physical appearance as a measure of value

- Accept that children are likely to have different eating habits from adults—they may require food more frequently during the day or go through periods of liking or disliking particular foods

- Children learn by example—don't skip meals, participate in fad diets or enforce diets upon children

- Encourage your child to express their feelings freely and encourage open communication in the home

- Allow your child to eat when they are hungry and stop when they are full—don't force them to eat everything on their plate

- Model acceptance of different body shapes and sizes, including your own

- Don't criticize or tease children about their appearance, or make comparisons to another child's appearance

- Encourage sport and regular exercise to foster their body confidence. Model a healthy lifestyle yourself by participating in regular exercise for enjoyment and fitness

- Reassure your child that it is normal and healthy to gain weight at the onset of puberty and throughout adolescence

- Help children develop a critical awareness of the images and messages they receive from television, magazines, the Internet and social media

- If you are concerned about a child restricting food groups or portion sizes, consult your general physician.

If You Are Worried about Your Child

It is essential to seek help immediately if you suspect your child is showing signs of developing an eating disorder. Children are more vulnerable to the effects of eating disorders than adults, and early detection and intervention is crucial. Talk to a psychologist or a general practitioner with experience in this area about your concerns, and they will help you with obtaining a diagnosis and assessment.

Do not blame yourself—eating disorders are *not* caused by parents.

Section 12.2

Most Teens with Eating Disorders Go without Treatment

This section includes text excerpted from "Most Teens with Eating Disorders Go without Treatment," National Institute of Mental Health (NIMH), March 7, 2011. Reviewed March 2016.

About 3 percent of U.S. adolescents are affected by an eating disorder, but most do not receive treatment for their specific eating condition, according to a study, funded by National Institute of Mental Health (NIMH), published online in the *Archives of General Psychiatry.*

Results of the Study

According to the data, 0.3 percent of youth have been affected by anorexia, 0.9 percent by bulimia, and 1.6 percent by binge eating disorder. The researchers also tracked the rate of some forms of eating disorders not otherwise specified (EDNOS), a catch-all category of symptoms that do not meet full criteria for specific disorders but still impact a person's life. EDNOS is the most common eating disorder diagnosis. Overall, another 0.8 percent had subthreshold anorexia, and another 2.5 percent had symptoms of subthreshold binge eating disorder.

In addition,

- Hispanics reported the highest rates of bulimia, while whites reported the highest rates of anorexia.

- The majority who had an eating disorder also met criteria for at least one other psychiatric disorder such as depression.

- Each eating disorder was associated with higher levels of suicidal thinking compared to those without an eating disorder.

Significance

The prevalence of these disorders and their association with coexisting disorders, role impairment, and suicidal thinking suggest that eating disorders represent a major public health concern. In addition, the significant rates of subthreshold eating conditions support the notion that eating disorders tend to exist along a spectrum and may be better recognized by doctors if they included a broader range of symptoms. In addition, the findings clearly underscore the need for better access to treatment specifically for eating disorders.

Section 12.3

Eating Disorders among Teens

This section includes text excerpted from "Teens and At-Risk Behaviors," U.S. Department of Health and Human Services (HHS), August 23, 2012. Reviewed March 2016.

Eating Disorders in Teens

Teenagers, particularly girls, are often overly focused on their bodies. They may spend hours obsessing over what they perceive as fat thighs or a too-big tummy. The result can be excessive dieting and, in the worst cases, eating disorders. The desire to maintain a normal weight is healthy, and a goal parents should encourage. However, teenagers' weights often fluctuate until they have reached their full height and mature body, something neither you nor your child should expect until sometime in the middle to late teen years. Consequently, it is important not to become overly focused on your child's weight, whether over- or underweight. However, if your child begins to show signs of an eating disorder, you will need to take appropriate action.

Table 12.1. Eating Disorders: Teens

Eating Disorders: Teens (Percent)	2013
By Total	
Total	16.70%
By Sex	
Male	10.40%
Female	23.00%
By Race/Ethnicity	
White only	15.80%
Black or African American only	17.50%
American Indian or Alaska Native only	25.80%
Asian only	15.40%
Native Hawaiian or Other Pacific Islander only	17.40%
2 or more races	17.60%
Hispanic or Latino	21.30%
Not Hispanic or Latino	15.40%
White only, non-Hispanic	14.90%
Black or African American only, non-Hispanic	17.10%
By Obesity Status	
Obese	22.70%
Not obese	15.30%
By Characteristic of School/Student	
9th grade	16.50%
10th grade	16.70%
11th grade	16.40%
12th grade	17.10%

Source: "Eating Disorders: Teens (Percent)," Health Indicators Warehouse (HIW), 2013.

Anorexia Nervosa

Anorexia nervosa, an eating disorder in which a person starves him or herself, typically appears in early to mid-adolescence. According to the National Eating Disorders Association, between one-half and one percent of American women suffer from anorexia nervosa. Though boys can also suffer from anorexia, it is far less common.

Many teens, particularly teenage girls, diet or practice unusual eating habits, and typically it is nothing to be alarmed about. However, if the behavior persists, or if you recognize any of the following symptoms of anorexia nervosa, speak to your teen and his or her doctor:

- Extreme weight loss

- Restricted food intake

- Absence of at least three periods (amenorrhea) in girls

- Constant irrational fear of getting fat

If left untreated, a teen who is suffering from anorexia may experience serious physical consequences and, in extreme cases, it may even result in death. According to the National Institutes of Mental Health (NIMH), medical complications due to the constant state of semi-starvation in anorexics may include:

- Damage to vital organs such as the heart and brain

- Drops in pulse and blood pressure rates

- Slowed thyroid functioning

- Brittle nails and hair

- Dry, yellowed skin which may become covered with soft hair called lanugo

- Excessive thirst and frequent urination

- Lowered body temperature and inability to withstand cold (caused by reduced body fat)

- Mild anemia

- Swollen joints

- Decrease in bone minerality (loss of calcium), making bones brittle and prone to breakage

- Shrinkage of the brain, which may cause personality changes

- Irregular heart rhythm and, in the most severe cases, heart failure

If you suspect that your teen has anorexia, seek medical help immediately—early treatment is crucial. No matter how well meaning, parents do not have the skills or training to handle this highly complex problem. Anorexia will not get better without medical intervention, and the potential consequences are too great to be ignored.

Bulimia Nervosa

Another eating disorder, with often serious consequences, is bulimia. Both boys and girls can become bulimic, but it is more common in girls. Those with bulimia may occasionally starve themselves as do anorexics, but much more typically, they binge and then purge shortly after ingesting the food by vomiting, using laxatives or both. In fact, in spite of chronic binge eating—sometimes enormous amounts of food—bulimics generally manage to keep their weight within 10 pounds of normal. Not surprisingly, the continuous purging can eventually cause erosion of tooth enamel, lesions on the esophagus, digestive problems, and chemical and hormonal imbalances. Those with bulimia, who tend to have outgoing, social personalities, often exercise excessively as well.

People who have bulimia are usually very embarrassed about it and will go to great lengths to hide it from others. This can make it difficult to recognize the symptoms, but parents should be aware of the following signs:

- Large amounts of food disappearing from the kitchen on a regular basis.

- Disappearing into the bathroom regularly and for prolonged periods of time. Some people with bulimia can't bear to wait more than a few minutes after eating even a modest meal to rid themselves of the food.

- A pattern of weight gains (up to 10 pounds in a month) that drop off quickly and seemingly effortlessly.

If you suspect your child is bulimic, talk to him or her about your concerns, but remember, he or she may not admit there is a problem. Seek medical help immediately if you have reason to suspect bulimia. Ask your child's doctor or contact your local hospital for a referral to an eating disorder specialist.

Overeating

Though not as extreme or severe as anorexia or bulimia, overeating can also be a problem for some teens. Though some children are overweight because they simply eat too much or don't exercise enough, in some cases, overeating can be a way of self-soothing, or dealing with the stress of being a teenager. This is a difficult situation for parents to address: Too much attention on weight can easily make a teen self-conscious, and can lead to overeating as a way of rebelling or comforting him or herself. Instead, try the following suggestions.

- **Set up an appointment with your child's doctor.** A discussion with the doctor about weight may make it easier for a teen to accept the information; if it comes from a parent, a child is more apt to be emotional and confrontational.

- **Avoid criticizing or commenting about your child's eating habits.** This can help keep food from turning into a hypersensitive issue in the household.

- **Stock your kitchen with healthy, low-fat foods** such as fruits, vegetables, whole grains and lean meats; avoid junk food.

- **Don't offer food as a reward or as a way to soothe feelings.** Many people spend a lifetime trying to unlearn the habit of using food to reward themselves or comfort emotions; you can help your child avoid starting the habit in the first place.

- **Encourage your child to develop interests outside the home such as theater, sports or volunteer projects.** These activities will help your child constructively fill his or her time, and enhance self-esteem.

Section 12.4

Eating Disorders among College Students

"Eating Disorders among College Students," © 2016
Omnigraphics, Inc. Reviewed March 2016.

Heading off to college is a challenging transitional period in the lives of young people. College students experience a sudden increase in independence and responsibility as they leave their parents' home and establish their own routines for eating, sleeping, exercising, and studying. They also face the pressures of living among peers in a dormitory environment, making new friends, and competing academically. Although the flurry of changes can be exciting, students who have trouble adjusting may feel overwhelmed and anxious, which can impact their physical and mental health.

The stressful nature of the transition to college life is reflected in the high incidence of eating disorders among college students. Studies have shown that of the estimated 30 million Americans with eating disorders, 95 percent are between the ages of 12 and 25. In addition, over 90 percent of women on college campuses report having dieted in an effort to control their weight, while 25 percent of college-aged women have engaged in bingeing and purging as a weight-management technique. Some studies suggest that upwards of 20 percent of college students develop eating disorders. Although the majority of people with eating disorders are female, research indicates that the prevalence rates are increasing among college-aged males as well.

Diagnosing College Students Eating Disorders

Early diagnosis and treatment of eating disorders is key to preventing the development of serious medical conditions and improving the chances of recovery. Some of the warning signs and behaviors that increase the risk of developing eating disorders include:

- symptoms of depression and anxiety relating to the adjustment to college life and the pressures of academia;

- changes in appearance, such as significant weight gain or loss;

- social withdrawal or pronounced changes in emotional state;

- associating with roommates, teammates, or sorority/fraternity members who have eating disorders, which may create peer pressure and establish norms of disordered eating;

- adopting unhealthy, extreme measures of weight management, such as skipping meals, exercising obsessively, taking diet pills, trying fad diets, substituting caffeine or tobacco for food, or purging after meals by inducing vomiting or abusing laxatives or diuretics;

- demonstrating bingeing behavior, such as not eating all day and then overeating at night or drinking excessively at parties, which is common on college campuses.

Eating disorders can be tricky to diagnose because college students often try to hide them. They may not believe their behavior is dangerous, or they may come to view extreme dieting, bingeing, or purging as normal because they see others engaging in it. Some individuals do not seek treatment for eating disorders because they feel shame or embarrassment, they are not aware of the treatment resources available, or they worry that treatment will not be covered by health insurance.

Educating college students and their families about eating disorders is an important way to help them determine whether they may be at risk. Many people recover from eating disorders when they are treated at an early stage. Left untreated, however, eating disorders can cause serious health problems and even death. Some tips for helping a college student who appears to have an eating disorder include:

- discussing concerns and mentioning specific observations of behavior;

- offering to provide help and support;

- contacting the family doctor and obtaining a referral to a nutritionist, therapist, or eating disorder treatment center;

- setting realistic goals for recovery and being prepared for the possibility that it may be too dangerous for the student to return to school.

References

1. "Eating Disorders among College Students," Walden Center, 2015.

2. Kramer, Jennie J. "Might Your College Student Have an Eating Disorder? How to Tell, What to Do," Huffington Post, December 12, 2014.

3. Wolf, Nancy L. "A Guide to Choosing a College for Teens with Eating Disorders," Noodle, May 21, 2015.

Chapter 13

Eating Disorders in Men

Diversity

Eating Disorders Don't Discriminate.

Eating disorders were once thought to affect only a narrow portion of the population in the teens and early twenties, but we now know that they affect people of every age, race, gender and socio-economic status.

Males

While women are more commonly affected by eating disorders, millions of men and boys battle all forms of the illness.

Anorexia Nervosa in Males

Anorexia nervosa is a severe, life-threatening disorder in which the individual refuses to maintain a minimally normal body weight, is intensely afraid of gaining weight, and exhibits a significant distortion in the perception of the shape or size of his body, as well as dissatisfaction with his body shape and size.

Behavioral Characteristics:

- Excessive dieting, fasting, restricted diet

This chapter includes text excerpted from "Diversity," © 2016 National Eating Disorders Association. For more information, visit www.nationaleatingdisorders. org. Reprinted with permission.

- Food rituals
- Preoccupation with body building, weight lifting, or muscle toning
- Compulsive exercise
- Difficulty eating with others, lying about eating
- Frequently weighing self
- Preoccupation with food
- Focus on certain body parts; e.g., buttocks, thighs, stomach
- Disgust with body size or shape
- Distortion of body size; i.e., feels fat even though others tell him he is already very thin

Emotional and Mental Characteristics:

- Intense fear of becoming fat or gaining weight
- Depression
- Social isolation
- Strong need to be in control
- Rigid, inflexible thinking, "all or nothing"
- Decreased interest in sex or fears around sex
- Possible conflict over gender identity or sexual orientation
- Low sense of self-worth—uses weight as a measure of worth
- Difficulty expressing feelings
- Perfectionistic—strives to be the neatest, thinnest, smartest, etc.
- Difficulty thinking clearly or concentrating
- Irritability, denial—believes others are overreacting to his low weight or caloric restriction
- Insomnia

Physical Characteristics:

- Low body weight (15% or more below what is expected for age, height, activity level)

- Lack of energy, fatigue
- Muscular weakness
- Decreased balance, unsteady gait
- Lowered body temperature, blood pressure, pulse rate
- Tingling in hands and feet
- Thinning hair or hair loss
- Lanugo (downy growth of body hair)
- Heart arrhythmia
- Lowered testosterone levels

Binge Eating Disorder in Males

Binge eating disorder (BED) is an eating disorder characterized by recurrent episodes of eating large quantities of food (often very quickly and to the point of discomfort); a feeling of a loss of control during the binge; experiencing shame, distress or guilt afterwards; and not regularly using unhealthy compensatory measures (e.g., purging) to counter the binge eating. Binge eating disorder is a severe, life-threatening and treatable eating disorder. Common aspects of BED include functional impairment, suicide risk and a high frequency of co-occurring psychiatric disorders.

Binge eating disorder is the most common eating disorder in the United States, affecting 3.5% of women, 2% of men, and up to 1.6% of adolescents. Estimates indicate that about 40% of people struggling with binge eating disorder are male.

Behavioral Characteristics:

Binge eating DSM-5 criteria includes:

- Eating in a discrete period of time, such as two hours, an amount of food that is considered larger than what most people would eat under similar circumstances.
- A sense of loss of control over how much a person is eating.

Additional behaviors might include:

- Eating even when full or not hungry.
- Eating rapidly during episodes of bingeing.

107

- Eating until uncomfortably full.

- Frequently eating alone or in secret.

- Repeatedly going on and off diets.

- Men may think of bingeing as normal masculine behavior, without an awareness that it can develop into BED.

- Restrictive eating is a common trigger for bingeing.

Emotional and Mental Characteristics:

- Feeling depressed, disgusted, ashamed, guilty or upset about eating behaviors.

- Men face a stigma for having any type of eating disorder, and this prevents them from getting treatment.

- Negative emotions (e.g., anger, anxiety, shame) often precede the initiation of the binge, which serves to numb those negative feelings.

- Men with BED commonly experience social isolation and body dissatisfaction.

- Feeling disgust about one's body size. Someone with BED may have been teased about their body while growing up.

Physical Characteristics:

- Weight gain may or may not be associated with BED. Although there is a correlation between BED and weight gain, not everyone who is classified as overweight or obese suffers from BED.

- Males with BED may have such physical symptoms as type II diabetes, high blood pressure and cholesterol, heart disease, gallbladder disease, osteoarthritis and gastrointestinal problems. They may avoid treatment detecting these issues.

- Warning signs include skipped meals, eating in secret, hidden wrappers, increased moodiness and depression.

Bulimia Nervosa in Males

Bulimia nervosa is a severe, life-threatening disorder characterized by recurrent episodes of binge eating followed by self-induced vomiting or other purging methods (e.g., laxatives, diuretics, excessive exercise, fasting) to prevent weight gain. An individual struggling with bulimia is intensely afraid of gaining weight and exhibits persistent dissatisfaction with his body and appearance, as well as a significant distortion in the perception of the size or shape of his body.

Behavioral Characteristics

- Recurrent episodes of binge eating: eating an amount of food that is definitely larger than most people would eat during a similar period of time and under similar circumstances

- A sense of lack of control over eating during binge episodes

- Recurrent purging or compensatory behavior to prevent weight gain: secretive self-induced vomiting, misuse of laxatives, diuretics, or fasting, compulsive exercise (possibly including excessive running, bodybuilding, or weight lifting)

- Hoarding of food, hiding food and eating in secret

- Frequently weighing self

- Preoccupation with food

- Focus on certain body parts; e.g., buttocks, thighs, stomach

- Disgust with body size or shape

- Distortion of body size; i.e., feels fat even though he may be thin

Emotional and Mental Characteristics

- Intense fear of becoming fat or gaining weight

- Performance and appearance oriented

- Works hard to please others

- Depression

- Social isolation

- Possible conflict over gender identity or sexual orientation

- Strong need to be in control

- Difficulty expressing feelings

- Feelings of worthlessness—uses weight, appearance, and achievement as measures of worth

- Rigid, inflexible "all or nothing" thinking

Physical Characteristics

- Weight fluctuations

- Loss of dental enamel due to self-induced vomiting

- Edema (fluid retention or bloating)

- Constipation

- Swollen salivary glands

- Cardiac arrhythmia due to electrolyte imbalances

- Esophageal tears, gastric rupture

- Lack of energy, fatigue

Enhancing Male Body Image

- **Recognize** that bodies come in all different sizes and shapes. There is no one "right" body size. Your body is not and should not be exactly like anyone else's. Try to see your body as a facet of your uniqueness and individuality.

- **Focus** on the qualities in yourself that you like that are not related to appearance. Spend time developing these capacities rather than letting your appearance define your identity and your worth.

- **Look** critically at advertisements that push the "bodybuilding" message. Our culture emphasizes the V-shaped muscular body shape ideal for men. Magazines targeted at men tend to focus on articles and advertisements promoting weight lifting, bodybuilding or muscle toning. Do you know men who have muscular, athletic bodies but who are not happy? Are there dangers in spending too much time focusing on your body? Consider giving up your goal of achieving the "perfect" male body and work at accepting your body just the way it is.

- **Remember** that your body size, shape, or weight does not determine your worth as a person, or your identity as a man. In other words, you are not just your body. Expand your idea of "masculinity" to include qualities such as sensitivity, cooperation, caring, patience, having feelings, being artistic. Some men may be muscular and athletic, but these qualities in and of themselves do not make a person a "man."

- **Find** friends who are not overly concerned with weight or appearance.

- **Be assertive** with others who comment on your body. Let people know that comments on your physical appearance, either positive or negative, are not appreciated. Confront others who tease men about their bodies or who attack their masculinity by calling them names such as "sissy" or "wimp."

- **Demonstrate respect** for men who possess body types or who display personality traits that do not meet the cultural standard for masculinity; e.g., men who are slender, short, or overweight, gay men, men who dress colorfully or who enjoy traditional "non-masculine" activities such as dancing, sewing or cooking.

- **Be aware** of the negative messages you tell yourself about your appearance or body. Respond to negative self-talk with an affirmation. For example, if you start giving yourself a message like, "I look gross," substitute a positive affirmation, "I accept myself the way I am," or "I'm a worthwhile person, fat and all."

- **Focus** on the ways in which your body serves you and enables you to participate fully in life. In other words, appreciate how your body functions rather than obsessing about its appearance. For example, appreciate that your arms enable you to hold someone you love, your thighs enable you to run, etc.

Aim for lifestyle mastery, rather than mastery over your body, weight, or appearance. Lifestyle mastery has to do with developing your unique gifts and potential, expressing yourself, developing meaningful relationships, learning how to solve problems, establishing goals, and contributing to life. View exercise and balanced eating as aspects of your overall approach to a life that emphasizes self-care.

Research on Males and Eating Disorders

Prevalence in Men

Prevalence figures for males with eating disorders (ED) are somewhat elusive. Many assessment tests have a gender bias, because they were created for females and underscore males. In the past, ED have been characterized as "women's problems" and men have been stigmatized from coming forward or have been unaware that they could have an ED. Studies have shown an increase in the numbers, although it is uncertain whether more males actually have eating disorders now or are becoming more aware of the gender-neutral nature of ED.

Additional research is needed, but several studies provide insight into the male experience of eating disorders:

- The most widely-quoted study estimates that males have a **lifetime prevalence** of 0.3% for anorexia nervosa (AN), 0.5% for bulimia nervosa (BN) and 2% for binge eating disorder (BED). These figures correspond to males representing 25% of individuals with AN and BN and 36% of those with BED. They are based on DSM-IV criteria.

- In the United States, **20 million women and 10 million men** will suffer from a clinically significant eating disorder at some time in their life, including anorexia nervosa, bulimia nervosa, binge eating disorder, or EDNOS [EDNOS is now recognized as OSFED, other specified feeding or eating disorder, per the DSM-5].

- In a study of 1,383 **adolescents**, the prevalence of any DSM-5 ED in males was reported to be 1.2% at 14 years, 2.6% at 17 years, and 2.9% at 20 years.

- A study of 2,822 **students on a large university campus** found that 3.6% of males had positive screens for ED. The female-to-male ratio was 3-to-1.

- In looking at **male sexuality and eating disorders**, higher percentage of gay (15%) than heterosexual males (5%) had diagnoses of ED, but when these percentages are applied to population figures, the majority of males with ED are heterosexual.

- **Subclinical eating disordered behaviors** (including binge eating, purging, laxative abuse and fasting for weight loss) are nearly as common among males as they are among females.

- Various studies suggest that risk of **mortality** for males with ED is higher than it is for females.

- Men with eating disorders often suffer from **comorbid conditions** such as depression, excessive exercise, substance disorders, and anxiety.

De-stigmatizing Male Eating Disorders

Eating disorders are gender neutral, but they have been routinely characterized as "women's problems." The stereotypical person with anorexia nervosa is a rich, white, adolescent girl; which is far from reality, because AN affects all genders, ages, races and socioeconomic classes.

Several factors lead to males being under- and undiagnosed for ED. Men can face a double stigma, for having a disorder characterized as feminine or gay and for seeking psychological help. Additionally, assessment tests with language geared to females have led to misconceptions about the nature of male ED.

A classic article by Richard Morton in 1689 described two cases—a man and a woman—of (what we now classify as) anorexia nervosa, and a case series by Sir William Gull in the 1860s noted that the illness can occur in males. However, an overwhelming majority of research, description, and treatment concentrated on females when the eating disorders field began to emerge in the 1970s, and that uneven focus continues to hold true. Virtually 99% of books on ED have a female bias.

Correcting false impressions that characterize ED as female disorders is necessary to remove stigmas about gender and ED. By de-stigmatizing ED, everyone will get better access to diagnosis and treatment.

Males and Body Image

There are numerous studies on male body image, and results vary widely. Many men have misconceived notions about their weight and physique, particularly the importance of muscularity. Findings include:

- Most males would like to be lean and muscular, which typically represents the ideal male body type. Exposure to these kinds of largely unattainable images leads to male body dissatisfaction. The sexual objectification of men and internalization of media images predicts drive for muscularity.

- The desire for increased musculature is not uncommon, and it crosses age groups; 25% of normal weight males perceive themselves to be underweight, 90% of teenaged boys exercised with the goal of bulking up, and among college-aged men, 68% say they have too little muscle.

- Muscle dysmorphia, a subtype of body dysmorphic disorder, is an emerging condition that primarily affects male bodybuilders. Such individuals obsess about being inadequately muscular. Compulsions include spending many hours in the gym, squandering excessive amounts of money on supplements, abnormal eating patterns, or use of steroids.

Treatment Considerations

Treatment is not one-size-fits-all. For any person, biological and cultural factors should be taken into consideration in order to provide an effective treatment environment.

- A gender-sensitive approach with recognition of different needs and dynamics for males is critical in effective treatment. Males in treatment can feel out of place when predominantly surrounded by females, and an all-male treatment environment is recommended—when possible.

- Males with anorexia nervosa usually exhibit low levels of testosterone and vitamin D, and they have a high risk of osteopenia and osteoporosis. Testosterone supplementation is often recommended.

Strategies for Prevention and Early Intervention of Male Eating Disorders

- **Recognize** that eating disorders do not discriminate on the basis of gender. Men can and do develop eating disorders.

- **Learn** about eating disorders and know the warning signs. Become aware of your community resources (treatment centers, self-help groups, etc.). Consider implementing an Eating Concerns Support Group in a school, hospital, or community setting to provide interested young men with an opportunity to learn more about eating disorders and to receive support. Encourage young men to seek professional help if necessary.

- **Understand** that athletic activities or professions that necessitate weight restriction (e.g., gymnastics, track, swimming, wrestling, rowing) put males at risk for developing eating disorders. Male wrestlers, for example, present with a higher rate of eating disorders than the general male population. Coaches need to be aware of and disallow any excessive weight control or body building measures employed by their young male athletes.

- **Talk** with young men about the ways in which cultural attitudes regarding ideal male body shape, masculinity, and sexuality are shaped by the media. Assist young men in expanding their idea of "masculinity" to include such characteristics as caring, nurturing, and cooperation. Encourage male involvement in traditional "non-masculine" activities such as shopping, laundry, and cooking.

- **Demonstrate** respect for gay men, and men who display personality traits or who are involved in professions that stretch the limits of traditional masculinity; e.g., men who dress colorfully, dancers, skaters, etc.

- **Never emphasize** body size or shape as an indication of a young man's worth or identity as a man. Value the person on the "inside" and help him to establish a sense of control in his life through self-knowledge and expression rather than trying to obtain control through dieting or other eating disordered behaviors.

- **Confront** others who tease men who do not meet traditional cultural expectations for masculinity. Confront anyone who tries to motivate or "toughen up" young men by verbally attacking their masculinity; e.g., calling names such as "sissy" or "wimp."

- **Listen** carefully to a young man's thoughts and feelings, take his pain seriously, allow him to become who he is.

- **Validate** a young man's strivings for independence and encourage him to develop all aspects of his personality, not only those that family and/or culture find acceptable. Respect a person's need for space, privacy, and boundaries. Be careful about being overprotective. Allow him to exercise control and make his own decisions whenever possible, including control over what and how much he eats, how he looks, and how much he weighs.

- **Understand** the crucial role of the father and other male influences in the prevention of eating disorders. Find ways to connect young men with healthy male role models.

Chapter 14

Eating Disorders in Older Adults

Older Adults

When eating disorders or body image conflicts are mentioned, the face we imagine is one of youth. It may be a preteen, an adolescent, or a young adult woman, but we rarely visualize an ageing face in that picture. Yet more and more older women, approaching or beyond "midlife," are admitting that they also struggle with their bodies and their eating and are seeking professional help.

What's Age Got to do with It?

Body Image Despair and Eating Disorders

Contemporary women experience unprecedented stress due to: their rapidly changing role in a globalized consumer culture; the strict cultural standards regarding women, weight, and appearance; unattainable media images; and the current fear of obesity. They find easy comfort in The Body Myth (Maine and Kelly, 2005), believing that the right appearance, weight, and eating can mitigate their stress and answer their relentless questions about their worth to self and to others.

This chapter includes text excerpted from "Diversity" © 2016 National Eating Disorders Association. For more information, visit www.nationaleatingdisorders. org. Reprinted with permission.

Once again, the old rules about eating disorders are no longer useful, but the dominant thinking of both the public and professionals does not reflect current reality. Western women live in a culture of Body Wars (Maine, 2000) that do not end when they turn 25 or 30. Just as women become invisible as they age, their problems are also discounted, minimized, and ignored. The picture of a young, vibrant teenager who succumbs to an eating disorder is tragic, but eating disorders are just as destructive in the lives of adult women.

The Face of Adult Eating Disorders and Body Image Despair

Although hard data on adult eating disorders are absent, researchers do have compelling information about the extent of dieting and body image concerns, both of which are precursors to clinical eating disorders. For example:

- One-third of inpatient admissions to a specialized treatment center for eating disorders were over 30 years old.

- About 43 million adult women in the United States are dieting to lose weight at any given time and another 26 million are dieting to maintain their weight.

- A major research project found that more than 20% of the women aged 70 and older were dieting, even though higher weight poses a very low risk for death at that age, and weight loss may actually be harmful.

- When asked what bothered them most about their bodies, a group of women aged 61 to 92 identified weight as their greatest concern.

- A survey of Swiss women found: 70% of women aged 30-74 were dissatisfied with their weight despite being at a normal weight; 62% of women over the age of 65 wanted to lose weight; 31% of them had dieted recently although most (62%) were normal in weight.

Other studies have found comparable levels of dieting and disordered eating across young and elderly age groups.

- About 60% of adult women have engaged in pathogenic weight control; 40% are restrained eaters; 40% are overeaters; only 20% are instinctive eaters; 50% say their eating is devoid of pleasure and causes them to feel guilty; 90% worry about their weight.

- Within three years after western television was introduced to Fiji, women, previously comfortable with their bodies and eating, developed serious problems: 74% felt "too fat;" 69% dieted to lose weight; 11% used self-induced vomiting; 29% were at risk for clinical eating disorders.

The Shape of Adult Eating Disorders

- Adults struggling with eating disorders have varying shapes, sizes, and severities, and may suffer from anorexia, bulimia, other specified feeding or eating disorder (OSFED), binge eating disorder, subclinical eating disorders, and/or orthorexia.

- Some struggled since youth and have never escaped the grip of these obsessions.

- Others have struggled, recovered, relapsed.

- Some have been preoccupied with food and weight for years, but never incapacitated until now.

- Some, faced with the challenges of adulthood and loss of status in a youth-obsessed world, develop rituals related to diet, exercise and appearance for the first time in their lives.

- **Co-existing issues:** women with eating disorders are 5 times more likely to abuse alcohol/drugs; women with alcohol/drug abuse are 11 times more likely to have eating disorders. 20–50% of women with eating disorders have history of trauma. Depression, anxiety disorders and personality disorders also co-exist.

Common Threads across Age

- The universal "language of fat"

- A shared ambivalence about their power and place as women

- Potentially deep conflicts between their masculine and feminine strivings

- The challenge of an overpowering consumer culture that teaches them to want and to need, but not to know their true wants and needs.

- Constant exposure to strict and unrealistic media images of beauty

- Uncertainty of the validity of their feelings
- Exposure to the "war on obesity" and the misinformation propagated by the diet industry.

Differences between the Young and Old

- Shame and embarrassment for having a "teenager's problem"
- More years speaking the "language of fat"
- Greater difficulty admitting the need for help
- More motivation for treatment
- Greater awareness of what they have lost due to their eating or body image issues
- More obstacles to treatment due to other responsibilities
- Increased anxiety about appearance/health due to natural aging process
- Multiple stressors and losses that accompany adult development.

Triggers to Adult Eating Disorders and Body Image Despair

- Pregnancy
- Childbirth
- Fertility/Infertility
- Menopause
- Natural Signs of Aging
- Death
- The Work Environment
- Work-Family Balance
- Competing with Younger Women
- Retirement
- Childrearing
- Deciding Not to Have Children
- Empty Nest
- Children's Marriage

- Becoming a Grandmother
- Aging Parents
- Infidelity
- Divorce

Medical Issues

- Same medical symptoms as younger patients: every system affected by malnutrition.
- Medical complications can emerge quickly despite long-term stability.
- Unique issues in adult women such as depleted fat stores increase menopausal symptoms.
- Muscle-wasting can reduce metabolic rate and hasten neuro-muscular decline.
- Anorexia nervosa has highest morbidity rate of any psychiatric illness with 10% mortality rate at 10 years of symptom duration and 20% at 20 years. The longer the duration of illness, the higher risk for death.
- Alcohol abuse increases the risk of death due to medical issues or suicide.

Women Over 50

Eating Disorder Behaviors and Weight Concerns are Common in Women Over 50

An online survey as part of the Gender and Body Image Study (GABI), published in the *International Journal of Eating Disorders*, found that there is no age limitation to disordered eating. The survey found eating disorder symptoms in 13% of women 50 and above over the past five years, with over 70% reporting they were attempting to lose weight. The study found that 62% of women felt their weight or shape had a negative impact on their life. To many people who are still under the false impression that eating disorders are the province of adolescent and young adult women, these results are a real eye-opener.

Although the exact symptoms of eating disorders in midlife do not differ much from eating disorders at a younger life stage, the context can be drastically different. For a woman struggling in her midlife, the disorder can affect her marriage or partnership, her children, her work, and even her parents if she is caring for them as they age. Treatment in younger women often includes family based therapy, which is not always appropriate for someone at a later stage of life who might not have the same support system as someone younger. Parents may no longer be alive and partners are often a replacement for the support and participation in therapy.

Health effects of eating disorders in older women are also of a high concern. As a woman's body becomes less resilient with age, older bodies have less ease in bouncing back from an eating disorder. There are greater numbers of gastrointestinal, cardiac, bone and even dental effects of eating disorders as women mature. This means clinicians should keep eating disorders on their radar screen regardless of the age of the patient—this means anorexia nervosa, bulimia nervosa, binge eating disorder, as well as symptoms of these disorders if a persona does not meet full diagnostic criteria. Many adult women are especially hesitant to bring up their eating disorder with their healthcare providers for fear of being told that they should have grown out of it, or that it is a young person's disorder.

Chapter 15

Eating Disorders in Athletes

Data suggest that athletes may be part of a unique subculture but that part of this group may, in fact, be vulnerable to eating disorders. Stress related to athletic and academic performance, desire to please, and insecurities associated with attempts to comply with the expectations of others may. For example, increase the likelihood that they will engage in unhealthy behaviors that could lead to a bona fide eating disorder. Therefore, athletes' environment may have a more predominant impact compared to other determinants of eating disorders and in relation to the general public.

The contention is that if the environment could be modified, the prevalence of anorexia nervosa and bulimia nervosa might be dramatically diminished among athletes. The three determinants of eating disorders, biogenetic, psychological, and sociological are reviewed below in accordance with the research literature relevant to athletes. The biogenetic and psychological determinants, however, are briefly reviewed. The major emphasis is on the sociological determinant. A sociological context is introduced to accomplish the following:

- understand and mitigate or abate problems related to eating disorders and athletes

- identify or develop interventions to alter negative environmental influences

---

This section includes text excerpted from "Eating Disorders among Athletes," U.S. Department of Education (ED), June 1, 2013.

- design or modify treatment programs to meet the needs of athletes
- stimulate research

Biogenetic Factors

The contribution of biogenetic factors to the initiation and perpetuation of eating disorders is the most evident of all the determinants, but less is known about this factor than any of the others. Historically, researchers interested in identifying determinants of eating disorders thought that anorexia nervosa and bulimia nervosa occurred because of the malfunction of the pituitary gland. More recent work has examined whether the biological abnormalities found in these disorders are secondary to the effects of starvation or whether they represent some underlying, primary pathophysiological disturbance that explains the pathogenesis of the illness. Other evidence suggests that bulimia may be a variant of a depressive disorder that may have a biogenetic basis.

Athletes who have abnormal and irregular eating patterns appear to follow in their parents' footsteps and also have altered brain neurotransmitters which change the release of the hypothalamic hormone. This hormone is important in producing normal menstruation and ovulation. Second, a reduction in body fat decreases the sensitivity of the hypothalamus to other influences that cause the hypothalamus to produce normal menstruation and ovulation. In addition, the opiods, endorphins produced in the "runner's high," have been linked to eating behaviors. Starvation, as well, has been known to increase opiod release. Finally, it has been noted that sustained and frequent exercise has been associated with amenorrhea.

Psychological Factors

A number of psychological factors have been identified that may contribute to eating disorders. Psychological research on puberty has suggested that sex differences in the impact of early versus late maturation may be important in identifying risk factors for bulimia nervosa. Other characteristics that have been studied concern the view that eating disorders, particularly bulimia nervosa, are basically substance abuse disorders, with food being one of many or the only substance abused.

In addition, researchers have found that women who experience more stress are at greater risk for binge eating. Stress is not an independent risk factor, but occurs in conjunction with other risk factors that may play a role in increasing the likelihood of developing an eating disorder.

Sociological / Environmental Factors

Central to an etiological analysis of eating disorders are sociological / environmental factors. Figure 15.1 depicts the determinants of eating disorders as three circles. Parts of the circles overlap to represent that some factors interact and are influenced by more than one determinant The circles can be conceptualized as the same sin hut their influence may be disproportionate. It is also recognized that all three determinants impact the athlete even though the focus is on the sociological determinant as indicated by the shading of the biogenetic and psychological determinants.

Figure 15.1. *Sociological influences in athletes*

The sociological determinant is divided into several factors and the athlete is placed in the center to represent the influence of each factor on the person. Although the segments of the circle are divided equally (or nearly so), the relative influence of each of the seven factors may vary depending on the individual athlete. The factors listed are not meant to be exhaustive but represent ones thought to have the greatest influence. In addition, the factors may be applicable to or interact with more than one determinant and apply to collegiate as well as to younger and older female and male athletes.

Culture

While the ideal body form has varied over time and between cultures, there is some support for the contention that the preferred shape for women in Western cultures has shifted toward a thinner ideal over the past 20 years. This is supported by the changes in accepted body type during this century from the ample mature figure in Rubens' paintings to the thin figure of Twiggy, the English model. Data from Playboy centerfolds and Miss America contestants from 1960 to 1980 revealed a significant trend toward a thinner standard. Garner et al. also noted over this period that the contestant group in general became taller and thinner, although during the same period biological studies have shown that the population has become taller and heavier. Finally, the trend for males has paralleled the trend for women. Men strive to be lean and muscular and are influenced by the emphasis on fitness and the athletic look of models, athletes, and nonathletes alike.

There is an expectation today to live up to the fitness/sport look. For example, it was noted that for women, fitness and exercise is related to weight control and for many, a development of a curveless body shape. In conjunction with this, it was also stated that men pursue fitness to attain certain health benefits (e.g., better cardiovascular functioning) while women predominantly pursue fitness to lose weight. This point is also illustrated by findings in which only 31% of the men pursued fitness to lose weight while over 50% of the women participated in fitness for this reason.

Media

The current focus of the media reflects the cultural emphasis on physical fitness and leanness. Athletes may be especially susceptible because they often model and epitomize the athletic or fitness look that is accentuated by the media. In addition, thinness is also equated in the media with sex appeal, popularity, status, self-esteem, happiness, control, achievement, and enhanced quality of life.

Athletes may also experience pressures to be thin that are designed to influence the general population. Popular women's magazines publicize diet articles and advertisements for light, fat free products; movies carry the same message indicating that thin is chic: and television carries the message, day in and day out, that one can only be loved and respected if slim.

The media may so influence the degree of body satisfaction among both the general population and athletes. In a glamor magazine survey of 33,000 women, 75% of the respondents reported feeling too fat, although according to height/weight charts, only 2514 were overweight. It is well publicized that over 80% of girls, before age 13, have been on a weight loss diet, in contrast to 10% of the boys. In a study of athletes, it was found that approximately one-seventh of the athletes thought they were fat even though they had lost weight and were not overweight.

Community

Pathology typically begins after a person has entered the athletic subculture. In addition, the occurrence of eating pathology in athletics seems to be linked to an emphasis on weight and appearance as opposed to the stressful nature of training and competition. Exercise or physical activity in and of itself, however, may not precipitate eating disorders but if fitness/sport programs are presented with an emphasis on body shape, they may well serve as a precipitator for individuals predisposed to an eating disorder.

The type of sport or level of competition, however. may also make a difference in possibly predisposing an athlete to an eating disorder. Individuals engaging in bodyfocused activities or lean-emphasizing sports were preoccupied with food and weight and had a tendency toward an eating disorder. Running is often a sport of choice for those with eating disorders. Isolation, self-regimentation, and self-deprivation, all which may increase the likelihood of eating disorders, are socially acceptable for runners. It was suggested that extreme exercise can serve to trigger anorexia nervosa in persons already at risk.

Peers

The influence of peers may be very important to athletes, especially with an emphasis on teamwork and team participation. The use of strategies to regulate weight or food intake may be a way to gain acceptance and feel included by one's peers in athletics. In some sports where there is pressure to maintain low body weight, peer pressure may be extreme as evidenced by the seemingly high prevalence of eating disorders among athletes in sports such as running, dance, and wrestling. In addition, athletes may teach each other unhealthy ways to manage weight or food consumption. Half of the women who reported vomiting knew another woman who vomited and many had been taught by them. There may be a contagious effect with eating disordered methods spreading among team members especially when less successful athletes prone to eating disorders observe more successful athletes who use unhealthy weight control methods. There may be a sense of comradery, and eating disorder behaviors may gain group acceptance.

Little is known about the impact of peer pressure specifically as it relates to athletes. It seems reasonable, however, that athletes would learn from fellow athletes about unhealthy weight control methods in the same way they learn from each other about aspects of their training such as techniques for skill acquisition, posturing, etc.

Coaches and Other Authority Figures

Coaches may play a key role in the physical, psychological, and social development of young athletes. Some coaches are genuinely concerned about the athlete's welfare, while others may be more concerned about winning than the athlete's physical and mental well-being. The U.S. Olympic Committee has raised several interesting points, one of which is that all coaches are in a position to have a profound influence on young, impressionable athletes, especially in the area of weight control. Some practices of coaches may serve to encourage eating disordered attitudes and behavior. For example, group or public weigh-ins as well as posting of percentage body fat may overemphasize low body weight. Many coaches have upper weight limits for athletes on their teams but not lower limits.

The message given to young athletes may be that low body weight is desirable and necessary for success. In addition, coaches' verbal statements may reinforce the necessity of unhealthy lower body weight. An innocent remark about an athlete being out of shape or overweight may lead to drastic actions by the athlete to prove otherwise. Comments that create an implied expectation with no guidance about how to proceed in a safe and effective manner may be harmful regardless of intent.

Coaches may not have an incentive to attend to anomalies in weight and eating habits. It is known that a coach's reputation is built on the ability to develop elite athletes. In addition, the competitive advantage may be lost for athletic scholarships due to excessive weight. Also, there may be concern among coaches that if an athlete enrolls in therapy for an eating disorder, that person may not be inclined to compete and participate in sport.

Family

The family may affect an athlete's susceptibility to an eating disorder in several ways. First, families may subtly sanction unhealthy behaviors and attitudes and the use of pathogenic weight loss methods. Second, family members may encourage athletes to be competitive and to succeed at their sport. Third, to gain family approval and recognition, young athletes may feel compelled to use pathogenic weight loss methods in order to achieve. Finally, an athlete is also at risk for developing an eating disorder if someone in the family specifically reinforces efforts to lose weight.

Family characteristics may predispose some athletes to an eating disorder. A study found a fourfold greater rate of alcoholism in the first-degree relatives of bulimic-anorexics than in relatives of (caloric) restricting anorexics (16% vs. 4%). Unipolar depression has been shown to occur two to four times more frequently in first-degree relatives of both anorexic and bulimic patients than in the general population. Studies have also shown the proportion of patients with positive family histories for eating disorders ranges from 4% to 7%. Kalucy. Crisp, and Harding reported peculiar dietary habits and anorexia or severe weight phobia in 27% of the mothers and 16% of the fathers in the 56 cases studied. In addition, Minuchin, Rosman, and Baker identified five primary personality characteristics of the family that are fairly common in anorexic families. They are enmeshment, overprotectiveness, rigidity, conflict avoidance, and poor conflict resolution skills.

Chapter 16

Eating Disorders in Other Specific Populations

Chapter Contents

Section 16.1

Eating Disorders in LGBT Populations

Lesbian, Gay, Bisexual, Transgender (LGBT)

The myriad of unique struggles related to sexuality and gender expression, such as coming out and harassment in schools or the workplace, can impact experiences of anxiety, depression, low self-esteem, trauma and developing unhealthy coping mechanisms such as substance abuse—all of which are common co-occurring conditions or contributing factors in the development of an eating disorder.

Eating Disorders in LGBT Populations

Eating disorders have historically been associated with straight, young, white females, but in reality, they affect people from all demographics and they are not caused by any single factor. They arise from a combination of long-standing behavioral, biological, emotional, psychological, interpersonal, and social factors. Research suggests that eating disorders disproportionately impact some segments of LGBT populations, though there is much research still to be done on the relationships between sexuality, gender identity, body image and eating disorders.

The myriad of unique stressors LGBT-identified people experience, such as coming out and harassment in schools or the workplace, can impact levels of anxiety, depression, low self-esteem, and unhealthy coping mechanisms such as substance abuse—all of which are common co-occurring conditions and can be contributing factors in the development of an eating disorder. Eating disorders among LGBT populations should be understood within the broader cultural context of oppression.

Potential factors that may interact with an LGBT person's predisposition for developing an eating disorder may include, but are not limited to:

- Coming out: Fear of rejection/experience of rejections by friends, family and co-workers

- Internalized negative messages/beliefs about oneself due to sexual orientation, non-normative gender expressions, or transgender identity

- Experiences of violence (gay bashing), contributing to development of posttraumatic stress disorder (PTSD), which research shows sharply increases vulnerability to an eating disorder

- Discrimination

- Being bullied

- Discordance between one's biological sex and gender identity

- Homelessness or unsafe home environment

- Up to 42% of homeless youth are LGBT-identified

- 33% of youth who are homeless or in the care of social services experienced violent assault when they came out

- Body image ideals within some LGBT cultural contexts

- LGBT people, in addition to experiencing unique contributing factors, may also face challenges for accessing treatment and support. Some of those barriers include:

- Lack of availability of culturally-competent treatment, which addresses the complexity of unique sexuality and gender identity issues

- Lack of family/friend support if not a part of an accepting family/community

- Insufficient eating disorder education among LGBT resource providers who are in a position to detect and intervene. The emergence of LGBT youth drop-in centers, gay-straight alliances, LGBT community centers and LGBT healthcare resources have created more safe spaces to access support and mental healthcare. However, many LGBT people still remain isolated in communities that do not offer such services/programs.

Research on LGBT Populations and Eating Disorders

- Research is limited and conflicting on eating disorders among lesbian and bisexual women.

- While research indicates that lesbian women experience less body dissatisfaction overall, research shows that beginning as

133

early as 12, gay, lesbian and bisexual teens may be at higher
risk of binge eating and purging than heterosexual peers.

- In one study, gay and bisexual boys reported being significantly
more likely to have fasted, vomited or taken laxatives or diet
pills to control their weight in the last 30 days. Gay males were
7 times more likely to report bingeing and 12 times more likely
to report purging than heterosexual males.

- Females identified as lesbian, bisexual or mostly heterosexual
were about twice as likely to report binge eating at least once
per month in the last year.

- Elevated rates of binge eating and purging by vomiting or laxative abuse was found for both males and females who identified
as gay, lesbian, bisexual or "mostly heterosexual" in comparison
to their heterosexual peers.

- Compared to other populations, gay men are disproportionately
found to have body image disturbances and eating disorder
behavior. Gay men are thought to only represent 5% of the total
male population but among men who have eating disorders, 42%
identify as gay.

- In a study of Lesbian, Gay and Bisexual (LGB)-identified participants, which was the first to assess DSM diagnostic categories,
rather than use measures that may be indicative of eating disorders (e.g., eating disorder symptoms), in community-based (versus those recruited from clinical or academic settings) ethnically/
racially diverse populations. Researchers found:

  - Compared with heterosexual men, gay and bisexual men had
  a significantly higher prevalence of lifetime full syndrome bulimia, subclinical bulimia, and any subclinical eating disorder.

  - There were no significant differences between heterosexual
  women and lesbians and bisexual women in the prevalence
  of any of the eating disorders.

  - Respondents aged 18–29 were significantly more likely than
  those aged 30–59 to have subclinical bulimia.

  - Black and Latino LGBs have at least as high a prevalence of
  eating disorders as white LGBs

  - A sense of connectedness to the gay community was related
  to fewer current eating disorders, which suggests that

feeling connected to the gay community may have a protective effect against eating disorders

Eating Disorders and Body Image: What Do Gender and Sexuality Have to Do With It?

Eating disorders are often associated with straight, young, white females, but in reality, they affect people from all demographics and they are not caused by any single factor. They arise from a combination of long-standing behavioral, biological, emotional, psychological, interpersonal, and social factors. Research suggests that eating disorders disproportionately impact some segments of LGBT populations, though there is much research still to be done on the relationship between sexuality, gender expression, body image and eating disorders. There is a strong genetic predisposition to the development of an eating disorder, but it interacts with the many contributing factors that can trigger onset.

LGBT people may also experience unique contributing factors such as trauma in the form of gay-bashing or harassment, losing social support, family, and potentially their home as a result of coming out (up to 42% of homeless youth are LGBT), and extreme anxiety or depression associated with their sexuality or gender expression. In one study, gay and bisexual boys reported being significantly more likely to have fasted, vomited or taken laxatives or diet pills to control their weight in the last 30 days. While research indicates that lesbian women experience less body dissatisfaction overall, recent research found that beginning as early as 12, gay, lesbian and bisexual teens may be at higher risk of binge eating and purging than heterosexual peers, with those identified as lesbian, bisexual or mostly heterosexual being about twice as likely to report binge eating at least once per month in the last year.

LGBT people, in addition to experiencing unique contributing factors, they may also face challenges for accessing treatment and support. In their own personal development, they always felt confused because they did not fit into the stereotypes of what it is to be a girl. In order for them to get the treatment they needed, addressing these complex issues of sexuality and gender would be crucial. LGBT people who struggle with body image issues and eating disorders need culturally competent care.

Section 16.2

Eating Disorders in Minority Populations

This section includes text excerpted from "Diversity"
© 2016 National Eating Disorders Association. For more information,
visit www.nationaleatingdisorders.org. Reprinted with permission.

Race, Ethnicity, and Culture

Eating disorders have historically been associated with young, white women of privilege. However, this is a myth—eating disorders do not discriminate. While more research is needed in this area, we do know that the prevalence of eating disorders is similar among Non-Hispanic Whites, Hispanics, African-Americans, and Asians in the United States, with the exception that anorexia nervosa is more common among Non-Hispanic Whites.

Eating Disorders Affect Us All

Research Results on Eating Disorders in Minority Populations

- Essence survey found that:
    - 71.5% of respondents reported being preoccupied with the desire to be thinner
    - 71.5% reported being "terrified" of being overweight
    - 64.5% were preoccupied with fat on their body
    - 52% reported being preoccupied with food
    - 46% reported feeling guilty after eating
    - 39% stated that food concerns virtually controlled their lives
- African American girls aged 11–14 consistently scored higher than white girls of the same age on all Eating Disorder Inventory (EDI) scales measuring features commonly associated with eating disorders except for body dissatisfaction and drive for thinness.

- Black girls may be especially vulnerable to developing eating disorders with binge eating features.

- African-American women feel tremendous pressure as role models, and that as a result, feel they must be perfect in order to counteract negative stereotypes.

- Asian and Asian-American women are becoming increasingly susceptible to eating and body image problems.

- Asian-American females are not immune to developing eating disorders.

- Among the leanest 25% of 6th and 7th grade girls, Hispanics and Asians reported significantly more body dissatisfaction than did white girls.

- Numerous studies of various Native American populations have shown a high incidence of disordered eating symptoms among adolescents.

- One study of adolescents belonging to the Chippewa tribe and living on a reservation in Michigan found that 74% were trying to lose weight, and of those, 75% were using at least one pathogenic weight control method.

- In studying Native American teenagers, it was found that 48.3% of girls and 30.5% of boys in grades 7–12 had dieted in the past year, and 28% of girls and 21% of boys reported purging behavior.

- In a study of Cuban American women, researchers found that close identification with Cuban culture was associated with lower Eating Attitudes Test (EAT) scores and may have a protective factor in the development of eating disorders.

- Researchers found that second-generation Mexican-American women—those born in the United States to foreign born parents—were the most acculturated and had the highest disordered eating patterns.

Eating Disorders in Women of Color: Explanations and Implications

Background

Over the past few years, there has been increasing evidence of disordered eating occurring among racial and ethnic minorities in the

United States. Contrary to the persistent belief that eating disorders affect only young, white women, analysis of the Minnesota Adolescent Health Study found that dieting was associated with weight dissatisfaction, perceived overweight, and low body pride in all ethnic groups.

In a survey of 6,504 adolescents, Asian, Black, Hispanic, and Caucasian youth all reported attempting to lose weight at similar rates, while among of Native American adolescents, 48.1% were attempting weight loss.

Research and Reporting Bias

Exact statistics on the prevalence of eating disorders among women of color are unavailable. Due to our historically biased view that eating disorders only affect white women, relatively little research has been conducted utilizing participants from racial and ethnic minority groups.

In spite of these factors, reports of eating disorders among women of color are on the rise. Some of this gain may simply reflect an increase in the reporting of these problems rather than actual increases. Three factors affect the rate of reporting among minority women: under-reporting of problems by the individual, under and misdiagnosing on the part of the treatment provider, and cultural bias of Diagnostic and Statistical Manual-IV criteria for eating disorders.

Acculturation Effects

It is sometimes speculated that women from racial and ethnic minority groups are "immune" to developing eating disorders because their cultural identity provides some amount of protection against body image disturbances. For example, it is frequently asserted that African-American culture embraces larger body types than does the dominant culture, thereby making Black women less prone to body dissatisfaction. Thus, it has been hypothesized that as women of color experience acculturation or assimilation of dominant ideals, they become more susceptible to eating disorders.

Kempa and Thomas define *acculturation* as "the process of shifting values to the host culture from the culture of origin." As this occurs, the dominant standards of beauty are internalized and women from minority groups adhere to standards similar to those of white women.

Research results regarding this theory have been mixed, with some evidence supporting the idea that highly acculturated women are more vulnerable to eating disorders. In one study of Cuban American women, it was found that close identification with Cuban culture was associated with lower EAT-26 scores, indicating less negative attitudes toward eating, and may have a protective factor in the development of eating disorders. Second-generation Mexican-American women, those born in the US to foreign-born parents, were the most acculturated and had the highest disordered eating patterns.

Other researchers have suggested that the influence of acculturation on body image formation is much more complex than previously stated. Researchers propose that the effect of acculturation is dependent upon which stage of the ethnic identity process the individual is in. Those in the conformity stage may internalize dominant values of beauty which could lead to eating disorders, while those in the dissonance stage may be highly sensitive to oppressive circumstances and subsequently develop eating problems to cope with these experiences.

Similarly, Lake, Staiger, and Glowiski postulate that eating disorders may result from either the process of assimilation or from the stress of trying to navigate two distinct cultures. Their study supported the "culture clash" argument; they found that "traditional" subjects (those with strong Chinese ethnic identity) were more influenced by western values than were the acculturated group members.

Therefore, acculturation does matter, but the level of acculturation is not always predictive of vulnerability to eating disorders. It is important to recognize that the differences in findings could be due to diversity within ethnic categories. In other words, there is no rigid formula for discerning how acculturation will affect an individual based solely upon their ethnicity.

Sociocultural Factors and Stress

Just as eating disorders have varying etiologies in Caucasian women, the same applies for women of color. Contemporary theories regarding the development of disordered eating include sociocultural, environmental, and genetic factors. These same factors are applicable to women of racial and ethnic minority groups as well.

Sociocultural factors, including the pervasive media images that embrace a narrowly defined conception of beauty, may be particularly disturbing for some women. Researchers notes that, "people furthest from the (dominant ideal of beauty), specifically women of color, may suffer the psychological effects of low self-esteem, poor body image, and eating disorders." Furthermore, it was found that African-American and Native-American women who were more accepting of white American culture (acculturated) showed significantly more symptoms of anorexia and bulimia than did those who were less accepting.

However, sociocultural influences are not the only significant factors in the development of eating disorders. Environmental stress can trigger the onset of disordered eating patterns as well. Among women of color, the process of acculturation can be one such source of stress. Davis and Katzman note that "by definition, acculturation is the process by which one group asserts its influence over another and what happens is likely to be difficult, reactive, and conflictual, affecting one's physical as well as psychological functioning."

Yet, women from racial and ethnic minority groups in the United States face substantially more stress resulting from their membership in multiple subordinate groups than that caused by acculturation alone. Thompson interviewed eighteen women of varying socio-economic status and race and found that eating disorders were frequently a response to environmental stress (i.e., abuse, racism, poverty). Therefore, given the multiple traumas that women of color are exposed to, they may, in fact, be more vulnerable to eating disorders.

Eating Disorders in the Jewish Community

Eating disorders, as with any mental illness, show no boundaries between demographics, with several studies indicating a rise in the problem for Jewish women. The Jewish community is not immune to the various diet and health misconceptions, pressure to be thin, and biological and environmental factors which contribute to the rising numbers of eating disorders, anorexia nervosa, bulimia nervosa and binge eating disorder. Eating disorders affect the entire Jewish community, from the irreligious to the ultra-orthodox.

There is no single reason for the growing number of cases. No matter how we try to shelter or protect our children, their ideas about being thin and desire for perfection seep into their lives. Eating disorders in the Jewish community arise and manifest themselves very similarly to eating disorders in the secular world, and can be potentially life-threatening. What differs however is the effect that culture has on the eating disorder as well as in the treatment and recovery process.

According to a recent article in the Washington Post, health experts say eating disorders are "underreported among orthodox Jewish women and to a lesser extent others in the Jewish community, as many families are reluctant to acknowledge the illness at all and often seek help only when a girl is on the verge of hospitalization." Reluctance to acknowledge an eating disorder is impacted by stigma of mental illness in orthodox Jewish communities, as well as the importance of being thin for marriage arrangements among the ultra-orthodox.

As with the community at large, Jewish girls may turn to an eating disorder in an attempt to achieve what they believe is perfection and control. In Jewish orthodox communities, an eating disorder may be used as a coping mechanism because it is perceived as more "socially acceptable" than other behaviors such as drug abuse.

Furthermore, just as with the general population, there are also individuals who unfortunately have suffered from various traumas and abuse and will turn to eating disorder behaviors as a way of expressing themselves. In the orthodox community, while the dating processes are different than in the secular world, girls have reported hearing their mothers or other community members discussing how being thin is important for dating. With society's notion that "thin is beautiful" surrounding us from all sides, it's no wonder young girls when starting to date tend to focus on being thin rather than finding their soul mate. In one study of ultra-orthodox and Syrian Jewish communities in Brooklyn, 1 out of 19 girls was diagnosed with an eating disorder, which is a rate about 50 percent higher than the general United States population.

Food is a central part of the Jewish culture and is prepared in abundance for Shabbat and holiday meals. Preoccupations with food can exacerbate eating disorder issues for those who struggle. Eating disorder thoughts and pressures tend to be stronger during holiday times. The individual might "save" her calories during the week in order to indulge at the Shabbat or holiday meal, however, this usually leads to either bingeing or further restricting, due to the intense fear of overeating. Those who struggle may begin to omit traditional Shabbat foods, or participate but purge later. The inability to participate in formal exercise on Shabbat or holidays may lead the individual to take extensive Shabbat/holiday walks or rush out to the gym as soon as Shabbat or the holiday is over.

With Shabbat, holidays, kashrut and other nuances of Orthodox Jewish life, the patient can often feel misunderstood or weary of clinicians from other backgrounds. Coupled with the stigma surrounding mental illness, these families are often unsure of where to turn and hesitant to take action. Therefore the needs of a Jewish patient often times require specific knowledge on the part of the treatment team. The Orthodox Jewish community is slowly taking action and addressing these issues. The community has become aware that eating disorders are very serious and can be life-threatening. The most effective treatment will be from individuals who are culturally sensitive and those that can collaborate with the appropriate treatment team.

Chapter 17

Problems Frequently Co-Occurring with Eating Disorders

Chapter Contents

Section 17.1

What Are Co-Occurring Disorders?

"What Are Co-Occurring Disorders?" © 2016
Omnigraphics, Inc. Reviewed March 2016.

Co-Occurring Disorders

Individuals suffering from eating disorders often tend to experience other emotional or behavioral issues, as well. These can include depression, anxiety disorder, and substance abuse. This accompanying condition is called a co-occurring disorder, and the two illnesses together are termed a dual diagnosis.

The co-occurring illness can sometimes be the actual cause of the eating disorder, so it is crucial to treat not just the eating disorder itself, but also to understand and address the factors that led to its development.

Unfortunately, serious coexisting conditions, such as depression, are often ignored, and an individual gets treated only for the eating disorder itself. Although a person may keep this disorder under control for a short time, unless the co-occurring illnesses are also addressed, he or she might soon revert back to poor eating habits once treatment stops. Hence, a comprehensive treatment strategy that focuses on both illnesses is vital to a successful outcome.

Reference

Ekern, Jacquelyn. "Dual Diagnosis and Co-Occurring Disorders," Eating Disorder Hope, April 25, 2012.

Section 17.2

Eating Disorders and Alcohol and Substance Abuse

"Eating Disorders and Alcohol and Substance Abuse," © 2016 Omnigraphics, Inc. Reviewed March 2016.

The uncontrolled use and abuse of alcohol and drugs can lead to dependence or addiction, which may have severe mental and physical consequences. Alcohol and substance addiction are caused by various biological, social, psychological, environmental, and physiological factors and can co-exist with other medical conditions, as well.

A three-year study by the National Center on Addiction and Substance Abuse (CASA) at Columbia University in 2003 showed a strong link between substance abuse and eating disorders—anorexia nervosa and bulimia nervosa, in particular—and identified shared risk factors and characteristics. The exhaustive report states that about 50 percent of those with eating disorders were likely to abuse alcohol and illicit drugs, and up to 35 percent of people with alcohol or drug dependency also had eating disorders.

Other studies have also confirmed that eating disorders and addiction frequently co-occur, noting that characteristics common to both conditions often include intense obsession with the substance (food, alcohol, or drugs), compulsive behavior, a tendency to keep the disorder a secret, social withdrawal, strong cravings, and risk for suicide. Both eating and substance-abuse disorders are more likely to occur in times of stress and depression, low self-esteem, anxiety, when unhealthy dieting behavior or substance abuse is present in the family, and when physical or sexual abuse has occurred in the past.

Both types of disorders are life-threatening, recurrent, and can have the same impact on the functioning of the brain. Some other severe psychiatric conditions associated with eating disorders, as well as substance and alcohol abuse, include obsessive-compulsive disorder and mood disorders.

Eating disorders and alcohol or substance abuse are similar in terms of their addictive nature, and issues related to both conditions tend to coincide. Hence, there is the need for comprehensive treatment that can effectively address the requirements of both disorders simultaneously. Dual-diagnosis treatment and 12-step programs are commonly used in many treatment centers to facilitate eating-disorder and substance-abuse rehabilitation.

References

1. "Eating Disorders and Other Health Problems," Eating Disorders Victoria, June 19, 2015.

2. Ekern, Jacquelyn. "Dual Diagnosis and Co-Occurring Disorders," Eating Disorder Hope, April 25, 2012.

Section 17.3

Eating Disorders and Diabetes

"Eating Disorders and Diabetes," © 2016
Omnigraphics, Inc. Reviewed March 2016.

In individuals suffering from type 1 diabetes, the pancreas is unable to produce insulin, which therefore must be administered daily. A healthy eating plan that balances the periodic insulin injections, physical activity, and food intake is crucial for an individual with this condition. The presence of an eating disorder can cause inadequate glucose control and an increase in the chances of developing secondary complications in the eyes, nerves, and kidneys. In addition to the long-term complications from extreme weight-loss, high blood glucose levels induced by omitted or reduced insulin doses can cause diabetic ketoacidosis (DKA), an acidic blood condition that may lead to coma.

Eating disorders that involve episodes of purging or restricting food intake can cause severe low blood sugar (hypoglycemia), which can make it difficult to determine the proper insulin dose for the individual. And those that involve "insulin-purging"—intentionally decreasing insulin dosage as a means of inducing weight loss—may result in a dangerously high blood sugar level (hyperglycemia).

Indications of an eating disorder in a diabetic individual include constant changes in weight, frequent changes in food intake, extreme fear of low blood glucose level (hypoglycemia), anxiety about injecting or injecting in private, and other signs of unusual eating behavior that may not be directly related to diabetes.

Although many diabetic individuals may be prone to developing eating disorders, the risks are higher for adolescents and young women, as the physical and hormonal changes occurring in the body can have an impact on blood sugar levels. It is important for a diabetic individual to seek professional help if even some of these symptoms are present.

Reference

"Eating Disorders and Other Health Problems," Eating Disorders Victoria, June 19, 2015.

Section 17.4

Eating Disorders and Obsessive-Compulsive Disorder

"Eating Disorders and Obsessive-Compulsive Disorder," © 2016
Omnigraphics, Inc. Reviewed March 2016.

A type of anxiety disorder, obsessive-compulsive disorder (OCD) is characterized by uncontrollable thoughts and repetitive behaviors. The individual often feels anxious and therefore engages in ritualistic or repetitive behaviors to reduce the feeling of uneasiness. OCD often co-occurs with other illnesses, including eating disorders and substance abuse.

Numerous indications of OCD, some more complex than others, may be observed in the behavior of an individual with an eating disorder. Examples include:

• Obsessive thoughts (about food, weight, and body image)

• An obsession with healthy eating and fear of food-borne impurities or diseases (called orthorexia)

• Rituals such as cutting food into tiny pieces or picking food items based on color or shape

- Hoarding large quantities of food
- Spitting out food immediately after chewing
- Excessive or compulsive exercise

These types of abnormal behaviors and thought patterns can take a significant toll on the quality of life, as they can be time-consuming and may create feelings of anxiety and discomfort, especially when in the company of others. Moreover, this situation can lead to a host of other problems, such as depression, irritability, and social isolation.

A strong relationship between eating disorders and OCD has been established, and therefore a comprehensive treatment plan that addresses both forms of illness is crucial. In addition to medication and therapy to treat eating disorders, various forms of psychotherapy may also be employed to bring about a change in the co-occurring unwanted behaviors and thought patterns.

Reference

Ekern, Jacquelyn. "Dual Diagnosis and Co-Occurring Disorders," Eating Disorder Hope, April 25, 2012.

Section 17.5

Eating Disorders and Self-Injury

"Eating Disorders and Self-Injury," © 2016
Omnigraphics, Inc. Reviewed March 2016.

Common forms of self-injury include cutting skin, scratching, beating or burning body parts, interfering with the healing of wounds, and the intake of poisonous substances. Self-injury can be caused by a combination of psychological, genetic, and social factors, along with a possible history of substance abuse and other destructive behavior. Rarely does an individual engage in self-harm with the intention of committing suicide, but these habits, if left unchecked, can increase the risk of death.

The reasons for self-injury can include establishing a sense of control, relieving negative emotions (such as anger, shame, distress, guilt, or loneliness), and attempting to escape traumatic memories. The consequences and complications of such behaviors may include depression, poor self-esteem, relationship difficulties, infections, hospitalization, or even death.

Self-injury is compulsive behavior that can also manifest as a co-occurring disorder. Signs of self-injury, such as fresh wounds, multiple scars, frequent withdrawal from friends and family, and covering wounds with long sleeves or pants, could be an indication of the presence of another illness.

The likelihood of engaging in self-injury is high for individuals with eating disorders. Similarly, certain behaviors associated with eating disorders—such as induced vomiting, excessive or compulsive exercise, and excessive consumption of laxatives—can be the cause self-harm. And self-injury could, alternatively, act as a means of expressing dissatisfaction with one's body, punishing oneself for not sticking to a routine, or even finding solace from a strict nutritional regimen.

During the diagnosis and treatment of eating disorders, identifying the signs of self-harm, as well as analyzing its causes, are essential for a successful outcome. Medication, along with various forms of psychotherapy, such as family intervention, group therapy, and cognitive-behavioral therapy (CBT), will aid in faster recovery from both eating disorders and self-injurious behavior.

Reference

Ekern, Jacquelyn. "Dual Diagnosis and Co-Occurring Disorders," Eating Disorder Hope, April 25, 2012.

Section 17.6

Eating Disorders and Trichotillomania

"Eating Disorders and Trichotillomania," © 2016
Omnigraphics, Inc. Reviewed March 2016.

Trichotillomania—sometimes called hair-pulling disorder—is characterized by a compulsive urge to pull one's own hair from the scalp, eyebrows, eyelashes, limbs, or pubic area. This impulse-control disorder is self-induced and is sometimes classified under OCD or self-injury. Research suggests that the hair-pulling behavior could be a way of relieving stress and anxiety. Some outward signs of trichotillomania, in addition to hair loss, include playing with, chewing, or eating pulled-out hair.

Current thinking suggests that trichotillomania is most likely caused by multiple factors—genetic, biological, and environmental—and could result in low self-esteem and social withdrawal. Complications include infections, permanent hair loss, and gastrointestinal blockage caused by the ingestion of hair, along with other disorders, such as anxiety, depression, and eating disorders.

Both eating disorders and trichotillomania are often attempts by an individual to cope with negative internal emotions or issues. Obsessive-compulsive behavior is a common trait in both disorders, and the individual suffering from an eating disorder might sense momentary relief when hair is pulled.

Treatment for trichotillomania primarily includes psychotherapy, along with medication and—in some cases—surgery to remove intestinal blockage. A comprehensive treatment method that focuses on resolving underlying issues is usually employed to help the individual heal from both disorders.

Reference

Ekern, Jacquelyn. "Dual Diagnosis and Co-Occurring Disorders," Eating Disorder Hope, April 25, 2012.

Section 17.7

Eating Disorders and Posttraumatic Stress Disorder

"Eating Disorders and Posttraumatic Stress Disorder," © 2016 Omnigraphics, Inc. Reviewed March 2016.

Posttraumatic stress disorder (PTSD) develops as a result of exposure to a terrifying or life-threatening event, such as abuse (physical, emotional, or sexual), the sudden death of a loved one, war, major accidents, or natural disasters. The symptoms of PTSD can fall into the following categories:

- **Re-experiencing the traumatic incident.** The individual could have "flashback" episodes, recurring nightmares, and/or reminders or distressing thoughts about the traumatic event, all of which can affect daily life.

- **Avoidance.** The individual may exhibit emotional detachment and avoid people, places, or situations that remind him or her about the event.

- **Stimulation.** These are called arousal symptoms and may include getting alarmed easily, trouble with focusing or sleeping, and sudden emotional outbursts.

- **Negative perceptions and emotions.** These symptoms may include the inability to remember certain parts of the traumatic incident, pessimistic thoughts about people or the world in general, lack of interest in formerly enjoyable activities, and momentary feelings of guilt or blame.

If left untreated, PTSD can have serious adverse effects on the individual. It can take a toll on the person's role in society, interpersonal relationships, the way he or she functions on a daily basis, the ability to learn, and also social and emotional development.

To help cope with the effects of PTSD, individuals frequently develop other disorders, such as drug or alcohol abuse, or an eating disorder. Eating disorders, in particular, have been observed in individuals with a history of trauma, who often perceive this as a way to distract themselves from, or attain a sense of control over, the distressing emotions associated with PTSD. It thus becomes essential to seek help from experienced professionals to treat both conditions simultaneously. A comprehensive treatment strategy may include a combination of medication, nutritional support, and therapy to help resolve the underlying causes of the disorders.

Reference

Ekern, Jacquelyn. "Dual Diagnosis and Co-Occurring Disorders," Eating Disorder Hope, April 25, 2012.

Section 17.8

Eating Disorders and Autism Spectrum Disorder

"Eating Disorders and Autism Spectrum Disorder," © 2016
Omnigraphics, Inc. Reviewed March 2016.

Autism spectrum disorder (ASD) is a type of developmental disorder that is characterized by difficulties in interacting or communicating with others, repetitive or constrained behavior, abnormal sensory responses, and occasional delays in cognition. The term "spectrum" refers to a wide range of symptoms, skills, and levels of impairment. Thus, each individual suffering from ASD is affected differently and requires a unique approach to care and support.

Individuals on the Autism spectrum can be extremely particular about what they eat. They may, for example, have an aversion to the physical properties of some food, such as texture, appearance, smell, and even the sound it makes when chewed. Another common symptom of those on the Autism spectrum is pica, or the tendency to consume non-food items, like paper, dirt, or soap. Some individuals might also experience such problems as difficulty in chewing and swallowing, or gastrointestinal issues. Such eating difficulties, combined with other behaviors associated with the spectrum, can often result in poor body weight and other characteristics of eating disorders.

A number of shared behavioral patterns and personality traits have been identified among individuals suffering from both anorexia and ASD. A study in 2013 established that girls with ASD and those with anorexia had lower empathy and a stronger tendency to systemize (construct and follow rules or patterns) than other people. Keen interest in details, strict behavior patterns, and an inclination to focus on self were some of the common features identified among the two groups.

Since the majority of people diagnosed with eating disorders are females—and since both ASD and anorexia are characterized by symptoms like low body weight, poor or disordered eating habits, and preoccupation with systems—some girls and young women with ASD are incorrectly diagnosed or neglected because the signs of anorexia are the ones most obvious to medical professionals.

Reference

"Eating Disorders and Other Health Problems," Eating Disorders Victoria, June 19, 2015.

Section 17.9

Eating Disorders, Anxiety, and Depression

Psychological conditions like depression and anxiety have been found to co-occur frequently in individuals suffering from eating disorders.

Depression

Depression is a mood disorder that comprises acute feelings of distress, helplessness, anxiety, and/or guilt. It is one of the most common mental-health problems, and it can seriously affect the overall well-being and productivity of the individual. Symptoms may include:

- Increased frustration
- Insomnia
- Reckless behavior
- Loss of interest in activities that were previously enjoyed
- Irritability
- Feelings of insignificance or self-hatred
- Tendency to abuse alcohol or drugs
- Frequent feelings of fatigue or pain
- Low energy level
- Fluctuations in eating habits and body weight

- Social withdrawal

- Poor concentration

- Delusions

- Suicidal thoughts

Depression can be caused by a number of factors, including hormonal imbalance, traumatic experiences, previous history of substance abuse, and side-effects of certain medication. It can either co-occur with, or lead to the development of other mental illnesses, such as anxiety, phobias, panic disorders, and eating disorders.

It is not clear whether eating disorders take root in an individual due to existing depression, or whether eating disorders cause depression. Since no two eating disorders are the same, and each is a complex condition on its own, both arguments are considered valid in different cases. For instance, feelings of worthlessness and moodiness are often identified as a sign of an eating disorder, which, on the other hand, may also be symptoms of depression. Likewise, a depressed person can indulge in emotional eating, which can subsequently lead to an eating disorder.

Anxiety

It is quite normal for people to feel anxious in stressful situations, but when an individual experiences an extreme and unreasonable level of anxiety, it is characterized as a disorder. Anxiety disorder is generally identified as a combination of psychological states, such as nervousness, fear, worry, and mistrust, that extends over a long period of time and considerably affects daily activities. Anxiety may be caused by a combination of environmental, social, psychological, genetic, and physiological factors. Some examples include:

- Hormonal imbalance

- Substance abuse, or withdrawal from an illicit drug

- History of mental illness in the family

- Traumatic episodes

- Current physical ailment

Types of anxiety disorders include generalized anxiety disorder (GAD), obsessive-compulsive disorder (OCD), phobias, social anxiety disorder, panic disorder, and posttraumatic stress disorder (PTSD). Each of them has its own unique symptoms, which are further categorized as physical, behavioral, emotional, and cognitive. These symptoms include sweating, irregular heartbeat, difficulty in breathing, headache, irregular sleeping patterns, nervous habits, irritability, restlessness, obsessive and unwanted thoughts, and irrational fear.

Like depression, anxiety disorder can co-occur with eating disorders. And similarly, an individual suffering from an anxiety disorder can develop an eating disorder as a means of coping with anxiety.

In most cases, anxiety precedes the onset of an eating disorder, such as when an individual briefly soothes symptoms of anxiety by trying to gain a sense of control over other aspects of life, like food, exercise, and weight. This, in the long run, can lead to the development of eating disorders.

Due to the complex nature of eating disorders in conjunction with depression or anxiety, there is the need for an intense treatment plan that analyzes the factors underlying these conditions. Since a number of similar factors can lead to the development of each of these illnesses, successful treatment requires an inclusive strategy that addresses the root cause of all the conditions and helps the individual learn to manage the co-occurring disorder separately and not associate it with food. In addition to medication and nutritional support, the treatment plan may also include various forms of therapy, such as group therapy, cognitive behavioral therapy (CBT), and music and art therapy.

References

1. "Eating Disorders and Other Health Problems," Eating Disorders Victoria, June 19, 2015.

2. Ekern, Jacquelyn. "Dual Diagnosis and Co-Occurring Disorders," Eating Disorder Hope, April 25, 2012

Part Three

Causes of Eating Disorders

Chapter 18

Identifying and Understanding the Causes of Eating Disorders

Chapter Contents

Section 18.1

What Causes Eating Disorders?

This section contains text excerpted from the following sources: Text under the heading "Causes of Eating Disorders" is excerpted from "Eating Disorders," © 1995–2016. The Nemours Foundation/ KidsHealth®. Reprinted with permission; Text under the heading "About Eating Disorders" is excerpted from "Body Image," Office on Women's Health (OWH), September 22, 2010. Reviewed March 2016.

Causes of Eating Disorders

The causes of eating disorders aren't entirely clear. However, a combination of psychological, genetic, social, and family factors are thought to be involved.

For kids with eating disorders, there may be a difference between the way they see themselves and how they actually look. People with anorexia or bulimia often have an intense fear of gaining weight or being overweight and think they look bigger than they actually are. Also, certain sports and activities (like cheerleading, gymnastics, ballet, ice skating, and wrestling) that emphasize certain weight classes may put some kids or teens at greater risk for eating disorders.

There is also an increased incidence of other problems among kids and teens with eating disorders, like anxiety disorders and obsessive-compulsive disorder. Sometimes, problems at home can put kids at higher risk of problem eating behaviors.

Some research suggests that media images contribute to the rise in the incidence of eating disorders. Most celebrities in advertising, movies, TV, and sports programs are very thin, and this may lead girls to think that the ideal of beauty is extreme thinness. Boys, too, may try to emulate a media ideal by drastically restricting their eating and compulsively exercising to build muscle mass.

Concerns about eating disorders are also beginning at an alarmingly young age. Research shows that 42% of first- to third-grade girls want to be thinner, and 81% of 10-year-olds are afraid of being fat. In fact, most kids with eating disorders began their disordered eating between the ages of 11 and 13.

Many kids who develop an eating disorder have low self-esteem and their focus on weight can be an attempt to gain a sense of control at a time when their lives feel more out-of-control.

About Eating Disorders

Eating disorders frequently develop during adolescence or early adulthood, but can occur during childhood or later in adulthood. Females are more likely than males to develop an eating disorder.

Eating disorders are more than just a problem with food. Food is used to feel in control of other feelings that may seem overwhelming. For example, starving is a way for people with anorexia to feel more in control of their lives and to ease tension, anger, and anxiety. Purging and other behaviors to prevent weight gain are ways for people with bulimia to feel more in control of their lives and to ease stress and anxiety.

Although there is no single known cause of eating disorders, several things may contribute to the development of these disorders:

- **Culture**. In the United States extreme thinness is a social and cultural ideal, and women partially define themselves by how physically attractive they are.

- **Personal characteristics.** Feelings of helplessness, worthlessness, and poor self-image often accompany eating disorders.

- **Other emotional disorders.** Other mental health problems, like depression or anxiety, occur along with eating disorders.

- **Stressful events or life changes.** Things like starting a new school or job or being teased and traumatic events like rape can lead to the onset of eating disorders.

- **Biology**. Studies are being done to look at genes, hormones, and chemicals in the brain that may have an effect on the development of, and recovery from eating disorders.

- **Families**. Parents attitudes about appearance and diet can affect their kids' attitudes. Also, if your mother or sister has bulimia, you are more likely to have it.

Section 18.2

Genetics and Anorexia

This section includes text excerpted from "Coming Together to
Calm the Hunger: Group Therapy Program for Adults Diagnosed
with Anorexia Nervosa," U.S. Department of
Education (ED), March 4, 2012. Reviewed March 2016.

The presence of eating disorders tends to be influenced by hereditary within families, with female relatives most often diagnosed. This
hereditary component may suggest that there is a genetic component
as well as environmental elements to the disorder onset. In terms of
the latter, the environmental factors that could be causes of an eating
disorder include the social pressure to be thin, high social class, high
social anxiety, elevated weight or obesity, high impulsivity, individual
differences in biological response to starvation, and individual differences in the reward value of starvation or eating.

It is important to recognize that a genetic component may play a
role in people struggling with disordered eating, particularly since the
diagnosis of anorexia nervosa (AN) is currently based solely on signs and
symptoms as opposed to objective measures. The criteria of AN remains
the subject of considerable debate, in large part because it fails to result
in clearly defined subgroups or to account for changing symptomatology
over the course of the illness. Many individuals who suffer from disordered eating do not meet the criteria for AN and bulimia nervosa, so they
are placed in a residual group known as eating disorder not otherwise
specified. It was stated that risk-factor studies that include both the
genetic and environmental factors present an untapped source of information of potential value for revising the current classification system.

Understanding the genetic components of AN is valuable for treatment. Treatment is best accomplished when the causes of a disorder
are known as this aids in the search for effective interventions. It is
interesting to note that some individuals with a family history of AN
do not develop AN, whereas others will develop disordered eating; it
has been asserted that this is a gene plus an environmental interaction
whereby varying genotypes would render individuals differentially
sensitive to environmental events.

An excellent example of this was provided where an individual with Genotype A might experiment with her first extreme diet, find the experience aversive and uncomfortable, and reject the behaviour on the basis of it not being at all reinforcing. In contrast, an individual with Genotype B might experience that first episode of severe caloric restriction to be highly reinforcing by reducing her innate dysphoria and anxiety, providing her with a sense of control over her own body weight and resulting in her receiving positive social attention for weight-loss attempts.

Identification of risk factors is important for determining high-risk groups for targeted interventions, designing prevention program content, and informing public policy.

Section 18.3

Mediating Factors for Anorexia

This section includes text excerpted from "Coming Together to Calm the Hunger: Group Therapy Program for Adults Diagnosed with Anorexia Nervosa," U.S. Department of Education (ED), March 4, 2012. Reviewed March 2016.

Various empirical and survey-based studies examined possible mediating factors that promote the onset and maintenance of AN. The topic of mediating factors is worthy of exploring as it might aid counsellors helping those with anorexia nervosa (AN) if an anorexic client has a history of childhood sexual abuse, obsessive-compulsive disorder (OCD), depression, borderline personality disorder, or Post-traumatic stress disorder. It is also a necessary to present the mediating factors, as they may help guide treatment options and intervention techniques.

Childhood Sexual Abuse

Clinicians have long argued that childhood sexual abuse is a risk factor for the development of AN. The issue is whether a meaningful relationship exists between the two phenomena, or whether it is merely an illusory one because of the prevalence of both in a female population. Some studies have failed to identify a link between childhood sexual abuse and eating disorders.

A study found that not all of the AN participants reported childhood sexual abuse and that some of the control participants did. What seemed to differentiate the two groups was the amount of abuse. The women with AN reported more separate instances and longer duration of sexual abuse than did healthy controls and were more likely to have been revictimized. Another study found that the individuals who had experienced both childhood sexual abuse and sexual assault in adulthood showed the highest rates of AN behaviour and associated impulsivity, which also support the concept that early trauma may sensitize an individual's reaction to later adversity or traumatic experience.

Obsessive-Compulsive Disorder (OCD)

OCD involves a combination of dysfunctional thoughts and behaviours. Furthermore, it was asserted that the obsessions of OCD are "persistent thoughts, impulses, or images that are intrusive or unwanted such that the client has some degree of insight that their worries are unrealistic". Individuals diagnosed with AN have persistent and intrusive thoughts about food and repetitive concerns about gaining weight. An individual with AN may avoid meals with friends or family in an attempt to reduce their anxiety; this type of behaviour is associated with an obsession characteristic of the disorder.

Compulsions, also part of OCD, are repetitive, purposeful actions that are usually intended to reduce anxiety raised by the obsessions. Compulsions and obsessions can also be identified within individuals diagnosed with AN. For example, an AN individual might disclose how she is frequently spending her time considering how she is going to structure her day around food avoidance.

It was identified that OCD is comorbid with AN, however, there appears to be distinct differences in the desire for change. The motivation for change is often a critical component of treatment of AN, in a way that is qualitatively different from OCD. In OCD clients, there may be high degree of motivation to change. However, those with AN may have difficulty identifying their behaviours and thoughts as being maladaptive and thus do not see a need to change.

Furthermore, it appears that clients with AN are unable to see the physical dangers associated with their dietary restrictions.

Depression

Depression has been found to coexist with AN at a relatively high rate such as 50%. Features that are common to both eating disorders and depression (i.e., weight change, social withdrawal, decreased self-esteem, sleep disturbance, and concentration problems) can make differential diagnosis of depression difficult. Depressive symptoms that do not meet full criteria for an affective disorder, such as low mood, sleep changes, and experiencing less pleasure in one's life, are also common in AN clients. Individuals suffering from depression are reported to have higher than expected rates of a history of trauma or victimization, and more often than not the trauma occurred during childhood or adolescence.

Posttraumatic Stress Disorder

Posttraumatic stress disorder (PTSD) is currently conceptualized as a complex anxiety disorder with an oscillation between reexperiencing the trauma in memories and dreams, on one hand, and generalized avoidance of stimuli reminiscent of the event on the other. Trauma-related symptoms are generally diagnosed under either acute stress disorder or posttraumatic stress disorder. Acute stress disorder and posttraumatic stress disorder are quite similar in symptomatology; however, acute stress disorder is only used for diagnosis during the first month after a traumatic event and acute stress disorder tends to have a great emphasis on dissociative symptoms. While a person with posttraumatic stress disorder may present with dissociative features, it is not a requirement for the diagnosis. It was stated that the individual who experiences a traumatic event may, soon after the experience, develop and present with a variety of symptoms including anxiety, depression, and dissociative symptoms along with other trauma-related symptoms.

Despite their apparent distance in presentation and clinical picture between PTSD and AN, there are similarities.

According to a study, both posttraumatic stress disorder and AN disorders contain ruminations, and these ruminations tend to be called obsessive by AN individuals and intrusive in posttraumatic stress disorder individuals. When compared with typical obsessions, both the intrusive thoughts of individuals with posttraumatic stress disorder and the obsessive thoughts of anorexics have a stronger link with objective external reality. The study asserted that in both AN and posttraumatic stress disorder the resulting aggravated symptoms may worsen self-esteem and depressive states and the interruption of this vicious circle is vital to improvement.

Borderline Personality Disorder

Highly variable rates of comorbidity, ranging from 21% to 57% have been reported for the presence of any personality disorder in patients with a range of eating disorder diagnoses. It has been asserted in a study that childhood trauma is a potential etiological factor in the development of both AN and borderline personality disorder. The relationship between childhood abuse and eating disorders may be mediated by personality dysfunction. It was further postulated that, "At the outset of life's journey, one's endowment with low adaptive genetics and exposure to an unstable family environment highlighted by abuse appears to establish the risk for personality disorder". In turn, this consolidated personality disorder may enhance the risk for AN. However, not all traumatized individuals develop personality disorders, and not all individuals with personality disorders develop AN.

Section 18.4

Congenital Leptin Deficiency and Obesity

This section includes text excerpted from "Congenital Leptin Deficiency," Genetics Home Reference (GHR), December 2013.

What Is Congenital Leptin Deficiency?

Congenital leptin deficiency is a condition that causes severe obesity beginning in the first few months of life. Affected individuals are of normal weight at birth, but they are constantly hungry and quickly gain weight. Without treatment, the extreme hunger continues and leads to chronic excessive eating (hyperphagia) and obesity. Beginning in early childhood, affected individuals develop abnormal eating behaviors such as fighting with other children over food, hoarding food, and eating in secret.

People with congenital leptin deficiency also have hypogonadotropic hypogonadism, which is a condition caused by reduced production of hormones that direct sexual development. Without treatment, affected individuals experience delayed puberty or do not go through puberty, and may be unable to conceive children (infertile).

How Common Is Congenital Leptin Deficiency?

Congenital leptin deficiency is a rare disorder. Only a few dozen cases have been reported in the medical literature.

What Genes Are Related to Congenital Leptin Deficiency?

Congenital leptin deficiency is caused by mutations in the *LEP* gene. This gene provides instructions for making a hormone called leptin, which is involved in the regulation of body weight. Normally, the body's fat cells release leptin in proportion to their size. As fat accumulates in cells, more leptin is produced. This rise in leptin indicates that fat stores are increasing.

Leptin attaches (binds) to and activates a protein called the leptin receptor, fitting into the receptor like a key into a lock. The leptin receptor protein is found on the surface of cells in many organs and tissues of the body including a part of the brain called the hypothalamus.

The hypothalamus controls hunger and thirst as well as other functions such as sleep, moods, and body temperature. It also regulates the release of many hormones that have functions throughout the body. In the hypothalamus, the binding of leptin to its receptor triggers a series of chemical signals that affect hunger and help produce a feeling of fullness (satiety).

LEP gene mutations that cause congenital leptin deficiency lead to an absence of leptin. As a result, the signaling that triggers feelings of satiety does not occur, leading to the excessive hunger and weight gain associated with this disorder. Because hypogonadotropic hypogonadism occurs in congenital leptin deficiency, researchers suggest that leptin signaling is also involved in regulating the hormones that control sexual development. However, the specifics of this involvement and how it may be altered in congenital leptin deficiency are unknown.

Congenital leptin deficiency is a rare cause of obesity.

How Do People Inherit Congenital Leptin Deficiency?

This condition is inherited in an autosomal recessive pattern, which means both copies of the gene in each cell have mutations. The parents of an individual with an autosomal recessive condition each carry one copy of the mutated gene, but they typically do not show signs and symptoms of the condition.

What Other Names Do People Use for Congenital Leptin Deficiency?

- LEPD
- leptin deficiency
- obesity due to congenital leptin deficiency
- obesity, morbid, due to leptin deficiency
- obesity, morbid, nonsyndromic 1
- obesity, severe, due to leptin deficiency

Chapter 19

Environmental Factors in Eating Disorder Development

Introduction

Researchers cannot pinpoint a single cause for eating disorders. Instead, they view eating disorders as complex illnesses that can have a variety of contributing causes, including genetic, biological, psychological, social, and environmental factors. Some of the environmental factors that may increase the likelihood of an individual developing an eating disorder include sociocultural pressures to attain a certain standard of thinness, media messages about diet and weight loss, exposure to traumatic events, stressful or chaotic family dynamics, and mothers who frequently express dissatisfaction with their own bodies or criticize their daughters' body shape or weight.

Sociocultural Ideals

American media and popular culture promote an image of the ideal or "perfect" body that is unattainable for most people. Fashion models, actors, and celebrities featured onscreen or in magazines tend to fall

"Environmental Factors in Eating Disorder Development," © 2016 Omnigraphics, Inc. Reviewed March 2016.

within a narrow set of norms that include only those who are extremely thin or extremely muscular, and editing technologies such as Photoshop and airbrushing are often employed to remove any blemishes, wrinkles, or love handles. When people internalize these unrealistic standards of beauty, it may contribute to the development of a negative body image, an obsession with weight and appearance, and eating disorders. Although many people who are exposed to sociocultural ideals of thinness do not develop eating disorders, studies have shown that some individuals are highly vulnerable to such environmental messages about weight and beauty.

Dieting

In response to societal pressures to attain a certain ideal body shape, many people resort to restrictive dieting or other extreme weight-loss measures. Americans spend an estimated $60 billion each year on fad diets and dangerous weight-loss products, despite the fact that 95 percent of people on diets fail to achieve permanent weight loss. In addition to their ineffectiveness, restrictive diets are also a common precipitating factor in the development of eating disorders. Dieting increases people's preoccupation with food and weight and generates feelings of guilt and shame surrounding eating. For some people, these feelings contribute to the development of eating disorders.

Traumatic Experiences

Studies have suggested that up to 50 percent of people with eating disorders have experienced a traumatic event, such as physical or sexual abuse. Such events often create feelings of guilt and shame and contribute to a negative body image. Some victims of trauma develop eating disorders as they restrict food in an attempt to regain control over their bodies or cope with the intense emotions generated by the event.

Family Dynamics

Stressful or chaotic family situations are another environmental factor that has been linked with an increase in the likelihood of eating disorders. While many people with eating disorders come from difficult family environments, however, there is no evidence to support the idea that certain family situations or parenting styles directly cause eating disorders. Instead, family dynamics are only one factor that may potentially contribute to the illness. In addition, research has found that the relationship may be reciprocal—the stress surrounding a member's struggle with an eating disorder may cause negative family dynamics to develop.

On the other hand, family support systems can also help young people ignore sociocultural pressures and establish a positive body image, which may help protect them from developing eating disorders. Finally, family involvement is a vital component in the treatment and recovery process.

The Mother-Daughter Relationship

Of all the family relationships, the one between mothers and daughters has been most extensively studied with respect to its impact on the development of eating disorders. Research has suggested a correlation between a mother's body image and eating behaviors and the likelihood of her daughter developing an eating disorder. Some of this the correlation may be explained by genetic predisposition, which is estimated to account for between 50 and 80 percent of eating disorder risk, yet many experts believe that behavior modeling also plays a role.

Studies have identified the following behaviors by mothers as factors that may increase the risk of daughters developing low self-esteem, negative body image, preoccupation with weight and appearance, and eating disorders:

- Mothers who have a negative body image or frequently express dissatisfaction with their own weight, shape, or size;

- Mothers who have disordered eating habits and attitudes, such as restrictive dieting or binge eating;

- Mothers who criticize or ridicule their daughters' food choices or eating habits;

- Mothers who make negative comments about their daughters' weight and appearance;

- Mothers who insist upon a relationship with their daughters that lacks boundaries and does not promote individual autonomy.

It is important to note that eating disorders never have a single cause. Even if mothers engage in one or more of the above behaviors, they should not be blamed for having a daughter with an eating disorder. But being aware of the risks associated with the mother-daughter relationship can help people adjust their behavior and build healthier family dynamics. Mothers who focus on health and inner beauty rather than weight and appearance can help counteract other environmental factors and protect their daughters against disordered eating behaviors.

References

1. Fielder-Jenks, Chelsea. "Mothers, Daughters, and Eating Disorders." Eating Disorder Hope, 2016.

2. Jones, Megan. "Factors that May Contribute to Eating Disorders." National Eating Disorders Association, n.d.

Chapter 20

Body Image and Eating Disorders

What Is Body Image?

Body image is how you think and feel about your body. It includes whether you think you look good to other people.

Body image is affected by a lot of things, including messages you get from your friends, family, and the world around you. Images we see in the media definitely affect our body image even though a lot of media images are changed or aren't realistic.

Why does body image matter? Your body image can affect how you feel about yourself overall. For example, if you are unhappy with your looks, your self-esteem may start to go down. Sometimes, having body image issues or low self-esteem may lead to depression, eating disorders, or obesity.

How Can I Deal with Body Image Issues?

Everyone has something they would like to change about their bodies. But you'll be happier if you focus on the things you like about your body—and your whole self. Check out some tips:

This chapter contains text excerpted from the following sources: Text beginning with the heading "What Is Body Image?" is excerpted from Office on Women's Health (OWH), January 7, 2015; Text under the heading "Where Does Body Image Come From?" is excerpted from "Where Does Body Image Come From?" U.S. Department of Health and Human Services (HHS), November 30, 2012. Reviewed March 2016.

- **List your great traits.** If you start to criticize your body, tell yourself to stop. Instead, think about what you like about yourself, both inside and out.

- **Know your power.** Hey, your body is not just a place to hang your clothes! It can do some truly amazing things. Focus on how strong and healthy your body can be.

- **Treat your body well.** Eat right, sleep tight, and get moving. You'll look and feel your best—and you'll be pretty proud of yourself too.

- **Give your body a treat.** Take a nice bubble bath, do some stretching, or just curl up on a comfy couch. Do something soothing.

- **Mind your media.** Try not to let models and actresses affect how you think you should look. They get lots of help from makeup artists, personal trainers, and photo fixers. And advertisers often use a focus on thinness to get people to buy stuff. Don't let them mess with your mind!

- **Let yourself shine.** A lot of how we look comes from how we carry ourselves. Feeling proud, walking tall, and smiling big can boost your beauty—and your mood.

- **Find fab friends.** Your best bet is to hang out with people who accept you for you! And work with your friends to support each other.

If you can't seem to accept how you look, talk to an adult you trust. You can get help feeling better about your body.

What Do You See?

A lot of our body image comes from pics we see in the media or on social media sites. But those images can be unhealthy, fixed up, or faked. Focusing on inner beauty makes more sense.

Stressing about Body Changes

During puberty and your teen years, your body changes a lot. All those changes can be hard to handle. They might make you worry about what other people think of how you look and about whether your body is normal. If you have these kinds of concerns, you are not alone.

Here are some common thoughts about changing bodies.

- Why am I taller than most of the boys my age?
- Why haven't I grown?
- Am I too skinny?
- Am I too fat?
- Will others like me now that I am changing?
- Are my breasts too small?
- Are my breasts too large?
- Why do I have acne?
- Do my clothes look right on my body?
- Are my hips getting bigger?

If you are stressed about your body, you may feel better if you understand why you are changing so fast—or not changing as fast as your friends.

During puberty, you get taller and see other changes in your body, such as wider hips and thighs. Your body will also start to have more fat compared to muscle than before. Each young woman changes at her own pace, and all of these changes are normal.

What Are Serious Body Image Problems?

If how your body looks bothers you a lot and you can't stop thinking about it, you could have body dysmorphic disorder, or BDD.

People with BDD think they look ugly even if they have a small flaw or none at all. They may spend many hours a day looking at flaws and trying to hide them. They also may ask friends to reassure them about their looks or want to have a lot of cosmetic surgery. If you or a friend may have BDD, talk to an adult you trust, such as a parent or guardian, school counselor, teacher, doctor, or nurse. BDD is an illness, and you can get help.

Where Does Body Image Come From?

Body image is all about how you see and judge your body. Chances are good that there are things about your body you really like and probably some things that aren't your favorite. If you find that you are mostly focusing on the things you don't like about how your body looks, you may have a negative body image. We get both positive and negative messages about our bodies all the time.

175

Here are some common sources that can affect how we view our bodies:

- Television, magazines, and movies

- Comments about how you look from family, friends and even strangers

- Worrying about whether others will think you're attractive

- Comparisons to other people—like your sister, best friend or even your former self, 10 to 20 years ago

- Changes to your body because of aging, menopause, illness, or disability

- Emotions like feeling unhappy or depressed

Everyone feels self-conscious, awkward, or ashamed about their bodies from time to time—even "skinny" people and people who are at their "ideal" weight. But when these feelings are how you usually feel about your body, it can take a toll on your confidence and how you take part in the rest of your life. The good news is that there are things you can do to improve your body image.

Chapter 21

Bullying and the Link to Eating Disorders

Weight-Based Bullying and Binge Eating Disorder

Binge eating disorder (BED) is a complex psychiatric disorder with countless risk factors, signs and symptoms, and potential accompanying physical and psychological complications (called co-morbidities)—and bullying can be a contributing factor.

Bullying has very serious consequences. Studies show bullying of any kind, but particularly weight-based bullying, leads to increased occurrence of low self-esteem, poor body image, social isolation, eating disorders, and poor academic performance.

Kids and teens who are overweight can be victims of many forms of bullying, including physical force, name calling, derogatory comments, being ignored or excluded, or being made fun of.

In a research, it was found that:

- Weight-based teasing predicted binge eating at five years of follow-up among both men and women, even after controlling for age, race/ethnicity, and socioeconomic status.

This chapter contains text excerpted from the following sources: Text beginning with the heading "Weight-Based Bullying and Binge Eating Disorder" is excerpted from U.S. Department of Health and Human Services (HHS), May 12, 2015; Text under the heading "Childhood Bullying Linked to Adult Psychiatric Disorders" is excerpted from "Childhood Bullying Linked to Adult Psychiatric Disorders," U.S. Department of Health and Human Services (HHS), February 18, 2014.

- Peer victimization can be directly predicted by weight.

- 64% of students enrolled in weight-loss programs reported experiencing weight-based victimization.

- One third of girls and one fourth of boys report weight-based teasing from peers, but prevalence rates increase to approximately 60% among the heaviest students.

- 84% of students observed students perceived as overweight being called names or getting teased during physical activities.

Bullying Is Trauma and Can Lead to BED

Bullying because of body size can have a major negative impact on this vulnerable population. BED has the highest rate of trauma of all eating disorders. That is, individuals who have binge eating disorder have experienced trauma at some point during their lives. Types of trauma include emotional, physical, and sexual abuse, a divorce or death, and, yes, bullying.

Trauma doesn't have to be catastrophic to have lasting catastrophic effects on a person's psychological, social, and physical health.

People living in larger bodies experience trauma every day by being assaulted by negative attitudes and messages about weight from all angles: in the media; at home, school, and work; even in doctors' offices. This increases stress and leads to internalized weight stigma, which further entrenches disordered eating patterns.

What Can We Do about It?

There are several things you can do to help stop weight-based bullying and all other types of bullying.

- Learn what bullying is and what it is not.

- Learn to recognize warning signs that your child is involved in bullying.

- Talk to your child about bullying and what to do if it happens.

Childhood Bullying Linked to Adult Psychiatric Disorders

It was discovered that victims of childhood bullying have a higher risk of developing mental health problems later in life. For a study, researchers followed more than 1,000 youth, starting at the ages of 9, 11, and 13. The youth were interviewed each year until they turned 16. Follow-up interviews were then conducted into adulthood.

Results of the study showed bullying elevated the rate of mental health problems. Some of the key findings were:

- Youth who were victims of bullying had a higher chance of having agoraphobia, anxiety and panic disorders.

- Youth who bullied were at risk for antisocial personality disorder.

- Youth who bullied who were also victims of bullying were at a higher risk for adult depression and panic disorder. For this group, there was an increased risk for agoraphobia in females and suicidality in males.

The link between bullying and mental illness is very real. This research brief only scratches the surface of this issue, and is not a synthesis of all mental health and bullying research. Bullying can have many different effects.

Bullying is a serious problem for all involved and can have a lasting impact on someone's entire life—but it doesn't have to. You can help youth heal from the harmful effects of bullying.

Chapter 22

The Media and Eating Disorders

Chapter Contents

Section 22.1

Media Influence and Eating Disorders

This section contains text excerpted from the following sources:
Text beginning with the heading "Weight Bias" is excerpted from
Centers for Disease Control and Prevention (CDC), March 22,
2013; Text under the heading "Six Media Questions" is excerpted
from "Six Media Questions," National Institute of Child Health
and Human Development (NICHD), 2013; Text under the heading
"Media, Body Image, and Eating Disorders" is excerpted from
"Media, Body Image, and Eating Disorders," © 2016 National
Eating Disorders Association. For more information, visit www.
nationaleatingdisorders.org. Reprinted with permission.

Weight Bias

Weight bias can be defined as the inclination to form unreasonable
judgments based on a person's weight. Stigma is the social sign that is
carried by a person who is a victim of prejudice and weight bias. Obese
children are at an increased risk for bias as a result of their weight.

Weight bias is caused by a general belief that stigma and shame
will motivate people to lose weight or the belief that people fail to lose
weight as a result of inadequate self-discipline or insufficient will-
power. The U.S. culture may not punish people who practice weight
bias because our culture values thinness. Society frequently blames
the victim rather than addressing environmental conditions that contribute to obesity.

Weight bias affects the child in multiple ways. Obese children are
often the brunt of teasing or discrimination. Bias exists in the adult
workplace and may affect children as they enter the workforce. Weight
bias also influences educational success and may affect how healthcare is delivered. Weight bias is promoted in the media and even by
parents of obese children. Curbing the obesity epidemic will require
new strategies that do not result in bias or prejudice.

Weight Bias and the Media

Children's media have a prevailing tendency to represent positive messages about being thin and negative messages about being

overweight. In children's entertainment, thin characters are ascribed desirable attributes and dominate central roles, whereas overweight characters are onscreen rarely or in minor stereotypical roles. Compared with thin characters appearing on television, heavier characters rarely are portrayed in romantic relationships (and never with thin characters), are more likely to be objects of humor and ridicule, and often engage in stereotypical eating behaviors.

Six Media Questions

Next time you watch an ad, ask yourself these 6 questions

1. Who is the author or sponsor?

2. What is the purpose?

3. Who is the audience?

4. What is the message?

5. What information is missing?

6. What techniques are used to attract your attention?

Media, Body Image, and Eating Disorders

We Live in a Media-Saturated World and Do Not Control the Message.

Mass media provides a significantly influential context for people to learn about body ideals and the value placed on being attractive.

- Over 80% of Americans watch television daily. On average, these people watch over three hours per day.

- American children engage in increasing amounts of media use, a trend fueled largely by the growing availability of Internet access through phones and laptops. On a typical day, 8–18-year-olds are engaged with some form of media about 7.5 hours. Most of this time is spent watching television, though children play video games more than an hour per day and are on their computers for more than an hour per day. Even media aimed at elementary school age children, such as animated cartoons and children's videos, emphasize the importance of being attractive. Sexually objectified images of girls and women in advertisements are most likely to appear in men's magazines. Yet the second most common source of such images is the advertisements in teen magazines directed at adolescent girls.

Effects of Media

There is no single cause of body dissatisfaction or disordered eating. But, research is increasingly clear that media does indeed contribute and that exposure to and pressure exerted by media increase body dissatisfaction and disordered eating.

- Numerous correlational and experimental studies have linked exposure to the thin ideal in mass media to body dissatisfaction, internalization of the thin ideal, and disordered eating among women.

- The effect of media on women's body dissatisfaction, thin ideal internalization, and disordered eating appears to be stronger among young adults than children and adolescents. This may suggest that long-term exposure during childhood and adolescence lays the foundation for the negative effects of media during early adulthood.

- Black-oriented television shows may serve a protective function; Hispanic and Black girls and women who watch more Black-oriented television have higher body satisfaction.

- Pressure from mass media to be muscular also appears to be related to body dissatisfaction among men. This effect may be smaller than among women but it is still significant.

- Young men seem to be more negatively affected by the media images than adolescent boys are.

Section 22.2

The Internet and Eating Disorders (Pro-ED Websites)

"The Internet and Eating Disorders (Pro-ED Websites),"
© 2016 Omnigraphics, Inc. Reviewed March 2016.

The Internet can be a valuable source of information and support for people who are working to recover from eating disorders. It can help them feel less isolated by enabling them to connect with others who share their experiences and understand their feelings. Yet the Internet also contains thousands of dangerous websites that advocate extreme weight loss methods and encourage disordered eating behaviors. Known as pro-anorexia (pro-ana), pro-bulimia (pro-mia), and pro-eating disorder (pro-ED) websites, these online communities can be harmful or even deadly for people who are vulnerable to their messages. Rather than promoting treatment and recovery, these sites spread strategies and ideas that may trigger or exacerbate an eating disorder.

The Dangers of Pro-ED Websites

Some pro-ED websites appear fairly innocuous on the surface. They may seem to promote clean eating, fitness, or a healthy lifestyle. The underlying message, however, is that controlling food intake, losing weight, and achieving a "perfect" body can resolve a myriad of social and emotional issues. For people who are struggling with an eating disorder, this message validates their unhealthy eating behaviors and makes their illness seem like an acceptable lifestyle choice.

Pro-ana and pro-mia websites offer praise, encouragement, and support for the "strength," "discipline," and "self-control" required to ignore the body's basic need for food and severely restrict or purge calories. Many sites also provide strategies or tips for eating less, purging more effectively, or hiding an eating disorder from concerned family members and friends. The sites may glorify extremely thin models and actresses and provide photos of emaciated people for "thinspiration," which has the effect of reinforcing negative, self-destructive body images.

A 2010 study showed that 83 percent of the websites that appeared in search results for such terms as "anorexia" and "support" included pro-ana/pro-mia ideas for dieting and staying thin. Research also indicates that exposure to such websites has a negative impact on the eating behaviors and self-esteem of people who view them. One study found that healthy college women with no history of eating disorders who were exposed to such sites for 1.5 hours reduced their caloric intake—most without even realizing it—during the week following their exposure. They also scored lower on measures of body image and feelings of attractiveness after viewing the pro-ED websites.

Counteracting Pro-ED with Pro-Recovery

Given the dangers of pro-ED websites, eating disorder experts argue that public education is needed to raise awareness of the sites and counteract their effects. The National Eating Disorder Association (NEDA) has worked with major online social networks, such as Facebook and Tumblr, to block pro-ana/pro-mia content, monitor Internet communities dedicated to eating disorders, and provide support and recovery resources for people who need help. NEDA also launched its own social media campaign, Proud2BMe, with a website dedicated to promoting healthy attitudes about food, weight, and body image.

Some eating disorder experts claim that banning pro-ED websites, blogs, forums, and images may be counterproductive. Since many of these sites are operated by people who have eating disorders, they believe that maintaining an open dialogue and providing support is a better response. The pro-recovery movement aims to counteract the effects of pro-ED materials online by offering an alternative source of understanding and community for people struggling with eating disorders. They work to expose the dangers of websites that make eating disorders seem glamorous or encourage people to employ harmful weight-loss methods. They also combat these negative messages with positive information about treatment, recovery, health, fitness, and self-esteem.

References

1. Bond, Emma. "Virtually Anorexic—Where's the Harm?" Nominet Trust, November 28, 2012.

2. Ekern, Jacquelyn and Karges, Crystal. "The Pro-Recovery Movement Fights the Pro-Ana and Pro-Mia Websites." Eating Disorder Hope, August 14, 2013.

3. Klimek, Amy M. "The Dangers of Pro-ED Websites." Eating Disorder Hope, November 11, 2014.

Part Four

Medical Complications of Eating Disorders

Chapter 23

Health Consequences of Eating Disorders

Eating disorders are serious, potentially life-threatening conditions that affect a person's emotional and physical health. They are not just a "fad" or a "phase." People do not just "catch" an eating disorder for a period of time. They are real, complex, and devastating conditions that can have serious consequences for health, productivity, and relationships. Anorexia nervosa, bulimia and binge eating disorder affect up to 5% of young women, are associated with high use of medical resources, but often go unrecognized in medical settings. Men with eating disorders are even more likely to elude detection.

People struggling with an eating disorder need to seek professional help. The earlier a person with an eating disorder seeks treatment, the greater the likelihood of physical and emotional recovery. All physicians should be alert to signs and symptoms of these relatively common behavioral disorders. Most patients respond to specialist treatment,

---

This chapter contains text excerpted from the following sources: Text under the heading "Health Consequences of Eating Disorders" is excerpted from "Health Consequences of Eating Disorders," © 2016 National Eating Disorders Association. For more information, visit www.nationaleatingdisorders.org. Reprinted with permission; Text under the heading "What All Medical Professionals Should Know About Eating Disorders" is excerpted from "What All Medical Professionals Should Know About Eating Disorders," © 2016 National Eating Disorders Association. For more information, visit www.nationaleatingdisorders.org. Reprinted with permission.

although rates of medical morbidity, functional impairment and mortality are high, especially for anorexia nervosa, which has the highest mortality of any psychiatric condition.

Health Consequences of Anorexia Nervosa

In anorexia nervosa's cycle of self-starvation, the body is denied the essential nutrients it needs to function normally. Thus, the body is forced to slow down all of its processes to conserve energy, resulting in serious medical consequences:

- Abnormally slow heart rate and low blood pressure, which mean that the heart muscle is changing. The risk for heart failure rises as the heart rate and blood pressure levels sink lower and lower.

- Reduction of bone density (osteoporosis), which results in dry, brittle bones.

- Muscle loss and weakness.

- Severe dehydration, which can result in kidney failure.

- Fainting, fatigue, and overall weakness.

- Dry hair and skin; hair loss is common.

- Growth of a downy layer of hair called lanugo all over the body, including the face, in an effort to keep the body warm.

Health Consequences of Bulimia Nervosa

The recurrent binge-and-purge cycles of bulimia can affect the entire digestive system and can lead to electrolyte and chemical imbalances in the body that affect the heart and other major organ functions. Some of the health consequences of bulimia nervosa include:

- Electrolyte imbalances that can lead to irregular heartbeats and possibly heart failure and death. Electrolyte imbalance is caused by dehydration and loss of potassium, sodium and chloride from the body as a result of purging behaviors.

- Potential for gastric rupture during periods of bingeing.

- Inflammation and possible rupture of the esophagus from frequent vomiting.

- Tooth decay and staining from stomach acids released during frequent vomiting.

- Chronic irregular bowel movements and constipation as a result of laxative abuse.

- Peptic ulcers and pancreatitis.

Health Consequences of Binge Eating Disorder

Binge eating disorder often results in many of the same health risks associated with clinical obesity. Some of the potential health consequences of binge eating disorder include:

- High blood pressure.

- High cholesterol levels.

- Heart disease as a result of elevated triglyceride levels.

- Type II diabetes mellitus.

- Gallbladder disease.

What All Medical Professionals Should Know about Eating Disorders

Anorexia nervosa, bulimia and binge eating disorder affect up to 5% of young women, are associated with high use of medical resources, but often go unrecognized in medical settings. Men with eating disorders are even more likely to elude detection. All physicians should be alert to signs and symptoms of these relatively common behavioral disorders. Most cases respond to specialist treatment, although rates of medical morbidity, functional impairment and mortality are high, especially for anorexia nervosa, which has the highest mortality of any psychiatric condition. Patients may deny they have an eating disorder; and some degree of symptom concealment is common, as these conditions are associated with high levels of ambivalence towards treatment, as well as feelings of shame, embarrassment and stigma.

Patients frequently present to a variety of medical specialists including pediatricians, internists, gastroenterologists, endocrinologists, gynecologists, neurologists, cardiologists, orthopedic specialists and psychiatrists seeking help for medical or psychiatric complications of their eating behavior, whether or not they acknowledge their diagnosis. They may avoid treatments focused on normalizing their eating behavior, favoring instead medical interventions that address consequences of their behavior without altering the underlying problem.

Medical professionals should be familiar with common presenting complaints, with diagnostic screening questions and with treatment options to optimally detect and manage these disorders. Collateral information from family is often very helpful in establishing the diagnosis. Onset of an eating disorder may be insidious, and may follow a viral or other illness. It is not uncommon for example for a bout of mononucleosis or viral gastroenteritis to evolve into anorexia nervosa or bulimia.

Complications of eating disorders are best thought of as consequences of starvation or of bingeing and purging behaviors. Patients who are underweight and who purge are therefore at highest risk for severe complications.

Eating disorders can affect all organ systems and presenting complaints are quite varied. The following Top 10 list reviews common medical presentations and laboratory values that may reflect an occult eating disorder. The vast majority of these symptoms reverse with normalization of weight and eating behavior, although symptomatic treatment alone is unlikely to alter their course, making identification and appropriate referral for treatment of the underlying behavioral disorder of paramount importance.

1. Metabolic or electrolyte abnormalities

- Rapid weight loss may indicate anorexia nervosa and rapid weight gain may result from new onset of binge eating disorder

- Hypokalemia can be a sign of regular self-induced vomiting, especially in the presence of low chloride and elevated bicarbonate. Laxative abuse may also lead to hypokalemia and can result in either metabolic acidosis or alkalosis. Diuretic abuse can result in hypokalemia and contraction alkalosis.

- Hypoglycemia may be starvation-related in anorexia nervosa

- Hyponatremia may result from excessive water intake, a behavior often used to suppress appetite and increase satiety or to artificially inflate weight gain.

- Hypophosphatemia may be detected on initial evaluation following weight loss, although more commonly a complication of refeeding

2. Gastrointestinal complaints

- Functional gastrointestinal disorders are present in the vast majority of inpatients with eating disorders treated on specialty behavioral units. Patients may also present with excessive and disabling preoccupations or idiosyncratic ideas regarding food intolerances or bowel regimens. Delayed gastric emptying and slowed whole gut transit times are typical of anorexia nervosa and gastroparesis is also commonly present in bulimia.

- Abdominal bloating, pain and constipation and other symptoms typical of irritable bowel syndrome are frequently associated with starvation or with binge intake of food.

- Gastrointestinal reflux disease (GERD), esophageal Mallory Weiss tears, bilateral parotid gland enlargement, dental caries and enamel erosion are all associated with self-induced vomiting. Most individuals who vomit regularly have lost the gag reflex and many can vomit spontaneously without inducing a gag.

- Transaminitis and elevated lipase and amylase are frequent consequences of anorexia nervosa and can be associated both with both starvation and refeeding.

- Acute gastric dilatation is a rare, life threatening presenting symptom in patients with anorexia nervosa who binge eat and may cause superior mesenteric artery syndrome.

- Rectal prolapse and hemorrhoids can be complications of laxative abuse.

3. Gynecologic and Obstetric complaints

- Hypothalamic amenorrhea and infertility are common in anorexia nervosa.

- Pregnancy may be associated with poor weight gain, intrauterine growth retardation or hyperemesis gravidarum in individuals who purge by vomiting.

- Postpartum rapid weight loss due to excessive breast pumping and milk wasting has been described.

4. Neurologic presentations

- Syncopal or presyncopal episodes and orthostasis due to fluid restriction or diuretic and laxative abuse may be presenting symptoms.

- Somatoform pain disorders especially abdominal pain complaints or headaches are common.

- Seizures may be due to hypoglycemia or excessive water intake and resultant hyponatremia.

- Wernicke-Korsakoff's syndrome can be a complication of refeeding in very low weight anorexia nervosa, especially when comorbid with alcohol abuse. Preventative thiamine supplementation is critically important in these cases.

5. *Cardiac presentations*

- Bradycardia is often detected in anorexia nervosa and can be severe with heart rates of 30 or below and may be associated with corrected QT (QTc) prolongation and increased risk of cardiac arrest.

- Orthostatic hypotension or tachycardia may reflect dehydration from purging or fluid restriction or from impaired vagal tone.

- A starvation cardiomyopathy and heart failure may occur in severe and chronic AN.

- Mitral valve prolapse due to atrophic cardiac muscle may be evident on exam.

- Arrthymias may occur due to electrolyte abnormalities or caffeine or ephedrine diet suppressant abuse.

6. *Endocrine presentations*

- Hypothalamic amenorrhea and infertility, as well as osteoporotic fractures are complications of anorexia nervosa.

- Sick euthryoid labs are commonly seen in anorexia nervosa with low T3 and rT3 and ration of T4 to rT3 is elevated. TSH and T4 may be suppressed.

- Hypercortisolemia is common in anorexia nervosa as a result of starvation related activation of the HPA axis and may contribute to bone loss and osteoporosis.

- Frequent ketoacidosis in a diabetic may reflect purging by underdosing insulin or insulin omission in order to waste calories.

7. Hematological presentations

Anemia, leukopenia and thrombocytopenia are all seen in severe anorexia nervosa as starvation is associated with bone marrow hypocellularity and fatty infiltration.

8. Psychiatric complications

Major depression, anxiety disorders and substance abuse are commonly comorbid with eating disorders and tend to worsen with the severity of the eating disorder.

9. Renal presentations

Although relatively uncommon, renal failure can be seen in cases of severe laxative and or diuretic abuse. Contraction alkalosis and dehydration may be evident. In starvation, blood urea nitrogen may be very low due to low protein intake and 24-hour creatinine clearance is often decreased and is lower for laxative abusers than for pure restrictors.

10. Opportunistic Infections

At severely low BMIs patients with anorexia nervosa can present with opportunistic infections. Case reports include mycobacterial infections and aspergillosis.

Tips to Diagnosing an Eating Disorder

- Asking questions about eating behavior and weight concerns is critical to making the diagnosis when an eating disorder is in the differential, the history should include direct questions that assess dieting behavior, binge eating, self-induced vomiting or regular laxative, diuretic or diet pill use in the service of weight control. Affirmative answers should be followed by clarifying questions regarding frequency and severity of each behavior. Collateral history from family regarding changes in exercise, dieting, bingeing or purging behaviors and weight or shape concern can be very helpful in confirming the diagnosis.

- Several screening instruments exist. The SCOFF is a rapid four question screening tool with good sensitivity and specificity that is easily included in a routine medical history.

- Additional probes for anorexia nervosa include questions regarding desired weight—"What would you like to weigh?" and dietary habits—"Tell me what you eat at each meal on a typical day". A desired maximum weight below a BMI of 19 in an adult is suggestive of anorexia nervosa. In anorexia nervosa and in bulimia the dietary repertoire is characterized by skipped meals and limited food choices, typical food choices are of low calorie density and fat content. In patients who binge, binges are usually secretive and involve intake of large quantities of high calorie density foods associated with a sense of loss of control over eating.

- Patients usually have tried and failed to change on their own. They may be demoralized and discouraged. The physician should reinforce that treatment is effective and refer patients to an eating disorder specialist. As an integral member, and often the coordinator of the treatment team, physicians can be instrumental in engaging the reluctant or anxious patient in seeking appropriate treatment.

Chapter 24

Symptoms and Complications of Eating Disorders

Chapter Contents

Section 24.1

Medical Symptoms and Complications Associated with Anorexia

This section includes text excerpted from "Eating
Disorders: About More than Food," National Institute
of Mental Health (NIMH), December 2014.

Anorexia Nervosa

Many people with anorexia nervosa see themselves as overweight,
even when they are clearly underweight. Eating, food, and weight
control become obsessions. People with anorexia nervosa typically
weigh themselves repeatedly, portion food carefully, and eat very small
quantities of only certain foods. Some people with anorexia nervosa
also may engage in binge eating followed by extreme dieting, excessive exercise, self-induced vomiting, or misuse of laxatives, diuretics,
or enemas.

Symptoms of anorexia nervosa include:

- Extremely low body weight

- Severe food restriction

- Relentless pursuit of thinness and unwillingness to maintain a
  normal or healthy weight

- Intense fear of gaining weight

- Distorted body image and self-esteem that is heavily influenced
  by perceptions of body weight and shape, or a denial of the seriousness of low body weight

- Lack of menstruation among girls and women.

Some who have anorexia nervosa recover with treatment after only
one episode. Others get well but have relapses. Still others have a more
chronic, or long-lasting, form of anorexia nervosa, in which their health
declines as they battle the illness.

Other symptoms and medical complications may develop over time, including:

- Thinning of the bones (osteopenia or osteoporosis)
- Brittle hair and nails
- Dry and yellowish skin
- Growth of fine hair all over the body (lanugo)
- Mild anemia, muscle wasting, and weakness
- Severe constipation
- Low blood pressure, or slowed breathing and pulse
- Damage to the structure and function of the heart
- Brain damage
- Multi-organ failure
- Drop in internal body temperature, causing a person to feel cold all the time
- Lethargy, sluggishness, or feeling tired all the time
- Infertility.

Section 24.2

Medical Symptoms and Complications Associated with Binge Eating Disorder

This section contains text excerpted from the following sources: Text under the heading "Binge Eating Disorder" is excerpted from "Eating Disorders: About More than Food," National Institute Mental Health (NIMH), 2014; Text under the heading "What Is Binge Eating Disorder?" is excerpted from "Binge Eating Disorder Fact Sheet," Office on Women's Health (OWH), July 16, 2012. Reviewed March 2016.

Binge Eating Disorder

People with binge eating disorder lose control over their eating. Periods of binge eating are not followed by compensatory behaviors like purging, excessive exercise, or fasting. As a result, people with binge eating disorder often are overweight or obese. People with binge eating disorder who are obese are at higher risk for developing cardio-vascular disease and high blood pressure. They also experience guilt, shame, and distress about their binge eating, which can lead to more binge eating.

What Is Binge Eating Disorder?

People with binge eating disorder often eat an unusually large amount of food and feel out of control during the binges. Unlike bulimia or anorexia, binge eaters do not throw up their food, exercise a lot, or eat only small amounts of only certain foods. Because of this, binge eaters are often overweight or obese. People with binge eating disorder also may:

- Eat more quickly than usual during binge episodes
- Eat until they are uncomfortably full
- Eat when they are not hungry
- Eat alone because of embarrassment
- Feel disgusted, depressed, or guilty after overeating

About 2 percent of all adults in the United States (as many as 4 million Americans) have binge eating disorder. Binge eating disorder affects women slightly more often than men.

What Are the Health Consequences of Binge Eating Disorder?

People with binge eating disorder are usually very upset by their binge eating and may become depressed. Research has shown that people with binge eating disorder report more health problems, stress, trouble sleeping, and suicidal thoughts than people without an eating disorder. People with binge eating disorder often feel badly about themselves and may miss work, school, or social activities to binge eat.

People with binge eating disorder may gain weight. Weight gain can lead to obesity, and obesity raises the risk for these health problems:

- Type 2 diabetes
- High blood pressure
- High cholesterol
- Gallbladder disease

- Heart disease

- Certain types of cancer

Obese people with binge eating disorder often have other mental health conditions, including:

- Anxiety

- Depression

- Personality disorders

Section 24.3

Medical Symptoms and Complications Associated with Bulimia

This section contains text excerpted from the following sources: Text under the heading "Bulimia Nervosa" is excerpted from "Eating Disorders: About More than Food," National Institute Mental Health (NIMH), 2014; Text under the heading "What Is Bulimia?" is excerpted from "Binge Eating Disorder Fact Sheet," Office on Women's Health (OWH), July 16, 2012. Reviewed March 2016.

Bulimia Nervosa

People with bulimia nervosa have recurrent and frequent episodes of eating unusually large amounts of food and feel a lack of control over these episodes. This binge eating is followed by behavior that compensates for the overeating such as forced vomiting, excessive use of laxatives or diuretics, fasting, excessive exercise, or a combination of these behaviors.

Unlike anorexia nervosa, people with bulimia nervosa usually maintain what is considered a healthy or normal weight, while some are slightly overweight. But like people with anorexia nervosa, they often fear gaining weight, want desperately to lose weight, and are intensely unhappy with their body size and shape. Usually, bulimic behavior is done secretly because it is often accompanied by feelings of disgust or shame. The binge eating and purging cycle can happen anywhere from several times a week to many times a day.

Other symptoms include:

- Chronically inflamed and sore throat
- Swollen salivary glands in the neck and jaw area
- Worn tooth enamel, and increasingly sensitive and decaying teeth as a result of exposure to stomach acid
- Acid reflux disorder and other gastrointestinal problems
- Intestinal distress and irritation from laxative abuse
- Severe dehydration from purging of fluids
- Electrolyte imbalance—too low or too high levels of sodium, calcium, potassium, and other minerals that can lead to a heart attack or stroke.

What Is Bulimia?

Bulimia nervosa, often called bulimia, is a type of eating disorder. A person with bulimia eats a lot of food in a short amount of time (bingeing) and then tries to prevent weight gain by getting rid of the food (purging). Purging might be done by:

- Making yourself throw up
- Taking laxatives (pills or liquids that speed up the movement of food through your body and lead to a bowel movement)

A person with bulimia feels he or she cannot control the amount of food eaten. Also, bulimics might exercise a lot, eat very little or not at all, or take pills to pass urine often to prevent weight gain.

Unlike anorexia, people with bulimia can fall within the normal range for their age and weight. But like people with anorexia, bulimics:

- Fear gaining weight
- Want desperately to lose weight
- Are very unhappy with their body size and shape

What Are Signs of Bulimia?

A person with bulimia may be thin, overweight, or have a normal weight. Also, bulimic behavior, such as throwing up, is often done in private because the person with bulimia feels shame or disgust. This makes it hard to know if someone has bulimia. But there are warning signs to look out for. Someone with bulimia may use extreme measures to lose weight by:

- Using diet pills, or taking pills to urinate or have a bowel movement
- Going to the bathroom all the time after eating (to throw up)
- Exercising a lot, even in bad weather or when hurt or tired

Someone with bulimia may show signs of throwing up, such as:

- Swollen cheeks or jaw area
- Calluses or scrapes on the knuckles (if using fingers to induce vomiting)
- Teeth that look clear
- Broken blood vessels in the eyes

People with bulimia often have other mental health conditions, including:

- Depression
- Anxiety
- Substance abuse problems

Someone with bulimia may also have a distorted body image, shown by thinking she or he is fat, hating her or his body, and fearing weight gain. Bulimia can also cause someone to not act like her or himself. She or he may be moody or sad, or may not want to go out with friends.

Chapter 25

Eating Disorders and Pregnancy

Adequate nutrition is vital during pregnancy to ensure the health and well-being of both mother and baby. As a result, pregnancy may present challenges for women who are struggling with or recovering from eating disorders. Pregnancy creates physical and emotional changes that can be stressful for anyone, but especially for women who have preexisting mental health conditions. Even women who believe they have put their disordered eating behaviors in the past may be vulnerable to relapse due to the bodily changes associated with pregnancy. The normal weight gain during pregnancy can trigger symptoms of anorexia, for instance, while the feelings of fullness as the baby grows can create an urge to purge among people with bulimia. The food cravings that often occur during pregnancy can also be problematic for people with binge eating disorder.

If left untreated during pregnancy, active eating disorders can cause serious complications that jeopardize the health of both mother and baby. Mothers with eating disorders are more likely to deliver by Caesarean section and experience postpartum depression. Meanwhile, babies born to mothers with eating disorders have a high risk of premature delivery, low birth weight, and small head circumference. On the other hand, some women find it easier to avoid disordered eating behavior during pregnancy as their focus shifts to protecting the health and welfare of the fetus. Given the importance of nutrition throughout pregnancy, however, women with eating disorders should seek professional advice and treatment to ensure that the condition does not interfere with the normal growth and development of the baby.

Recognizing the Signs of Eating Disorders

Eating disorders may impact a woman's reproductive health even before she becomes pregnant. Women with anorexia or bulimia often experience irregularity or cessation of menstrual cycles, for instance, which can affect fertility and reduce the likelihood of conception. Therefore, doctors recommend that women bring eating disorders under control and maintain a healthy weight for several months before trying to get pregnant. Even in such cases, however, some women find that the bodily changes associated with pregnancy may trigger or exacerbate the symptoms of eating disorders. Some of the common signs that a woman is struggling with an eating disorder during pregnancy include:

- weight loss or very limited weight gain throughout the pregnancy
- anxiety about being overweight
- restricting food intake, skipping meals, or eliminating major food groups
- vomiting or purging to get rid of calories consumed
- extreme (to the point of exhaustion) or excessive exercising to stay thin
- chronic fatigue, dizziness, or fainting
- depression, lack of interest in socializing, or avoidance of family and friends

If these signs appear during pregnancy, it is important to seek treatment to ensure a healthy outcome for both mother and baby.

Understanding the Risks of Eating Disorders

Left untreated, eating disorders can have debilitating effects on the health of both the pregnant woman and the unborn baby. Understanding the risks posed by eating disorders may encourage expectant mothers to get the help they need to have a healthy pregnancy. Some of the potential health risks for a pregnant woman with an eating disorder include:

- severe dehydration or malnutrition
- high blood pressure (preeclampsia), gestational diabetes, or anemia
- cardiac irregularities
- miscarriage, stillbirth, or premature labor
- complications during delivery and increased risk of Caesarean section
- extended time required to heal from childbirth
- postpartum depression
- difficulties breastfeeding
- low self-esteem and poor body image
- social withdrawal, isolation, and marital or family conflicts

Eating disorders also carry a number of serious risks for the developing baby, including:

- malnutrition, abnormal fetal growth, or poor development
- premature birth
- respiratory distress
- small head circumference
- low birth weight (with anorexia or bulimia)
- high birth weight (with binge eating disorder)
- feeding difficulties

The seriousness of these risks, along with the natural maternal instinct to protect the developing baby, enables some women to effectively manage their eating disorders during pregnancy.

Managing Eating Disorders in Pregnancy

For some women, on the other hand, the physical and emotional changes that occur during pregnancy may trigger or worsen eating disorder symptoms. Those with anorexia, for instance, may struggle with their inability to fully control their eating and weight gain while pregnant.

Pregnant women who are struggling with eating disorders should see a counselor or therapist to help guide them through pregnancy-related changes, fears about weight gain, and concerns about body image. In addition, they should work with a nutritionist or dietitian to learn about nutritional requirements during pregnancy, ensure that caloric intake is sufficient to support fetal development, and create appropriate meal plans. Finally, they should inform their obstetrician about their eating disorder and make regular visits to track prenatal growth. The pregnancy may be classified as "high risk" so that the healthcare provider can carefully monitor the health of both mother and baby. Additional tips to help alleviate concerns and manage eating disorders during pregnancy include:

- remember that the source of weight gain is a growing baby

- avoid the scale, and ask the healthcare provider not to share your weight during checkups

- try to ignore, or at least not dwell on, comments others make about your pregnant body

- avoid looking at magazines that feature unrealistic postnatal weight-loss stories

Maintaining Health after Childbirth

Even when women with eating disorders manage to keep them under control during pregnancy, many tend to suffer relapses following childbirth. Women face extreme social pressure to lose pregnancy weight as quickly as possible. As a result, many women feel that they must begin a weight-loss diet or exercise regimen immediately after their baby has been born. This pressure to shed pounds can trigger disordered eating behaviors. Experts recommend focusing instead on the remarkable physical accomplishment of growing and delivering a healthy baby. This focus can help women accept the changes in body shape and appearance that may have resulted from pregnancy and childbirth.

Experts also stress that it is important for women to take care of their own health following childbirth. Women with eating disorders are particularly susceptible to postnatal depression, so they should watch out for symptoms and seek professional help if they appear. Many women with eating disorders also express concerns about their ability to breastfeed. As long as the eating disorder is under control, it should not affect breastfeeding. But it is important to remember that restricting caloric intake during breastfeeding can reduce both the quantity and quality of breastmilk. Adequate nutrition is also important to ensure that new mothers have the energy, health, and well-being necessary to love, care for, and enjoy their infant.

References

1. "Eating Disorders and Pregnancy." Eating Disorder Hope, May 25, 2013.

2. "Eating Disorders and Pregnancy." Eating Disorders Victoria, June 24, 2015.

3. "Pregnancy and Eating Disorders." American Pregnancy Association, July 2015.

Chapter 26

Eating Disorders and Oral Health

Dental Complications of Eating Disorders

Dietary habits can and do play a role in oral health. Everyone has heard from their dentist that eating too much sugar can lead to cavities, but did you know that high intake of acidic "diet" foods can have an equally devastating effect on your teeth? Changes in the mouth are oftentimes the first physical signs of an eating disorder. The harmful habits and nutritional deficiencies that often accompany disordered eating can have severe consequences on one's dental health.

An eating disorder may cause lingering or even permanent damage to the teeth and mouth. Early detection of eating disorders may ensure a smoother and more successful recovery period for the body and the teeth. Damage to the teeth and mouth can be tempered by arming yourself with the right information and receiving appropriate guidance from your oral health professional.

If you or your loved one has struggled with an eating disorder, make sure you ask questions about your dental provider's qualifications, their experience, the kinds of cases they have treated and their treatment philosophies. It is important that like all of your relationships with healthcare providers, your relationship with your oral healthcare

This chapter includes text excerpted from "Dental Complications of Eating Disorders," © 2016 National Eating Disorders Association. For more information, visit www.nationaleatingdisorders.org. Reprinted with permission.

provider be candid and honest. They can only provide as much help as you allow them to provide.

If you are experiencing any dental symptoms, talk with your dentist about ways to care for your teeth and mouth. If you notice these symptoms in a loved one, you may use your observations to initiate a respectful conversation about your concerns. There are methods for improving oral health while seeking help to change harmful eating habits.

Dental Effects of Eating Disorders

- Without the proper nutrition, gums and other soft tissue inside your mouth may bleed easily. The glands that produce saliva may swell. Individuals may experience chronic dry mouth.

- Food restriction often leads to nutritional deficiency. Nutrients that promote oral health include calcium, iron and B vitamins. Insufficient calcium promotes tooth decay and gum disease; even if an anorexia patient does consume enough calcium, they also need enough vitamin D to help the body absorb it. Insufficient iron can foster the development of sores inside the mouth. Insufficient amounts of vitamin B3 (also known as niacin) can contribute to bad breath and the development of canker sores. Gums can become red and swollen—almost glossy-looking—which is often a sign of gingivitis. The mouth can also be extremely dry, due to dehydration, and lips may become reddened, dry and cracked.

- Frequent vomiting leads to strong stomach acid repeatedly flowing over the teeth. The tooth's outer covering (enamel) can be lost and teeth can change in color, shape and length, becoming brittle, translucent and weak. Eating hot or cold food or drink may become uncomfortable. Tissue loss and erosive lesions on the surface of the mouth may occur. The edges of teeth often become thin and break off easily. In extreme cases the pulp can be exposed and cause infection, discoloration or even pulp death. Tooth decay can actually be aggravated by extensive tooth brushing or rinsing following vomiting.

- Degenerative arthritis within the temporomandibular joint in the jaw is a dental complication often associated with eating disorders. This joint is found where the lower jaw hinges to the skull. When arthritis begins in this joint it may create pain in the joint area, chronic headaches and problems chewing and opening/closing the mouth.

- Purging can lead to redness, scratches and cuts inside the mouth, especially on the upper surface commonly referred to as the 'soft palate.' Such damage is a warning sign for dental professionals, because healthy daily behaviors rarely cause harm to this area. Soft palate damage is often accompanied by cuts or bruises on the knuckles as a result of an individual's teeth placing pressure on the skin while attempting to purge.

- A frequent binge-and-purge cycle can cause an enlargement of the salivary glands. Enlarged glands can be painful and are often visible to others, which can lead to emotional distress.

Treatment of the Oral Health Consequences of Eating Disorders

- Maintain meticulous oral health care related to tooth brushing and flossing, as well as frequent and appropriate communication and examination by your dentist. A confidential relationship should always be maintained between the dentist and patient, and therefore, the patient should feel that the dental office is a "safe" place to disclose their ED struggles and progress towards recovery.

- Individuals in treatment may still engage in purging behaviors, and should be honest with their treatment team about these behaviors. To maintain oral care while curbing these behaviors, after purging patients should immediately rinse their mouth with water or use a sugar-free mouth rinse. Patients should swish only water around their mouth due to the high acidic content in the oral cavity. It has also been recommended that brushing be halted for an hour to avoid actually scrubbing the stomach acids deeper into the tooth enamel.

- A dry mouth, or xerostomia, may result from vomiting and/or poor overall nutrition. Xerostomia will also frequently lead to tooth decay. Moisturizing the mouth with water, or other specified products, will help keep recurrent decay at a minimum.

- Consult with your dentist about your specific treatment needs. Fluoride rinses may be prescribed as well as desensitizing or re-mineralizing agents.

Chapter 27

Anorexia Nervosa and Osteoporosis

What Is Anorexia Nervosa?

Anorexia nervosa is an eating disorder characterized by an irrational fear of weight gain. People with anorexia nervosa believe that they are overweight even when they are extremely thin.

Individuals with anorexia become obsessed with food and severely restrict their dietary intake. The disease is associated with several health problems and, in rare cases, even death. The disorder may begin as early as the onset of puberty. The first menstrual period is typically delayed in girls who have anorexia when they reach puberty. For girls who have already reached puberty when they develop anorexia, menstrual periods are often infrequent or absent.

What Is Osteoporosis?

Osteoporosis is a condition in which the bones become less dense and more likely to fracture. Fractures from osteoporosis can result in significant pain and disability. In the United States, more than 53 million people either already have osteoporosis or are at high risk due to low bone mass.

This chapter includes text excerpted from "What People with Anorexia Nervosa Need to Know about Osteoporosis," National Institutes of Health (NIH), April 2015.

Risk factors for developing osteoporosis include:

- thinness or small frame
- family history of the disease
- being postmenopausal and particularly having had early menopause
- abnormal absence of menstrual periods (amenorrhea)
- prolonged use of certain medications, such as those used to treat lupus, asthma, thyroid deficiencies, and seizures
- low calcium intake
- lack of physical activity
- smoking
- excessive alcohol intake.

Osteoporosis often can be prevented. It is known as a silent disease because, if undetected, bone loss can progress for many years without symptoms until a fracture occurs. Osteoporosis has been called a childhood disease with old age consequences because building healthy bones in youth helps prevent osteoporosis and fractures later in life. However, it is never too late to adopt new habits for healthy bones.

The Link between Anorexia Nervosa and Osteoporosis

Anorexia nervosa has significant physical consequences. Affected individuals can experience nutritional and hormonal problems that negatively impact bone density. Low body weight in females causes the body to stop producing estrogen, resulting in a condition known as amenorrhea, or absent menstrual periods. Low estrogen levels contribute to significant losses in bone density.

In addition, individuals with anorexia often produce excessive amounts of the adrenal hormone cortisol, which is known to trigger bone loss. Other problems, such as a decrease in the production of growth hormone and other growth factors, low body weight (apart from the estrogen loss it causes), calcium deficiency, and malnutrition, contribute to bone loss in girls and women with anorexia. Weight loss, restricted dietary intake, and testosterone deficiency may be responsible for the low bone density found in males with the disorder.

Studies suggest that low bone mass (osteopenia) is common in people with anorexia and that it occurs early in the course of the disease.

Girls with anorexia are less likely to reach their peak bone density and therefore may be at increased risk for osteoporosis and fracture throughout life.

Osteoporosis Management Strategies

Up to one-third of peak bone density is achieved during puberty. Anorexia is typically identified during mid to late adolescence, a critical period for bone development. The longer the duration of the disorder, the greater the bone loss and the less likely it is that bone mineral density will ever return to normal. The primary goal of medical therapy for individuals with anorexia is weight gain and, in females, the return of normal menstrual periods. However, attention to other aspects of bone health is also important.

Nutrition. A well-balanced diet rich in calcium and vitamin D is important for healthy bones. Good sources of calcium include low-fat dairy products; dark green, leafy vegetables; and calcium-fortified foods and beverages. Supplements can help ensure that people get adequate amounts of calcium each day, especially in people with a proven milk allergy. The Institute of Medicine recommends a daily calcium intake of 1,000 mg (milligrams) for men and women up to age 50. Women over age 50 and men over age 70 should increase their intake to 1,200 mg daily.

Vitamin D plays an important role in calcium absorption and bone health. Food sources of vitamin D include egg yolks, saltwater fish, and liver. Many people may need vitamin D supplements to achieve the recommended intake of 600 to 800 International Units (IU) each day.

Exercise. Like muscle, bone is living tissue that responds to exercise by becoming stronger. The best activity for your bones is weight-bearing exercise that forces you to work against gravity. Some examples include walking, climbing stairs, lifting weights, and dancing.

Although walking and other types of regular exercise can help prevent bone loss and provide many other health benefits, these potential benefits need to be weighed against the risk of fractures, delayed weight gain, and exercise-induced amenorrhea in people with anorexia and those recovering from the disorder.

Healthy lifestyle. Smoking is bad for bones as well as the heart and lungs. In addition, smokers may absorb less calcium from their diets. Alcohol also can have a negative effect on bone health. Those who drink heavily are more prone to bone loss and fracture, because of both poor nutrition and increased risk of falling.

Bone density test. A bone mineral density (BMD) test measures bone density in various parts of the body. This safe and painless test can detect osteoporosis before a fracture occurs and can predict one's chances of fracturing in the future. The BMD test can help determine whether medication should be considered.

Medication. There is no cure for osteoporosis. However, medications are available to prevent and treat the disease in postmenopausal women, men, and both women and men taking glucocorticoid medication. Some studies suggest that there may be a role for estrogen preparations among girls and young women with anorexia. However, experts agree that estrogen should not be a substitute for nutritional support.

Part Five

Recognizing and Treating Eating Disorders

Chapter 28

Physical, Psychological, and Behavioral Effects of Eating Disorders

Anorexia Nervosa

Anorexia nervosa is a psychological illness with devastating physical consequences. Anorexia nervosa is characterized by low body weight and body image distortion with an obsessive fear of gaining weight which manifests itself through depriving the body of food. It often coincides with increased levels of exercise.

Anorexia nervosa usually develops during adolescence and generally has an earlier age of onset than bulimia nervosa and binge eating disorder (the latter are often developed during late adolescence or early adulthood). However like all eating disorders, anorexia nervosa can be developed at any age or stage of life for both males and females.

Anorexia nervosa is the most fatal of all psychiatric illnesses. Extreme food restriction can lead to starvation, malnutrition and a dangerously low body weight—all of which are synonymous with a host of health problems, and in some cases death.

Text in this chapter is excerpted from "What Is an Eating Disorder?" © 2016 Eating Disorders Victoria. For more information, visit www.eatingdisorders.org. au. Reprinted with permission.

Types of Anorexia Nervosa

There are two main subtypes of anorexia:

1. **Restricting type:** this is the most commonly known type of anorexia nervosa whereby a person severely restricts their food intake. Restriction may take many forms (e.g. maintaining very low calorie count; restricting types of food eaten; eating only one meal a day) and may follow obsessive and rigid rules (e.g. only eating food of one color).

2. **Binge eating or purging type:** less recognized; a person restricts their intake as above, but also during some bouts of restriction the person has regularly engaged in binge eating or purging behaviour (e.g. self-induced vomiting, over-exercise, misuse of laxatives, diuretics or enemas).

Physical Effects

Most physical symptoms associated with anorexia nervosa are related to malnutrition. A person may experience some or all of the following symptoms, which tend to become more severe the longer the disorder remains untreated.

- Dry skin
- Dry or chapped lips
- Poor circulation resulting in pins and needles (paresthesia) and/or purple extremities
- Headaches
- Brittle fingernails
- Bruising easily
- Frail appearance
- Endocrine disorder leading to cessation of periods in girls (amenorrhoea)
- Decreased libido; impotence in males
- Reduced metabolism
- Abnormally slow heart rate
- Low blood pressure
- Hypotension

- Hypothermia
- Anaemia (iron deficiency)
- Abdominal pain
- Oedema (retention of fluid giving a "puffy" appearance)
- Stunting of height and growth
- Fainting
- Abnormality of mineral and electrolyte levels
- Thinning of the hair
- Lanugo (growth of fine hair layer all over the body to promote warmth)
- Constantly feeling cold
- Zinc deficiency
- Reduction in white blood cell count
- Reduced immune system function
- Pallid complexion and sunken eyes
- Reduction of bone density that results in dry and brittle bones (osteoporosis)
- Constipation or diarrhoea
- Tooth decay

Psychological Effects

- Distorted body image
- Self-evaluation based largely or entirely in terms of weight and appearance
- Pre-occupation or obsessive thoughts about food and weight
- Refusal to accept that one's weight is dangerously low despite warnings from family, friends and/or health professionals
- Low self-esteem
- Mood swings
- Clinical depression
- Withdrawal from interpersonal relationships in favor of social isolation

Behavioral Effects

- Excessive exercise and/or food restriction
- Secretive behaviour surrounding eating or exercise
- Overly sensitive to references about weight or appearance
- Obsessive interest in cooking or preparing food for others
- Refusal to eat in the presence of others
- Aggressive when forced to eat "forbidden foods"
- Self-harm
- Substance abuse
- Suicide attempts
- About 40 percent of people with anorexia nervosa will later develop bulimia nervosa.

Bulimia Nervosa

Bulimia nervosa is a serious psychiatric illness characterised by recurrent binge eating episodes (the consumption of abnormally large amounts of food in a relatively short period of time), followed by compensatory behaviors (purging or over-exercising). Binge episodes are associated with a sense of loss of control and immediately followed by feelings of guilt and shame, which leads the person to compensatory behaviors (purging) such as self-induced vomiting, fasting, over-exercising and/or the misuse of laxatives, enemas or diuretics.

A person with bulimia nervosa usually maintains an average weight, or may be slightly above or below average weight for height, which often makes it less recognizable than serious cases of anorexia nervosa. Many people, including some health professionals, incorrectly assume that a person must be underweight and thin if they have an eating disorder. Because of this, bulimia nervosa is often missed and can go undetected for a long period of time.

Bulimia nervosa often starts with weight-loss dieting in the "pursuit for thinness.". The resulting food deprivation and inadequate nutrition can trigger what is, in effect, a starvation reaction—an overriding urge to eat. Once the person gives in to this urge, the desire to eat is uncontrollable, leading to a substantial binge on whatever food is available—often foods with high fat and sugar content, which is followed by compensatory behaviours. A repeat of weight-loss dieting often follows, perhaps even more strictly—which leads to a frantic binge/purge/exercise cycle which becomes more compulsive and uncontrollable overtime.

Physical Effects

There are many physical symptoms associated with bulimia nervosa, many of which are similar to the effects of anorexia nervosa. Some of the physical symptoms associated with bulimia include:

- Tooth decay
- Dehydration
- Stomach and intestinal ulcers
- Inflammation and rupture of the oesophagus
- Irregular or slow heartbeat
- Heart failure
- Erosion of dental enamel from vomiting
- Swollen salivary glands
- The possibility of a ruptured stomach
- Chronic sore throat and gullet
- Sore throat, indigestion, heartburn and reflux
- Abdominal pain and bloating
- Electrolyte imbalance resulting in cardiac arrhythmia, muscle fatigue and cramps
- Bowel problems, constipation, diarrhoea, cramps

Psychological Effects

- Difficulties with activities which involve food
- Loneliness due to self-imposed isolation and a reluctance to develop personal relationships
- Deceptive behaviours relating to food
- Fear of the disapproval of others if the illness becomes known
- Mood swings, changes in personality, emotional outbursts or depression

- Self-harm, substance abuse or suicide attempts

- Overly sensitive to references about weight or appearance

- Guilt, self-disgust, self-loathing

- Anxiety

- Depression

Behavioural Effects

- Frequent trips to the bathroom, especially after eating. The length of time taken for these bathroom trips can depend on the amount of food consumed and the need felt by the sufferer to purge themselves of it.

- Food avoidance, dieting behaviour. This may be because of a fear of gaining weight (as in anorexia nervosa) and it may also be to avoid the unpleasant ritual of purging afterwards.

- Fluctuations in weight

- Erratic behaviour

- Mood swings

Binge Eating Disorder

Binge eating disorder is a psychological illness characterized by frequently eating excessive amounts of food, often when not hungry. Binges represent a distraction that allows a person to avoid thinking about the real root of their problems. Feelings of guilt, disgust and depression often follow a bingeing episode.

Binge eating disorder is similar to, but not the same as bulimia nervosa. Where people experiencing bulimia nervosa will partake in purging activities after bingeing, binge eating disorder is characterized by an absence of purging, despite suffering similar feelings of intense guilt, shame and self-hatred after binges. While a lack of purging is evident, a person experiencing binge eating disorder will often participate in sporadic fasts and repetitive diets in response to the negative sensations which follow a binge episode.

"People who overeat compulsively may struggle with anxiety, depression, and loneliness, which can contribute to their unhealthy episodes of binge eating. Body weight may vary from normal to mild, moderate, or severe obesity."

Physical Effects

Most of the physical signs and symptoms associated with binge eating disorder are long-term, and these can include:

- Weight gain, often leading to obesity
- High blood pressure
- High cholesterol
- Chronic kidney problems or kidney failure
- Osteoarthritis
- Diabetes
- Stroke
- Complications during pregnancy
- Gallbladder disease
- Irregular menstrual cycle
- Skin disorders
- Heart disease
- Certain types of cancer

Psychological Effects

- Difficulties with activities involving food which may lead to self-imposed isolation
- Low self-esteem and embarrassment over physical appearance
- Feeling extremely distressed, upset and anxious during and after a binge episode
- Fear of the disapproval of others
- Self-harm or suicide attempts
- Overly sensitive to references about weight or appearance
- Guilt, self-disgust, self-loathing
- Anxiety
- Depression

Behavioural Effects

- An overwhelming sense of lack of control regarding eating behaviour

- Eating more rapidly than normal

- Periods of uncontrolled, impulsive or continuous eating whereby a person may consume many thousands of calories, often to the point of feeling uncomfortably full

- Eating when not physically hungry

- Repeated episodes of binge eating that often results in feelings of shame or guilt

- Eating in secret

- Avoiding social situations, particularly those involving food.

- Eating "normal" quantities in social settings, and gorging when alone

Chapter 29

Confronting a Person with an Eating Disorder

About Eating Disorders

Every year, thousands of teens (and adults, too) develop eating disorders and disordered eating behaviors. In fact, an estimated 24 million Americans meet the criteria for an eating disorder.

In our image-obsessed culture, it can be easy to become critical of the way we look. Taking good care of our health and physical fitness is important for all of us.

But some people can take being fit too far, which can lead to an eating disorder. Some go on diets that become more and more restricted or extreme, leading to anorexia. Others may eat way too much food (known as binge eating). And people with bulimia may try to make up for their eating by vomiting, using laxatives or other medicines, fasting, or exercising compulsively.

Although eating disorders are much more common in girls, guys can get them, too.

What's Going On?

Eating disorders can be caused by—and lead to—complicated physical and psychological illnesses. Many people with an eating disorder

This chapter includes text excerpted from "I Think My Friend May Have an Eating Disorder. What Should I Do?" © 1995–2016. The Nemours Foundation/ KidsHealth®. Reprinted with permission.

also have problems with anxiety (excessive worry) and depression (feeling sad, hopeless, and withdrawn).

Many people who try to lose weight feel successful and in control when they become thin. But people with eating disorders can become seriously ill and even die. They might start out dieting successfully and be happy with their weight loss, but then they find they can't stop. For some, losing weight feels like an addiction and they continue to restrict their food intake to an extreme degree (in anorexia) or exercise excessively to try to burn off food they've eaten.

Signs of Eating Disorders

So how do you know if a friend has an eating disorder? It can be hard to tell—after all, someone who has lost a lot of weight may have another type of health condition or might have been overweight and deliberately tried to eat better and exercise more.

Friends and Eating Disorders: Top Things to Know

- It can be hard to tell if a friend has an eating disorder

- Eating disorders are more than about food and weight—they can be caused by complicated emotions or psychological conditions.

- If you're worried about a friend who isn't getting better, talk to a parent, counselor, school nurse, or other adult.

But Certain Signs Can Indicate a Problem, Such as If a Friend:

- Has an obsession with weight and food. It might seem like all your friend thinks (and talks) about is food, calories, fat grams, weight, and being thin.

- Feels the need to exercise all the time, even when sick or exhausted, and might talk about compensating for eating too much by exercising or burning off calories.

- Avoids hanging out with you and other friends during meals and always comes up with an excuse not to eat lunch at school or go out to eat.

- Starts to wear big or baggy clothes as a way to hide his or her body and shape.

- Goes on extreme or highly restrictive diets (for example, eating only clear soup or only raw veggies), cuts food into tiny pieces, moves food around on the plate instead of eating it, and is very precise about how food is arranged on the plate.

- Seems to compete with others about how little he or she eats. If a friend proudly tells you she only had a diet drink for breakfast and a few grapes for lunch, it's a red flag that she could be developing a problem.

- Goes to the bathroom a lot, especially right after meals, or you've heard your friend vomiting after eating.

- Always talks about how fat he or she is, despite losing a lot of weight, and sometimes focuses on body parts he or she doesn't like (such as the stomach, thighs, or arms) to the point of excess.

- Appears to be gaining a lot of weight even though you never see him or her eat much.

- Is very defensive or sensitive about his or her weight loss or eating habits.

- Buys or takes stimulants, diet pills, laxatives, steroids, herbal supplements, or other medicines to lose weight.

- Has a tendency to faint, bruises easily, is very pale, or starts complaining of being cold more than usual (this can be a symptom of being underweight).

How to Help?

- **Start by talking to your friend privately about what you've noticed.** Explain that you're worried. Be as gentle as possible, and try to really listen to and be supportive about what your friend is going through.

- **If your friend opens up about what's going on, ask how you can help.** Tell your friend you want to help him or her get healthy again. Try not to make statements like "If you'd just eat (or stop working out so much), you'll get better." Instead, simply asking "How can I help?" shows you can listen and be supportive without judging.

- **Find out as much as you can about eating disorders from reliable sources.** Many organizations, books, websites, hotlines, and other resources are devoted to helping people who are battling eating disorders. Learning more can help you better understand what your friend is going through. Share what you learn with your friend if he or she is open to it, but don't preach or try to tell your friend what's best for him or her.

- **Try not to be too watchful of your friend's eating habits, food amounts, and choices.** It can be tempting to try to get a friend to eat more, but eating disorders are complicated, so it often does no good. And it may push your friend away if he or she thinks you're judging, lecturing, or just trying to make him or her regain lost weight.

- **Know your limits.** Being concerned and trying to help is part of a good friendship. But don't take it on yourself to fix things. Telling your friend what to do or how to act probably won't work. You can talk to your parents or school counselor about your concerns and get advice on what to do next.

- **Focus on inner qualities.** Try not to talk about food, weight, diets, or body shape (yours, your friend's, or even a popular celebrity's). Focus instead on people's strengths—like how someone is a good friend, has a fun personality, or has talents in something like math or art.

- **Offer to go with your friend to a support group or be there when your friend talks to a counselor.**

- **Remind your friend that you're there no matter what.** Listen and be supportive. Sometimes you'd be surprised how asking a simple question (like "What would make you feel better?") can lead to a great conversation about how you can help your friend heal.

People with eating disorders often have trouble admitting that they have a problem—even to themselves. They may feel guarded and private and worry that people will try to make them eat or gain weight.

It can be hard trying to help someone who isn't ready or doesn't think help is needed. Try not to get angry or frustrated. Remind your friend that you care. If your friend tells you it's none of your business or that there is no problem, trust your instincts and be the best friend you can be, even if that means telling your parents or another trusted adult about your concerns.

Chapter 30

Diagnosing Eating Disorders

Chapter Contents

Section 30.1

Identifying Eating Disorders

This section includes text excerpted from "Clients with
Substance Use and Eating Disorders," Substance Abuse
and Mental Health Services Administration (SAMHSA),
February 2011. Reviewed March 2016.

Screening Patients for Eating Disorders

Little is known about ideal screening for eating disorders (EDs)
in substance use disorder (SUD) treatment programs. Researchers
recommend that SUD treatment programs screen for EDs, along with
other behavioral health disorders, at intake and intermittently during
treatment of all patients in SUD treatment. An analysis of National
Treatment Center Study data notes that programs that screen for
EDs do so during intake and assessment.

About half these programs screen all admissions for EDs, and half
screen only when an ED is suspected. Screening for EDs only when one
is suspected can be complex, because signs and symptoms of EDs can
overlap with those of SUDs or with those of other behavioral health
problems. For example, weight loss, lethargy, changes in eating habits, and depressed mood can indicate an SUD or an affective disorder.
In addition, signs may not be readily observable to counselors, because
people with EDs often go to great lengths to disguise and hide their
disorder. However, counselors should be aware of common red flags
for EDs that tend not to overlap with those of other behavioral health
disorders. Given below are some indications (in addition to DSM criteria) that an ED may be present.

Screening all patients for EDs will likely result in identification
of more patients in need of further assessment and treatment. SUD
treatment counselors can easily (and unobtrusively) incorporate some
ED screening into the SUD assessment in a number of ways:

- As part of the drug use assessment, ask patients about their use
  of over-the-counter and prescription laxatives, diuretics, and
  diet pills.

- As part of taking a medical history, ask patients about past hospitalizations and behavioral health treatment history, including for EDs.

- As part of assessing daily activities, ask patients how often and for how long they exercise.

- Ask patients, "Other than those we've discussed so far, are there any health issues that concern you?"

Counselors also can use a standardized screening instrument. The SCOFF questionnaire discussed later in this section is a screening tool that was originally developed and validated in the United Kingdom and has been validated for use in the United States. Other validated brief screening instruments include:

- Eat-26 (The Eating Attitudes Test, a 26-item version of the original 40-question Eating Attitudes Test)

- The Bulimia Test—Revised (BULIT—R)

Patients in SUD treatment may be confused or defensive about being asked questions regarding their eating and body image. Counselors can prepare patients by:

- Explaining that EDs commonly co-occur with SUDs.

- Explaining that it is important to have a clear picture of the patient's overall health status.

- Asking the patient for permission to pursue ED screening (e.g., "May I ask you some questions about your eating habits?").

Screening does not end at intake. Counselors should remain alert for signs of EDs, including changes in weight that may appear later in treatment or recovery.

The SCOFF Questionnaire

1. Do you make yourself **S**ick [induce vomiting] because you feel uncomfortably full?

2. Do you worry you have lost **C**ontrol over how much you eat?

3. Have you recently lost more than **O**ne stone (14 pounds) in a 3-month period?

4. Do you believe yourself to be **F**at when others say you are too thin?

5. Would you say that **F**ood dominates your life?

Two or more "yes" responses indicate that an ED is likely.

Body Mass Index (BMI)

BMI is a number derived from a calculation based on a person's weight and height. For most people, BMI correlates with their amount of body fat. Measuring BMI is an inexpensive and easy alternative to a direct measurement of body fat percentage and is a useful method of screening for weight categories that may lead to health problems. BMI categories are:

- Underweight: BMI score of less than 18.5

Table 30.1. BMI Score for Underweight

Severe thinness	BMI score of less than 16
Moderate thinness	BMI score between 16.00 and 16.99
Mild thinness	BMI score between 17.00 and 18.49

- Normal range: BMI score between 18.5 and 24.9
- Overweight: BMI score between 25.0 and 29.9
- Obese: BMI score of 30.0 or more

BMI in children and adolescents is calculated somewhat differently from BMI in adults.

DSM-IV-TR Diagnostic Criteria for Anorexia Nervosa

1. Refusal to maintain body weight at or above a minimally normal weight for age and height (e.g., weight loss leading to maintenance of body weight less than 85% of that expected; or failure to make expected weight gain during period of growth, leading to body weight less than 85% of that expected).

2. Intense fear of gaining weight or becoming fat, even though underweight.

3. Disturbance in the way in which one's body weight or shape is experienced, undue influence of body weight or shape on

self-evaluation, or denial of the seriousness of the current low body weight.

4. In postmenarcheal females, amenorrhea, i.e., the absence of at least three consecutive menstrual cycles. (A woman is considered to have amenorrhea if her periods only occur following hormone therapies, e.g., estrogen administration.)

DSM-IV-TR Diagnostic Criteria for Bulimia Nervosa

1. Recurrent episodes of binge eating. An episode of binge eating is characterized by both of the following:

   - Eating, in a discrete period of time (e.g., within any 2-hour period), an amount of food that is definitely larger than most people would eat during a similar period of time and under similar circumstances

   - A sense of lack of control over eating during the episode (e.g., a feeling that one cannot stop eating or control what or how much one is eating)

2. Recurrent inappropriate compensatory behavior in order to prevent weight gain, such as self-induced vomiting; misuse of laxatives, diuretics, enemas, or other medications; fasting; or excessive exercise.

3. The binge eating and inappropriate compensatory behaviors both occur, on average, at least twice a week for 3 months.

4. Self-evaluation is unduly influenced by body shape and weight.

5. The disturbance does not occur exclusively during episodes of anorexia nervosa.

Proposed DSM-5 Diagnostic Criteria for Binge Eating Disorder

1. Recurrent episodes of binge eating. An episode of binge eating is characterized by both of the following:

   - Eating, in a discrete period of time (for example, within any 2-hour period), an amount of food that is definitely larger than most people would eat in a similar period of time under similar circumstances

- A sense of lack of control over eating during the episode (for example, a feeling that one cannot stop eating or control what or how much one is eating)

2. The binge eating episodes are associated with three (or more) of the following:

   - Eating much more rapidly than normal

   - Eating until feeling uncomfortably full

   - Eating large amounts of food when not feeling physically hungry

   - Eating alone because of being embarrassed by how much one is eating

   - Feeling disgusted with oneself, depressed, or very guilty afterwards

3. Marked distress regarding binge eating is present.

4. The binge eating occurs, on average, at least once a week for three months.

5. The binge eating is not associated with the recurrent use of inappropriate compensatory behavior (for example, purging) and does not occur exclusively during the course of anorexia nervosa, bulimia nervosa, or avoidant/restrictive food intake disorder.

Section 30.2

Suggested Medical Tests in Diagnosing Eating Disorders

"Suggested Medical Tests in Diagnosing Eating Disorders,"
© 2016 Omnigraphics, Inc. Reviewed March 2016.

Many people with eating disorders either deny that a problem exists or try to hide it from friends, family members, and medical professionals. As a result, diagnosing an eating disorder can be a difficult process, and such conditions as anorexia nervosa, bulimia nervosa, and binge eating disorder often go undetected for long periods of time. However, doctors have a variety of assessment tools and medical tests available to aid in the diagnosis of eating disorders. If an eating disorder is suspected, the diagnostic process is likely to include the following:

- a full medical history, including information about both physical and emotional health;

- a mental health screening to look for underlying psychological problems, evaluate eating habits, and assess attitudes about food and body image;

- a complete physical examination to check for signs of eating disorders as well as health problems related to malnutrition;

- additional medical tests—including X-rays and chemical analysis of blood and urine—to look for evidence of damage to the heart, kidneys, gastrointestinal tract, and other organs.

In the process of diagnosing eating disorders, doctors must rule out other health conditions that may present similar symptoms, such as hyperthyroidism, inflammatory bowel syndrome, immunodeficiency, chronic infection, diabetes, and cancer. In addition, doctors must look for evidence of diseases that often co-exist with eating disorders, such as depression, anxiety, obsessive-compulsive disorder, schizophrenia, and substance abuse.

Commonly Used Medical Tests

The initial step in diagnosing eating disorders usually involves administering questionnaires and conducting interviews to gather information about the patient's eating history, body image, and attitudes about food. Interviews are often conducted by a psychologist or psychiatrist in the presence of a supportive friend or family member of the patient. Medical professionals may also administer psychometric tests that are specifically designed to elicit information about eating disorders, such as the Eating Disorders Examination (EDE), the Eating Disorders Examination-Questionnaire (EDE-Q), and the SCOFF questionnaire. The results of these screening assessments help doctors determine whether further testing and evaluation is appropriate.

The next step in diagnosing eating disorders may involve administering a number of different medical tests to detect and rule out physical symptoms and health complications related to eating disorders. Some of the most commonly used tests include:

- a complete blood count, including levels of cholesterol, protein, and electrolytes;

- a urinalysis to evaluate kidney function;

- an oral glucose tolerance test (OGTT) to assess the body's ability to metabolize sugar;

- an enzyme-linked immunosorbent assay (ELISA) to check for antibodies to various viruses and bacteria;

- a secretin-CCK test to evaluate pancreas and gall bladder function;

- a blood urea nitrogen (BUN) test to evaluate protein metabolism and kidney function;

- a BUN-to-creatinine ratio to check for evidence of severe dehydration, kidney failure, congestive heart failure, cirrhosis of the liver, and other serious conditions;

- a serum cholinesterase test to assess liver function and check for signs of malnutrition;

- a luteinizing hormone (Lh) response to gonadotropin-releasing hormone (GnRH) to evaluate pituitary gland function;

- thyroid-stimulating hormone (TSH) and parathyroid hormone (PTH) tests to assess thyroid function;

- a creatine kinase test to evaluate enzyme levels in the heart, brain, and muscles;

- an echocardiogram or electrocardiogram (EKG) to assess heart function;

- an electroencephalogram (EEG) to measure electrical activity in the brain;

- an upper GI series to look for problems in the upper gastrointestinal tract;

- X-rays or a barium enema to assess issues in the lower gastrointestinal tract.

Making a Diagnosis

The results of these various medical tests can help medical professionals diagnose an eating disorder as well as pinpoint the specific type of disorder in order to provide effective treatment. To receive a diagnosis of anorexia nervosa, a patient typically has a distorted self-image and an intense fear of gaining weight, which translates into an inability or refusal to maintain a healthy weight for their age, height, and body type. Severely restricting food intake, abusing laxatives or diuretics in an effort to eliminate calories, and exercising excessively are common symptoms of anorexia. In females, the loss of menstrual function for at least three months is another key indicator.

The criteria for diagnosing bulimia nervosa include patterns of purging food from the body through self-induced vomiting or other methods at least twice a week for three months. Bulimia can be difficult to diagnose because patients usually binge and purge secretly and deny that they have a problem. In addition, most people with bulimia fall within their normal weight range. Dental and gum problems, stomach and digestive issues, dehydration, fatigue, and other symptoms related to repeated vomiting are key factors in the diagnosis of bulimia.

The diagnosis of binge eating disorder often occurs when a patient seeks medical help with losing weight or dealing with an obesity-related health problem. Medical tests aid in the diagnosis by ruling out physical illnesses and detecting health consequences of the eating disorder. With all types of eating disorders, early diagnosis is important to reduce the patient's risk of long-term health problems and improve the chances of successful treatment and recovery.

References

1. "Anorexia Nervosa—Exams and Tests," WebMD, November 14, 2014.

2. "Bulimia Nervosa—Exams and Tests," WebMD, November 14, 2014.

3. "Diagnosing Binge Eating Disorder," WebMD, 2016.

4. Mandal, Ananya. "Eating Disorders Diagnosis," News Medical, 2016.

Chapter 31

Choosing an Eating Disorders Treatment Facility or Therapist

Selecting a Treatment Center for Your Loved One

If your loved one is struggling with outpatient treatment or needs a higher level of care, you will need to consider several different options. Finding a program or physician that has expertise in treating all aspects of eating disorders is crucial.

Selecting an Appropriate Eating Disorders Treatment Program

First, you will need to find a treatment program that meets your loved one's needs. Consulting with their current treatment providers should give you a good idea of what level of care is most appropriate and what aspects of the eating disorder most need addressing.

Second, determine whether a particular level of care and specific treatment center is covered by your insurance carrier, and whether the treatment facility accepts insurance. If the treatment center is not part of the health insurer's system (out-of-network), the insurer may pay a percentage of the treatment costs, with the patient responsible for the remainder. It is best to negotiate this percentage with the insurer before starting treatment. If your insurance does not provide any coverage, you need to determine whether you and/or your loved one will be able to pay for treatment without insurance. A small number of treatment centers offer financial assistance; but most do not. However, inquiring whether a facility is able to work with your current financial situation may be worth investigating if the patient does not have financial resources or insurance.

Third, determine the philosophy of the treatment facility and the type of care they provide. Is the center's view of eating disorders supported by up-to-date research? Does it support ideas of eating disorder causes and recovery that are congruent with your family's situation? Does it encourage or require a high level of family involvement?

In addition, "evidence-based treatment" is increasingly emphasized, meaning that many eating disorder programs advertise that they use these types of treatments. It's important to check how frequently these therapies are used, and the qualifications of the therapists providing them. Many facilities have also begun advertising their efficacy via outcome studies. However, residential treatment hasn't been studied for efficacy in randomized control trials, and long-term outcomes have not been followed. Some treatment centers will only evaluate people who were not discharged prematurely, or they may only assess individuals who returned surveys, which could be biased towards individuals who are doing well. The eating disorder community also does not have a standard definition of what recovery looks like, which can make interpreting these studies even harder. Don't ignore these data, but interpret them with caution.

Lastly, think about what will happen after discharge. Does the program have a step-down program or is there another one that you intend to use? Discharge plans can be complicated and require much coordination of care among different healthcare providers. That takes time. Effective discharge planning needs to start much earlier than a day or two before the patient is expected to be discharged from a facility.

Other factors to consider when selecting a treatment center include religious affiliation (if any), multidisciplinary approach to care, distance from home, staff/patient ratio, professional qualifications of staff, their experience in treating eating disorders and adjunct therapies offered. Some treatment centers provide therapies in addition to psychiatric counseling and pharmacotherapy, like equine therapy, massage, dance or art therapy. These therapies may be appealing, although there is no evidence for these being essential to treatment response, and they may not be covered by your health insurance.

Determining Quality of Care

Determining the quality of care offered by a center is difficult at this time. No organization yet exists to specifically accredit treatment centers for the quality and standard of eating disorder-specific care. Leaders within the national eating disorders community organized in mid-2006 to develop care standards and a process for accrediting eating disorder centers. That effort is ongoing. One national organization, the Joint Commission on Accreditation of Healthcare Organizations (JCAHO), provides generic accreditation for healthcare facilities, and some eating disorder centers advertise "JCAHO accreditation." JCAHO accreditation does not link directly to quality of care for treatment of eating disorders; it assesses safety and credentials of staff.

Another issue regarding quality of care is that much care is delivered on an outpatient basis. For individual psychotherapists in private practice, no special credentialing or specialty certification exists regarding treatment of eating disorders. Thus, any mental healthcare professional can offer to treat an eating disorder whether or not he/she has experience or training in this specific area. Therefore, it is important to ask a prospective therapist about his/her knowledge about eating disorders and years of experience treating them.

Questions to Ask When Considering a Treatment Center

- Does the center accept the patient's insurance? If so, how much will it cover?

- Does the center offer help in obtaining reimbursement from the insurer?

- Does the center offer financial assistance?

- How long has the center been in business?

- What is its treatment philosophy?

- Does the center have any religious affiliations and what role do they play in treatment philosophy?

- Does the center provide multidisciplinary care?

- Who will be coordinating my loved one's treatment?

- Is the location convenient for the patient and his/ her support people who will be involved through recovery?

- If family cannot participate in treatment in-person, what alternatives are there?

- What security does the facility have in place to protect my loved one?

- How quickly will you complete a full assessment of the patient?

- Prior to traveling to the treatment center: what are your specific medical criteria for admission and will you talk with my insurance company before we arrive to determine eligibility for benefits?

- What is expected of the family during the person's stay?

- **Anorexic-specific:** Please describe your strategy for accomplishing refeeding and weight gain, and please include anticipated time frame.

- How are target weights determined?

- How do you handle food refusal?

- What steps do you take to prevent purging? Compulsive exercise?

- What happens if my loved one needs a higher level of care? How do you make that decision?

- If my loved one does not start to make progress, what will happen?

- Who is the best person to whom I should fax my loved one's treatment history and medical records?

- What are the visiting guidelines for family or friends?

- What levels of care does the center provide? Please define criteria for each level mentioned.

- What types of professionals participate on the care team and what is each person's role?

- What are the credentials and experience of the staff?

- How many hours of treatment are provided to a patient each day and week?

- Which professional serves as team leader?

- What types of therapy does the center consider essential?
- What types of therapy does the center consider optional?
- What is the patient-staff ratio?
- What is the rate of turnover (staff resigning) for clinical staff?
- How is that handled with patients?
- Who will the patient have the most contact with on a daily basis?
- What is the mealtime support philosophy?
- Who will update key family or friends? How often?
- How is care coordinated for the patient inside the center and outside if needed?
- How does the center communicate with the patient's family doctors and other doctors who may routinely provide care?
- What are your criteria for determining whether a patient needs to be partially or fully hospitalized?
- What happens in counseling sessions? Will there be individual and group sessions?
- Will there be family sessions?
- How will family be prepared for the patient's discharge?
- How does the care team measure success for the patient?
- How do you decide when a patient is ready to leave?
- How is that transition managed with the patient and family?
- What after-care plans do you have in place and at what point do you begin planning for discharge?
- What follow-up care after discharge is needed and who should deliver it?
- Does the patient have a follow-up appointment in hand before being discharged? Is the follow-up appointment within seven days of the discharge date?
- When is payment due?

Chapter 32

Determining the Types of Treatment Needed for Eating Disorders

Chapter Contents

Section 32.1

Determining Level of Care for Eating Disorder

"Determining Level of Care for Eating Disorder" © 2016
Omnigraphics, Inc. Reviewed March 2016.

There is no effective "one size fits all" approach to the treatment of eating disorders. Even though different people may suffer from the same type of disorder, they will often respond favorably to different types of treatment, and therefore prescribed therapies may employ a combination of various kinds of interventions and levels of care tailored to suit individual requirements.

The term "level of care" refers to the intensity of services provided for a patient undergoing treatment for an eating disorder. The level of care prescribed for an individual primarily depends on the severity of the illness and the degree of functional loss resulting from the condition. More serious illnesses and greater loss of functionality will require more intensive levels of care to meet the individual's clinical needs and treatment goals.

While treatment settings are required to be the least restrictive possible, the level of care is decided on the basis of the patient's initial diagnosis. For instance, an adult patient whose weight is less than 80 percent of his or her estimated ideal body weight may require a highly structured program in a restrictive setting—such as inpatient care—to gain weight.

That being said, inpatient care may be deemed appropriate even for those whose weight is above 80 percent of their healthy body weight. For example, this could be prescribed when psychosocial parameters, such as behavior and co-occurring psychological issues, are taken into consideration. Therefore, regular evaluation of the patient's condition and needs is necessary to determine whether the patient is ready to be moved to a different level of care, clinically appropriate with his or her current nutritional and medical status.

Broadly, the two traditional levels of care include the outpatient setting and the inpatient setting. However, in reality, these settings form the two ends of a continuum of services, which includes both distinctive and overlapping components aimed at providing the best type of treatment and rehabilitative options based on individual needs.

Outpatient Treatment for Eating Disorders

The least restrictive level of care, outpatient treatment is partic-ularly useful for those who do not want the therapy to interfere with their occupation or school. This is also suitable for those who cannot afford higher levels of care but require assistance to stay in recovery. The duration of treatment in an outpatient setting may depend on the severity of the eating disorder, as well as the prognosis, and it may range from a few weeks to a few months, following which the visits may be reduced in frequency. Outpatient settings can offer intensive care in the form of supervised meals and a structured treatment plan provided by a professional team, which may include a primary-care physician, a psychotherapist, and a registered nutritionist or dietician.

Partial Hospitalization

Partial hospitalization is a type of outpatient care in which the level of intensity falls somewhere between 24-hour care and an outpatient setting. This means the patient may require hospitalization for a few hours per day at a hospital or a residential facility. Often referred to as a "day hospital," these settings offer a range of ambulatory services that can compare with acute inpatient settings. The treatment team in a day hospital usually comprises a primary-care physician, a psy-chotherapist/family therapist, and a nutrition counselor, and this type of setting also offers ample opportunity for group therapies. Partial hospitalization may take anywhere from a week to a few months, and based on the progress made, the patient may be moved to an outpa-tient setting.

Inpatient/Hospital Treatment

Inpatient settings offer intensive care for eating disorders and may include hospitals or treatment facilities offering different levels of specialization. While hospitals offer 24-hour acute care services, resi-dential-care facilities focus less on clinical treatment and more on reha-bilitation. Inpatient settings provide a wide range of services, and the duration of treatment may range from a few days to several months, depending on the patient's physical and psychological treatment goals.

Hospitals generally offer a structured treatment program for eat-ing disorders, which may start with stabilizing the patient's physical symptoms. Some of the symptoms that could require immediate medi-cal attention include electrolyte imbalance, hypotension, hypothermia, osteoporosis, and edema, among others. Regular laboratory tests are performed to regulate and monitor metabolic functions. The patient receives one-on-one psychotherapy, which motivates them to participate actively in the treatment program and also work towards developing healthy patterns of behavior. Nutritionists formulate a diet plan for the patient based on individual needs, and nursing staff supervise the patient's meal time and snacks. Hospitals also may provide group therapy sessions and family support groups.

Residential Care

Residential care is usually recommended for children and adolescents who require 24-hour support to treat their eating disorders and other associated behavioral and psychosocial conditions. Residential care offers a comfortable and informal setting and is less restrictive than a hospital. Treatment is based on a predefined time limit, individual needs, and clear goals and is supervised by a team of professionals, including medical physicians, psychiatrists, psychologists, nurses, dieticians, and occupational therapists. Residential-care facilities also may bring in registered therapists to offer art-based psychotherapies, such as painting, sculpting, music, dance, and drama. And some also offer academic support to help children with eating disorders continue their academic pursuits while in active therapy or rehabilitation.

Reference

Eating Disorder Hope. "Types of Treatment and Therapy," June 12, 2012.

Section 32.2

Types of Therapy for Eating Disorder

"Types of Therapy for Eating Disorder," © 2016
Omnigraphics, Inc. Reviewed March 2016.

Eating disorders are health conditions with serious physical, psychological, and social consequences. What starts out as an urge to eat less or more in response to a distorted perception of body image, may spiral out of control and become a debilitating or chronic medical illness. Early intervention is key to successful treatment outcomes and may avoid the fatal or life-threatening conditions often associated with eating disorders, such as anorexia nervosa. Studies have shown that multiple factors—genetic, biological, psychological, and social—determine the cause of eating disorders, and efforts are underway to develop specific psychotherapies and medications that can control eating behavior by targeting specific centers in the brain.

Typically, treatment goals involve formulating a healthy nutrition plan, restoring body weight to a prescribed level, and stopping such behaviors as binge eating and purging. Treatment plans are tailored to meet individual requirements and also treat co-existing conditions, such as depression, substance abuse, or personality disorders. While some types of psychotherapy can be provided on an outpatient basis, others may require hospitalization to treat the more severe effects of malnutrition.

The treatment protocol for eating disorders is highly dependent on the type and severity of the disorder and any associated conditions. It may include one or a combination of the following:

- Individual, family, or group psychotherapy
- Medical care and monitoring
- Nutritional counselling
- Medications (for example, antidepressants)

Some Common Types of Therapy Available for Eating Disorders

Cognitive Behavioral Therapy (CBT)

CBT is one of the most widely practiced forms of psychological intervention for treating eating disorders. Developed by psychotherapist Aaron Beck, M.D., in the 1960s, CBT combines two therapies, cognitive therapy (CT) and behavioral therapy, and is based on the theory that negative thoughts and negative behavior are interlinked. This kind of therapy focuses on helping individuals recognize the irrational thinking patterns associated with food and body image, then develop positive and healthy behavior patterns.

The treatment plan usually includes three phases and requires the active participation of both patient and therapist. The first phase is called the behavioral phase, in which the therapist and the patient devise a plan to stabilize eating behavior, treat symptoms, and learn coping mechanisms with the help of in-session activities. The second phase, the cognitive phase, involves restructuring techniques intended to change harmful and problematic thinking patterns and replace them with new perspectives and ideas. This phase also assesses other psychological and social factors, such as relationship problems or low self-esteem, that may underlie the eating problem. The final phase of CBT is the relapse prevention phase. Here the focus is on eliminating triggers and maintaining the progress made thus far. CBT is almost always incorporated into the treatment plan for eating disorders because of its adaptability in creating individualized therapy to achieve personal goals and promote holistic healing.

Medical Nutrition Therapy (MNT)

This type of treatment, an essential part of the treatment plan for eating disorders, focuses on helping patients normalize their eating patterns. Creating a healthy eating regimen includes maintaining a nutritious and balanced diet, promoting a harmonious and sustainable relationship with food devoid of negative or harmful rationale, and learning to trust the body's natural response to feelings of hunger or fullness.

MNT can be implemented in all kinds of treatment settings, including inpatient, outpatient, and residential care facilities. In all cases, a registered dietician formulates a structured meal plan on the basis of the patient's medical history, as well as his or her dietary and laboratory evaluations, and supervises the implementation of the dietary plan. The dietitian also educates the patient on the importance of following the prescribed diet plan and avoiding dysfunctional eating behavior and may also modify the plan to address specific deficiencies or medical conditions.

Dialectical Behavioral Therapy (DBT)

Dialectical behavior therapy is a form of CBT originally developed to treat people with borderline personality disorder. The term "dialectical" refers to a discussion that takes place between two people holding opposing views until they find common ground or achieve a balance between the two extreme views. In a treatment setting, the therapist engages in a philosophical exercise with the patient and tries to make him or her responsible for disruptive behavior, while at the same time assuring the patient that illogical thoughts and actions are understandable and not necessarily destructive.

In recent years, DBT has often been incorporated into treatment plans for eating disorders—in both individual and group therapy sessions—and is known to have better outcomes than CBT, which is based more on the premise that the patient's thoughts have to be controlled or changed. In contrast, DBT is based more on acceptance of the patient's extreme behavior and gradual progress toward recognizing triggers, learning to perceive when boundaries are overstepped, and acquiring skills to deal with conflict and stress.

This form of psychotherapy accepts the fact that the patient has spent months – even years – developing eating-disorder patterns and would find it difficult to switch them off in a day. For instance, an anorexic's "I am fat" mindset is not something he or she can unlearn quickly, but developing a heightened awareness of thought processes can help control negative emotions and shift focus to healthy and positive emotions. DBT relies greatly on a close relationship between patient and therapist, and while patients learn new skills during individual sessions, they get an opportunity to practice their newly acquired skills at group sessions.

Expressive or Creative Arts Therapy

Expressive or creative arts therapy uses the creative process to help people treat depression and eating disorders. Used in conjunction with other traditional therapies, this approach has been particularly beneficial in people with a history of trauma.

Art therapy is based on developing self-awareness and centers on the experiences and perceptions of the individual. The process of creating an image of one's thoughts, emotions, and conflicts through the medium of art—say sculpting or painting—is often called "concretization.," which can help the patient accept and recognize his or her inner self through the use of symbols. These symbols of self-expression may also help the therapist in diagnosis, in addition to providing research material for this relatively new field.

Art provides a creative outlet for self-expression and offers a coping mechanism for self-destructive behavior, such as bingeing or purging. A licensed creative-arts therapist can assess, evaluate, and provide therapeutic intervention for the treatment of eating disorders through the use of such activities as drawing, painting, sculpting, photography, music, dance, and drama.

Animal-Assisted Therapy

Although early studies have shown that companion animals contribute significantly to mental and emotional well-being, it is only recently that animal-assisted therapy has begun to be used in conjunction with established therapies to treat many types of mental disorders. Working or playing with animals, such as cats, dogs, or horses, is increasingly being incorporated into the treatment of behavioral problems, particularly in pediatric settings.

For example, equine-assisted psychotherapy is being used as an effective treatment for such disorders as anxiety, attention deficit hyperactivity disorder (ADHD), depression, eating disorders, and post-traumatic stress disorder (PTSD). Caring for animals has been shown to improve self-image in people with eating disorders, and patients also forge an emotional bond with animals, which provides them with a means of self-expression while also teaching them coping mechanisms to deal with self-injurious thoughts and emotions.

Play Therapy

Play therapy is commonly used as a therapeutic intervention, particularly in children and adolescents, as it provides them with an opportunity to express and communicate at their own pace. Toys and games help children make developmentally appropriate responses and also allows the therapist to gain insight into the child's inner world.

Studies have shown that each child's personal experience plays a role in determining the child's self-image as well as the behavioral tendencies that he or she develops to function in the world. Play therapy helps focus on the child's effort to develop coping mechanisms to resolve social or emotional conflict, both in the present and the future. More recently, play therapy has gained momentum as an effective treatment tool for behavioral disorders, including binge eating and anorexia nervosa, as it offers a safe environment in which children can work toward finding their sense of emotional stability without having to relive past traumas.

Family-Based Therapy

Family-based therapy was developed from the premise that involving family and improving relationships between family members increases the likelihood of a positive treatment outcome. Therapists work at resolving conflicts within the family, educating relatives about the patient's condition and early signs of problems, and charting out an action plan to manage the condition effectively.

Studies have shown favorable outcomes with family-focused therapy in terms of both stabilizing treatment and preventing relapse. Moreover, this kind of therapy builds better understanding and communication and has been effective in preventing "burn out" in family caregivers, which could in turn result in apathy to the patient's condition.

The Maudsley Approach

One type of family-based therapy, called the Maudsley approach for its development at Maudsley Hospital in London, has proven to be effective in the long-term improvement of anorexia nervosa and bulimia nervosa, particularly in adolescents. This approach is characterized by three distinct procedural stages:

- Weight restoration

- Returning control over eating to the teen

- Establishing healthy adolescent identity

In the first phase, the parents are made responsible for helping the teen adopt a healthy eating plan. They are also counseled on the child's condition and how to refrain from criticism. The second phase involves getting the patient to assume responsibility for his or her eating habits. Here, there is a gradual shift away from parental control, and the patient is encouraged to develop the cognitive processes required to take responsibility for healthy nutrition. The third stage begins after the patient reaches and maintains a healthy body weight. During this stage, the therapist helps the patient develop a healthy identity and resolve adolescent and family issues that may underlie the eating disorder. The therapist also helps the patient develop autonomy while helping caregivers cope with high anxiety and stress, which may be counterproductive to the success of family-based therapies.

Despite this method gaining popularity as a treatment regime for binge eating and anorexia, Maudsley studies have shown that the model has had mixed outcomes with older adolescents, adults, and the chronically ill. Moreover, the high degree of parental involvement in the treatment and recovery process may sometimes further exacerbate dysfunctional patterns in adolescents and make it difficult for the patient to gain autonomy, something crucial to the recovery phase. And yet, notwithstanding these issues, the Maudsley approach continues to be a popular therapeutic modality studied by researchers across the United States and Europe.

Photo Therapy

Bright light therapy has traditionally been used in the treatment of seasonal affective disorder (SAD), a form of depression associated with imbalances of melatonin, a hormone that regulates the sleep and wake cycles, often referred to as the circadian rhythm. SAD may also be attributed to a fall in the levels of serotonin, a neurotransmitter responsible for maintaining mood, sleep and appetite.

Melatonin is produced nocturnally by the pineal gland, and its production stops with exposure to sunlight. It has been proven that exposure to bright light or natural sunlight during the day triggers early nocturnal production of melatonin, thereby enhancing sleep cycle, appetite, and mood. Serotonin is a precursor of melatonin and is also influenced by sunlight. Although it is produced during the day, the conversion of serotonin to melatonin occurs at night. Short days and long nights in winter not only lower serotonin production during the day, but also causes delayed nighttime melatonin production, both of which negatively impact energy levels, sleep, and sense of well-being.

Light therapy is administered by exposing the patient to bright light for prescribed periods of time. In recent years, light therapy has been used to treat eating disorders, in conjunction with other established therapies. Disorders such as bulimia nervosa or binge eating share certain features with SAD, in that symptoms are seasonal and depression is a coexisting condition. Although more studies are needed before drawing definitive conclusions on the efficacy of light therapy, it is being used to treat eating disorders, particularly in cases where antidepressants and established psychotherapies fail to be effective.

References

1. National Institute of Mental Health (NIMH). "Psychotherapies," October 2008.

2. Sholt, Michal and Gavron, Tami. "Therapeutic Qualities of Clay-work in Art Therapy and Psychotherapy: A Review" Journal of the American Art Therapy Association, 2006.

3. Eating Disorder Hope. "Eating Disorder Treatment," November 2015.

4. Wilson, George F. and Philips, Kelley L. "Concepts and Definitions Used in Quality Assurance and Utilization Review" *Manual of Psychiatric Quality Assurance*, American Psychiatric Association, 2005.

Chapter 33

Psychotherapeutic Approach for Eating Disorders

What Is Psychotherapy?

Psychotherapy, or "talk therapy," is a way to treat people with a mental disorder by helping them understand their illness. It teaches people strategies and gives them tools to deal with stress and unhealthy thoughts and behaviors. Psychotherapy helps patients manage their symptoms better and function at their best in everyday life.

Sometimes psychotherapy alone may be the best treatment for a person, depending on the illness and its severity. Other times, psychotherapy is combined with medications. Therapists work with an individual or families to devise an appropriate treatment plan.

This chapter contains text excerpted from the following sources: Text beginning with the heading "What Is Psychotherapy?" is excerpted from "Mental Health Information," National Institute of Mental Health (NIMH), October 19, 2008. Reviewed March 2016; Text under the heading "Psychotherapeutic Treatment for Anorexia" is excerpted from "Mental Health Illnesses," Office on Women's Health (OWH), March 29, 2010. Reviewed March 2016; Text under the heading "Psychotherapeutic Treatment for Bulimia" is excerpted from "Mental Health Illnesses," Office on Women's Health (OWH), March 29, 2010. Reviewed March 2016.

What Are the Different Types of Psychotherapy?

Many kinds of psychotherapy exist. There is no "one-size-fits-all" approach. In addition, some therapies have been scientifically tested more than others. Some people may have a treatment plan that includes only one type of psychotherapy. Others receive treatment that includes elements of several different types. The kind of psychotherapy a person receives depends on his or her needs.

Patients should talk to their doctor or a psychotherapist about planning treatment that meets their needs.

Cognitive Behavioral Therapy

Cognitive behavioral therapy (CBT) is a blend of two therapies: cognitive therapy (CT) and behavioral therapy. CT was developed by psychotherapist Aaron Beck, M.D., in the 1960's. CT focuses on a person's thoughts and beliefs, and how they influence a person's mood and actions, and aims to change a person's thinking to be more adaptive and healthy. Behavioral therapy focuses on a person's actions and aims to change unhealthy behavior patterns.

CBT helps a person focus on his or her current problems and how to solve them. Both patient and therapist need to be actively involved in this process. The therapist helps the patient learn how to identify distorted or unhelpful thinking patterns, recognize and change inaccurate beliefs, relate to others in more positive ways, and change behaviors accordingly.

CBT can be applied and adapted to treat many specific mental disorders.

CBT for Eating Disorders

Eating disorders can be very difficult to treat. However, some small studies have found that CBT can help reduce the risk of relapse in adults with anorexia who have restored their weight. CBT may also reduce some symptoms of bulimia, and it may also help some people reduce binge eating behavior.

Psychotherapeutic Treatment for Anorexia

Some forms of psychotherapy can help make the psychological reasons for anorexia better. Psychotherapy is sometimes known as "talk therapy." It uses different ways of communicating to change a patient's thoughts or behavior. This kind of therapy can be useful for treating eating disorders in young patients who have not had anorexia for a long time.

Individual counseling can help someone with anorexia. If the patient is young, counseling may involve the whole family. Support groups may also be a part of treatment. In support groups, patients, and families meet and share what they've been through.

Some researchers point out that prescribing medicines and using psychotherapy designed just for anorexic patients works better at treating anorexia than just psychotherapy alone. Whether or not a treatment works, though, depends on the person involved and his or her situation. Unfortunately, no one kind of psychotherapy always works for treating adults with anorexia.

Psychotherapeutic Treatment for Bulimia

Someone with bulimia can get better. A health care team of doctors, nutritionists, and therapists will help the patient recover. They will help the person learn healthy eating patterns and cope with their thoughts and feelings. Treatment for bulimia uses a combination of options. Whether or not the treatment works depends on the patient.

To stop a person from bingeing and purging, a doctor may recommend the patient:

- Receive nutritional advice and psychotherapy, especially cognitive behavioral therapy (CBT)

- Be prescribed medicine

CBT is a form of psychotherapy that focuses on the important role of thinking in how we feel and what we do. CBT that has been tailored to treat bulimia has shown to be effective in changing bingeing and purging behavior, and eating attitudes. Therapy for a person with bulimia may be one-on-one with a therapist or group-based.

Chapter 34

Pharmacotherapy: Medications for Eating Disorders

Pharmacotherapy

Although medication alone cannot cure eating disorders, pharmacotherapy often plays a role in the treatment and recovery process. When used along with psychotherapy and nutritional guidance, medications such as antidepressants can help patients with eating disorders stabilize their mental and physical condition and control their symptoms. Prescription drugs may help people with bulimia suppress their urges to binge and purge, for instance, and may help people with anorexia manage their obsessive thinking about food and weight. A medication that benefits one patient might not work effectively for another, however, so it is important to consider different options. In addition, all medications involve side effects, so patients must weigh the risks of each drug against its possible health benefits.

There are three main categories of medications that are commonly used in the treatment of eating disorders:

- medications to restore body chemistry and manage the physical damage done by severe caloric restriction or repeated bingeing and purging episodes;

- medications to treat physical and mental health conditions that frequently co-exist with eating disorders and complicate treatment;

- psychiatric medications to treat the underlying depression, anxiety, obsessive-compulsive disorder, and other mental health conditions that often affect people with eating disorders.

Medications to Manage Physical Damage

Several types of medication may be prescribed to help manage the harmful physical effects of severe food restriction. To prevent health complications involving the kidneys, heart, and brain, for instance, patients with anorexia and bulimia may need medication to restore the proper electrolyte balance in their bodies. Medications commonly used to replenish electrolytes include potassium chloride, potassium phosphate, and calcium gluconate. For patients with binge eating disorder who experience health complications related to obesity, medications may be prescribed to promote weight loss. Examples include appetite suppressants like sibutramine (Meridia) and fat blockers like orlistat (Xenical). These medications may involve side effects, however, such as increases in blood pressure, insomnia, dry mouth, and loose, oily stools.

Medications to Address Coexisting Conditions

A variety of physical and mental health conditions often coexist with eating disorders and complicate the treatment process. Many people with eating disorders also have clinical psychiatric disorders such as depression, anxiety, bipolar, obsessive-compulsive, attention deficit, and posttraumatic stress. Medications are available to help patients manage the symptoms of these conditions in order to improve their ability to recover from eating disorders. Physical health conditions such as diabetes and celiac disease may also coexist with eating disorders. The special nutritional requirements associated with these conditions may impede the treatment of eating disorders. Medication can help patients manage their symptoms and eat a normal diet.

Psychiatric Medications for Eating Disorders

Antidepressants, mood stabilizers, and other psychiatric medications are often prescribed to treat eating disorders. Eating disorders are considered a form of psychiatric illness, and many people with eating disorders also have symptoms of depression, anxiety, and other psychiatric conditions. The most common types of psychiatric medications used in the treatment of eating disorders include:

- ## Selective serotonin reuptake inhibitors (SSRI)

This category of antidepressant drugs works by increasing the level of serotonin (a chemical that affects mood) in the brain. SSRIs are commonly used to treat depression, anxiety, and obsessive-compulsive disorder. Fluoxetine (Prozac) is the only medication approved by the U.S. Food and Drug Administration for the treatment of bulimia. Research suggests that fluoxetine may also help people with anorexia overcome underlying depression and maintain a healthy weight once they have brought their eating under control. Other commonly prescribed SSRIs include sertraline (Zoloft), fluvoxamine (Luvox), citalopram (Celexa), and paroxetine (Paxil). Although SSRIs well-tolerated by most people, some experience such side effects as drowsiness, weight gain, agitation, and loss of interest in sex.

- ## Tricyclic antidepressants (TCAs) and monoamine oxidase inhibitors (MAOIs)

These categories of antidepressant drugs have long been used to treat depression, panic disorder, and chronic pain. There is also some evidence that they may be effective in treating eating disorders, especially bulimia. They have more side effects than SSRIs, however, including dry mouth, headaches, blurred vision, dizziness, nausea, drowsiness, and insomnia. Examples include imipramine (Tofranil) and despiramine (Norpramin).

- ## Other antidepressants

Other types of antidepressants that are not related to SSRIs, TCAs, and MAOIs are also prescribed in the treatment of eating disorders. Medications like bupropion (Wellbutrin) and trazodone (Desyrel) work by increasing the levels of certain neurotransmitters, like norephinephrine, serotonin, and dopamine.

- ## Mood stabilizers

Mood stabilizers, such as lithium, are typically used in treating manic-depressive and bipolar disorders. Some research has indicated that they may also be helpful for patients with bulimia. Since these medications may cause weight loss, however, they are not usually considered for patients with anorexia.

- **Antipsychotics**

Olanzapine (Zyprexa) is an antipsychotic drug that is often pre-scribed for schizophrenia. Research has shown that it can also help some anorexia patients gain weight and overcome their obsessive thinking about food. Although many people tolerate olanzapine well, there is a risk of lightheadedness, dizziness, drowsiness, weakness, and tardive dyskinesia (a movement disorder).

- **Anticonvulsants**

The anti-seizure medication topiramate (Topamax) has been shown to help some people with bulimia suppress their urge to binge and purge and reduce their preoccupation with eating and weight. It can involve side effects, however, such as nausea, constipation or diarrhea, dizziness, drowsiness, insomnia, loss of appetite, and weight loss.

- **Central nervous system stimulants**

Lisdexamfetamine dimesylate (Vyvanse), a medication that was developed to treat attention deficit hyperactivity disorder (ADHD), received FDA approval for the treatment of binge eating disorder in 2015. It has been shown to help adults who compulsively overeat to manage their urge to binge. However, Vyvanse is not approved as a medication to promote weight loss.

References

1. Marks, Hedy. "How Medication Treats Eating Disorders." Everyday Health, May 10, 2010.

2. "Medications/Drugs to Treat Eating Disorders." Eating Disorder Referral and Information Center, n.d.

3. Tracy, Natasha. "Medications for Eating Disorders." Healthy Place, January 10, 2012.

Chapter 35

Recovery from an Eating Disorder

Chapter Contents

Section 35.1

Overcoming Negative Thoughts

This section includes text excerpted from "Changing
Negative Thinking Patterns," U.S. Department of
Veterans Affairs (VA), August 2013.

Changing Negative Thinking Patterns

When bad things happen in our lives, it's normal to have negative
thoughts—like expecting the worst, or seeing the worst in people
or situations. Negative thoughts like these can be useful during a
traumatic or stressful event. But after the event has passed, con-
tinuing to have negative thoughts may no longer be helpful. Always
having negative thoughts can make you feel bad. And it can stress
your body. If you can identify thinking patterns you may have, and
challenge the ones that are not helpful, you can open yourself up to
new and different ways of looking at the situation, which can help
you feel better.

Negative Thinking Styles

Indicate which of these negative thinking styles sometimes apply
to you:

- **All-or-nothing thinking:** People who engage in this kind of
  thinking see the world in all-or-nothing terms. Things are either
  black or white, but never (or rarely) gray.

- **Emotional thinking:** This thinking happens when what you
  feel controls what you think. Feelings are important, but your
  feelings can play tricks on you. In fact, if you are anxious most
  of the time, your feelings are almost certainly sending you the
  wrong message.

- **Overestimating risk:** This happens when you assess the risk
  associated with a situation as higher than it really is. This way
  of thinking can lead to feeling a lot of anxiety.

- **"Must" or "Should" thinking:** These are unwritten rules or expectations for how you ought to behave that are based on myths rather than facts. They are standards that you feel you must or should live up to.

- **Self-blame:** People who engage in this style of thinking blame themselves when bad things happen. They take responsibility for things they often had little or no control over.

- **Expecting the worst:** Some people always expect the worst to happen. Many times their fears are triggered by "what if" thoughts.

- **Over-generalization:** People who over-generalize believe that because something happened once it will happen again and again.

Here Are Some Questions You Can Ask Yourself Any Time You Need to Combat Negative Thinking:

- Is there any other way of looking at the situation?

- Is there any other explanation?

- How would someone else, like a friend, think about the situation? Or what would you tell a friend who had the thought?

- Am I using all or nothing thinking? Is there a middle ground?

- Am I expecting more of myself than I do of other people?

- Am I overestimating (or underestimating) how much control and responsibility I have in this situation?

- What is the most realistic thing that would happen if my thought came true?

- Do I have other ways of handling the problem?

- Am I overestimating the risk involved?

- Am I predicting the future as if I have a crystal ball?

Section 35.2

Relapse Prevention

This section contains text excerpted from the following sources: Text
beginning with the heading "What is a Relapse?" is excerpted from
"Lifestyle Coach Facilitation Guide: Post-Core," Centers for Disease
Control and Prevention (CDC), June 14, 2012. Reviewed March 2016;
Remaining text in this chapter is "Slips, Lapses and Relapses,"
© 2016 National Eating Disorders Association. For more information,
visit www.nationaleatingdisorders.org. Reprinted with permission.

What is a Relapse?

Weight regain usually starts with a lapse.

A lapse might be overeating during dinner for a day or two, or skipping your physical activity for a week while you are on vacation. Lapses
are a natural part of weight management. At some point, everyone
has lapses—small slips, moments, or brief periods of time when they
return to an old habit.

A lapse is a brief and small slip in your weight loss efforts.

REMEMBER that by itself, a lapse will not cause you to gain back
the weight you have lost.

A lapse left unchecked, however, can grow into a relapse. A relapse
usually results from a series of several small lapses that snowball into
a full-blown relapse. The most effective way to prevent a relapse is
to identify the lapses early and deal with them before they turn into
a relapse.

A relapse is a return to previous eating and activity habits and is
associated with significant weight regain.

The Relapse Chain

The relapse chain is a series—or chain reaction—of events that can
lead to a full relapse.

1. High risk situation
2. No plan for the situation
3. Small lapse occurs
4. Negative thinking and no plan for lapse

5. Another relapse and no comeback plan
6. Full relapse

Keeping a Lapse from Becoming a Relapse

In order to deal most effectively with lapses, it is important to be prepared for them.

A lapse (or a single occasion of uncontrolled eating or not being physically active) is not likely—by itself—to cause you to slip back into old habits and regain weight. However, when people eat something they know they shouldn't or stop being active, they often have self-defeating thoughts.

Step 1: The first step in dealing with lapses is to recognize that 99.9% of all people trying to lose weight and be active experience lapses. Lapses can and should be useful learning experiences.

Step 2: The second step is to resist the tendency to think negative thoughts. You are not a failure if you lapse—you are normal!

Step 3: Next, ask yourself what happened. Use the chance to learn from the lapse. Was it a special occasion? If so, is it likely to happen again soon? Did you eat because of social pressure? Did you skip physical activity because you were too busy with other things, or because of work and family pressures? Review the situation and think about it neutrally. Then plan a strategy for dealing more effectively with similar situations in the future.

Step 4: The fourth step is to regain control of your eating or physical activity at the very next opportunity. Do not tell yourself, "Well, I blew it for the day," and wait until the next day to get back on track. Getting back on track without delay is important in preventing lapses from becoming relapses.

Step 5: Talk to someone supportive. Call your lifestyle coach, or another friend or loved one and discuss your new strategy for handling lapses.

Step 6: Finally, remember you are making life-long changes. Weight loss is a journey with lots of small decisions and choices every day that add up over time. Focus on all the positive changes you have made and realize that you can get back on track.

Relapse is a natural part of the recovery process. Even when you have an excellent plan to handle your slips and high-risk situations,

271

you cannot always prevent or avoid lapses. This does not mean you have failed or that you will regain your weight. In the event that you feel that you may be in a situation where you have fallen back to eating disorder behavior, there are some things to remember:

- Seek professional help immediately.

- Relapse does not mean failure.

- Reflect on your progress. Remember your purpose.

- Remember that a short period of overeating or skipped activity will not erase all of your progress.

- You have been through this before and you can get through it again.

- Be kind to yourself and give yourself time to recover.

- Refer often to your values and strive to live by them.

- Work on self-approval, which is not dependent on weight.

- Accept your personal limitations.

- Create an environment of respect, optimism, trust and honesty with yourself and others.

- Know that "failure" neither dooms nor defines you. You are just a person who is willing to take on challenges.

- Practice, practice, practice!

- Stay calm and listen to your positive self-talk (while sending away negative thoughts). How you think about your lapse is the most important part of the process. If you use it as a learning opportunity, you will succeed. If you give up and stop trying to make changes, then you are at risk for a relapse.

Comeback Plan

- Start using your Food and Activity Tracker daily

Make sure you write down everything that you eat and drink, taking care to be as exact in your portion size as possible.

- Budget fewer calories

Decrease your calorie intake or increase your physical activity for several days to make up for your lapse.

- Plan your meals

Start planning what you will eat at your next meal. Plan what you will eat for the next several days, including snacks. You might consider using pre-packaged frozen meals so that you know exactly what and how much you are eating.

- Seek support

Call your lifestyle coach, or a good friend for a pep talk to help you start your comeback plan and to feel positive about your success.

Your Comeback Plan

Think about what will be the most effective comeback plan for you to recover from a lapse and prevent a full relapse. Write down these steps and keep your written plan in a place where you can easily find it when you need it.

1. What two steps can I take immediately after a lapse to get back on track?

2. What negative thinking might get in the way of putting my comeback plan into action?

3. What positive thoughts will I use to keep myself going with my comeback plan?

4. How will I reward myself when I get back on track?

Tips for Challenging Situations

Sustained recovery requires careful planning, and a team approach. For many patients, that means utilizing the full continuum of care. Typically, recovery does not happen once, but takes place over years of mindful application of the lessons learnt in treatment. In other words, care goes hand and hand with aftercare.

It can be challenging to re-enter into the environment that one's eating disorder had previously developed. However, going back with a realistic treatment plan can help facilitate the recovery process.

Trust your team. Follow their recommendations for when it is time to step down. It is important to not cut yourself off from support, even when you feel like things are going "fine". Challenges will come up, and while you might have the skills to respond to them without eating disorder behavior it's helpful to have a professional as "backup". They will be able to help you create a plan that includes being aware of what may have triggered you in the past, and help you to work towards creating effective and healthy coping skills.

Some Signs That Might Indicate Relapse:

- Your thoughts keep turning to food, dieting and weight.

- You have been dishonest with your eating disorder treatment professionals or if you feel compelled to hide information or behaviors.

- You worry that you are losing control and may overcompensate with perfectionism.

- You feel as if you have no outlet for your stress.

- You feel hopeless and wonder what you're going to do with your life.

- With diet and exercise, your primary goal is to look good rather than to be healthy.

- You believe that you'll never be happy unless you're thin.

- You see yourself as overweight or obese.

- Friends or family indicate to you that your self-image is inaccurate.

- You look in the mirror frequently and weigh yourself often.

- You skip meals or find ways to purify yourself after eating.

- You get irritable around the issue of food.

- You feel an overwhelming sense of guilt or shame after eating.

- You avoid events that involve food.

- You isolate yourself or engage in increasingly secretive behaviors.

- You hold contempt for people who are overweight or don't eat well according to your standards.

Steps to Help Prevent Relapse

- Seek help from a professional.

- Develop self-acceptance through practicing compassion toward self.

- Develop a positive and self-nurturing internal dialogue.

- Get treatment for co-occurring disorders such as anxiety and depression.

- Practice mindfulness and living in the moment.

- Listen to and honor your feelings.

- Eat well and listen to your body's hunger and fullness signs.

- Accept your genetic makeup and appreciate your body.

- Have a relapse prevention or correction plan.

Chapter 36

Insurance Coverage for Eating Disorders Treatment

Health Insurance Coverage

Eating disorders are serious, life-threatening illnesses, but studies have shown that early intervention and a full course of treatment can lead to recovery for many patients. Despite these promising results, however, many health insurance providers deny coverage for eating disorder treatment. Some insurance policies exclude psychiatric conditions in general, while some exclude eating disorders specifically. Other health insurance policies only cover a small portion of expenses for procedures that are deemed "medically necessary" or establish low daily payment limits that are insufficient for inpatient treatment. The denial of insurance coverage leaves countless eating disorder patients not only fighting for recovery, but also battling with insurance companies to obtain reimbursement for medical costs.

Why Eating Disorder Treatment Should Be Covered

Advocates for people with eating disorders make a number of arguments for covering treatment costs in health insurance policies. They point out, for instance, that federal mental health parity laws require insurance plans to provide the same coverage limits for mental health

"Insurance Coverage for Eating Disorders Treatment," © 2016 Omnigraphics, Inc. Reviewed March 2016.

benefits as for other medical conditions. Anorexia nervosa is one of the deadliest forms of mental illness, with a mortality rate of up to 10 percent, so denying patients access to treatment can affect their very survival.

Advocates also note that early diagnosis and intervention can significantly reduce the long-term cost of treatment and improve the chances of recovery for people with eating disorders. Studies of patients with bulimia nervosa have shown that 80 percent of patients recover when they begin treatment within five years of symptoms appearing, while only 20 percent recover when they begin treatment after experiencing fifteen years of symptoms. Insurance coverage increases the likelihood that people with eating disorders will seek medical treatment promptly.

Eating disorder treatment is a long, intensive process that must be administered in stages to address the complex medical and psychiatric components of the illness. Yet research has shown that a full course of specialized treatment is cost-effective in the long run, because shortening the length of treatment reduces successful outcomes and increases readmissions. Some insurance providers insist that patients be discharged from inpatient treatment programs as soon as their weight or body mass index (BMI) reaches a certain target figure, even though many other factors determine the severity of an eating disorder and the effectiveness of treatment.

Although the costs associated with treating eating disorders are high, effective treatment helps patients avoid many indirect costs associated with long-term health complications and disabilities. Eating disorders can compromise patients' physical and emotional health to the point that they cannot hold jobs or be productive members of society. In addition, untreated eating disorders can contribute to the development of expensive, ongoing medical problems such as depression, substance abuse, dehydration, electrolyte imbalance, osteoporosis, organ damage, cognitive losses, gastrointestinal problems, and cardiac arrest.

Tips for Obtaining Insurance Coverage

Obtaining insurance coverage for eating disorder treatment, or contesting the denial of coverage, can be a complicated and frustrating process. But it is vital for patients to receive all the healthcare benefits to which they are entitled in order to gain access to life-saving treatments and make a full recovery. The following tips can help patients and their advocates navigate the process of obtaining insurance coverage:

- Read your health insurance policy and understand the coverage and benefits it provides before beginning treatment. Employers and insurance providers are required to provide subscribers with copies of their policy upon request. Get advice from a doctor's office or an attorney if you have trouble understanding what is covered. It may also be helpful to become familiar with applicable federal and state laws relating to health insurance coverage and mental health parity.

- Keep records of all communication with doctors, therapists, treatment centers, and insurance representatives, including detailed notes on every telephone conversation and copies of all email messages, written correspondence, and receipts. Ask healthcare professionals to provide reports or letters explaining why specific treatments are medically necessary and why specific facility choices are appropriate.

- Follow the medical advice of your treatment team and do not allow the insurance provider to make healthcare determinations for you. Although eating disorder treatment can be very costly, it is important to remain in treatment even if your insurance company denies coverage. In order to pursue legal action to recover unpaid benefits, you must continue treatment and pay out of pocket. Some treatment providers are willing to negotiate a reduction in fees during the insurance appeal process.

- If your insurance company denies coverage, find out the reason for the denial and get it in writing. Appeal the decision immediately by phone and by sending a letter to the provider's medical director. Explain the medical necessity of treatment and provide documentation to support your claims. Although the appeal process can be complicated and stressful, remember that a denial of coverage is not the final word.

- If your appeal is not resolved to your satisfaction, seek assistance from an attorney. Sometimes a letter from a law firm is enough to get the attention of an insurance company. Also consider contacting the state insurance or consumer rights commission, your legislators, or the local media and asking for support.

- If no health insurance coverage is available, seek treatment from alternative sources that may offer services at a reduced cost, such as community mental health agencies, university medical schools, or government-funded clinics. Also inquire about free clinical trials and research programs available through such organizations as the National Institute of Mental Health, the Academy of Eating Disorders, or the American Academy of Child and Adolescent Psychiatry.

References

1. Andersen, Arnold. "How to Fight Insurance Discrimination?" National Association of Anorexia Nervosa and Related Disorders, 2016.

2. Teicher, Rachel. "What You Should Know about Insurance Coverage and Eating Disorder Treatment." Eating Disorder Hope, June 5, 2013.

Part Six

Preventing Eating Disorders and Achieving a Healthy Weight

Chapter 37

Eating Disorder Prevention

Contributing Factors and Prevention

National Eating Disorders Association (NEDA) offers many programs and efforts designed to prevent the occurrence of eating disorders before they begin, as well as programs designed to promote the early identification and treatment of eating disorders.

Eating disorders are complex conditions that arise from a combination of long-standing behavioral, biological, emotional, psychological, interpersonal, and social factors. While eating disorders are sometimes associated solely with food and weight preoccupations, they are complex diseases with a variety of causes. Those suffering from them may try to use food and the control of food to cope with feelings and emotions that may otherwise seem overwhelming. For some, dieting, bingeing and purging may begin as a way to cope with painful emotions and to feel in control of one's life.

Ultimately, though, these behaviors will damage a person's physical and emotional health, self-esteem and sense of competence and control. Scientists and researchers are still learning about the underlying causes of these emotionally and physically damaging conditions. There is general agreement, however, around some of the issues that may contribute to the development of an eating disorder. NEDA acknowledges that there may be a difference of opinion among experts and in the literature on this topic, and we encourage readers to explore the topic further, using all reliable sources available to them.

What Is Prevention and Does It Work?

Prevention is any systematic attempt to change the circumstances that promote, initiate, sustain or intensify problems like eating disorders. Eating disorders arise from a variety of physical, emotional and social issues, all of which must be addressed for effective prevention and treatment. Prevention efforts may involve reducing negative risk factors, such as body dissatisfaction, depression or basing self-esteem on appearance; or increasing protective factors, such as a non-appearance-oriented self-definition and replacing dieting and body snarking with intuitive eating and appreciation for the body's functionality.

What are Prevention Programs?

Prevention programs are systems and trainings developed in order to prevent eating disorder onset in a population. Prevention programs vary based on the size and nature of the group for whom the programming is intended. The Mental Health Intervention Spectrum, developed by the National Academy of Sciences, classifies different types of prevention programs according to their goals, methods and audiences:

Universal prevention: Designed to change public policy, institutions and normative cultural attitudes and practices. The aim is to prevent the development of eating disorders in large groups with varying degrees of risk (e.g., all adolescents in New York). Universal prevention may involve education, policy or legal action, and other environmental and larger social actions.

Selective prevention: Intended to prevent eating disorders by targeting individuals who do not yet have symptoms of a disorder and are at risk for an eating disorder due to biological, psychological or sociocultural factors (e.g., girls aged 10 to 13 who are facing puberty, experience sociocultural pressure for thinness and have a parent with a history of an eating disorder). Selective prevention typically involves multisession, interactive curriculum.

Indicated / targeted prevention: Targets people who are at high risk due to warning signs (e.g., mild eating disorder symptoms) and/or clear risk factors (e.g., high levels of body dissatisfaction). The audience does not yet have an eating disorder. The goal is to stop the development of a serious problem and is aimed at the individual, rather than at effecting change in social policies, systems or interpersonal behavior. Indicated prevention overlaps with traditional steps of clinical treatment: case identification to intervention to aftercare.

What Can You Do to Help Prevent Eating Disorders?

There are many studies evaluating a variety of eating disorders and disordered eating prevention programs. Some of the major findings are:

General Findings

- Prevention programs can alter knowledge, attitudes and behaviors associated with eating disorders and disordered eating.

- Various programs have successfully discouraged the development of eating problems in children, adolescents and young adults.

- Much more research is needed concerning prevention.

Findings on Program Types

- Universal, selective and indicated/targeted prevention programs have enjoyed some success, though targeted programs may have had more success. Universal prevention is often difficult to research due to its focus on large-scale policy and normative attitudinal changes.

- There is particularly good evidence that targeted programs using a social learning theory, cognitive behavioral, media literacy and cognitive dissonance approaches are effective with adolescents and young adult women from various ethnic groups.

- The cognitive dissonance approach encourages girls and women to question the media and cultural messages by asking them to speak out against the thin ideal or other eating disorder risk factors through verbal, written and behavioral exercises. The conflict between one's beliefs and actions creates psychological discomfort, motivating the individual to change their beliefs to match their actions.

- Programs that have shown some success include, but are not limited to, programs that adopt an ecological approach, involving not only individual change but also changing the environment of teacher and peer behavior; media literacy programs; and programs that emphasize health.

We can all be advocates for eating disorders prevention: taking steps to educate ourselves and others, challenging the notion that there's a 'right' way to look and spreading the word about eating disorders can be powerful actions with far-reaching effects.

Educate Yourself

- Learn all you can about anorexia nervosa, bulimia nervosa, binge eating disorder and other specified feeding or eating disorder (OSFED). Genuine awareness will help you avoid judgmental or mistaken attitudes about food, weight, body shape and eating disorders.

- Avoid categorizing foods as "good/safe" vs. "bad/dangerous." Remember, we all need to eat a balanced variety of foods.

Challenge the Thin Ideal

- Choose to challenge the false belief that thinness, weight loss and/or muscularity are desirable, while body fat and weight gain are shameful or indicate laziness, worthlessness or immorality.

- Avoid attitudes or actions that communicate, "I will like you better if you lose weight, don't eat so much or change your body shape."

- Discourage the idea that a particular diet, weight or body size will automatically lead to happiness and fulfillment.

- Decide to avoid judging others and yourself on the basis of body weight or shape. Turn off the voices in your head that tell you that a person's body weight or muscularity says anything about their character, personality or value as a person.

Talk about It

- Be a model of healthy self-esteem and body image. Recognize that others pay attention and learn from the way you talk about yourself and your body. Choose to talk about yourself with respect and appreciation. Choose to value yourself based on your goals, accomplishments, talents and character. Refrain from letting the way you feel about your body weight and shape determine the course of your day. Embrace the natural diversity of human bodies and celebrate your body's unique shape and size.

- If you think someone has an eating disorder, express your concerns in a forthright, caring manner. Gently but firmly encourage the person to seek trained professional help.

Take Action!

- Become a critical viewer of the media and its messages about self-esteem and body image. Talk back to the television when you hear a comment or see an image that promotes a certain body ideal at all costs. Rip out (or better yet, write to the editor about) advertisements or articles in magazines that make you feel bad about your body shape or size.

- Support local and national nonprofit eating disorders organizations—like the National Eating Disorders Association—by volunteering your time or giving a tax-deductible donation.

Personal Prevention Toolkit

Losing the 3Ds: Dieting, Drive for Thinness and Body Dissatisfaction

The '3Ds' are dieting, drive for thinness and body dissatisfaction—unhealthy actions and ideals that are often communicated to us and internalized from a young age. Once internalized, we may inadvertently perpetuate the cycle by passing those same ideals onto others—including children, students, patients and communities. This harmful cycle can be stopped before disordered thinking turns into disordered eating; shedding the 3Ds and encouraging a happy and healthy relationship with your body are vital tools in eating disorders prevention. NEDA's recommendations on how to curb disordered thinking—and how to avoid passing those messages to others—were developed by Michael Levine, PhD, Paula Levine, PhD, and Linda Smolak, PhD. Please note that these tips are intended to adjust mindsets in order to prevent the spread of unhealthy attitudes and beliefs. If you or someone you know is struggling with an eating disorder, please seek individualized professional guidance.

Changing Your Thinking

- Examine your own attitudes, beliefs, prejudices and behaviors about food, weight, body image, physical appearance, health and exercise. Identify any unhealthy attitudes derived from dieting, drive for thinness and body dissatisfaction. Try to change these attitudes in your everyday life—for example, if you edit photos of yourself before posting them on social media, consider why you do so, how you feel when you do it, and what message you're communicating to yourself and others. Honestly examining your thoughts and feelings is the first step to replacing unhealthy attitudes with healthy ones.

- Mindful eating and healthy physical activity are part of a well-rounded lifestyle. Assess your eating and exercise habits; strive for balance and moderation over extreme measures.

- Encourage balanced eating of a variety of foods in moderation. Don't treat food as a reward or punishment; such behaviors set food up as a potential weapon for control. Discourage the idea that a particular diet or body size will lead to happiness and fulfillment. Encourage eating in response to body hunger. Allow all foods in your home.

- Don't constantly criticize your own shape (e.g., "I'm so fat—I've got to lose weight."). This type of self-criticism implies that appearance is more important than character, and that there is always room to 'improve' one's appearance. Promote and celebrate body positivity.

Modeling Healthy Attitudes for Young People

- Set a positive example of a healthy and balanced relationship with food. Don't talk about or behave as if you are constantly dieting; encourage eating a broad variety of foods in response to body hunger. Don't equate food with positive or negative behavior. The dieting parent who says she was "good" today because she didn't "eat much" teaches that eating is bad, and that avoiding food is good. Similarly, "don't eat that—it will make you fat" teaches that being fat makes one unlikable. Learn about and discuss with your sons and daughters the dangers of trying to alter their body shape through dieting. Trust your children's appetites; never try to limit their caloric intake—unless requested to do so by a physician for a medical problem.

- Help children accept and enjoy their bodies and encourage physical activity. Love, accept, acknowledge, appreciate and value your children—out loud—no matter what they weigh. Convey to children that weight and appearance are not the most critical aspects of their identity and self-worth. Do not communicate the message that you cannot dance, swim, wear shorts, or enjoy a summer picnic because you do not look a certain way or weigh a certain amount. Notice often and in a complimentary way how varied people are—how they come in all colors, shapes, and sizes. Show appreciation for diversity and a respect for nature. Link respect for diversity in weight and shape with respect for diversity in race, gender, ethnicity, intelligence, etc. Educate your children about the existence, the experience and the ugliness of prejudice and oppression—whether it is directed against people of color or people who are overweight.

- Devote yourself to raising non-sex-stereotyped children by modeling and living gender equality. Develop a historical perspective on the politics of the control of women's bodies. Work toward and speak out for women's rights: to fair pay, to safety, to respect, and to control of their bodies. Demonstrate a respect for women as they age, in order to work against the cultural glorification of youth and a tightly controlled ideal body type. Take women seriously for what they say, feel and do, and focus less on the way they look. Give boys and girls the same opportunities and encouragement (in assignment of chores, choosing a sport, etc.) and avoid restricting children to gender-specific activities (boys can enjoy cooking and girls can fix cars). Remain close to and supportive of your sons and daughters as they experiment and struggle with body image, grooming and cosmetic issues, flirtatiousness and sexuality, etc. Talk to your sons and daughters about the way body shape and sexuality are manipulated by the media and the struggle their brothers, sisters, boyfriends or girlfriends have in trying to conform or not to conform.

- Build self-esteem. The most important gift adults can give children is self-esteem. When adults show children that they value and love them unconditionally, children can withstand the perils of childhood and adolescence with fewer scars and traumas. Self-esteem is a universal vaccine that can immunize a youngster from eating problems, body image distortion, exercise abuse, and many other problems. Providing self-esteem is the responsibility of both parents. Girls especially need support and validation from their fathers.

- Encourage children to talk openly and honestly and really listen to them. Encourage open communication and teach children how to communicate. Recognize that sociocultural pressures

289

surrounding drugs, sexuality, body image and perfectionism require great character strength, self-assurance and decision-making in young children. Let them know that their opinions and feelings are valued. Encouraging young people to assert themselves helps them say no to pressures to conform. Feeling loved and confident allows them to accept that they are unique individuals.

- Encourage critical thinking. The only sure antidote to the tendency to conform to the powerful seduction of the media and peer pressure is the ability to think critically. Become a critical consumer of the media—pay attention to and openly challenge media messages. Talk with your children about the pressures they see, hear, and feel to diet and to "look good." Parents have to encourage critical thinking early, and educators have to continue the mission. We need to teach kids how to think, not what to think, and to encourage them to disagree, challenge, brainstorm alternatives, etc. Girls especially need to learn that men are not the ultimate authorities and that they themselves have something important to contribute.

- Develop a value system based on internal values. Help children understand the importance of equating personal worth with care and concern for others, wisdom, loyalty, fairness, self-care and self-respect, personal fulfillment, curiosity, self-awareness, the capacity for relationships, connectedness and intimacy, individuality, confidence, assertiveness, a sense of humor, ambition, motivation, etc. Model this value system; examine, explore, and, if necessary, modify any appearance expectations you have about your child or the children you work with (e.g., 'will she grow up to be pretty?').

- Teach children about good relationships and how to deal with difficulties when they arise. Males and females alike may use food to express or numb themselves instead of dealing with difficult feelings or relationships. Because of messages that suggest that the perfect body will dissolve all relationship problems, young people often put energy into changing their bodies instead of their feelings or their relationships.

- Be aware of some of the warning signs of eating disorders. Understand that these warning signs can appear before puberty. Watch for: refusing typical family meals, skipping meals, comments about self and others like "I'm too fat; she's too fat," clothes shopping that becomes stressful, withdrawal from friends, irritability and depression, or any signs of extreme dieting, bingeing or purging.

- Educate your community about the risks of the 3Ds and the dangers of eating disorders. At the same time, be careful not to promote or teach young people how to become eating disordered.

Listen to Your Body

When was the last time you truly had fun dieting? Most likely you won't remember it as a pleasurable experience. After all, it doesn't feel so great to get hungry for lunch but force yourself to wait an extra hour. Do you remember feeling irritable? Did you get a headache or feel your stomach growling? The reason strict diets don't work and aren't much fun is because your body needs food for energy, just like a car needs gas to drive. Food is fuel for your body! Your body knows what it needs in order to keep running efficiently—it needs the fuel of vitamin and nutrient-rich foods from a variety of food groups. That's why it's important to listen to your body and respond to its natural hunger. It will tell you what it needs. And if you don't listen, it will find ways to keep reminding you—like headaches, a growling stomach and obsessing about food.

Three Keys to Listening to Your Body

- **The first key to listening to your body is being able to detect when you are getting hungry.** If you are indeed truly hungry, and not just looking for food to cure your boredom, stress or loneliness, then it is time to refuel.

- **The second key is being able to know when you have had enough.** Listen to your body. When you begin to feel full, you will know that you have had enough to eat. The goal is to feel content—not uncomfortably stuffed but not starving either. For some people this means planning five or six smaller, well-balanced meals a day instead of three large meals. And remember, it takes about 20 minutes for your body to realize it's full. Be aware of what you are eating—eat sitting down, chew slowly, and enjoy the tastes, smells, and textures of your food.

- **The third key is moderation, nothing to extremes.** Often people hear this advice and think it means they can eat whatever they crave, all the time. Obviously we cannot survive on potato chips or peanut butter cookies alone. And if you tried, chances are you'd probably start to crave a balanced meal or fresh fruit or vegetables after awhile. These cravings are your body's way of helping you get the nutrients it knows you need.

- **Eat what you want, when you are truly hungry. Stop when you're full.** And eat exactly what appeals to you. Do this instead of any diet, and you're likely to maintain a healthy weight and avoid eating disorders.

Chapter 38

Promoting Positive Self-Esteem

Chapter Contents

Section 38.1

What Is Self-Esteem?

This section includes text excerpted from "Self-Esteem,"
U.S. Department of Veterans Affairs (VA), July 2013.

- Self-esteem is a way of thinking, feeling, and acting that implies that you accept, respect, and believe in yourself.

- When you accept yourself, you are okay with both the good and not so good things about yourself.

- When you respect yourself, you treat yourself well in much the same way you would treat someone else you respect.

- To believe in yourself means that you feel you deserve to have the good things in life. It also means that you have confidence that you can make choices and take actions that will have a positive effect on your life.

- Part of self-esteem is knowing that you are important enough to take good care of yourself by making good choices for yourself. For example, choosing nutritious food for your body, exercising, giving yourself time to relax, etc.

- Self-esteem doesn't mean you think you are better or more important than other people are, it means that you respect and value yourself as much as other people.

- Self-esteem needs to come from within and not be dependent on external sources such as material possessions, your status, or approval from others.

- Having self-esteem also means you don't have to put other people down to feel good about yourself.

Self-Esteem

- Self-esteem is a way of thinking, feeling, and acting that implies that you accept, respect, and believe in yourself.

- When you accept yourself, you are okay with both the good and not so good things about yourself.

- When you respect yourself, you treat yourself well in much the same way you would treat someone else you respect.

- To believe in yourself means that you feel you deserve to have the good things in life. It also means that you have confidence that you can make choices and take actions that will have a positive effect on your life.

- Part of self-esteem is knowing that you are important enough to take good care of yourself by making good choices for yourself. For example, choosing nutritious food for your body, exercising, giving yourself time to relax, etc.

- Self-esteem doesn't mean you think you are better or more important than other people are, it means that you respect and value yourself as much as other people.

- Self-esteem needs to come from within and not be dependent on external sources such as material possessions, your status, or approval from others.

- Having self-esteem also means you don't have to put other people down to feel good about yourself.

Signs of Low and High Self-Esteem

Signs of low self-esteem

- Lack of confidence
- Negative view of life
- Perfectionistic attitude
- Mistrusting others inappropriately
- Blaming behavior
- Fear of taking appropriate risks
- Feelings of being unloved and unlovable
- Dependence on others to make decisions
- Fear of being ridiculed

Signs of high self-esteem

- Confidence

- Self-direction

- Non-blaming behavior

- Awareness of personal strengths

- Ability to make mistakes and learn from them

- Ability to accept mistakes from others

- Optimism

- Ability to solve problems

- Independent and cooperative attitude

- Feeling comfortable with a wide range of emotions

- Ability to appropriately trust others

- Good sense of personal limitations

- Ability to set boundaries and say no

- Good self-care

Causes of Low Self-Esteem

Nobody is born with low self-esteem; it's something that is learned. It is the result of filtering opinions, comments, looks, suggestions, and actions of those around us through a person's own feelings and self-image.

Some possible early causes of low self-esteem:

- Overly critical parents (never good enough, feelings of inferiority or self-criticism)

- Significant childhood losses (abandonment, insecurity)

- Parental abuse, alcoholism, neglect, or rejection (unreliable family atmosphere resulting in lack of trust, insecurity, inadequacy or worthlessness, anger, guilt, denying feelings)

- Parental overprotectiveness (lack of confidence)

- Parental overindulgence (feelings of being cheated and insecure because life does not continue to provide what they learnt to expect as a child)

Some possible later contributors to low self-esteem:

- Negative or controlling personal relationships

- Negative experiences on the job

- Messages from society

- Even if low self-esteem had its roots in childhood, you can learn to identify and challenge the assumptions you consciously or unconsciously have about yourself.

- Take notice of and become more consciously aware of your needs.

- Acknowledge the importance of self-nurturing and self-care activities and take appropriate steps in that direction.

- Recognize and take pride in your accomplishments.

- Focus on problem solving.

Section 38.2

Developing Your Self-Esteem

This section includes text excerpted from "Boost Your Self-Esteem and Self-Confidence," Office on Women's Health (OWH), January 7, 2015.

Boost Your Self-Esteem and Self-Confidence

Do you want to feel better about yourself? You can learn how to build self-esteem and raise your self-confidence. Try these tips:

- Check out new activities. You'll feel proud for stretching your wings. Does trying something new on your own seem too scary? Maybe see if a friend will go along.

- Be your own BFF. Make a list of things you love about you. Are you friendly, funny, creative, or hard-working, for example?

- Celebrate your successes. Try to really enjoy your achievements. Record them in a journal, tell your friends, or hang up pictures or other reminders.

- Tell your inner critic to be quiet. If you have a mean thought about yourself, see if you can change it to something positive instead. For example, if you think, "I'm dumb," try remembering a time you did something smart.

- Don't compare yourself to others. Someone else may have tons of online friends or a "great" body. But everyone has strengths and weaknesses.

- Practice being assertive. Try to express your thoughts, opinions, and needs. It feels great to know you can speak up for yourself! (Of course, you want to do this without stomping on other people's feelings.)

- Find ways to feel like you're contributing. It feels great to help. You might do chores at home or volunteer in your community.

- Set realistic goals. Aim for a goal that you think you can reach. Then make a plan for how to get there. If you pick something very hard, you may get frustrated and quit.

- Forgive yourself when you fail. Nobody is perfect. The important thing is to learn from your mistakes. And it's good to know you can pick yourself up and keep going!

- Find true friends. Hang out with people who make you feel good about yourself. Real friends like you for you.

- Honor your background. It can be great to feel proud of who you are and where you come from.

If you try working on your self-esteem for a while and still don't feel good about yourself, reach out for help. Talk to a parent or guardian, doctor, school counselor, school nurse, teacher, or other trusted adult. An adult may be able to suggest other things you can try, and it may help just to talk about how you're feeling. Also, sometimes low self-esteem can increase your risk for depression and other emotional problems. An adult you trust could help you get treatment if you need it.

Chapter 39

Promoting a Healthy Body Image

Chapter Contents

Section 39.1

The ABC's of Positive Body Image

This section includes text excerpted from "The ABC's of Positive Body Image," U.S. Department of Health and Human Services (HHS), November 30, 2012. Reviewed March 2016.

Feeling comfortable in your own skin can be difficult. And because your body goes through changes throughout your life, learning to appreciate and accept your body can be a lifelong process. It's important to remember that even if you are able to lose the weight you want to lose, this may not lead you to body image bliss.

Having a more positive body image involves seeing yourself as a whole person (not just how you look or how much you weigh) and learning to accept, appreciate, and even love the parts that you wish were different. This can be a challenge, but you can take charge of how you feel about yourself by creating a more positive body image:

- **A**ppreciate your body
- **B**e aware of when you compare
- **C**reate a positive environment

Appreciate Your Body

Our culture focuses so much on how our bodies look that we sometimes lose sight of what our bodies do. Our bodies allow us to do amazing things every day. Not sure what counts as "amazing"?

Check this out:

- **Getting around and doing stuff.**

  Think about the things that your body allows you to do every day. Whether you are cooking a meal, helping a friend get settled in their new place, or changing a flat tire, your body helps you carry out your daily activities and do the things you want to do. Remember to appreciate all the "little things" your body helps you do every day.

- **Your body as repair shop.**

  Your body has an amazing capacity to heal. From everyday cuts and bruises to more serious injuries, our bodies can recover from all kinds of things without us doing anything. And, even when our bodies need medicines or other treatments to help us heal, they still manage to keep everything going while we recover.

- **The power of touch.**

  Whether you're giving your main squeeze a quick kiss, giving a friend a comforting pat, or greeting your kids with a hug, your touch is powerful! Research shows that touch helps lower blood pressure, soothe anxiety, and release feel-good hormones. Your body does that!

Focusing on the powerful things your body can do is one way to break the cycle of negative body image.

Be Aware of When You Compare

One of the keys to building a positive body image is to be aware of when—and to whom—you compare your body. Whether you compare yourself to your best friend, a stranger in a store, a woman in a magazine, or to your 20-something self, it can be tough to see your own beauty when you're focused on others.

People often think "if I just looked like her" or "if I just was more like my old self," I would feel better and others would give me more attention. Remember that one of the most attractive things to others is self-confidence. And self-confidence comes from being proud of who you are no matter what shape or size you are.

Being aware of when you compare yourself is an important part of creating a more positive body image. Another important step is to be kind to, not critical of, yourself. Quieting those judgments starts with you!

Create a Positive Environment

Family, friends, coworkers, and others who you interact with can affect how you feel about yourself. This includes how you feel about your body. So, one of the keys to creating a more positive body image is to create a more positive environment for yourself by focusing on:

- **Surrounding yourself with positive relationships.**

Part of creating a positive environment is surrounding yourself with people who support you, especially when you're struggling with your body image, staying smokefree, or other parts of your life. This also means spending less time with the people who make you feel bad about yourself.

- **Finding what you enjoy.**

Whether it's a new dance workout, volunteering with a local charity, or starting a book club with a small group of close friends, having activities in your life that are fun and that you value is another way to create a positive environment for yourself. When you're enjoying life, you will have less time to focus on negative thoughts about how you look.

- **Helping others to find their strength and beauty.**

How can you help others to appreciate their bodies? Whether it's shifting your focus to feeling better—and not just looking better—or thinking about the amazing things our bodies do, creating a positive environment for others can be another way to create a positive environment for yourself.

Section 39.2

Promoting Positive Body Image in Children: A Guide for Parents

This section contains text excerpted from the following sources: Text beginning with the heading "Your Body Image Plays a Role in Theirs" is excerpted from "Body Image and Your Kids: Your Body Image Plays a Role in Theirs," U.S. Department of Health and Human Services (HHS), June 19, 2012. Reviewed March 2016; Text beginning with the heading "Encouraging a Healthy Body Image" is excerpted from "Encouraging a Healthy Body Image," © 1995–2016. The Nemours Foundation/KidsHealth®. Reprinted with permission.

Your Body Image Plays a Role in Theirs

"On a diet, you can't eat." That is what one 5-year-old girl had to say in a study on girls' ideas about dieting. This and other research have shown that daughters are more likely to have ideas about dieting when their mothers diet. Children pick up on comments about dieting concepts that may seem harmless, such as limiting high-fat foods or eating less. Yet, as girls enter their teen years, having ideas about dieting can lead to problems. Many things can spark weight concerns for girls and impact their eating habits in potentially unhealthy ways:

- Having mothers concerned about their own weight
- Having mothers who are overly concerned about their daughters' weight and looks
- Natural weight gain and other body changes during puberty
- Peer pressure to look a certain way
- Struggles with self-esteem
- Media images showing the ideal female body as thin

Many teenage girls of average weight think they are overweight and are not satisfied with their bodies. Having extreme weight concerns—and acting on those concerns—can harm girls' social, physical, and emotional growth. Actions such as skipping meals or taking diet pills can lead to poor nutrition and difficulty learning. For some, extreme efforts to lose weight can lead to eating disorders such as anorexia or bulimia. For others, the pressure to be thin can actually lead to binge eating disorder: overeating that is followed by extreme guilt. What's more, girls are more likely to further risk their health by trying to lose weight in unhealthy ways, such as smoking.

Although not as common, boys are also at risk of developing unhealthy eating habits and eating disorders. Body image becomes an important issue for teenage boys as they struggle with body changes and pay more attention to media images of the "ideal" muscular male.

Help Your Child Have a Healthy Body Image

Your children pay attention to what you say and do—even if it doesn't seem like it sometimes. If you are always complaining about your weight or feel pressure to change your body shape, your children may learn that these are important concerns. If you are attracted to new "miracle" diets, they may learn that restrictive dieting is better than making healthy lifestyle choices. If you tell your daughter that she would be prettier if she lost weight, she will learn that the goals of weight loss are to be attractive and accepted by others.

Parents are role models and should try to follow the healthy eating and physical activity patterns that you would like your children to follow—for your health and theirs. Extreme weight concerns and eating disorders, as well as obesity, are hard to treat. Yet, you can play an important role in preventing these problems for your children.

Follow these steps to help your child develop a positive body image and relate to food in a healthy way:

- Make sure your child understands that weight gain is a normal part of development, especially during puberty.

- Avoid negative statements about food, weight, and body size and shape.

- Allow your child to make decisions about food, while making sure that plenty of healthy and nutritious meals and snacks are available.

- Compliment your child on her or his efforts, talents, accomplishments, and personal values.

- Restrict television viewing, and watch television with your child and discuss the media images you see.

- Encourage your school to enact policies against size and sexual discrimination, harassment, teasing, and name-calling; support the elimination of public weigh-ins and fat measurements.

- Keep the communication lines with your child open.

Encouraging a Healthy Body Image

It seems like just yesterday that you had to coax your daughter to bathe. But then she turned 11 and started spending hours in the bathroom and sizing herself up in every mirror she passes. She seems consumed by her looks. What happened? And is it healthy?

As they approach the teen years, it's common and natural for kids to become more interested in appearances—their own and others'—seemingly all of a sudden. Their bodies are going through some big changes as they grow and go through puberty. As preteens change physically, they become more aware of how they look.

Growing and puberty affect more than a preteen's outward appearance—body image is affected, too. Having a healthy body image means that most of your feelings, ideas, and opinions about your body and appearance are positive. It means accepting and appreciating your body and feeling mostly satisfied with your appearance.

Developing a healthy body image happens over time. It can be influenced by experiences and shaped by the opinions and feedback of others and by cultural messages.

Body Image and Appearance

Body image can be especially vulnerable during the preteen and teen years because appearances change so much and cultural messages that fuel dissatisfaction can be very strong. Being criticized or teased about appearance can be particularly hurtful at this age.

Preteens and teens often compare their looks with others' or with media images of the "right" way to look. In cultures where looks seem to matter so much—and ideal images are so unrealistic—it's all too common to be dissatisfied with some aspect of appearance.

But feeling too self-critical about appearance can interfere with body image. And poor body image can hurt a teen's overall self-image, too.

Beyond Appearances

As teens mature mentally and emotionally, they will develop a more complex self-image—one that incorporates their interests, talents, unique qualities, values, aspirations, and relationships. But during the early teen years, the image they see in the mirror makes up a big part of their self-image.

And while it's true that appearance isn't everything, feeling satisfied with appearance means a lot. If you're wondering why your child suddenly seems so focused on appearance, keep in mind that preteens are:

- **Adapting to a new reflection.** Spending extra time grooming, making comparisons with friends and celebrities, and experimenting with clothing, hair, and makeup can be ways of getting to know and like the new self reflected in the mirror.

- **Making a fashion statement.** When preteens and teens express their taste in clothes and hairstyles, they're making statements about themselves. Experimenting with and defining their styles is one way to express their interests, personality, independence, and identity.

- **Finding a way to belong.** Peers, groups, and cliques—which take center stage during the teen years—can also play a role in heightening young teens' concerns about appearances. Dressing a certain way might be a way of feeling included, fitting in, standing out, or belonging to a group of peers.

Boys and Body Image

It's not just girls who become focused on appearance. Boys might not be as vocal about it, but they can worry just as much about their looks. They may spend the same amount of time in front of the mirror, weighing where to part their hair, what kind of product to use, assessing acne, and deciding whether or not to shave. And when your son emerges wearing pants that sag as if he hasn't quite finished getting dressed, he may in fact have spent hours getting them to hang at that exact angle.

Self-Critical Feelings

Feeling satisfied with appearance isn't always easy. Many kids who have positive body images become self-conscious or self-critical as they enter the teen years. It's not uncommon for preteens and teens to express dissatisfaction about their appearance or to compare themselves with their friends, celebrities, or people they see in ads.

Our culture emphasizes the need to look just right. Ads for everything from makeup and hair products to clothing and toothpaste send messages that people need to look a certain way to be happy. It's hard not to be influenced by that.

You might hear your son or daughter fret about anything from height and hair to the shape of their nose or the size of their ears—any aspect that doesn't match the "ideal."

Body shape and size can concern them, too. It's important for preteens or teens to eat nutritious foods, limit junk foods, and get plenty of physical activity, but it's not advisable for them to diet. Being overly concerned about weight, restricting food, or exercising excessively can be signs of an eating disorder. Talk to your doctor if you notice any of these signs in your kids.

Self-criticism that seems constant or excessive or causes daily distress that lasts might signal an extreme body image problem known as body dysmorphic disorder. This condition involves obsessions and compulsions about slight or imagined imperfections in appearance.

A Natural Transition

In most cases, the focus on appearance is a very natural and common part of becoming a teenager. Usually, these expressions of frustration clear up quickly and don't warrant concern—just plenty of patience, empathy, support, and perspective from parents.

Still, parents can be frustrated when looks seem to matter so much to kids. It can be a delicate balance to help preteens feel confident and satisfied with their looks while encouraging them not to be overly concerned with the superficial. It's important to encourage teens to take pride in their appearance but also to emphasize the deeper qualities that matter more.

Boosting Body Image

As preteens try on different looks, parents can help by being accepting and supportive, providing positive messages, and encouraging other qualities that keep looks in perspective. Be sure to:

- **Accept and understand.** Recognize that being concerned about looks is as much a part of the teen years as a changing voice and learning to shave. You know that in the grand scheme of things your daughter's freckles don't matter, but to her they might seem critical. As frustrating as it can be when they hog the bathroom, avoid criticizing kids for being concerned about appearances. As they grow, concern about their looks will stop dominating their lives.

- **Give lots of compliments.** Provide reassurance about kids' looks *and* about all their other important qualities. As much as they may seem not to notice or care, simple statements like "you've got the most beautiful smile" or "that shirt looks great on you" really do matter. Compliment them on other physical attributes, such as strength, speed, balance, energy, or grace. Appreciating physical qualities and capabilities helps build a healthy body image.

- **Compliment what's inside too.** Notice out loud all the personal qualities that you love about your kids—how generous your son is to share with his little sister, the determined way that your daughter studies for her tests, or how your son stood by his best friend. Reassure them when they express insecurity. When you hear "I hate my hair" or "I'm so little," provide valuable counterpoint.

- **Talk about what appearances mean.** Guide your kids to think a little more deeply about appearances and how people express themselves. Talk about the messages that certain styles might convey. One outfit may send the message "I'm ready to party!" while others might say "I'm heading to school" or "I'm too lazy to do laundry."

- **Set reasonable boundaries.** Be patient, but also set boundaries on how much time your kids can spend on grooming and dressing. Tell them it's not OK to inconvenience others or let chores go. Limits help kids understand how to manage time, be considerate of others' needs, share resources, exercise a little self-discipline, and keep appearances in perspective.

- **Be a good role model.** How you talk about your own looks sets a powerful example. Constantly complaining about or fretting over your appearance teaches your kids to cast the same critical eye on themselves. Almost everyone is dissatisfied with certain elements of their appearance, but talk instead about what your body can *do*, not just how it looks. Instead of griping about how big your legs are, talk about how they're strong enough to help you hike up a mountain.

Having a healthy and positive body image means liking your body, appreciating it, and being grateful for its qualities and capabilities. When parents care for and appreciate their own bodies, they teach their kids to do the same.

Section 39.3

Body Image during Pregnancy: Loving Your Body at All Stages

This section contains text excerpted from the following sources:
Text beginning with the heading "How Pregnancy Can Affect Body
Image?" is excerpted from "Body Image," Office on Women's Health
(OWH), September 22, 2009. Reviewed March 2016; Remaining text
in this section is "Body Image: Learning to Love the New You," U.S.
Department of Health and Human Services (HHS), June 22, 2015.

How Pregnancy Can Affect Body Image

For some women, body image is a huge concern, especially during
pregnancy. Some women welcome their pregnant bodies, while others
are in complete shock over the different changes. Naturally, your body
is going to be different than it was before you were pregnant. Hormone fluctuations will cause your uterus to expand, your breasts to
grow, your feet to enlarge, and your skin to break out. You may suffer
increased fatigue and incredible food cravings. Let's not even mention
varicose veins and mood swings!

Loving your body before pregnancy can help you get through the
physical and emotional changes during pregnancy. Changing your body
image while you are pregnant is a pretty tough thing to do, especially
if it was already low to begin with. Here are some ideas to try and help
you love and accept your pregnant body:

- Take up prenatal yoga. Yoga focuses not on how your body looks,
  but on the link between your body and your mind.

- Practice self-massage. Touching your own body will help you to
  become more familiar and accepting of it.

- If you are really having serious issues, seek out mental health
  counseling.

The American Pregnancy Association suggests exercising as
a way to help you get your pre-pregnancy body back. Join a gym
that offers childcare or load up your stroller and walk through the

neighborhood. This will also help get you out of the house so you can feel refreshed.

Body Image: Learning to Love the New You

Your body goes through a lot of changes to accommodate your baby during and after pregnancy. These changes are natural and healthy, but they might affect the way you feel about your looks. Even if you didn't like your body before, recognize the great feat it has accomplished—it produced another human being!

Here are some ideas to help you love and accept your post-pregnancy body:

- **Concentrate on your baby.** Your body changed to help your baby grow and develop. It is a natural process.

- **Express your feelings.** Talk with your partner, family, or friends about how you are feeling. Don't keep your feelings bottled up.

- **Try to get out for some enjoyable exercise.** Physical activity helps improve your mood throughout the postpartum period.

- **Learn as much as you can about pregnancy and being a new mom.** By educating yourself, you will know what to expect and feel more in control.

Your body has to adjust and return to a non-pregnant body. Don't expect a flat belly after your delivery. Remember, your body has been through a lot in giving birth and needs time to recover.

Give yourself some time to rest, especially if being active doesn't feel good. Eat well, exercise when you can, and be good to yourself!

Section 39.4

Bullying and Body Image

This section contains text excerpted from the following sources: Text beginning with the heading "Bullying" is excerpted from "What Is Bullying?" U.S. Department of Health and Human Services (HHS), March 17, 2012. Reviewed March 2016; Remaining text in this section is "Bullying and Body Image," U.S. Department of Health and Human Services (HHS), July 1, 2013.

Bullying

Bullying is unwanted, aggressive behavior among school aged children that involves a real or perceived power imbalance. The behavior is repeated, or has the potential to be repeated, over time. Both kids who are bullied and who bully others may have serious, lasting problems.

In order to be considered bullying, the behavior must be aggressive and include:

- **An Imbalance of Power:** Kids who bully use their power—such as physical strength, access to embarrassing information, or popularity—to control or harm others. Power imbalances can change over time and in different situations, even if they involve the same people.

- **Repetition:** Bullying behaviors happen more than once or have the potential to happen more than once.

Bullying includes actions such as making threats, spreading rumors, attacking someone physically or verbally, and excluding someone from a group on purpose.

Types of Bullying

There are three types of bullying:
1. **Verbal bullying** is saying or writing mean things. Verbal bullying includes:
   - Teasing

- Name-calling
- Inappropriate sexual comments
- Taunting
- Threatening to cause harm

2. **Social bullying**, sometimes referred to as relational bullying, involves hurting someone's reputation or relationships. Social bullying includes:

- Leaving someone out on purpose
- Telling other children not to be friends with someone
- Spreading rumors about someone
- Embarrassing someone in public

3. **Physical bullying** involves hurting a person's body or possessions. Physical bullying includes:

- Hitting/kicking/pinching
- Spitting
- Tripping/pushing
- Taking or breaking someone's things
- Making mean or rude hand gestures

Where and When Bullying Happens?

Bullying can occur during or after school hours. While most reported bullying happens in the school building, a significant percentage also happens in places like on the playground or the bus. It can also happen travelling to or from school, in the youth's neighborhood, or on the Internet.

Frequency of Bullying

There are two sources of federally collected data on youth bullying:

- The 2010–2011 School Crime Supplement (National Center for Education Statistics and Bureau of Justice Statistics) indicates that, nationwide, 28% of students in grades 6–12 experienced bullying.

- The 2013 Youth Risk Behavior Surveillance System (Centers for Disease Control and Prevention) indicates that, nationwide, 20% of students in grades 9–12 experienced bullying.

Research on cyberbullying is growing. However, because kids' technology use changes rapidly, it is difficult to design surveys that accurately capture trends.

Bullying and Body Image

Although bullying can occur among individuals of any weight, overweight and underweight children tend to be at higher risk for bullying. Targets of verbal bullying based on weight, sometimes referred to as "weight teasing," can experience a number of negative consequences, including a change in body perception.

Weight teasing by both family and peers has been associated with high levels of anxiety and low self-esteem among adolescents. Having low self-esteem because of peer criticism can change an individual's body image. Body image is the positive or negative feelings you have about the way you look.

A study in the *Journal of Pediatric Psychology* found that adolescents teased about weight tended to have a body image that was more negative than those not teased because of weight. Victims of weight teasing who have a negative body image may be at a higher risk for developing unhealthy eating and exercising habits. This could lead to disorders such as anorexia, bulimia, or binge eating.

How Can You Encourage a Healthy Body Image among Adolescents?

- Promote healthy eating and exercise habits.

- Encourage adolescents not to compare themselves to their peers.

- Set a good example by not criticizing your own body or the bodies of others.

- Help victims of bullying boost self-esteem by focusing on their positive attributes.

- Encourage them to do the things they love. This boosts confidence and builds healthy friendships.

Chapter 40

Determining a Healthy Weight

Chapter Contents

315

Section 40.1

How to Assess Your Weight?

This section includes text excerpted from "Assessing Your Weight,"
Centers for Disease Control and Prevention (CDC), May 15, 2015.

A high amount of body fat can lead to weight-related diseases and
other health issues and being underweight can also put one at risk for
health issues. BMI and waist circumference are two measures that
can be used as screening tools to estimate weight status in relation
to potential disease risk. However, BMI and waist circumference are
not diagnostic tools for disease risks. A trained healthcare provider
should perform other health assessments in order to evaluate disease
risk and diagnose disease status.

How to Measure and Interpret Weight Status?

Adult Body Mass Index or BMI

Body Mass Index (BMI) is a person's weight in kilograms divided
by the square of height in meters. A high BMI can be an indicator of
high body fatness and having a low BMI can be an indicator of having
too low body fatness. BMI can be used as a screening tool but is not
diagnostic of the body fatness or health of an individual.

Determine your BMI by finding your height and weight in the BMI
Index Chart (www.nhlbi.nih.gov/health/educational/lose_wt/BMI/
bmi_tbl.htm).

- If your BMI is less than 18.5, it falls within the underweight
  range.

- If your BMI is 18.5 to 24.9, it falls within the normal or Healthy
  Weight range.

- If your BMI is 25.0 to 29.9, it falls within the overweight range.

- If your BMI is 30.0 or higher, it falls within the obese range.

Weight that is higher than what is considered as a healthy weight
for a given height is described as overweight or obese. Weight that is

lower than what is considered as healthy for a given height is described as underweight.

At an individual level, BMI can be used as a screening tool but is not diagnostic of the body fatness or health of an individual. A trained healthcare provider should perform appropriate health assessments in order to evaluate an individual's health status and risks.

How to Measure Height and Weight for BMI?

Height and weight must be measured in order to calculate BMI. It is most accurate to measure height in meters and weight in kilograms. However, the BMI formula has been adapted for height measured in inches and weight measured in pounds. These measurements can be taken in a healthcare provider's office, or at home using a tape measure and scale.

Waist Circumference

Another way to estimate your potential disease risk is to measure your waist circumference. Excessive abdominal fat may be serious because it places you at greater risk for developing obesity-related conditions, such as type 2 diabetes, high blood pressure, and coronary artery disease. Your waistline may be telling you that you have a higher risk of developing obesity-related conditions if you are:

- A man whose waist circumference is more than 40 inches

- A non-pregnant woman whose waist circumference is more than 35 inches

Waist circumference can be used as a screening tool but is not diagnostic of the body fatness or health of an individual. A trained healthcare provider should perform appropriate health assessments in order to evaluate an individual's health status and risks.

How to Measure Your Waist Circumference?

To correctly measure waist circumference:

- Stand and place a tape measure around your middle, just above your hipbones

- Make sure tape is horizontal around the waist

- Keep the tape snug around the waist, but not compressing the skin

- Measure your waist just after you breathe out

About Adult BMI

What Is BMI?

BMI is a person's weight in kilograms divided by the square of height in meters. BMI does not measure body fat directly, but research has shown that BMI is moderately correlated with more direct measures of body fat obtained from skinfold thickness measurements, bioelectrical impedance, densitometry (underwater weighing), dual-energy X-ray absorptiometry (DXA) and other methods. Furthermore, BMI appears to be as strongly correlated with various metabolic and disease outcome as are these more direct measures of body fatness. In general, BMI is an inexpensive and easy-to-perform method of screening for weight category, for example underweight, normal or healthy weight, overweight, and obesity.

How Is BMI Used?

A high BMI can be an indicator of high body fatness. BMI can be used as a screening tool but is not diagnostic of the body fatness or health of an individual.

To determine if a high BMI is a health risk, a healthcare provider would need to perform further assessments. These assessments might include skinfold thickness measurements, evaluations of diet, physical activity, family history, and other appropriate health screenings.

What Are the BMI Trends for Adults in the United States?

The prevalence of adult BMI greater than or equal to 30 kg/m^2 (obese status) has greatly increased since the 1970s. Recently, however, this trend has leveled off, except for older women. Obesity has continued to increase in adult women who are age 60 years and older.

Why Is BMI Used to Measure Overweight and Obesity?

BMI can be used for population assessment of overweight and obesity. Because calculation requires only height and weight, it is inexpensive and easy to use for clinicians and for the general public. BMI can be used as a screening tool for body fatness but is not diagnostic.

What Are Some of the Other Ways to Assess Excess Body Fatness Besides BMI?

Other methods to measure body fatness include skinfold thickness measurements (with calipers), underwater weighing, bioelectrical impedance, dual-energy X-ray absorptiometry (DXA), and isotope dilution. However, these methods are not always readily available, and they are either expensive or need to be conducted by highly trained personnel. Furthermore, many of these methods can be difficult to standardize across observers or machines, complicating comparisons across studies and time periods.

How Is BMI Calculated?

BMI is calculated the same way for both adults and children. The calculation is based on the following formulas:

Table 40.1. BMI Calculation

Measurement Units	Formula and Calculation
Kilograms and meters (or centimeters)	Formula: weight (kg) / [height (m)]^2 With the metric system, the formula for BMI is weight in kilograms divided by height in meters squared. Because height is commonly measured in centimeters, divide height in centimeters by 100 to obtain height in meters. Example: Weight = 68 kg, Height = 165 cm (1.65 m) Calculation: 68 ÷ (1.65)^2 = 24.98
Pounds and inches	Formula: weight (lb) / [height (in)]^2 x 703 Calculate BMI by dividing weight in pounds (lbs) by height in inches (in) squared and multiplying by a conversion factor of 703. Example: Weight = 150 lbs, Height = 5'5" (65") Calculation: [150 ÷ (65)^2] x 703 = 24.96

How Is BMI Interpreted for Adults?

For adults 20 years old and older, BMI is interpreted using standard weight status categories. These categories are the same for men and women of all body types and ages.

The standard weight status categories associated with BMI ranges for adults are shown in the following table.

Table 40.2. Weight Status Categories Associated with BMI

BMI	Weight Status
Below 18.5	Underweight
18.5–24.9	Normal or Healthy Weight
25.0–29.9	Overweight
30.0 and Above	Obese

For example, here are the weight ranges, the corresponding BMI ranges, and the weight status categories for a person who is 5' 9".

Table 40.3. Weight Ranges, the Corresponding BMI Ranges, and the Weight Status

Height	Weight Range	BMI	Weight Status
5' 9"	124 lbs or less	Below 18.5	Underweight
	125 lbs to 168 lbs	18.5 to 24.9	Normal or Healthy Weight
	169 lbs to 202 lbs	25.0 to 29.9	Overweight
	203 lbs or more	30 or higher	Obese

Is BMI Interpreted the Same Way for Children and Teens as It Is for Adults?

BMI is interpreted differently for children and teens, even though it is calculated using the same formula as adult BMI. Children and teen's BMI need to be age and sex-specific because the amount of body fat changes with age and the amount of body fat differs between girls and boys. The CDC BMI-for-age growth charts take into account these differences and visually show BMI as a percentile ranking. These percentiles were determined using representative data of the United States population of 2- to 19-year-olds that was collected in various surveys from 1963–65 to 1988–94.

Obesity among 2- to 19-year-olds is defined as a BMI at or above the 95th percentile of children of the same age and sex in this 1963 to 1994 reference population. For example, a 10-year-old boy of average height (56 inches) who weighs 102 pounds would have a BMI of 22.9 kg/m². This would place the boy in the 95th percentile for BMI—meaning that his BMI is greater than that of 95% of similarly aged boys in this reference population—and he would be considered to have obesity.

How Good Is BMI as an Indicator of Body Fatness?

The correlation between the BMI and body fatness is fairly strong but even if 2 people have the same BMI, their level of body fatness may differ.

In general,

• At the same BMI, women tend to have more body fat than men.

• At the same BMI, Blacks have less body fat than do Whites, and Asians have more body fat than do Whites.

- At the same BMI, older people, on average, tend to have more body fat than younger adults.

- At the same BMI, athletes have less body fat than do non-athletes.

The accuracy of BMI as an indicator of body fatness also appears to be higher in persons with higher levels of BMI and body fatness. While, a person with a very high BMI (e.g., 35 kg/m^2) is very likely to have high body fat, a relatively high BMI can be the results of either high body fat or high lean body mass (muscle and bone). A trained healthcare provider should perform appropriate health assessments in order to evaluate an individual's health status and risks.

If an Athlete or Other Person with a Lot of Muscle Has a BMI over 25, Is That Person Still Considered to Be Overweight?

According to the BMI weight status categories, anyone with a BMI between 25 and 29.9 would be classified as overweight and anyone with a BMI over 30 would be classified as obese.

However, athletes may have a high BMI because of increased muscularity rather than increased body fatness. In general, a person who has a high BMI is likely to have body fatness and would be considered to be overweight or obese, but this may not apply to athletes. A trained healthcare provider should perform appropriate health assessments in order to evaluate an individual's health status and risks.

What Are the Health Consequences of Obesity for Adults?

People who are obese are at increased risk for many diseases and health conditions, including the following:

- All-causes of death (mortality)

- High blood pressure (Hypertension)

- High LDL (Low-Density Lipoprotein) cholesterol, low HDL (High-Density Lipoprotein) cholesterol, or high levels of triglycerides (Dyslipidemia)

- Type 2 diabetes

- Coronary heart disease

- Stroke

- Gallbladder disease

- Osteoarthritis (a breakdown of cartilage and bone within a joint)

- Sleep apnea and breathing problems

- Chronic inflammation and increased oxidative stress

- Some cancers (endometrial, breast, colon, kidney, gallbladder, and liver)

- Low quality of life

- Mental illness such as clinical depression, anxiety, and other mental disorders

- Body pain and difficulty with physical functioning

About Child and Teen BMI

What Is a BMI Percentile and How Is It Interpreted?

After BMI is calculated for children and teens, it is expressed as a percentile which can be obtained from either a graph or a percentile calculator. These percentiles express a child's BMI relative to children in the United States who participated in national surveys that were conducted from 1963-65 to 1988-944. Because weight and height change during growth and development, as does their relation to body fatness, a child's BMI must be interpreted relative to other children of the same sex and age.

The BMI-for-age percentile growth charts are the most commonly used indicators to measure the size and growth patterns of children and teens in the United States. BMI-for-age weight status categories and the corresponding percentiles were based on expert committee recommendations and are shown in the following table.

Table 40.4. BMI-for-Age Weight Status Categories and the Corresponding Percentiles

Weight Status Category	Percentile Range
Underweight	Less than the 5th percentile
Normal or Healthy Weight	5th percentile to less than the 85th percentile
Overweight	85th to less than the 95th percentile
Obese	Equal to or greater than the 95th percentile

The following is an example of how sample BMI numbers would be interpreted for a 10-year-old boy.

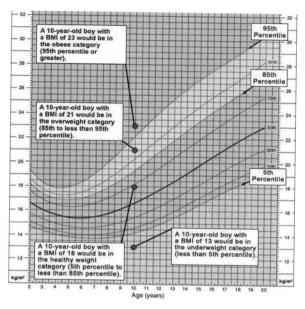

Figure 40.1. *Body Mass Index-for-Age Percentiles: Boys, 2 to 20 Years*

How Is BMI Used with Children and Teens?

For children and teens, BMI is not a diagnostic tool and is used to screen for potential weight and health-related issues. For example, a child may have a high BMI for their age and sex, but to determine if excess fat is a problem, a healthcare provider would need to perform further assessments. These assessments might include skinfold thickness measurements, evaluations of diet, physical activity, family history, and other appropriate health screenings. The American Academy of Pediatrics recommends the use of BMI to screen for overweight and obesity in children beginning at 2 years old.

Why Can't Healthy Weight Ranges Be Provided for Children and Teens?

Normal or healthy weight status is based on BMI between the 5th and 85th percentile on the CDC growth chart. It is difficult to provide healthy weight ranges for children and teens because the interpretation of BMI depends on weight, height, age, and sex.

What Are the BMI Trends for Children and Teens in the United States?

The prevalence of children and teens who measure in the 95th percentile or greater on the CDC growth charts has greatly increased over the past 40 years. Recently, however, this trend has leveled off and has even declined in certain age groups.

How Can I Tell If My Child Is Overweight or Obese?

CDC and the American Academy of Pediatrics (AAP) recommend the use of BMI to screen for overweight and obesity in children and teens age 2 through 19 years. For children under the age of 2 years old, consult the WHO standards. Although BMI is used to screen for overweight and obesity in children and teens, BMI is not a diagnostic tool. To determine whether the child has excess fat, further assessment by a trained health professional would be needed.

Can I Determine If My Child or Teen Is Obese by Using an Adult BMI Calculator?

In general, it's not possible to do this.

The adult calculator provides only the BMI value (weight/height^2) and not the BMI percentile that is needed to interpret BMI among children and teens. It is not appropriate to use the BMI categories for adults to interpret the BMI of children and teens.

However, if a child or teen has a BMI of $\geq$ 30 kg/m^2, the child is almost certainly obese. A BMI of 30 kg/m^2 is approximately the 95th percentile among 17-year-old girls and 18-year-old boys.

My Two Children Have the Same BMI Values, but One Is Considered Obese and the Other Is Not. Why Is That?

The interpretation of BMI varies by age and sex. So if the children are not the same age and the same sex, the interpretation of BMI has different meanings. For children of different age and sex, the same BMI could represent different BMI percentiles and possibly different weight status categories.

See the following graphic for an example for a 10-year-old boy and a 15-year-old boy who both have a BMI-for-age of 23. (Note that two children of different ages are plotted on the same growth chart to illustrate a point. Normally the measurement for only one child is plotted on a growth chart.)

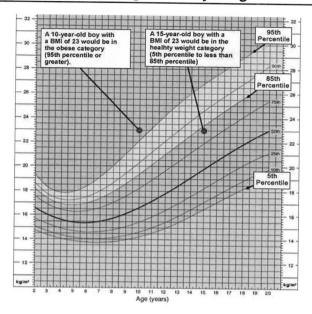

Figure 40.2. *Body Mass Index-for-Age Percentiles: Boys, 2 to 20 Years*

What Are the Health Consequences of Obesity during Childhood?

Health Risks Now

- Childhood obesity can have a harmful effect on the body in a variety of ways.

- High blood pressure and high cholesterol, which are risk factors for cardiovascular disease (CVD). In one study, 70% of obese children had at least one CVD risk factor, and 39% had two or more.

- Increased risk of impaired glucose tolerance, insulin resistance and type 2 diabetes.

- Breathing problems, such as sleep apnea, and asthma.

- Joint problems and musculoskeletal discomfort.

- Fatty liver disease, gallstones, and gastro-esophageal reflux (i.e., heartburn).

- Psychological stress such as depression, behavioral problems, and issues in school.

- Low self-esteem and low self-reported quality of life.

- Impaired social, physical, and emotional functioning.

Health Risks Later

- Obese children are more likely to become obese adults. Adult obesity is associated with a number of serious health conditions including heart disease, diabetes, and some cancers.

- If children are overweight, obesity in adulthood is likely to be more severe.

Section 40.2

Weight Cycling: An Unhealthy Pattern

This section includes text excerpted from "Weight Cycling,"
National Institute of Diabetes and Digestive and Kidney
Diseases (NIDDK), March 2006. Reviewed March 2016.

What Is Weight Cycling?

Weight cycling is the repeated loss and regain of body weight. This sometimes happens to people who go on weight-loss diets. A small cycle may include loss and regain of 5 to 10 lbs. In a large cycle, weight can change by 50 lbs or more.

Is Weight Cycling Harmful to My Health?

Experts are not sure if weight cycling leads to health problems. However, some studies suggest a link to high blood pressure, high cholesterol, gallbladder disease, and other problems. One study showed other problems may be linked to weight cycling as well. This study showed that women who weight cycle gain more weight over time than women who do not weight cycle. Binge eating (when a person eats a lot of food while feeling out of control) was also linked to women who weight cycle. The same study showed that women who weight cycle were also less likely to use physical activity to control their weight.

Weight cycling may affect your mental health too. People who weight cycle may feel depressed about their weight. However, weight cycling should not be a reason to "feel like a failure." If you feel down, try to focus on making changes in your eating and physical activity habits. Keeping a good attitude will help you stay focused.

If I Weight Cycle after a Diet, Will I Gain More Weight than I Had Before the Diet? Will I Have Less Muscle?

Studies do not show that fat tissue increases after a weight cycle. Studies do not support decreases in muscle either. Many people simply regain the weight they lost while on the diet—they have the same amount of fat and muscle as they did before the weight cycle.

Some people worry that weight cycling can put more fat around their stomach area. This is important since people who carry extra body weight around this area are more likely to develop type 2 diabetes. Studies show that people do not have more fat around their stomachs after a weight cycle. However, other studies suggest that women who are overweight and have a history of weight cycling have thicker layers of fat around their stomachs—compared to women who do not weight cycle. It is not clear how this relates to weight cycling.

If I Regain Lost Weight, Will It Be Even Harder to Lose It Again?

Losing weight after a weight cycle should not be harder. Studies show weight cycling does not affect how fast you burn food energy, which is called your "metabolic rate." This rate slows as we get older, but a healthy diet and regular physical activity can still help you achieve a healthy weight.

Is Staying Overweight Healthier than Weight Cycling?

This is a hard question to answer since experts are not sure whether weight cycling causes health problems. However, experts are sure that if you are overweight, losing weight is a good thing. Being overweight or obese is associated with the following health problems:

- high blood pressure
- heart disease
- stroke
- gallbladder disease

- fatty liver disease

- type 2 diabetes

- certain types of cancer

- arthritis

- breathing problems, such as sleep apnea (when breathing stops for short periods during sleep)

Not everyone who is overweight or obese has the same risk for these problems. Risk is affected by several factors: your gender, family history of disease, the amount of extra weight you have, and where fat is located on your body. You can improve your health with a modest weight loss. Losing just 10 percent of your body weight over 6 months will help.

How Can I Manage Weight and Avoid Weight Cycling?

Experts recommend different strategies for different people. The goal for everyone is to achieve a healthy weight. This can help prevent the health problems linked to weight cycling.

People who are not overweight or obese, and have no health problems related to weight, should maintain a stable weight.

People who are overweight or obese should try to achieve and maintain a modest weight loss. An initial goal of losing 10 percent of your body weight can help in your efforts to improve overall health.

If you need to lose weight, be ready to make lifelong changes. A healthy diet and physical activity are the keys to your efforts. Focus on making healthful food choices, such as eating more high-fiber foods like fruits and vegetables and cutting down on foods that are high in saturated or trans fats. Walking, jogging, or other activities can help keep you be active and feeling good.

Section 40.3

Are You Overweight?

This section includes text excerpted from "Keeping Children at a Healthy Weight," Agency for Healthcare Research and Quality (AHRQ), September 19, 2013.

What Might Lead to a Child Becoming Overweight or Obese?

Many things can lead to a child becoming overweight or obese, including:

- Unhealthy eating habits. Children may eat too much, eat too many unhealthy foods, or drink too many sugary drinks.

- Not getting enough sleep. Children who do not get enough sleep each night are more likely to become overweight.

- Family history. Children from overweight families may be more likely to become overweight. This could be due to a child's genes or learned family eating habits.

- Not enough physical activity. Children may not get enough physical activity. Children should be active for at least 1 hour each day.

- Too much screen time. Children may have too much screen time during the day. Some children may eat while watching television or playing on the computer.

- Environment. Children may spend time in an environment (such as with relatives, with friends, in childcare, or at school) where healthy eating choices or opportunities for physical activity are not available.

What Needs to Be Done?

There are ways parents can help prevent obesity and support healthy growth in children.

Eat Healthy

- Cook healthy meals at home with foods from each food group.
- The food groups include fruits, vegetables, grains, protein foods (such as meats, eggs, fish, tofu, and beans), and low-fat or non-fat dairy.
- Be sure to eat a healthy breakfast every day.
- Eat at the table as a family instead of in front of a screen (television, computer, cell phone, or tablet).
- Limit or do not keep unhealthy foods and drinks at home.
- Replace unhealthy snacks such as cookies, candy, or chips with healthy snacks such as fruits and vegetables.
- Replace unhealthy sugary drinks such as sodas, sports drinks, or juices with healthy drinks such as water and low-fat or non-fat milk.
- Eat most meals at home instead of at restaurants. At home, you are better able to limit the amount of fat, sugar, and salt in your meals.
- Be sure to eat the right amount of food.

Be Physically Active

- Give your child a chance to run around and play—at least 1 hour a day.
- Plan fun activities like bicycling, walking to the park, playing ball, or swimming.
- Encourage everyone in the family to be active during the day.
- For example, take the stairs instead of the elevator and walk or bike places instead of driving or taking the bus.
- Limit the amount of screen time each day.
- In addition to being physically active, make sure your child gets enough sleep each night.

Addressing Obesity Can Start in the Home, but Also Requires the Support of Communities

States, communities, schools, and parents can work together to help make the healthy choice the easy choice for children, teens, and their families.

In School

In addition to eating healthy and being physically active at home, school programs can help keep children at a healthy weight. School programs could include things such as:

- Lessons about the importance of healthy eating and physical activity
- Information sessions for parents to learn ways to help keep their child at a healthy weight
- Healthy breakfast and lunch options in the cafeteria with the right portion sizes
- Healthy snacks and drinks in vending machines and at parties and events
- Filtered water coolers to encourage drinking water instead of soft drinks or sports drinks
- Adult-led walk-to-school or bike-to-school groups
- A longer physical education (PE) period in which children are physically active
- Gym equipment such as balls and jump ropes for use during recess

In the Community

In addition to home and school, things can also be done in the community to help keep children at a healthy weight. Communities and community centers can:

- Improve community parks, sidewalks, and biking paths.
- Take steps to make parks, sidewalks, and biking paths safe.
- Advertise community events such as health fairs, 5K walks, sports events at local parks, community garden programs, and local farmers markets. This can be done on posters, in local newspapers, and on local television and radio stations.
- Offer programs in which families can get advice on healthy eating and being physically active.

What Have Researchers Found about Doing Things at Home, in School, and in the Community to Help Keep Children from Becoming Overweight or Obese?

Healthy eating and physical activity are very important in keeping children from becoming overweight or obese.

Researchers found that:

- Programs at schools to help children eat healthy and be physically active can keep children from becoming overweight or obese.

- Along with school programs, additional steps at home and in the community can also help.

Talking with Your Child's Doctor, School, and Community Centers

Examples of Questions to Ask Your Child's Doctor

- Is my child at a healthy weight?
- What are the most important things for me to do at home to help keep my child at a healthy weight?
- How can I get my child to eat healthy foods?
- How much of each type of food should my child eat?
- How much physical activity does my child need each day?
- What are the best types of physical activity for my child?
- How much screen time should I allow my child each day?
- How much sleep should my child get each night?
- Do you have any resources that can help me keep my child at a healthy weight?
- Do you know of any community resources that can help?
- If there are no grocery stores nearby or healthy food is too expensive for me, do you know of any resources that could help me?
- If there is no safe place for my child to play outside, how can I help my child stay active?

Examples of Questions to Ask Your Child's School Principal, Nurse, or Counselor

- Does the school offer programs to help keep children from becoming overweight or obese? If not, how can we start some?
- In the cafeteria and in vending machines, are healthy foods such as fruits and vegetables available instead of sugary drinks and salty or fatty foods?

- How much time is my child given during PE, recess, and throughout the day to be physically active?

- Does the school ever use PE or other physical activity as punishment?

- Do you have adult-led walk-to-school or bike-to-school programs or other physical activity programs for children?

- Are there information sessions that I can attend to learn more about helping my child stay at a healthy weight?

- What can I do at home to help reinforce what my child is taught about healthy eating and physical activity at school?

- Do you know of any community resources that can help?

Examples of Questions to Ask Your Local Community or Recreation Center

- Do you have any resources or programs on healthy eating or physical activities for children?

- Do you keep a calendar of community events such as health fairs, 5K walks, or sports events at local parks?

- Do you have a list of local community gardens or farmer's markets?

- Do you know of any programs that can give me advice on how to help my family eat healthy and be physically active?

Chapter 41

Maintaining Your Weight

Chapter Contents

335

Section 41.1

Balancing Calories

This section includes text excerpted from "Finding a Balance,"
Centers for Disease Control and Prevention (CDC), May 15, 2015.

Finding a Balance

There's a lot of talk about the different components of food. Whether you're consuming carbohydrates, fats or proteins, all of them contain calories. If your diet focus is on any one of these alone, you're missing the bigger picture.

The Caloric Balance Equation

When it comes to maintaining a healthy weight for a lifetime, the bottom line is—**calories count!** Weight management is all about balance—balancing the number of calories you consume with the number of calories your body uses or "burns off."

A *calorie* is defined as a unit of energy supplied by food. A calorie is a calorie regardless of its source. Whether you're eating carbohydrates, fats, sugars, or proteins, all of them contain calories.

Caloric balance is like a scale. To remain in balance and maintain your body weight, the calories consumed (from foods) must be balanced by the calories used (in normal body functions, daily activities, and exercise).

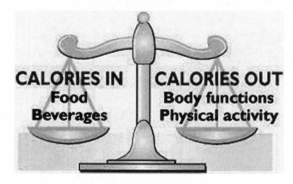

Figure 41.1. *Caloric balance scale*

Table 41.1. Caloric Balance Status

If you are...	Your caloric balance status is...
Maintaining your weight	**"in balance."** You are eating roughly the same number of calories that your body is using. Your weight will remain **stable.**
Gaining weight	**"in caloric excess."** You are eating more calories than your body is using. Your body will store these extra calories as fat and you'll **gain** weight.
Losing weight	**"in caloric deficit."** You are eating fewer calories than you are using. Your body is pulling from its fat storage cells for energy, so your weight is **decreasing.**

Am I in Caloric Balance?

If you are maintaining your current body weight, you are in caloric balance. If you need to gain weight or to lose weight, you'll need to tip the balance scale in one direction or another to achieve your goal.

If you need to tip the balance scale in the direction of losing weight, keep in mind that it takes approximately 3,500 calories below your calorie needs to lose a pound of body fat. To lose about 1 to 2 pounds per week, you'll need to reduce your caloric intake by 500–1000 calories per day.

To learn how many calories you are currently eating, begin writing down the foods you eat and the beverages you drink each day. By writing down what you eat and drink, you become more aware of everything you are putting in your mouth. Also, begin writing down the physical activity you do each day and the length of time you do it.

Physical activities (both daily activities and exercise) help tip the balance scale by increasing the calories you expend each day.

Recommended Physical Activity Levels

- 2 hours and 30 minutes (150 minutes) of moderate-intensity aerobic activity (i.e., brisk walking) every week and muscle-strengthening activities on 2 or more days a week that work all major muscle groups (legs, hips, back, abdomen, chest, shoulders, and arms).

- Increasing the intensity or the amount of time that you are physically active can have even greater health benefits and may be needed to control body weight.

• Encourage children and teenagers to be physically active for at least 60 minutes each day, or almost every day.

The bottom line is each person's body is unique and may have different caloric needs. A healthy lifestyle requires balance, in the foods you eat, in the beverages you consume, in the way you carry out your daily activities, and in the amount of physical activity or exercise you include in your daily routine. While counting calories is not necessary, it may help you in the beginning to gain an awareness of your eating habits as you strive to achieve energy balance. The ultimate test of balance is whether or not you are gaining, maintaining, or losing weight.

Questions and Answers about Calories

Q: Are Fat-Free and Low-Fat Foods Low in Calories?

A: Not always. Some fat-free and low-fat foods have extra sugars, which push the calorie amount right back up. Always read the Nutrition Facts food label to find out the calorie content. Remember, this is the calorie content for **one serving** of the food item, so be sure and check the serving size. If you eat more than one serving, you'll be eating more calories than is listed on the food label.

Q: If I Eat Late at Night, Will These Calories Automatically Turn into Body Fat?

A: The time of day isn't what affects how your body uses calories. It's the overall number of calories you eat and the calories you burn over the course of 24 hours that affects your weight.

Q: I've Heard It Is More Important to Worry about Carbohydrates than Calories. Is This True?

A: By focusing only on carbohydrates, you can still eat too many calories. Also, if you drastically reduce the variety of foods in your diet, you could end up sacrificing vital nutrients and not be able to sustain the diet over time.

Q: Does It Matter How Many Calories I Eat as Long as I'm Maintaining an Active Lifestyle?

A: While physical activity is a vital part of weight control, so is controlling the number of calories you eat. If you consume more calories than you use through normal daily activities and physical activity, you will still gain weight.

Q: What Other Factors Contribute to Overweight and Obesity?

A: Besides diet and behavior, environment, and genetic factors may also have an effect in causing people to be overweight and obese.

Section 41.2

Cutting Calories

This section includes text excerpted from "Cutting Calories,"
Centers for Disease Control and Prevention (CDC), May 15, 2015.

Once you start looking, you can find ways to cut calories for your meals, snacks, and even beverages. Here are some examples to get you started.

Eat More, Weigh Less?

How to Manage Your Weight without Being Hungry

Have you tried to lose weight by cutting down the amount of food you eat? Do you still feel hungry and not satisfied after eating? Or have you avoided trying to lose weight because you're afraid of feeling hungry all the time? If so, you are not alone. Many people throw in the towel on weight loss because they feel deprived and hungry when they eat less. But there is another way. Aim for a slow, steady weight loss by decreasing calorie intake while maintaining an adequate nutrient intake and increasing physical activity. You can cut calories without eating less nutritious food. The key is to eat foods that will fill you up without eating a large amount of calories.

If I Cut Calories, Won't I Be Hungry?

Research shows that people get full by the *amount of food* they eat, not the *number of calories* they take in. You can cut calories in your favorite foods by lowering the amount of fat and or increasing the amount of fiber-rich ingredients, such as vegetables or fruit.

Let's take macaroni and cheese as an example. The original recipe uses whole milk, butter, and full-fat cheese. This recipe has about 540 calories in one serving (1 cup).

Here's how to remake this recipe with fewer calories and less fat:

- Use 2 cups non-fat milk instead of 2 cups whole milk.

- Use 8 ounces light cream cheese instead of 2 1/4 cups full-fat cheddar cheese.

- Use 1 tablespoon butter instead of 2 or use 2 tablespoons of soft trans-fat free margarine.

- Add about 2 cups of fresh spinach and 1 cup diced tomatoes (or any other veggie you like).

Your redesigned mac and cheese now has 315 calories in one serving (1 cup). You can eat the same amount of mac and cheese with 225 fewer calories.

What Foods Will Fill Me Up?

To be able to cut calories without eating less and feeling hungry, you need to replace some higher calorie foods with foods that are lower in calories and fat and will fill you up. In general, this means foods with lots of water and fiber in them. The chart below will help you make smart food choices that are part of a healthy eating plan.

Table 41.2. Food items with less calories and more calories

These foods will fill you up with less calories. Choose them *more* often...	These foods can pack more calories into each bite. Choose them *less* often...
Fruits and Vegetables (prepared without added fat)	**Fried foods**
Spinach, broccoli, tomato, carrots, watermelon, berries, apples	Eggs fried in butter, fried vegetables, French fries
Low-fat and fat-free milk products	**Full-fat milk products**
Low-fat- or fat-free, low-fat- or fat-free yogurt, low-fat- or fat-free cottage cheese	Full-fat cheese, full-fat ice cream, whole and 2% milk
Broth-based soup	**Dry snack foods**

Table 41.2. Continued

These foods will fill you up with less calories. Choose them *more* often...	These foods can pack more calories into each bite. Choose them *less* often...
Vegetable-based soups, soups with chicken or beef broth, tomato soups (without cream)	Crackers or pretzels, cookies, chips, dried fruits
Whole grains	**Higher-fat and higher-sugar foods**
Brown rice, whole wheat bread, whole wheat pastas, popcorn	Croissants, margarine, shortening and butter, doughnuts, candy bars, cakes and pastries
Lean meat, poultry and fish	**Fatty cuts of meat**
Grilled salmon, chicken breast without skin, ground beef (lean or extra lean)	Bacon, brisket, ground beef (regular)
Legumes (beans and peas)	
Black, red kidney and pinto beans (without added fat), green peas, black-eyed peas	

A Healthy Eating Plan Is One That:

- Emphasizes fruits, vegetables, whole grains, and fat free or low-fat milk and milk products.

- Includes lean meats, poultry, fish, beans, eggs, and nuts.

- Is low in saturated fats, trans fats, cholesterol, salt (sodium), and added sugars.

- Stays within your calorie needs.

Technically Speaking

The number of calories in a particular amount or weight of food is called "calorie density" or "energy density." Low-calorie-dense foods are ones that don't pack a lot of calories into each bite. Foods that have a lot of water or fiber and little fat are usually low in calorie density. They will help you feel full without an unnecessary amount of calories.

Here are some more ideas for cutting back on calories without eating less and being hungry:

Table 41.3. Some more ideas for cutting back on calories

Instead of...	Try...
Fried chicken sandwich with 1 tbsp. mayonnaise = 599 calories	**Grilled chicken salad with low-fat dressing** 2 cups lettuce, 2 oz. grilled chicken breast, 2 tbsp. light balsamic vinaigrette dressing = 178 calories
Cream-based soup 1 cup mushroom bisque = 400 calories	**Broth-based soup** 1 cup minestrone = 112 calories
Chips or pretzels 1.5 oz. pretzels = 162 calories	**Baby carrots with hummus** 16 baby carrots with 1 tbsp. hummus = 75 calories

Rethink Your Drink

When it comes to weight loss, there's no lack of diets promising fast results. There are low-carb diets, high-carb diets, low-fat diets, grapefruit diets, cabbage soup diets, and blood type diets, to name a few. But no matter what diet you may try, to lose weight, you must take in fewer calories than your body uses. Most people try to reduce their calorie intake by focusing on food, but another way to cut calories may be to think about what you drink.

What Do You Drink? It Makes More Difference than You Think!

Calories in drinks are not hidden (they're listed right on the Nutrition Facts label), but many people don't realize just how many calories beverages can contribute to their daily intake. As you can see in the example below, calories from drinks can really add up. But there is good news: you have plenty of options for reducing the number of calories in what you drink.

Table 41.4. Substitutes for high-calorie drinks

Occasion	Instead of...	Calories	Try...	Calories
Morning coffee shop run	Medium café latte (16 ounces) made with whole milk	265	Small café latte (12 ounces) made with fat-free milk	125

Table 41.4. Continued

Occasion	Instead of...	Calories	Try...	Calories
Lunchtime combo meal	20-oz. bottle of nondiet cola with your lunch	227	Bottle of water or diet soda	0
Afternoon break	Sweetened lemon iced tea from the vending machine (16 ounces)	180	Sparkling water with natural lemon flavor (not sweetened)	0
Dinnertime	A glass of nondiet ginger ale with your meal (12 ounces)	124	Water with a slice of lemon or lime, or seltzer water with a splash of 100% fruit juice	0 calories for the water with fruit slice, or about 30 calories for seltzer water with 2 ounces of 100% orange juice.
Total beverage calories:		796		125–155

(*USDA National Nutrient Database for Standard Reference*)

- Substituting no- or low-calorie drinks for sugar-sweetened beverages cuts about 650 calories in the example above.

- Of course, not everyone drinks the amount of sugar-sweetened beverages shown above. Check the list below to estimate how many calories you typically take in from beverages.

Table 41.5. Calorie count in beverages

Type of Beverage	Calories in 12 ounces	Calories in 20 ounces
Fruit punch	192	320
100% apple juice	192	300
100% orange juice	168	280
Lemonade	168	280

Table 41.5. Continued

Type of Beverage	Calories in 12 ounces	Calories in 20 ounces
Regular lemon/lime soda	148	247
Regular cola	136	227
Sweetened lemon iced tea (bottled, not homemade)	135	225
Tonic water	124	207
Regular ginger ale	124	207
Sports drink	99	165
Fitness water	18	36
Unsweetened iced tea	2	3
Diet soda (with aspartame)	0*	0*
Carbonated water (unsweetened)	0	0
Water	0	0

Some diet soft drinks can contain a small number of calories that are not listed on the nutrition facts label.
(USDA National Nutrient Database for Standard Reference)

Milk contains vitamins and other nutrients that contribute to good health, but it also contains calories. Choosing low-fat or fat-free milk is a good way to reduce your calorie intake and still get the nutrients that milk contains.

Table 41.6. Calories in various types of milk

Type of Milk	Calories per cup (8 ounces)
Chocolate milk (whole)	208
Chocolate milk (2% reduced-fat)	190
Chocolate milk (1% low-fat)	158
Whole Milk (unflavored)	150
2% reduced-fat milk (unflavored)	120
1% low-fat milk (unflavored)	105
Fat-free milk (unflavored)	90

Some diet soft drinks can contain a small number of calories that are not listed on the nutrition facts label.
(USDA National Nutrient Database for Standard Reference)

Learn to Read Nutrition Facts Labels Carefully

Be aware that the Nutrition Facts label on beverage containers may give the calories for only part of the contents. The example below shows the label on a 20-oz. bottle. As you can see, it lists the number of calories in an 8-oz. serving (100) even though the bottle contains 20 oz. or 2.5 servings. To figure out how many calories are in the whole bottle, you need to multiply the number of calories in one serving by the number of servings in the bottle (100 x 2.5). You can see that the contents of the entire bottle actually contain 250 calories even though what the label calls a "serving" only contains 100. This shows that you need to look closely at the serving size when comparing the calorie content of different beverages.

Table 41.7. Nutrition Facts Label

Nutrition Facts Label
Serving Size 8 fl. oz. Servings Per Container **2.5**
Amount per serving
Calories **100**

Sugar by Any Other Name: How to Tell Whether Your Drink Is Sweetened?

Sweeteners that add calories to a beverage go by many different names and are not always obvious to anyone looking at the ingredients list. Some common caloric sweeteners are listed below. If these appear in the ingredients list of your favorite beverage, you are drinking a sugar-sweetened beverage.

- High-fructose corn syrup
- Fructose
- Fruit juice concentrates
- Honey
- Sugar
- Syrup
- Corn syrup
- Sucrose
- Dextrose

High-Calorie Culprits in Unexpected Places

Coffee drinks and blended fruit smoothies sound innocent enough, but the calories in some of your favorite coffee-shop or smoothie-stand items may surprise you. Check the website or in-store nutrition information of your favorite coffee or smoothie shop to find out how many calories are in different menu items. And when a smoothie or coffee craving kicks in, here are some tips to help minimize the caloric damage:

At the coffee shop:

• Request that your drink be made with fat-free or low-fat milk instead of whole milk

• Order the smallest size available.

• Forgo the extra flavoring—the flavor syrups used in coffee shops, like vanilla or hazelnut, are sugar-sweetened and will add calories to your drink.

• Skip the Whip. The whipped cream on top of coffee drinks adds calories and fat.

• Get back to basics. Order a plain cup of coffee with fat-free milk and artificial sweetener, or drink it black.

At the smoothie stand:

• Order a child's size if available.

• Ask to see the nutrition information for each type of smoothie and pick the smoothie with the fewest calories.

• Hold the sugar. Many smoothies contain added sugar in addition to the sugar naturally in fruit, juice, or yogurt. Ask that your smoothie be prepared without added sugar: the fruit is naturally sweet.

Better Beverage Choices Made Easy

Now that you know how much difference a drink can make, here are some ways to make smart beverage choices:

• Choose water, diet, or low-calorie beverages instead of sugar-sweetened beverages.

• For a quick, easy, and inexpensive thirst-quencher, carry a water bottle and refill it throughout the day.

- Don't "stock the fridge" with sugar-sweetened beverages. Instead, keep a jug or bottles of cold water in the fridge.

- Serve water with meals.

- Make water more exciting by adding slices of lemon, lime, cucumber, or watermelon, or drink sparkling water.

- Add a splash of 100% juice to plain sparkling water for a refreshing, low-calorie drink.

- When you do opt for a sugar-sweetened beverage, go for the small size. Some companies are now selling 8-oz. cans and bottles of soda, which contain about 100 calories.

- Be a role model for your friends and family by choosing healthy, low-calorie beverages.

How to Avoid Portion Size Pitfalls to Help Manage Your Weight

When eating at many restaurants, it's hard to miss that portion sizes have gotten larger in the last few years. The trend has also spilled over into the grocery store and vending machines, where a bagel has become a BAGEL and an "individual" bag of chips can easily feed more than one. Research shows that people unintentionally consume more calories when faced with larger portions. This can mean significant excess calorie intake, especially when eating high-calorie foods. Here are some tips to help you avoid some common portion-size pitfalls.

Portion control when eating out. Many restaurants serve more food than one person needs at one meal. Take control of the amount of food that ends up on your plate by splitting an entrée with a friend. Or, ask the wait person for a "to-go" box and wrap up half your meal as soon as it's brought to the table.

Portion control when eating in. To minimize the temptation of second and third helpings when eating at home, serve the food on individual plates, instead of putting the serving dishes on the table. Keeping the excess food out of reach may discourage overeating.

Portion control in front of the TV. When eating or snacking in front of the TV, put the amount that you plan to eat into a bowl or container instead of eating straight from the package. It's easy to overeat when your attention is focused on something else.

Go ahead, spoil your dinner. We learned as children not to snack before a meal for fear of "spoiling our dinner." Well, it's time to forget that old rule. If you feel hungry between meals, eat a healthy snack, like a piece of fruit or small salad, to avoid overeating during your next meal.

Be aware of large packages. For some reason, the larger the package, the more people consume from it without realizing it. To minimize this effect:

- Divide up the contents of one large package into several smaller containers to help avoid over-consumption.

- Don't eat straight from the package. Instead, serve the food in a small bowl or container.

Out of sight, out of mind. People tend to consume more when they have easy access to food. Make your home a "portion friendly zone."

- Replace the candy dish with a fruit bowl.

- Store especially tempting foods, like cookies, chips, or ice cream, out of immediate eyesight, like on a high shelf or at the back of the freezer. Move the healthier food to the front at eye level.

- When buying in bulk, store the excess in a place that's not convenient to get to, such as a high cabinet or at the back of the pantry.

How to Use Fruits and Vegetables to Help Manage Your Weight

Fruits and vegetables are part of a well-balanced and healthy eating plan. There are many different ways to lose or maintain a healthy weight. Using more fruits and vegetables along with whole grains and lean meats, nuts, and beans is a safe and healthy one. Helping control your weight is not the only benefit of eating more fruits and vegetables. Diets rich in fruits and vegetables may reduce the risk of some types of cancer and other chronic diseases. Fruits and vegetables also provide essential vitamins and minerals, fiber, and other substances that are important for good health.

To Lose Weight, You Must Eat Fewer Calories than Your Body Uses

This doesn't necessarily mean that you have to eat less food. You can create lower-calorie versions of some of your favorite dishes by substituting low-calorie fruits and vegetables in place of higher-calorie ingredients. The water and fiber in fruits and vegetables will add volume to your dishes, so you can eat the same amount of food with fewer calories. Most fruits and vegetables are naturally low in fat and calories and are filling.

Here are some simple ways to cut calories and eat fruits and vegetables throughout your day:

Breakfast: Start the Day Right

- Substitute some spinach, onions, or mushrooms for one of the eggs or half of the cheese in your morning omelet. The vegetables will add volume and flavor to the dish with fewer calories than the egg or cheese.

- Cut back on the amount of cereal in your bowl to make room for some cut-up bananas, peaches, or strawberries. You can still eat a full bowl, but with fewer calories.

Lighten Up Your Lunch

- Substitute vegetables such as lettuce, tomatoes, cucumbers, or onions for 2 ounces of the cheese and 2 ounces of the meat in your sandwich, wrap, or burrito. The new version will fill you up with fewer calories than the original.

- Add a cup of chopped vegetables, such as broccoli, carrots, beans, or red peppers, in place of 2 ounces of the meat or 1 cup of noodles in your favorite broth-based soup. The vegetables will help fill you up, so you won't miss those extra calories.

Dinner

- Add in 1 cup of chopped vegetables such as broccoli, tomatoes, squash, onions, or peppers, while removing 1 cup of the rice or pasta in your favorite dish. The dish with the vegetables will be just as satisfying but have fewer calories than the same amount of the original version.

- Take a good look at your dinner plate. Vegetables, fruit, and whole grains should take up the largest portion of your plate. If they do not, replace some of the meat, cheese, white pasta, or rice with legumes, steamed broccoli, asparagus, greens, or another favorite vegetable. This will reduce the total calories in your meal without reducing the amount of food you eat. BUT remember to use a normal—or small-size plate—not a platter. The total number of calories that you eat counts, even if a good proportion of them come from fruits and vegetables.

Smart Snacks

Most healthy eating plans allow for one or two small snacks a day. Choosing most fruits and vegetables will allow you to eat a snack with only 100 calories.

About 100 Calories or Less:

- a medium-size apple (72 calories)

- a medium-size banana (105 calories)

- 1 cup steamed green beans (44 calories)

- 1 cup blueberries (83 calories)

- 1 cup grapes (100 calories)

- 1 cup carrots (45 calories), broccoli (30 calories), or bell peppers (30 calories) with 2 tbsp. hummus (46 calories)

Instead of a high-calorie snack from a vending machine, bring some cut-up vegetables or fruit from home. One snack-sized bag of corn chips (1 ounce) has the same number of calories as a small apple, 1 cup of whole strawberries, AND 1 cup of carrots with 1/4 cup of low-calorie dip. Substitute one or two of these options for the chips, and you will have a satisfying snack with fewer calories.

Remember: Substitution is the key.

It's true that fruits and vegetables are lower in calories than many other foods, but they do contain some calories. If you start eating fruits and vegetables in addition to what you usually eat, you are adding calories and may gain weight. The key is substitution. Eat fruits and vegetables instead of some other higher-calorie food.

More Tips for Making Fruits and Vegetables Part of Your Weight Management Plan

Eat fruits and vegetables the way nature provided—or with fat-free or low-fat cooking techniques.

Try steaming your vegetables, using low-calorie or low-fat dressings, and using herbs and spices to add flavor. Some cooking techniques, such as breading and frying, or using high-fat dressings or sauces will greatly increase the calories and fat in the dish. And eat your fruit raw to enjoy its natural sweetness.

Canned or frozen fruits and vegetables are also good options.

Frozen or canned fruits and vegetables can be just as nutritious as the fresh varieties. However, be careful to choose those without added sugar, syrup, cream sauces, or other ingredients that will add calories.

Choose whole fruit over fruit drinks and juices. Fruit juices have lost fiber from the fruit.

It is better to eat the whole fruit because it contains the added fiber that helps you feel full. One 6-ounce serving of orange juice has 85 calories, compared to just 65 calories in a medium orange.

Whole fruit gives you a bigger size snack than the same fruit dried—for the same number of calories.

A small box of raisins (1/4 cup) is about 100 calories. For the same number of calories, you can eat 1 cup of grapes.

Ideas for Every Meal

Table 41.8. Ideas for Every Meal

Breakfast	Substitution	Calories Reduced by
Top your cereal with low fat or fat-free milk instead of 2% or whole milk.	1 cup of fat-free milk instead of 1 cup of whole milk	63
Use a non-stick pan and cooking spray (rather than butter) to scramble or fry eggs	1 spray of cooking spray instead of 1 pat of butter	34
Choose reduced-calorie margarine spread for toast rather than butter or stick margarine.	2 pats of reduced calorie margarine instead of 2 pats of butter	36
Lunch	**Substitution**	**Calories Reduced by**
Add more vegetables such as cucumbers, lettuce, tomato, and onions to a sandwich instead of extra meat or cheese.	2 slices of tomatoes, ¼ cup of sliced cucumbers, and 2 slices of onions instead of an extra slice (3/4 ounce) of cheese and 2 slices (1 ounce) of ham	154

Table 41.8. Continued

Lunch	Substitution	Calories Reduced by
Accompany a sandwich with salad or fruit instead of chips or French fries.	½ cup diced raw pineapple instead of 1 ounce bag of potato chips	118
Choose vegetable-based broth soups rather than cream- or meat-based soups.	1 cup of vegetable soup instead of 1 cup cream of chicken soup	45
When eating a salad, dip your fork into dressing instead of pouring lots of dressing on the salad.	½ TBSP of regular ranch salad dressing instead of 2 TBSP of regular ranch dressing	109
When eating out, substitute a broth-based soup or a green lettuce salad for French fries or chips as a side dish	A side salad with a packet of low-fat vinaigrette dressing instead of a medium order of French fries	270
Dinner	**Substitution**	**Calories Reduced by**
Have steamed or grilled vegetables rather than those sautéed in butter or oil. Try lemon juice and herbs to flavor the vegetables. You can also sauté with non-stick cooking spray.	½ cup steamed broccoli instead of ½ cup broccoli sautéed in 1/2 TBSP of vegetable oil.	62
Modify recipes to reduce the amount of fat and calories. For example, when making lasagna, use part-skim ricotta cheese instead of whole-milk ricotta cheese. Substitute shredded vegetables, such as carrots, zucchini, and spinach for some of the ground meat in lasagna.	1 cup of part-skim ricotta cheese instead of 1 cup whole milk ricotta cheese	89
When eating out, have a cocktail or dessert instead of both during the same eating occasion.	Choosing one or the other saves you calories. A 12-ounce beer has about 153 calories. A slice of apple pie (1/6 of a 8" pie) has 277 calories.	153 if you have the apple pie without the drink; 277 if you have a drink and no pie.
When having pizza, choose vegetables as toppings and just a light sprinkling of cheese instead of fatty meats.	One slice of a cheese pizza instead of one slice of a meat and cheese pizza	60

Table 41.8. Continued

Snacks	Substitution	Calories Reduced by
Choose air-popped popcorn instead of oil-popped popcorn and dry-roasted instead of oil-roasted nuts.	3 cups of air-popped popcorn instead of 3 cups of oil-popped popcorn	73
Avoid the vending machine by packing your own healthful snacks to bring to work. For example, consider vegetable sticks, fresh fruit, low fat or nonfat yogurt without added sugars, or a small handful of dry-roasted nuts.	An eight-ounce container of no sugar added nonfat yogurt instead of a package of 6 peanut butter crackers	82
Choose sparkling water instead of sweetened drinks or alcoholic beverages.	A bottle of carbonated water instead of a 12-ounce can of soda with sugar	136
Instead of cookies or other sweet snacks, have some fruit for a snack.	One large orange instead of 3 chocolate sandwich cookies	54

Section 41.3

Helping Children Maintain a Healthy Weight

This section includes text excerpted from "Tips for Parents—Ideas to Help Children Maintain a Healthy Weight," Centers for Disease Control and Prevention (CDC), May 15, 2015.

Why Is Childhood Obesity Considered a Health Problem?

Doctors and scientists are concerned about the rise of obesity in children and youth because obesity may lead to the following health problems:

- Heart disease, caused by:
- high cholesterol and/or

- high blood pressure
- Type 2 diabetes
- Asthma
- Sleep apnea
- Social discrimination

Childhood obesity is associated with various health-related consequences. Obese children and adolescents may experience immediate health consequences and may be at risk for weight-related health problems in adulthood.

Psychosocial Risks

Some consequences of childhood and adolescent overweight are psychosocial. Obese children and adolescents are targets of early and systematic social discrimination. The psychological stress of social stigmatization can cause low self-esteem which, in turn, can hinder academic and social functioning, and persist into adulthood.

Cardiovascular Disease Risks

Obese children and teens have been found to have risk factors for cardiovascular disease (CVD), including high cholesterol levels, high blood pressure, and abnormal glucose tolerance. In a population-based sample of 5- to 17-year-olds, almost 60% of overweight children had at least one CVD risk factor while 25 percent of overweight children had two or more CVD risk factors.

Additional Health Risks

Less common health conditions associated with increased weight include asthma, hepatic steatosis, sleep apnea and type 2 diabetes.

- Asthma is a disease of the lungs in which the airways become blocked or narrowed causing breathing difficulty. Studies have identified an association between childhood overweight and asthma.

- Hepatic steatosis is the fatty degeneration of the liver caused by a high concentration of liver enzymes. Weight reduction causes liver enzymes to normalize.

- Sleep apnea is a less common complication of overweight for children and adolescents. Sleep apnea is a sleep-associated breathing disorder defined as the cessation of breathing during sleep that lasts for at least 10 seconds. Sleep apnea is characterized by loud snoring and labored breathing. During sleep apnea, oxygen levels in the blood can fall dramatically. One study estimated that sleep apnea occurs in about 7% of overweight children.

- Type 2 diabetes is increasingly being reported among children and adolescents who are overweight. While diabetes and glucose intolerance, a precursor of diabetes, are common health effects of adult obesity, only in recent years has type 2 diabetes begun to emerge as a health-related problem among children and adolescents. Onset of diabetes in children and adolescents can result in advanced complications such as CVD and kidney failure.

In addition, studies have shown that obese children and teens are more likely to become obese as adults.

What Can I Do as a Parent or Guardian to Help Prevent Childhood Overweight and Obesity?

To help your child maintain a healthy weight, balance the calories your child consumes from foods and beverages with the calories your child uses through physical activity and normal growth.

Remember that the goal for overweight and obese children and teens is to reduce the rate of weight gain while allowing normal growth and development. Children and teens should NOT be placed on a weight reduction diet without the consultation of a healthcare provider.

Balancing Calories: Help Kids Develop Healthy Eating Habits

One part of balancing calories is to eat foods that provide adequate nutrition and an appropriate number of calories. You can help children learn to be aware of what they eat by developing healthy eating habits, looking for ways to make favorite dishes healthier, and reducing calorie-rich temptations.

Encourage Healthy Eating Habits.

There's no great secret to healthy eating. To help your children and family develop healthy eating habits:

- Provide plenty of vegetables, fruits, and whole-grain products.

- Include low-fat or nonfat milk or dairy products.

- Choose lean meats, poultry, fish, lentils, and beans for protein.

- Serve reasonably-sized portions.

- Encourage your family to drink lots of water.

- Limit sugar-sweetened beverages.

- Limit consumption of sugar and saturated fat.

Remember that small changes every day can lead to a recipe for success!

Look for ways to make favorite dishes healthier.

The recipes that you may prepare regularly, and that your family enjoys, with just a few changes can be healthier and just as satisfying.

Remove calorie-rich temptations!

Although everything can be enjoyed in moderation, reducing the calorie-rich temptations of high-fat and high-sugar, or salty snacks can also help your children develop healthy eating habits. Instead only allow your children to eat them sometimes, so that they truly will be treats! Here are examples of easy-to-prepare, low-fat and low-sugar treats that are 100 calories or less:

- A medium-size apple

- A medium-size banana

- 1 cup blueberries

- 1 cup grapes

- 1 cup carrots, broccoli, or bell peppers with 2 tbsp. hummus

Balancing Calories: Help Kids Stay Active

Another part of balancing calories is to engage in an appropriate amount of physical activity and avoid too much sedentary time. In addition to being fun for children and teens, regular physical activity has many health benefits, including:

- Strengthening bones

- Decreasing blood pressure

- Reducing stress and anxiety

- Increasing self-esteem
- Helping with weight management

Help kids stay active.

Children and teens should participate in at least 60 minutes of moderate intensity physical activity most days of the week, preferably daily. Remember that children imitate adults. Start adding physical activity to your own daily routine and encourage your child to join you.

Some examples of moderate intensity physical activity include:

- Brisk walking
- Playing tag
- Jumping rope
- Playing soccer
- Swimming
- Dancing

Reduce sedentary time.

In addition to encouraging physical activity, help children avoid too much sedentary time. Although quiet time for reading and home-work is fine, limit the time your children watch television, play video games, or surf the web to no more than 2 hours per day. Additionally, the American Academy of Pediatrics (AAP) does not recommend tele-vision viewing for children age 2 or younger. Instead, encourage your children to find fun activities to do with family members or on their own that simply involve more activity.

Chapter 42

Weight Gain Guidelines

If You Need to Gain Weight

If your doctor tells you that you are underweight, it's important you try to gain some weight. Sometimes being underweight can be just as hard to handle as being overweight. Here are some tips for gaining weight in a healthy way:

- **Eat more healthy fats.** Choose unsaturated fats. You can find these in nuts, avocados, olives, and "fatty" fish. Add extra olive oil to your pasta dish. Add more salad dressing to your salad, and more mayonnaise to your tuna.

- **Eat more healthy carbohydrates.** Select sweets that also provide nutrients, such as bran muffins, yogurt with fruit, fruit pies or juice, and granola bars.

- **Think about your drink.** Try drinks with extra calories and nutrients, like a smoothie made with milk or juice. And don't fill up on a drink at mealtime.

This chapter contains text excerpted from the following sources: Text under the heading "If You Need to Gain Weight" is excerpted from "If You Need to Gain Weight," Office on Women's Health (OWH), November 5, 2013; Text beginning with the heading "Are You at a Healthy Body Weight?" is excerpted from "NIH Clinical Center Patient Education Materials: Eating Well and Maintaining a Healthy Body Weight with Pulmonary Non-TB Mycobacterial Disease (NTM)," National Institutes of Health (NIH), June 6, 2015.

Are You at a Healthy Body Weight?

Body mass index or BMI is a calculation of weight relative to height and is an indicator of overall health. To determine if you need to gain or lose weight, find your BMI on the chart using your current height and weight.

Table 42.1. BMI Calculation

BMI = (Weight in Kilograms / (Height in Meters x Height in Meters))
BMI = (Weight in Pounds / (Height in inches x Height in inches)) x 703

- If your BMI is below 18.5 (underweight), you should focus on gaining weight.

- If your BMI is between 18.5 and 29.9 (normal or overweight), you should focus on maintaining your weight.

- If your BMI is 30 or greater (obese), you may need to lose weight—talk with your physician and Registered Dietitian (RD) for further guidance.

Are You Eating a Healthy, Well–Balanced Diet?

Eating a healthy, well–balanced diet, such as the USDA's (U.S. Department of Agriculture) MyPlate (www.choosemyplate.gov), will help meet your overall nutrition goals. MyPlate shows the five food groups using a familiar mealtime picture, a place setting.

Figure 42.1. *Well–Balanced Diet*

Key messages include:

- Include foods from all 5 food groups every day.
- Make half of your plate fruits and vegetables.
- Make at least half of your grains whole.
- Vary your protein choices (lean meat, poultry, seafood, eggs, beans, nuts and seeds).

What If You Need to Gain Weight?

The best way to gain weight is to eat and drink more energy or calories.

If You Need to Eat More Calories:

- Eat 5–6 small meals per day.
- Keep your favorite foods on hand.
- Choose high calorie beverages such as whole milk, 100% fruit juice, sweetened soda, milkshakes, Boost® and Ensure®.
- Add fat to foods by including butter, margarine, vegetable oils, nuts, peanut butter, mayonnaise, sauces, gravies, cheese and salad dressings.
- Sweeten foods and beverages with sugar, jam, jelly and honey.
- Use full-fat or regular versions of foods instead of low-fat or fat-free.
- Avoid foods that say "lite," diet" or "low-calorie."

If You Feel Full Quickly:

- Drink fluids between meals rather than with meals.
- Eat high calorie foods first at a meal—avoid filling up on low calorie items such as salads.

If You Feel Nauseous:

- Try cold or room temperature foods that have fewer odors.
- Try dry, starchy or salty foods such as pretzels, saltines or potatoes.

If You Are Experiencing Taste Changes:

- Try adding spices and condiments to foods to make them more appealing.

- Eat with plastic utensils if you have a metallic taste in your mouth.

If You Feel Fatigued:

- Ask family members and friends to help with grocery shopping and food preparation.

- Focus on convenience foods that require little or no preparation (yogurt, nuts, nut butters, trail mix, string cheese, etc).

What Should You Do Next?

If you have an underweight BMI, are experiencing unexplained weight loss or just want to discuss a healthy diet, ask to meet with a Registered Dietitian.

Chapter 43

Healthy Weight Loss Guidelines

Chapter Contents

Section 43.1

What is Healthy Weight Loss?

This section includes text excerpted from "Losing Weight,"
Centers for Disease Control and Prevention (CDC), May 15, 2015.

It's natural for anyone trying to lose weight to want to lose it very quickly. But evidence shows that people who lose weight gradually and steadily (about 1 to 2 pounds per week) are more successful at keeping weight off. Healthy weight loss isn't just about a "diet" or "program." It's about an ongoing lifestyle that includes long-term changes in daily eating and exercise habits.

To lose weight, you must use up more calories than you take in. Since one pound equals 3,500 calories, you need to reduce your caloric intake by 500–1000 calories per day to lose about 1 to 2 pounds per week.

Once you've achieved a healthy weight, by relying on healthful eating and physical activity most days of the week (about 60–90 minutes, moderate intensity), you are more likely to be successful at keeping the weight off over the long term. Losing weight is not easy, and it takes commitment.

Even Modest Weight Loss Can Mean Big Benefits

The good news is that no matter what your weight loss goal is, even a modest weight loss, such as 5 to 10 percent of your total body weight, is likely to produce health benefits, such as improvements in blood pressure, blood cholesterol, and blood sugars.

For example, if you weigh 200 pounds, a 5 percent weight loss equals 10 pounds, bringing your weight down to 190 pounds. While this weight may still be in the "overweight" or "obese" range, this modest weight loss can decrease your risk factors for chronic diseases related to obesity.

So even if the overall goal seems large, see it as a journey rather than just a final destination. You'll learn new eating and physical activity habits that will help you live a healthier lifestyle. These habits may help you maintain your weight loss over time.

In addition to improving your health, maintaining a weight loss is likely to improve your life in other ways. For example, a study of participants in the National Weight Control Registry found that those who had maintained a significant weight loss reported improvements in not only their physical health, but also their energy levels, physical mobility, general mood, and self-confidence.

Section 43.2

Why Diets Don't Work

This section includes text excerpted from "Why Diets Don't Work," © 2016 Eating Disorders Victoria. For more information, visit www.eatingdisorders.org.au. Reprinted with permission.

Weight-loss and fad diets involve restricting food intake to levels which often leave a person constantly hungry and in some cases, lacking the necessary nutrients they need to maintain physical health and energy levels. The restrictive nature of dieting does not work, as fad diets do not provide a sustainable meal plan for the long term. Ninety-five percent of people who diet regain the weight and more within two years. Aside from the dangers of dieting, there are a number of physical and emotional reasons why diets do not work:

Famine Response

When food intake is reduced, bodies respond as if they are in famine or starvation situation. As a survival instinct, the body can adjust its metabolism or the amount of energy it uses to maintain bodily functions. Although it is very difficult to increase the body's metabolism (increase the rate we burn energy), the body attempts to protect itself against famine by reducing the metabolic rate, which can happen within 48 hours of restricting either the type and/or the amount of food, and can decrease by as much as 40 per cent.

Leptin

Leptin is a hormone produced by the fat cells in our bodies. It exists in the body in proportionate amounts to our weight. When body fat decreases, so do leptin levels. Bodies want to compensate for this loss in leptin and respond by increasing hunger urges and decreasing metabolism, which reduces the rate at which energy is burned.

Rising Obesity Rates Coinciding with Growth of Weight-Loss Industry

The past few decades have seen a marked increase in the size and profitability of the weight-loss industry, with a boom in the number and sales of countless diet plans. However over this time, we have also seen a significant increase in obesity rates across first world countries. While there is no hard evidence of this correlation, it seems the more pre-occupied and diet-obsessed we as a society become, the more we see these weight loss efforts fail as evident in rising obesity rates.

Food in Social Settings

Food is often associated with many social occasions and family gatherings, such as going out to dinner or a BBQ. People who are dieting often avoid social situations and family mealtimes, leading to feelings of isolation and a loss of support.

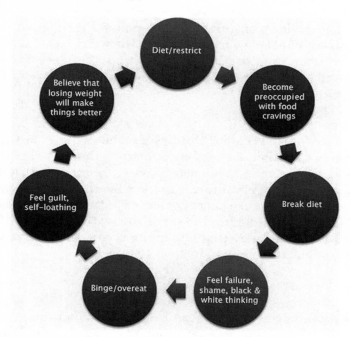

Figure 43.1. *The Diet/Binge Cycle*

Abstinence Leads to Bingeing

When food intake is restricted, a person experiences physical and emotional deprivation. This compels a person to eat, which commonly leads to overeating or bingeing. As a result, a person is likely to feel sensations of guilt and failure. This often becomes a cycle which is difficult to break and has devastating effects on a person's self-esteem, as demonstrated in Figure 43.1.

Section 43.3

Are Detox Diets Safe?

What Is a Detox Diet?

The name sounds reassuring—everyone knows that anything toxic is bad for you. Plus, these diets encourage you to eat natural foods and involve lots of water and veggies—all stuff you know is good for you. You hear about celebrities going on detox diets, and people who go into drug or alcohol rehabs are said to be detoxing. So shouldn't a detox diet be a good bet?

Not really. Like many other fad diets, detox diets can have harmful side effects, especially for teens.

A toxin is a chemical or poison that is known to have harmful effects on the body. Toxins can come from food or water, from chemicals used to grow or prepare food, and even from the air that we breathe. Our bodies process those toxins through organs like the liver and kidneys and eliminate them in the form of sweat, urine, and feces.

Although detox diet theories have not been proven scientifically, the people who support them believe that toxins don't always leave our bodies properly during the elimination of waste. Instead, they think toxins hang around in our digestive, lymph, and gastrointestinal systems as well as in our skin and hair causing problems like tiredness, headaches, and nausea.

The basic idea behind detox diets is to temporarily give up certain kinds of foods that are thought to contain toxins. The idea is to purify and purge the body of all the "bad" stuff. But the truth is, the human body is designed to purify itself.

Detox diets vary. Most involve some version of a fast: that is, giving up food for a couple of days and then gradually reintroducing certain foods into the diet. Many of these diets also encourage people to have colonic irrigation or enemas to "clean out" the colon. (An enema flushes out the rectum and colon using water.) Others recommend that you take special teas or supplements to help the "purification" process.

There are lots of claims about what a detox diet can do, from preventing and curing disease to giving people more energy or focus. Of course, eating a diet lower in fat and added sugars and higher in fiber can help many people feel healthier. But people who support detox diets claim that this is because of the elimination of toxins. There's no scientific proof that these diets help rid the body of toxins faster or that the elimination of toxins will make you a healthier, more energetic person.

What Should You Watch Out For?

Detox diets are supposedly to help "clean out the system" but many people think they will lose weight if they try these diets. Here's the truth:

- Detox diets are not recommended for teens. Normal teenagers need lots of nutritional goodies—like enough calories and protein to support rapid growth and development. So diets that involve fasting and severe restriction of food are not a good idea. Some sports and physical activities require ample food, and fasting does not provide enough fuel to support them. For these reasons, detox diets can be especially risky for teenagers.

- Detox diets aren't for people with health conditions. They're not recommended for people with diabetes, heart disease, or other chronic medical conditions. Detox diets should be avoided if you are pregnant or have an eating disorder.

- Detox diets can be addicting. That's because there's a certain feeling that comes from going without food or from having an enema—for some, it's almost like the high other people get from nicotine or alcohol. This can become a dangerous addiction that leads to health problems, including serious eating disorders, heart problems, and even death.

- Detox supplements can have side effects. Many of the supplements used during detox diets are actually laxatives, which are designed to make people go to the bathroom more often, and that can get messy. Laxative supplements are never a good idea because they can cause dehydration, mineral imbalances, and problems with the digestive system.

- Detox diets don't help people lose fat. People who fast for several days may drop pounds, but most of it will be water and some of it may be muscle. Most people regain the weight they lost soon after completing the program.

Detox diets are for short-term purposes only. In addition to causing other health problems, fasting for long periods can slow down a person's metabolism, making it harder to keep the weight off or to lose weight later.

Eat Right, and Your Body Does the Rest

Of course, it's a great idea to eat lots of fruits and veggies, get lots of fiber, and drink water. But you also need to make sure you're getting all of the nutrients you need from other foods, including protein (from sources such as lean meats, fish, eggs, and beans) and calcium (from foods like low-fat or fat-free milk or yogurt).

The human body is designed to purify itself. You can help by eating a variety of healthy foods. If you have questions about detox diets or are concerned about your weight, talk to your doctor or a registered dietitian.

Section 43.4

Skip the Fad Diet—Go the Healthy Way

This section includes text excerpted from "Skip the Fad Diet—Go the Healthy Way," U.S. Department of Veterans Affairs (VA), March 18, 2014.

How Can I Tell If a Diet Is a "Fad" Diet?

Signs of a Fad Diet Include:

- Miraculous claims and testimonials
- Promises of fast weight loss
- Rules that make you avoid certain food groups
- A food plan that does not consider your preferences and lifestyle

Do Fad Diets Work?

No! They can make you lose weight over the short-term, but you will gain it back. To lose weight and keep it off, you have to change your eating and physical activity and make this part of your lifestyle. Fad diets don't result in long-term weight loss and may be bad for your health.

Will Over-the-Counter Weight Loss Supplements Help Me?

No. Many over-the counter products contain questionable, if not frankly dangerous substances. Some of these over-the-counter products actually contain medications that should require a prescription or are illegal in the United States. These substances can also interact with your prescribed medications.

There are a small number of prescription medications that are approved by the Food and Drug Administration (FDA) for weight management. If you feel you would benefit from a weight loss medication, let your healthcare team know. They can help, but they are also not fast solutions.

Are All Diets Bad?

No. Eating healthier is always good for you. Your healthcare team or dietitian may recommend a special diet. These diets do work in managing problems like diabetes. They also help you manage your weight.

The current medical opinion is that one should choose a healthy diet and stick with it now and in the future. Find a healthy diet that works for you.

What Does Work?

Eating in more healthy ways and gradually increasing your physical activity works.

Section 43.5

Weight Loss and Nutrition Myths

This section includes text excerpted from "Weight-Loss and Nutrition Myths," National Institute of Diabetes and Digestive and Kidney Diseases (NIDDK), October 2014.

"Lose 30 pounds in 30 days!"
"Eat as much as you want and still lose weight!"
"Try the thigh buster and lose inches fast!"

Have you heard these claims before? A large number of diets and tools are available, but their quality may vary. It can be hard to know what to believe.

Here, we discuss myths and provide facts and tips about weight loss, nutrition, and physical activity. This information may help you make healthy changes in your daily habits. You can also talk to your healthcare provider. She or he can help you if you have other questions or you want to lose weight. A registered dietitian may also give you advice on a healthy eating plan and safe ways to lose weight and keep it off.

Weight-loss and Diet Myths

Myth: Fad diets will help me lose weight and keep it off.

371

Fact: Fad diets are not the best way to lose weight and keep it off. These diets often promise quick weight loss if you strictly reduce what you eat or avoid some types of foods. Some of these diets may help you lose weight at first. But these diets are hard to follow. Most people quickly get tired of them and regain any lost weight.

Fad diets may be unhealthy. They may not provide all of the nutrients your body needs. Also, losing more than 3 pounds a week after the first few weeks may increase your chances of developing gallstones (solid matter in the gallbladder that can cause pain). Being on a diet of fewer than 800 calories a day for a long time may lead to serious heart problems.

TIP: Research suggests that safe weight loss involves combining a reduced-calorie diet with physical activity to lose 1/2 to 2 pounds a week (after the first few weeks of weight loss). Make healthy food choices. Eat small portions. Build exercise into your daily life. Combined, these habits may be a healthy way to lose weight and keep it off. These habits may also lower your chances of developing heart disease, high blood pressure, and type 2 diabetes.

Myth: Grain products such as bread, pasta, and rice are fattening. I should avoid them when trying to lose weight.

Fact: A grain product is any food made from wheat, rice, oats, cornmeal, barley, or another cereal grain. Grains are divided into two subgroups, whole grains and refined grains. Whole grains contain the entire grain kernel—the bran, germ, and endosperm. Examples include brown rice and whole-wheat bread, cereal, and pasta. Refined grains have been milled, a process that removes the bran and germ. This is done to give grains a finer texture and improve their shelf life, but it also removes dietary fiber, iron, and many B vitamins.

People who eat whole grains as part of a healthy diet may lower their chances of developing some chronic diseases. Government dietary guidelines advise making half your grains whole grains. For example, choose 100 percent whole-wheat bread instead of white bread, and brown rice instead of white rice.

TIP: To lose weight, reduce the number of calories you take in and increase the amount of physical activity you do each day. Create and follow a healthy eating plan that replaces less healthy options with a mix of fruits, veggies, whole grains, protein foods, and low-fat dairy:

- Eat a mix of fat-free or low-fat milk and milk products, fruits, veggies, and whole grains.

- Limit added sugars, cholesterol, salt (sodium), and saturated fat.
- Eat low-fat protein: beans, eggs, fish, lean meats, nuts, and poultry.

Healthy habits may help you lose weight.

- Make healthy food choices. Half of your plate should be fruits and veggies.
- Eat small portions. Use a smaller plate, weigh portions on a scale, or check the Nutrition Facts label for details about serving sizes.
- Build exercise into your daily life. Garden, go for family walks, play a pickup game of sports, start a dance club with your friends, swim, take the stairs, or walk to the grocery store or work.

Combined, these habits may be a safe, healthy way to lose weight and keep it off.

Meal Myths

Myth: Some people can eat whatever they want and still lose weight.

Fact: To lose weight, you need to burn more calories than you eat and drink. Some people may seem to get away with eating any kind of food they want and still lose weight. But those people, like everyone, must use more energy than they take in through food and drink to lose weight.

A number of factors such as your age, genes, medicines, and lifestyle habits may affect your weight. If you would like to lose weight, speak with your healthcare provider about factors that may affect your weight. Together, you may be able to create a plan to help you reach your weight and health goals.

Eat the Rainbow!

When making half of your plate fruits and veggies, choose foods with vibrant colors that are packed with fiber, minerals, and vitamins.

Red: bell peppers, cherries, cranberries, onions, red beets, strawberries, tomatoes, watermelon,

Green: avocado, broccoli, cabbage, cucumber, dark lettuce, grapes, honeydew, kale, kiwi, spinach, zucchini

Orange and yellow: apricots, bananas, carrots, mangoes, oranges, peaches, squash, sweet potatoes

Blue and purple: blackberries, blueberries, grapes, plums, purple cabbage, purple carrots, purple potatoes

TIP: When trying to lose weight, you can still eat your favorite foods as part of a healthy eating plan. But you must watch the total number of calories that you eat. Reduce your portion sizes. Find ways to limit the calories in your favorite foods. For example, you can bake foods rather than frying them. Use low-fat milk in place of cream. Make half of your plate fruits and veggies.

Myth: "Low-fat" or "fat-free" means no calories.

Fact: A serving of low-fat or fat-free food may be lower in calories than a serving of the full-fat product. But many processed low-fat or fat-free foods have just as many calories as the full-fat versions of the same foods—or even more calories. These foods may contain added flour, salt, starch, or sugar to improve flavor and texture after fat is removed. These items add calories.

TIP: Read the Nutrition Facts label (see Figure 43.2) on a food package to find out how many calories are in a serving. Check the serving size, too—it may be less than you are used to eating.

Myth: Fast foods are always an unhealthy choice. You should not eat them when dieting.

Fact: Many fast foods are unhealthy and may affect weight gain. However, if you do eat fast food, choose menu options with care. Both at home and away, choose healthy foods that are nutrient rich, low in calories, and small in portion size.

TIP: To choose healthy, low-calorie options, check the nutrition facts. These are often offered on the menu or on restaurant websites. And know that the nutrition facts often do not include sauces and extras. Try these tips:

- Avoid "value" combo meals, which tend to have more calories than you need in one meal.

- Choose fresh fruit items or nonfat yogurt for dessert.

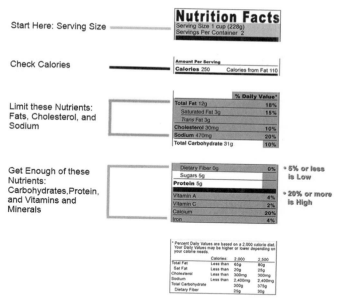

Figure 43.2. *Nutrition Facts Label*

- Limit your use of toppings that are high in fat and calories, such as bacon, cheese, regular mayonnaise, salad dressings, and tartar sauce.

- Pick steamed or baked items over fried ones.

- Sip on water or fat-free milk instead of soda.

Myth: If I skip meals, I can lose weight.

Fact: Skipping meals may make you feel hungrier and lead you to eat more than you normally would at your next meal. In particular, studies show a link between skipping breakfast and obesity. People who skip breakfast tend to be heavier than people who eat a healthy breakfast.

TIP: Choose meals and snacks that include a variety of healthy foods. Try these examples:

- For a quick breakfast, make oatmeal with low-fat milk, topped with fresh berries. Or eat a slice of whole-wheat toast with fruit spread.

- Pack a healthy lunch each night, so you won't be tempted to rush out of the house in the morning without one.

- For healthy nibbles, pack a small low-fat yogurt, a couple of whole-wheat crackers with peanut butter, or veggies with hummus.

Myth: Eating healthy food costs too much.

Fact: Eating better does not have to cost a lot of money. Many people think that fresh foods are healthier than canned or frozen ones. For example, some people think that spinach is better for you raw than frozen or canned. However, canned or frozen fruits and veggies provide as many nutrients as fresh ones, at a lower cost. Healthy options include low-salt canned veggies and fruit canned in its own juice or water-packed. Remember to rinse canned veggies to remove excess salt. Also, some canned seafood, like tuna, is easy to keep on the shelf, healthy, and low-cost. And canned, dried, or frozen beans, lentils, and peas are also healthy sources of protein that are easy on the wallet.

TIP: Check the nutrition facts on canned, dried, and frozen items. Look for items that are high in calcium, fiber, potassium, protein, and vitamin D. Also check for items that are low in added sugars, saturated fat, and sodium.

What Is the Difference between a Serving and a Portion?

The U.S. Food and Drug Administration (FDA) Nutrition Facts label appears on most packaged foods (see Figure 43.2 below). It tells you how many calories and servings are in a box or can. The serving size varies from product to product.

A portion is how much food you choose to eat at one time, whether in a restaurant, from a package, or at home. Sometimes the serving size and portion size match; sometimes they do not.

You can use the Nutrition Facts label

- to track your calorie intake and number of servings

- to make healthy food choices by serving smaller portions and selecting items lower in fats, salt, and sugar and higher in fiber and vitamins

Physical Activity Myths

Myth: Lifting weights is not a good way to lose weight because it will make me "bulk up."

Fact: Lifting weights or doing activities like push-ups and crunches on a regular basis can help you build strong muscles, which can help you burn more calories. To strengthen muscles, you can lift weights, use large rubber bands (resistance bands), do push-ups or sit-ups, or do household or yard tasks that make you lift or dig. Doing strengthening activities 2 or 3 days a week will not "bulk you up." Only intense strength training, along with certain genetics, can build large muscles.

TIP: Government guidelines for physical activity recommend that adults should do activities at least two times a week to strengthen muscles. The guidelines also suggest that adults should get 150 to 300 minutes of moderately intense or vigorous aerobic activity each week—like brisk walking or biking. Aerobic activity makes you sweat and breathe faster.

Myth: Physical activity only counts if I can do it for long periods of time.

Fact: You do not need to be active for long periods to achieve your 150 to 300 minutes of activity each week. Experts advise doing aerobic activity for periods of 10 minutes or longer at a time. You can spread these sessions out over the week.

TIP: Plan to do at least 10 minutes of physical activity three times a day on 5 or more days a week. This will help you meet the 150-minute goal. While at work, take a brief walking break. Use the stairs. Get off the bus one stop early. Go dancing with friends. Whether for a short or long period, bursts of activity may add up to the total amount of physical activity you need each week.

Don't Just Sit There!

Americans spend a lot of time sitting in front of computers, desks, hand-held devices, and TVs. Break up your day by moving around more and getting regular aerobic activity that makes you sweat and breathe faster.

- Get 150 to 300 minutes of moderately intense or vigorous physical activity each week. Basketball, brisk walks, hikes, hula hoops, runs, soccer, tennis—choose whatever you enjoy best! Even 10 minutes of activity at a time can add up over the week.

- Strengthen your muscles at least twice a week. Do push-ups or pull-ups, lift weights, do heavy gardening, or work with rubber resistance bands.

Food Myths

Myth: Eating meat is bad for my health and makes it harder to lose weight.

Fact: Eating lean meat in small amounts can be part of a healthy plan to lose weight. Chicken, fish, pork, and red meat contain some cholesterol and saturated fat. But they also contain healthy nutrients like iron, protein, and zinc.

TIP: Choose cuts of meat that are lower in fat, and trim off all the fat you can see. Meats that are lower in fat include chicken breast, pork loin and beef round steak, flank steak, and extra lean ground beef. Also, watch portion size. Try to eat meat or poultry in portions of 3 ounces or less. Three ounces is about the size of a deck of cards.

Myth: Dairy products are fattening and unhealthy.

Fact: Fat-free and low-fat cheese, milk, and yogurt are just as healthy as whole-milk dairy products, and they are lower in fat and calories. Dairy products offer protein to build muscles and help organs work well, and calcium to strengthen bones. Most milk and some yogurts have extra vitamin D added to help your body use calcium. Most Americans don't get enough calcium and vitamin D. Dairy is an easy way to get more of these nutrients.

TIP: Based on Government guidelines, you should try to have 3 cups a day of fat-free or low-fat milk or milk products. This can include soy beverages fortified with vitamins. If you can't digest lactose (the sugar found in dairy products), choose lactose-free or low-lactose dairy products or other foods and beverages that have calcium and vitamin D:

- calcium: soy-based beverages or tofu made with calcium sulfate; canned salmon; dark leafy greens like collards or kale
- vitamin D: cereals or soy-based beverages

Myth: "Going vegetarian" will help me lose weight and be healthier.

Fact: Research shows that people who follow a vegetarian eating plan, on average, eat fewer calories and less fat than non-vegetarians. Some research has found that vegetarian-style eating patterns are associated with lower levels of obesity, lower blood pressure, and a reduced risk of heart disease.

Vegetarians also tend to have lower body mass index (BMI) scores than people with other eating plans. (The BMI measures body fat based on a person's height in relation to weight.) But vegetarians—like others—can make food choices that impact weight gain, like eating large amounts of foods that are high in fat or calories or low in nutrients.

The types of vegetarian diets eaten in the United States can vary widely. Vegans do not consume any animal products, while lacto-ovo vegetarians eat milk and eggs along with plant foods. Some people have eating patterns that are mainly vegetarian but may include small amounts of meat, poultry, or seafood.

TIP: If you choose to follow a vegetarian eating plan, be sure you get enough of the nutrients that others usually take in from animal products such as cheese, eggs, meat, and milk. Nutrients that may be lacking in a vegetarian diet are listed in the sidebar, along with foods and beverages that may help you meet your body's needs for these nutrients.

Table 43.1. Nutrients and Common Sources

Nutrient	Common Sources
Calcium	dairy products, soy beverages with added calcium, tofu made with calcium sulfate, collard greens, kale, broccoli
Iron	cashews, spinach, lentils, chickpeas, bread or cereal with added iron
Protein	eggs, dairy products, beans, peas, nuts, seeds, tofu, tempeh, soy-based burgers
Vitamin B12	eggs, dairy products, fortified cereal or soy beverages, tempeh, miso (tempeh and miso are foods made from soybeans)
Vitamin D	foods and beverages with added vitamin D, including milk, soy beverages, or cereal
Zinc	whole grains (check the ingredients list on product labels for the words "whole" or "whole grain" before the grain ingredient's name), nuts, tofu, leafy greens (spinach, cabbage, lettuce)

Section 43.6

Weighing the Claims in Diet Ads

This section includes text excerpted from "Weighing
the Claims in Diet Ads," Federal Trade Commission (FTC),
July 15, 2012. Reviewed March 2016.

Whether it's a pill, patch, or cream, there's no shortage of ads promising quick and easy weight loss without diet or exercise. But the claims just aren't true, and some of these products could even hurt your health. The best way to lose weight is to eat fewer calories and get more exercise. Don't be hooked by promises, testimonials, or supposed endorsements from reporters; all you'll lose is money.

Will I Really Lose Weight?

Wouldn't it be nice if you could lose weight simply by taking a pill, wearing a patch, or rubbing in a cream? Unfortunately, claims that you can lose weight without changing your habits just aren't true.

Doctors, dietitians, and other experts agree that the best way to lose weight is to eat fewer calories and be more active. That's true even for people taking pills approved by U.S. Food and Drug Administration (FDA) to help them lose weight. For most people, a reasonable goal is to lose about a pound a week, which means:

- cutting about 500 calories a day from your diet

- eating a variety of nutritious foods

- exercising regularly

The Truth Behind Weight Loss Ads

Claims to watch out for include:

Lose weight without diet or exercise!

Getting to a healthy weight takes work. Take a pass on any product that promises miraculous results without the effort. The only thing you'll lose is money.

Lose weight no matter how much you eat of your favorite foods!

Beware of any product that claims that you can eat all the high-calorie food you want and still lose weight. Losing weight requires sensible food choices. Filling up on healthy vegetables and fruits can make it easier to say no to fattening sweets and snacks.

Lose weight permanently! Never diet again!

Even if you're successful in taking weight off, permanent weight loss requires permanent lifestyle changes. Don't trust any product that promises once-and-for-all results without ongoing maintenance.

Just take a pill!

Doctors, dietitians, and other experts agree that there's simply no magic way to lose weight without diet or exercise. Even pills approved by FDA to block the absorption of fat or help you eat less and feel full are to be taken with a low-calorie, low-fat diet and regular exercise.

Lose 30 pounds in 30 days!

Losing weight at the rate of a pound or two a week is the most effective way to take it off and keep it off. At best, products promising lightning-fast weight loss are a scam. At worst, they can ruin your health.

Everybody will lose weight!

Your habits and health concerns are unique. There is no one-size-fits-all product guaranteed to work for everyone. Team up with your healthcare provider to design a nutrition and exercise program suited to your lifestyle and metabolism.

Lose weight with our miracle diet patch or cream!

You've seen the ads for diet patches or creams that claim to melt away the pounds. Don't believe them. There's nothing you can wear or apply to your skin that will cause you to lose weight.

Acai Berry Supplements in the "News"

More and more, scam artists are exploiting people's trust in well-known news organizations by setting up fake news sites with the logos of legitimate news organizations to peddle their wares. In particular, sites claiming to be objective news sources may describe a so-called "investigation" of the effectiveness of acai berry dietary supplements for weight loss. These sites are a marketing ploy created to sell acai berry supplements.

Tainted Weight Loss Products

In the last few years, FDA has discovered hundreds of dietary supplements containing drugs or other chemicals, often in products for weight loss and bodybuilding. These extras generally aren't listed on the label—and might even be sold with false and misleading claims like "100% natural" and "safe." They could cause serious side effects or interact in dangerous ways with medicines or other supplements you're taking.

The Skinny on Electronic Muscle Stimulators

You might have seen ads for electronic muscle stimulators claiming they will tone, firm, and strengthen abdominal muscles, help you lose weight, or get rock hard abs. But according to FDA, while these devices may temporarily strengthen, tone, or firm a muscle, no electronic muscle stimulator device alone will give you "six-pack" abs.

Section 43.7

Tips for Losing Weight Safely

This section contains text excerpted from the following sources: Text beginning with the heading "If You Need to Lose Weight" is excerpted from "If You Need to Lose Weight," Office on Women's Health (OWH), November 5, 2013; Text beginning with the heading "What You Need to Know Before Getting Started" is excerpted from "Interested in Losing Weight?" U.S. Department of Agriculture (USDA), January 26, 2016; Text beginning with the heading "What Should I Look for in a Weight-Loss Program?" is excerpted from "Choosing a Safe and Successful Weight-Loss Program," National Institute of Diabetes and Digestive and Kidney Diseases (NIDDK), December 2012. Reviewed March 2016.

If You Need to Lose Weight

Lots of people need to lose some weight. If your doctor tells you that you are overweight or obese, it's important that you try to lose weight. You can ask your doctor and perhaps a dietitian about ways to lose weight. It can be a bit harder for some people to lose weight because of their genes or because of things around them, such as the food choices in their house. But with the right support and a good plan, you can get to a healthy weight. Learn more about losing weight:

Great Ways to Lose Weight

You don't need a special diet like a low-carb or high-protein diet to lose weight. The best way to lose weight is to get the right mix of nutrients and energy your body needs. Here are some tips for losing weight in a healthy way:

- **Follow a food guide.** It can be hard to know which foods to choose. The MyPlate guide (www.choosemyplate.gov) can be a big help. It will encourage you to eat whole grains, vegetables, and fruits. These foods are full of fiber, which can help you feel full. And keeping a record can help, so try the ChooseMyPlate tracking tool (www.supertracker.usda.gov).

- **Cut back on fats.** You need some fat, but even small amounts of fats have lots of calories. Read labels to see how much fat a food has. And try to cut back on fried foods and on meats that are high in fat, such as burgers.

- **Eat fewer sweets and unhealthy snacks.** Candy, cookies, and cakes often have a lot of sugar and fat and not many nutrients.

- **Avoid sugary drinks.** Try not to drink a lot of sugary sodas, energy drinks, and sports drinks. They can add a lot of calories. (There are about 10 packets of sugar in 12 ounces of soda.) Also try not to drink a lot of fruit juice. Water is a great choice instead. Add a piece of lemon or a splash of juice for more flavor.

- **Get enough sleep at night.** Many teens stay up too late. Staying up late often increases night-time snacking and low energy the next morning (which you might be tempted to beat with some extra food).

- **Limit fast food meals.** Studies show that the more fast food you eat each week, the greater the risk of gaining extra weight. So try to limit fast food meals to once a week or less.

- **Tackle hunger with fiber and protein.** Don't wait until you are so hungry that it gets hard to make smart food choices. Instead, when you start to feel hungry, eat a small snack that combines a protein with a food that's high in fiber, such as a whole-grain cracker with low-fat cheese. These are filling but not packed with calories.

- **Be aware of how much you are eating.** If you're not sure how much is considered one serving, you can learn how to read labels. You also may eat less if you use a smaller plate. Try not to eat straight from a big package of food—it's easy to lose track that way. And if you're at a restaurant, see if you can take home some leftovers.

- **Think about why you are eating.** Sometimes we eat to fill needs other than hunger, such as being bored, stressed, or lonely. If you do that, see if you can think of some other ways to meet those needs. Consider calling a friend or listening to some great music. And if think you may be having emotional problems, talk to an adult you trust.

- **Get moving.** One great way to lose weight is by being physically active. You should aim for a total of 60 minutes of moderate or vigorous physical activity each day. If you haven't been active in a while, start slowly.

- **Cut down on sitting around.** This means less TV, Internet, and other forms of screen time. Instead, aim for your "hour a day of active play."

Remember that losing weight is about making healthy changes in your life that you can stick with—and not just a one-time diet.

How Not to Lose Weight

It can be tempting to look for a quick fix if you need to lose weight. Remember, though, that if something sounds too good to be true, it probably is. Keep these tips in mind:

- **Avoid fad diets.** Fad diets often allow only a few types of food. That means you are not getting all the nutrients you need. And these diets may cause you to lose weight for a short time, but then you likely will gain it back quickly.

- **Avoid weight-loss pills and other quick-loss products.** Most weight-loss pills, drinks, supplements, and other products you can buy without a prescription have not been shown to work. And they can actually be very dangerous. If you are thinking about taking weight-loss pills or similar products, talk to your doctor first.

- **Don't eat too little.** Your body needs fuel to grow and be healthy. If you eat fewer than 1,600 calories each day, you may not get the nutrients you need. And don't skip breakfast. Some research suggests that teens who skip breakfast are more likely to be overweight.

- **Don't try to get rid of food you eat.** Some people think they can lose weight by making themselves vomit or taking laxatives (pills that make you go to the bathroom). These are very dangerous steps and signs of eating disorders. Your body is too precious to treat this way, so get help if you think you may have an eating disorder.

- **Don't expect to lose weight quickly.** Losing about one to two pounds a week is a healthy rate of weight loss. If you are taking extreme steps to lose weight faster, you will probably gain most or all of it back.

What You Need to Know before Getting Started

Weight loss can be achieved either by eating fewer calories or by burning more calories with physical activity, preferably both.

A healthy weight loss program consists of:

- A reasonable, realistic weight loss goal

- A reduced calorie, nutritionally-balanced eating plan

- Regular physical activity

- A behavior change plan to help you stay on track with your goals

Keep in Mind

- Calories count

- Portions count

- Nutrition counts

- Even a small amount of weight loss can lead to big health benefits

- Strive to develop good habits to last a lifetime

- Discuss weight loss with your doctor before getting started

Getting Started

- Check your Body Mass Index (BMI)—an indicator of body fat—and see where it fits within the BMI categories.

- Discuss weight loss with your doctor and decide on a goal. If you have a lot of weight to lose, set a realistic intermediate goal, maybe to lose 10 pounds. Remember that even a small amount of weight loss can lead to big health benefits.

- Estimate your calorie needs. Using U.S. Department of Agriculture's (USDA's) online Adult Energy Needs and BMI Calculator (www.bcm.edu/cnrc-apps/caloriesneed.cfm), you can determine the number of calories needed each day to maintain your current weight. To lose about 1 pound per week, subtract 500 calories each day from the daily amount. To lose about 2 pounds per week, subtract 1000 calories daily.

- Score your current food intake and physical activity level using MyPlate SuperTracker (www.supertracker.usda.gov). Taking a good look at your current habits will help you determine what changes you might make as well as what you are doing right.

How Do I Know Which Weight Loss Plan is Right for Me?

- Keep in mind that you want to develop lifestyle habits that will help you maintain your weight in a healthy range. A short-term "diet" that you "go on" and then "go off" is not the answer to long-term weight management.

- In choosing how to go about losing weight, keep in mind key habits of people who have lost weight and kept in off. These people are called "Successful Losers" by the weight control experts who have studied them.

Key Behaviors of Successful Losers

- Getting regular physical activity
- Reducing calorie and fat intake
- Eating regular meals, including breakfast
- Weighing themselves regularly
- Not letting small "slips" turn into large weight regain

- Ask your doctor if you should have a referral to a Registered Dietitian (RD). An RD can provide personalized dietary advice taking into consideration other health issues, lifestyle, and food likes and dislikes.

What Should I Look for in a Weight-Loss Program?

Successful, long-term weight control must focus on your overall health, not just on what you eat. Changing your lifestyle is not easy, but adopting healthy habits may help you manage your weight in the long run.

Effective weight-loss programs include ways to keep the weight off for good. These programs promote healthy behaviors that help you lose weight and that you can stick with every day.

Safe and effective weight-loss programs should include

- a plan to keep the weight off over the long run

- guidance on how to develop healthier eating and physical activity habits

- ongoing feedback, monitoring, and support

- slow and steady weight-loss goals—usually ½ to 2 pounds per week (though weight loss may be faster at the start of a program)

Some weight-loss programs may use very low-calorie diets (up to 800 calories per day) to promote rapid weight loss among people who have a lot of excess weight. This type of diet requires close medical supervision through frequent office visits and medical tests.

Questions to Ask Your Healthcare Provider

About Your Weight

- What is a healthy weight for me?

- Do I need to lose weight?

- How much weight should I lose? Could my extra weight be caused by a health problem or by a medicine I am taking?

About Ways to Lose Weight

- What kind of eating habits may help me control my weight?

- How much physical activity do I need?

- How can I exercise safely?

- Could a weight-loss program help me?

- Should I take weight-loss drugs?

- Is weight-loss surgery right for me?

What If the Program Is Offered Online?

Many weight-loss programs are now being offered online—either fully or partly. Not much is known about how well these programs work. However, experts suggest that online weight-loss programs should provide the following:

- structured, weekly lessons offered online or by podcasts

- support tailored to your personal goals

- self-monitoring of eating and physical activity using handheld devices, such as cell phones or online journals

- regular feedback from a counselor on goals, progress, and results, given by email, phone, or text messages social support from a group through bulletin boards, chat rooms, and/or online meetings

Whether the program is online or in person, you should get as much background as you can before deciding to join.

What Questions Should I Ask about the Program?

Professionals working for weight-loss programs should be able to answer questions about the program's features, safety, costs, and results. The following are sample questions you may want to ask.

What Does the Weight-Loss Program Include?

- Does the program offer group classes or one-on-one counseling that will help me develop healthier habits?

- Do I have to follow a specific meal plan or keep food records?

- Do I have to buy special meals or supplements?

- If the program requires special foods, can I make changes based on my likes, dislikes, and food allergies (if any)?

- Will the program help me be more physically active, follow a specific physical activity plan, or provide exercise guidelines?

- Will the program work with my lifestyle and cultural needs? Does the program provide ways to deal with such issues as social or holiday eating, changes to work schedules, lack of motivation, and injury or illness?

- Does the program include a plan to help me keep the weight off once I've lost weight?

What Are the Staff Credentials?

- Who supervises the program?

- What type of weight-control certifications, education, experience, and training do the staff have?

Does the Product or Program Carry Any Risks?

- Could the program hurt me?

- Could the suggested drugs or supplements harm my health?

- Do the people involved in the program get to talk with a doctor?

- Does a doctor or other certified health professional run the program?

- Will the program's doctor or staff work with my healthcare provider if needed (for example, to address how the program may affect an existing medical issue)?

- Is there ongoing input and follow-up from a healthcare provider to ensure my safety while I take part in the program?

How Much Does the Program Cost?

- What is the total cost of the program?

- Are there other costs, such as membership fees, fees for weekly visits, and payments for food, meal replacements, supplements, or other products?

- Are there other fees for medical tests?

- Are there fees for a follow-up program after I lose weight?

What Results Do People in the Program Typically Have?

- How much weight does the average person lose?

- How long does the average person keep the weight off?
- Do you have written information on these results?

If It Seems Too Good to Be True... It Probably Is!

In choosing a weight-loss program, watch out for these false claims:

- Lose weight without diet or exercise!
- Lose weight while eating all of your favorite foods!
- Lose 30 pounds in 30 days!
- Lose weight in specific problem areas of your body

Other warning signs include

- very small print
- asterisks and footnotes
- before-and-after photos that seem too good to be true

What If I Need More Help?

If a weight-loss program is not a good option for you, ask your healthcare provider about other types of treatment. Prescription drugs, combined with lifestyle changes, may help some people lose weight. For some people who have obesity, bariatric surgery on the stomach and/or intestines may be an option.

Section 43.8

Dietary Supplements for Weight Loss— Factsheet for Consumers

This section includes text excerpted from "Dietary
Supplements for Weight Loss: Fact Sheet for Consumers,"
National Institutes of Health (NIH), April 1, 2015.

What Are Weight-Loss Dietary Supplements and What Do They Do?

The proven ways to lose weight are by eating healthful foods, cutting calories, and being physically active. But making these lifestyle changes isn't easy, so you might wonder if taking a dietary supplement that's promoted for weight loss might help.

This section describes what's known about the safety and effectiveness of many ingredients that are commonly used in weight-loss dietary supplements. Sellers of these supplements might claim that their products help you lose weight by blocking the absorption of fat or carbohydrates, curbing your appetite, or speeding up your metabolism. But there's little scientific evidence that weight-loss supplements actually work. Many are expensive, some can interact or interfere with medications, and a few might be harmful.

If you're thinking about taking a dietary supplement to lose weight, talk with your healthcare provider. This is especially important if you have high blood pressure, diabetes, heart disease, or other medical conditions.

What Are the Ingredients in Weight-Loss Dietary Supplements?

Weight-loss supplements contain many ingredients—like herbs, fiber, and minerals—in different amounts and in many combinations. Sold in forms such as capsules, tablets, liquids, and powders, some products have dozens of ingredients.

Common ingredients in weight-loss supplements are described below in alphabetical order. You'll learn what's known about whether

391

each ingredient works and is safe. Figuring out whether these ingredients really help you lose weight safely is complicated, though. Most products contain more than one ingredient, and ingredients can work differently when they're mixed together.

You may be surprised to learn that makers of weight-loss supplements rarely carry out studies in people to find out whether their product really works and is safe. And when studies are done, they usually involve only small numbers of people taking the supplement for just a few weeks or months. To know whether a weight-loss supplement can really help people lose weight safely and keep it off, larger groups of people need to be studied for a longer time.

Bitter Orange

Bitter orange contains synephrine (a stimulant), and is claimed to burn calories, increase the breakdown of fat, and decrease appetite. Products with bitter orange usually also contain caffeine and other ingredients. Bitter orange is in some weight loss dietary supplements that used to contain ephedra, another stimulant-containing herb that was banned from the U.S. market in 2004.

Does It Work?

Bitter orange might slightly increase the number of calories you burn. It might also reduce your appetite a little, but whether it can help you lose weight is unknown.

Is It Safe?

Bitter orange might not be safe. Supplements with bitter orange can cause chest pain, anxiety, a faster heart rate, and higher blood pressure.

Caffeine

Caffeine is a stimulant that can make you more alert, give you a boost of energy, burn calories, and increase the breakdown of fat. Often added to weight-loss dietary supplements, caffeine is found naturally in tea, guarana, kola nut, yerba mate, and other herbs. The labels of supplements that contain caffeine don't always list it, so you might not know if a supplement has caffeine.

Does It Work?

Weight-loss dietary supplements with caffeine might help you lose a little weight or gain less weight over time. But when you use caffeine regularly, you develop a tolerance to it. This tolerance might lessen any effect of caffeine on body weight over time.

Is It Safe?

Caffeine is safe at low doses. But it can make you feel nervous, jittery, and shaky. It can also affect your sleep. At high doses (above about 400 milligrams [mg] a day for adults), it can cause nausea, vomiting, rapid heartbeat, and seizures. Combining caffeine with other stimulant ingredients can increase caffeine's effects.

Calcium

Calcium is a mineral you need for healthy bones, muscles, nerves, blood vessels and many of your body's functions. It's claimed to burn fat and decrease fat absorption.

Does It Work?

Calcium—either from food or in weight-loss dietary supplements—probably does not help you lose weight or prevent weight gain.

Is It Safe?

Calcium is safe at the recommended amounts of 1,000 to 1,200 mg a day for adults. Too much calcium (more than 2,000–2,500 mg a day) can cause constipation and decrease your body's absorption of iron and zinc. Also, too much calcium from supplements (but not foods) may increase your risk of kidney stones.

Chitosan

Chitosan comes from the shells of crabs, shrimp, and lobsters. It's claimed to bind fat in the digestive tract so that your body can't absorb it.

Does It Work?

Chitosan binds only a tiny amount of fat, not enough to help you lose much weight.

Is It Safe?

Chitosan seems to be safe. But it can cause flatulence, bloating, mild nausea, constipation, indigestion, and heartburn. If you're allergic to shellfish, you could have an allergic reaction to chitosan.

Chromium

Chromium is a mineral that you need to regulate your blood sugar levels. It's claimed to increase muscle mass and fat loss and decrease appetite and food intake.

Does It Work?

Chromium might help you lose a very small amount of weight and body fat.

Is It Safe?

Chromium in food and supplements is safe at recommended amounts, which range from 20 to 35 micrograms a day for adults. In larger amounts, chromium can cause watery stools, headache, weakness, nausea, vomiting, constipation, dizziness, and hives.

Coleus forskohlii

Coleus forskohlii is a plant that grows in India, Thailand, and other subtropical areas. Forskolin, made from the plant's roots, is claimed to help you lose weight by decreasing your appetite and increasing the breakdown of fat in your body.

Does It Work?

Forskolin hasn't been studied much. But so far, it doesn't seem to have any effect on body weight or appetite.

Is It Safe?

Forskolin seems to be fairly safe. But people have taken it for only a few weeks in the studies done to date.

Conjugated Linoleic Acid (CLA)

CLA is a fat found mainly in dairy products and beef. It's claimed to reduce your body fat.

Does It Work?

Studies lasting up to one year show that CLA may help you lose a very small amount of weight and body fat.

Is It Safe?

CLA appears to be fairly safe. It can cause an upset stomach, constipation, diarrhea, loose stools, and indigestion. In some people, CLA supplements decrease high-density lipoprotein (HDL) ("good") cholesterol levels and increase insulin resistance (a risk factor for diabetes).

Ephedra

Ephedra (also called ma huang) is a plant that's native to China. It contains substances that stimulate your nervous system, increase the amount of energy you burn, increase weight loss, and may suppress your appetite. Once found in weight-loss supplements, ephedra was taken off the market in the United States in 2004 because of safety concerns.

Does It Work?

Ephedra may help you lose weight over the short term. But its long-term effects are unknown.

Is It Safe?

Ephedra is not safe. It can cause nausea, vomiting, anxiety, mood changes, high blood pressure, abnormal heartbeat, stroke, seizures, heart attack, and even death.

Fucoxanthin

Fucoxanthin is a substance that's found in brown seaweed and other algae. It's claimed to help with weight loss by burning calories and decreasing fat.

Does It Work?

Fucoxanthin may help you lose weight. But it hasn't been studied alone as a weight-loss aid. Only one study in people included fucoxanthin (the other studies were in animals).

Is It Safe?

Fucoxanthin seems to be safe, but it hasn't been studied enough to know for sure if it really is safe.

Garcinia cambogia

Garcinia cambogia is a tree that grows throughout Asia, Africa, and the Polynesian islands. Hydroxycitric acid in the fruit is claimed to decrease the number of new fat cells your body makes, suppress your appetite and reduce the amount of food you eat, and limit the amount of weight you gain.

Does It Work?

Garcinia cambogia has little to no effect on weight loss.

Is It Safe?

Garcinia cambogia seems to be fairly safe. But it can cause headache, nausea, and symptoms in the upper respiratory tract, stomach, and intestines. A few people who were taking weight-loss supplements containing *Garcinia cambogia* developed liver damage.

But experts don't know whether this ingredient or the combination of ingredients in the weight-loss supplements was responsible.

Glucomannan

Glucomannan is a soluble dietary fiber from the root of the konjac plant. It's claimed to absorb water in the gut to help you feel full.

Does It Work?

Glucomannan has little to no effect on weight loss. But it might help lower total cholesterol, low-density lipoprotein (LDL) ("bad") cholesterol, triglyceride, and blood sugar levels.

Is It Safe?

Most forms of glucomannan appear to be safe. When used for a short time, it can cause loose stools, flatulence, diarrhea, constipation, and abdominal discomfort. Glucomannan's safety when it's used for a longer time is unknown. Tablet forms of glucomannan can block the esophagus, which is a serious problem.

Green Coffee Bean Extract

Green coffee beans are unroasted coffee beans. Green coffee bean extract is claimed to decrease fat accumulation and help convert blood sugar into energy that your cells can use.

Does It Work?

Green coffee bean extract might help you lose a small amount of weight.

Is It Safe?

The safety of green coffee bean extract has not been studied. It might cause headache and urinary tract infections. Green coffee beans contain the stimulant caffeine. Caffeine can cause problems at high doses or when it's combined with other stimulants.

Green Tea and Green Tea Extract

Green tea (also called *Camellia sinensis*) is a common beverage all over the world. Green tea and green tea extract in some weight-loss supplements are claimed to reduce body weight by increasing the calories your body burns, breaking down fat cells, and decreasing fat absorption and the amount of new fat your body makes.

Does It Work?

Green tea may help you lose weight, but only slightly.

Is It Safe?

Drinking green tea is safe. But taking green tea extract might not be safe. It can cause nausea, constipation, abdominal discomfort, and increased blood pressure. In some people, taking green tea extract has been linked to liver damage.

Guar Gum

Guar gum is a soluble dietary fiber in some dietary supplements and food products. It's claimed to make you feel full, lower your appetite, and decrease the amount of food you eat.

Does It Work?

Guar gum probably does not help you lose weight.

Is It Safe?

Guar gum seems to be safe when it is taken with enough fluid. But it can cause abdominal pain, flatulence, diarrhea, nausea, and cramps.

Hoodia

Hoodia is a plant that grows in southern Africa, where it's used as an appetite suppressant.

Does It Work?

There hasn't been a lot of research on hoodia, but it probably won't help you eat less or lose weight. In the past, analyses showed that some "hoodia" supplements contained very little hoodia or none at all. It's not known whether this is true for hoodia supplements sold today.

Is It Safe?

Hoodia might not be safe. It can cause rapid heart rate, increased blood pressure, headache, dizziness, nausea, and vomiting.

Pyruvate

Pyruvate is naturally present in your body. Pyruvate in weight-loss supplements is claimed to increase fat breakdown, reduce body weight and body fat, and improve exercise performance.

Does It Work?

Pyruvate in supplements might help you lose only a small amount of weight.

Is It Safe?

Pyruvate's safety hasn't been well studied. It can cause gas, bloating, diarrhea, and rumbling noises in the intestines (due to gas).

Raspberry Ketone

Raspberry ketone, found in red raspberries, is claimed to be a "fat burner."

Does It Work?

Raspberry ketone has not been studied alone as a weight-loss aid, only in combination with other ingredients. Its effects on body weight are unknown.

Is It Safe?

Raspberry ketone has not been studied enough to tell if it's safe

White Kidney Bean / Bean Pod

White kidney bean or bean pod (also called *Phaseolus vulgaris*) is a legume grown around the world. An extract of this bean is claimed to block the absorption of carbohydrates and suppress your appetite.

Does It Work?

Phaseolus vulgaris extract might help you lose a small amount of weight and body fat.

Is It Safe?

Phaseolus vulgaris seems to be fairly safe. But it might cause headaches, soft stools, flatulence, and constipation.

Yohimbe

Yohimbe is a West African tree. Yohimbe extract is an ingredient in supplements used to improve libido, increase muscle mass, and treat male sexual dysfunction. Yohimbe is also found in some weight-loss supplements and is claimed to increase weight loss.

Does It Work?

Yohimbe doesn't help you lose weight.

Is It Safe?

Yohimbe might not be safe. Only use it with guidance from your healthcare provider because the side effects can be severe. Yohimbe can cause headaches, high blood pressure, anxiety, agitation, rapid heartbeat, heart attack, heart failure and even death.

How Are Weight-Loss Dietary Supplements Regulated?

The U.S. Food and Drug Administration (FDA) regulates weight-loss supplements differently from prescription or over-the-counter drugs. As with other dietary supplements, the FDA does not test or approve weight-loss supplements before they are sold. Manufacturers are responsible for making sure that their supplements are safe and that the label claims are truthful and not misleading.

When the FDA finds an unsafe dietary supplement, it may remove the supplement from the market, or ask the supplement maker to recall it. The FDA and the Federal Trade Commission may also take action against companies that make false weight-loss claims about their supplements; add pharmaceutical drugs to their supplements; or claim that their supplements can diagnose, treat, cure, or prevent a disease.

Can Weight-Loss Dietary Supplements Be Harmful?

Weight-loss supplements, like all dietary supplements, can have harmful side effects and might interact with prescription and over-the-counter medications. Almost all weight-loss supplements have several ingredients that have not been tested in combination with one another, and their combined effects are unknown.

Tell your healthcare providers about any weight-loss supplements or other supplements you take. This information will help them work with you to prevent supplement-drug interactions, harmful side effects, and other risks.

Interactions with Medications

Like most dietary supplements, some weight-loss supplements may interact or interfere with other medicines or supplements you take. For example, caffeine's effect may be stronger if you take it with other stimulants (such as bitter orange), and chitosan might increase the blood-thinning effects of warfarin (Coumadin®) to dangerous levels.

If you take dietary supplements and medications on a regular basis, be sure to talk about this with your healthcare provider.

Fraudulent and Adulterated Products

Be very cautious when you see weight-loss supplements with tempting claims, such as "magic diet pill," "melt away fat," and "lose weight without diet or exercise." If the claim sounds too good to be true, it probably is. These supplements may not help you lose weight—and they could be dangerous.

Weight-loss supplements are sometimes adulterated with prescription drug ingredients or controlled substances. Because U.S. law doesn't allow these ingredients to be in dietary supplements, they won't be listed on the product label and they could harm you. Weight-loss supplements can be sold without being tested or approved by the FDA. Once a supplement that's suspected of causing serious health problems is on the market, the FDA can recall that product.

Choosing a Sensible Approach to Weight Loss

Weight-loss supplements can be expensive, and they might not work. The best way to lose weight and keep it off is to follow a healthy eating plan, reduce calories, and exercise regularly under the guidance of your healthcare provider.

As a bonus, lifestyle changes that help you lose weight might also improve your mood and energy level and lower your risk of heart disease, diabetes, and some types of cancer.

Chapter 44

Guidelines for Healthy Eating

Chapter Contents

Section 44.1

The Importance of Healthy Eating

This section contains text excerpted from the following sources: Text
under the heading "Dietary Guidelines Advisory Committee (DGAC)
2015 Overarching Themes" is excerpted from "Scientific Report of
the 2015 Dietary Guidelines Advisory Committee," Office of Disease
Prevention and Health Promotion (ODPHP), February 19, 2015; Text
beginning with the heading "Benefits of Eating Well" is excerpted
from "Eating Well as You Get Older," National Institute
on Aging (NIA), November 2014.

Dietary Guidelines Advisory Committee (DGAC) 2015 Overarching Themes

- **The Problem.** About half of all American adults—117 million
  individuals—have one or more preventable, chronic diseases
  that are related to poor quality dietary patterns and physical inactivity, including cardiovascular disease, hypertension,
  type 2 diabetes and diet-related cancers. More than two-thirds
  of adults and nearly one-third of children and youth are overweight or obese, further exacerbating poor health profiles and
  increasing risks for chronic diseases and their co-morbidities.
  High chronic disease rates and elevated population disease risk
  profiles have persisted for more than two decades and disproportionately affect low-income and underserved communities.
  These diseases focus the attention of the U.S. healthcare system
  on disease treatment rather than prevention; increase already
  strained healthcare costs; and reduce overall population health,
  quality of life, and national productivity. Other less common, but
  important, diet- and lifestyle-related health problems, including
  poor bone health and certain neuropsychological disorders and
  congenital anomalies, pose further serious concerns.

- **The Gap.** The dietary patterns of the American public are
  suboptimal and are causally related to poor individual and population health and higher chronic disease rates. Few, if any,
  improvements in consumers' food choices have been seen in

recent decades. On average, the U.S. diet is low in vegetables, fruits, and whole grains, and high in sodium, calories, saturated fat, refined grains, and added sugars. Underconsumption of the essential nutrients such as vitamin D, calcium, potassium, and fiber are public health concerns for the majority of the U.S. population, and iron intake is of concern among adolescents and premenopausal females. Health disparities exist in population access to affordable healthy foods. Eating behaviors of individuals are shaped by complex but modifiable factors, including individual, personal, household, social/cultural, community/environmental, systems/sectorial and policy-level factors. However, a dynamic and rapidly evolving food environment epitomized by the abundance of highly processed, convenient, lower-cost, energy-dense, nutrient-poor foods makes it particularly challenging to implement health promoting diet-related behavior changes at individual and population levels.

- **The Dietary Patterns.** Current research provides evidence of moderate to strong links between healthy dietary patterns, lower risks of obesity and chronic diseases, particularly cardiovascular disease, hypertension, type 2 diabetes and certain cancers. Emerging evidence also suggests that relationships may exist between dietary patterns and some neurocognitive disorders and congenital anomalies. **The overall body of evidence examined by the 2015 DGAC identifies that a healthy dietary pattern is higher in vegetables, fruits, whole grains, low- or non-fat dairy, seafood, legumes, and nuts; moderate in alcohol (among adults); lower in red and processed meats; and low in sugar-sweetened foods and drinks and refined grains.** Additional strong evidence shows that it is not necessary to eliminate food groups or conform to a single dietary pattern to achieve healthy dietary patterns. Rather, individuals can combine foods in a variety of flexible ways to achieve healthy dietary patterns, and these strategies should be tailored to meet the individual's health needs, dietary preferences and cultural traditions. Current research also strongly demonstrates that regular physical activity promotes health and reduces chronic disease risk.

In summary, the research base reviewed by the 2015 DGAC provides clear and consistent evidence that persistent, prevalent, preventable health problems, notably overweight and obesity, cardiovascular

405

diseases, diabetes, and certain cancers, have severely and adversely affected the health of the U.S. population across all stages of the lifespan for decades and raise the urgency for immediate attention and bold action. Evidence points to specific areas of food and nutrient concern in the current U.S. diet. Moderate to strong evidence pinpoints the characteristics of healthy dietary and physical activity patterns established to reduce chronic disease risk, prevent and better manage overweight and obesity, and promote health and well-being across the lifespan.

Benefits of Eating Well

Eating well is vital for everyone at all ages. Whatever your age, your daily food choices can make an important difference in your health and in how you look and feel.

Eating Well Promotes Health

Eating a well-planned, balanced mix of foods every day has many health benefits. For instance, eating well may reduce the risk of heart disease, stroke, type 2 diabetes, bone loss, some kinds of cancer, and anemia. If you already have one or more of these chronic diseases, eating well and being physically active may help you better manage them. Healthy eating may also help you reduce high blood pressure, lower high cholesterol, and manage diabetes.

Eating well gives you the nutrients needed to keep your muscles, bones, organs, and other parts of your body healthy throughout your life. These nutrients include vitamins, minerals, protein, carbohydrates, fats, and water.

Eating Well Promotes Energy

Eating well helps keep up your energy level, too. By consuming enough calories—a way to measure the energy you get from food—you give your body the fuel it needs throughout the day. The number of calories needed depends on how old you are, whether you're a man or woman, your height and weight, and how active you are.

Food Choices Can Affect Weight

Consuming the right number of calories for your level of physical activity helps you control your weight, too. Extra weight is a concern for older adults because it can increase the risk for diseases such as type 2 diabetes and heart disease and can increase joint problems.

Eating more calories than your body needs for your activity level will lead to extra pounds.

If you become less physically active as you age, you will probably need fewer calories to stay at the same weight. Choosing mostly nutrient-dense foods—foods which have a lot of nutrients but relatively few calories—can give you the nutrients you need while keeping down calorie intake.

Food Choices Affect Digestion

Your food choices also affect your digestion. For instance, not getting enough fiber or fluids may cause constipation. Eating more whole-grain foods with fiber, fruits and vegetables or drinking more water may help with constipation.

Make One Change at a Time

Eating well isn't just a "diet" or "program" that's here today and gone tomorrow. It is part of a healthy lifestyle that you can adopt now and stay with in the years to come.

To eat healthier, you can begin by taking small steps, making one change at a time. For instance, you might

- take the salt shaker off your table. Decreasing your salt intake slowly will allow you to adjust.

- switch to whole-grain bread, seafood, or more vegetables and fruits when you shop.

These changes may be easier than you think. They're possible even if you need help with shopping or cooking, or if you have a limited budget.

Checking with Your Doctor

If you have a specific medical condition, be sure to check with your doctor or registered dietitian about foods you should include or avoid.

You Can Start Today

Whatever your age, you can start making positive lifestyle changes today. Eating well can help you stay healthy and independent—and look and feel good—in the years to come.

Section 44.2

Healthy Eating for a Healthy Weight

This section contains text excerpted from the following sources: Text beginning with heading "Healthy Eating Plan" is excerpted from "Healthy Eating for a Healthy Weight," Centers for Disease Control and Prevention (CDC), November 9, 2015; Text beginning with the heading "What is MyPlate?" is excerpted from "MyPlate," U.S. Department of Agriculture (USDA), January 7, 2016.

Healthy Eating Plan

A healthy lifestyle involves many choices. Among them, choosing a balanced diet or healthy eating plan. So how do you choose a healthy eating plan? Let's begin by defining what a healthy eating plan is.

According to the *Dietary Guidelines for Americans* 2010, a healthy eating plan:

- Emphasizes fruits, vegetables, whole grains, and fat-free or low-fat milk and milk products

- Includes lean meats, poultry, fish, beans, eggs, and nuts

- Is low in saturated fats, *trans* fats, cholesterol, salt (sodium), and added sugars

- Stays within your daily calorie needs

Eat Healthfully and Enjoy It!

A healthy eating plan that helps you manage your weight includes a variety of foods you may not have considered. If "healthy eating" makes you think about the foods you **can't** have, try refocusing on all the new foods you **can** eat—

- **Fresh, Frozen, or Canned Fruits**—don't think just apples or bananas. All fresh, frozen, or canned fruits are great choices. Be sure to try some "exotic" fruits, too. How about a mango? Or a juicy pineapple or kiwi fruit! When your favorite fresh fruits aren't in season, try a frozen, canned, or dried variety of a fresh fruit you enjoy. One caution about canned fruits is that they may contain added sugars or syrups. Be sure and choose canned varieties of fruit packed in water or in their own juice.

- **Fresh, Frozen, or Canned Vegetables**—try something new. You may find that you love grilled vegetables or steamed vegetables with an herb you haven't tried like rosemary. You can sauté (pan-fry) vegetables in a non-stick pan with a small amount of cooking spray. Or try frozen or canned vegetables for a quick side dish—just microwave and serve. When trying canned vegetables, look for vegetables without added salt, butter, or cream sauces. Commit to going to the produce department and trying a new vegetable each week.

- **Calcium-rich foods**—you may automatically think of a glass of low-fat or fat-free milk when someone says "eat more dairy products." But what about low-fat and fat-free yogurts without added sugars? These come in a wide variety of flavors and can be a great dessert substitute for those with a sweet tooth.

- **A new twist on an old favorite**—if your favorite recipe calls for frying fish or breaded chicken, try healthier variations using baking or grilling. Maybe even try a recipe that uses dry beans in place of higher-fat meats. Ask around or search the Internet and magazines for recipes with fewer calories—you might be surprised to find you have a new favorite dish!

Do I Have to Give up My Favorite Comfort Food?

No! Healthy eating is all about balance. You can enjoy your favorite foods even if they are high in calories, fat or added sugars. The key is eating them only once in a while, and balancing them out with healthier foods and more physical activity.

Some general tips for comfort foods:

- **Eat them less often.** If you normally eat these foods every day, cut back to once a week or once a month. You'll be cutting your calories because you're not having the food as often.

- **Eat smaller amounts.** If your favorite higher-calorie food is a chocolate bar, have a smaller size or only half a bar.

- **Try a lower-calorie version.** Use lower-calorie ingredients or prepare food differently. For example, if your macaroni and cheese recipe uses whole milk, butter, and full-fat cheese, try remaking it with non-fat milk, less butter, light cream cheese, fresh spinach and tomatoes. Just remember to not increase your portion size.

What Is MyPlate?

MyPlate guide (www.choosemyplate.gov) is a reminder to find your healthy eating style and build it throughout your lifetime. Everything you eat and drink matters. The right mix can help you be healthier now and in the future. This means:

- Focus on variety, amount, and nutrition.
- Choose foods and beverages with less saturated fat, sodium, and added sugars.
- Start with small changes to build healthier eating styles.
- Support healthy eating for everyone.

Eating healthy is a journey shaped by many factors, including our stage of life, situations, preferences, access to food, culture, traditions, and the personal decisions we make over time. All your food and beverage choices count. MyPlate guide (www.choosemyplate.gov) offers ideas and tips to help you create a healthier eating style that meets your individual needs and improves your health.

Build a Healthy Eating Style

All Food and Beverage Choices Matter—Focus on Variety, Amount, and Nutrition.

- Focus on making healthy food and beverage choices from all five food groups including fruits, vegetables, grains, protein foods, and dairy to get the nutrients you need.
- Eat the right amount of calories for you based on your age, sex, height, weight, and physical activity level.
- Building a healthier eating style can help you avoid overweight and obesity and reduce your risk of diseases such as heart disease, diabetes, and cancer.

Choose an Eating Style Low in Saturated Fat, Sodium, and Added Sugars.

- Use Nutrition Facts labels and ingredient lists to find amounts of saturated fat, sodium, and added sugars in the foods and beverages you choose.
- Look for food and drink choices that are lower in saturated fat, sodium, and added sugar.

- Eating fewer calories from foods high in saturated fat and added sugars can help you manage your calories and prevent overweight and obesity. Most of us eat too many foods that are high in saturated fat and added sugar.

- Eating foods with less sodium can reduce your risk of high blood pressure.

Make Small Changes to Create a Healthier Eating Style.

- Think of each change as a personal "win" on your path to living healthier. Each MyWin is a change you make to build your healthy eating style. Find little victories that fit into your lifestyle and celebrate as a MyWin!

  - Start with a few of these small changes.

  - Make half your plate fruits and vegetables.

    - Focus on whole fruits.

    - Vary your veggies.

- Make half your grains whole grains.

  - Move to low-fat and fat-free dairy.

  - Vary your protein routine.

  - Eat and drink the right amount for you.

Support Healthy Eating for Everyone.

- Create settings where healthy choices are available and affordable to you and others in your community.

- Professionals, policymakers, partners, industry, families, and individuals can help others in their journey to make healthy eating a part of their lives.

Fruits

What Foods Are in the Fruit Group?

Any fruit or 100% fruit juice counts as part of the Fruit Group. Fruits may be fresh, canned, frozen, or dried, and may be whole, cut-up, or pureed.

411

How Much Fruit Is Needed Daily?

The amount of fruit you need to eat depends on age, sex, and level of physical activity. Recommended daily amounts are shown in the table below.

What Counts as a Cup of Fruit?

In general, 1 cup of fruit or 100% fruit juice, or ½ cup of dried fruit can be considered as 1 cup from the Fruit Group.

Vegetables

What Foods Are in the Vegetable Group?

Any vegetable or 100% vegetable juice counts as a member of the Vegetable Group. Vegetables may be raw or cooked; fresh, frozen, canned, or dried/dehydrated; and may be whole, cut-up, or mashed.

Based on their nutrient content, vegetables are organized into 5 subgroups: dark-green vegetables, starchy vegetables, red and orange vegetables, beans and peas, and other vegetables.

How Many Vegetables Are Needed?

The amount of vegetables you need to eat depends on your age, sex, and level of physical activity.

Vegetable subgroup recommendations are given as amounts to eat WEEKLY. It is not necessary to eat vegetables from each subgroup daily. However, over a week, try to consume the amounts listed from each subgroup as a way to reach your daily intake recommendation.

What Counts as a Cup of Vegetables?

In general, 1 cup of raw or cooked vegetables or vegetable juice, or 2 cups of raw leafy greens can be considered as 1 cup from the Vegetable Group.

Grains

What Foods Are in the Grains Group?

Any food made from wheat, rice, oats, cornmeal, barley or another cereal grain is a grain product. Bread, pasta, oatmeal, breakfast cereals, tortillas, and grits are examples of grain products.

Grains are divided into 2 subgroups, Whole Grains and Refined Grains. Whole grains contain the entire grain kernel—the bran, germ, and endosperm. Examples of whole grains include whole-wheat flour, bulgur (cracked wheat), oatmeal, whole cornmeal, and brown rice. Refined grains have been milled, a process that removes the bran and germ. This is done to give grains a finer texture and improve their shelf life, but it also removes dietary fiber, iron, and many B vitamins. *Some examples of refined grain products* are white flour, degermed cornmeal, white bread, and white rice.

Most refined grains are enriched. This means certain B vitamins (thiamin, riboflavin, niacin, folic acid) and iron are added back after processing. Fiber is not added back to enriched grains. Check the ingredient list on refined grain products to make sure that the word "enriched" is included in the grain name. Some food products are made from mixtures of whole grains and refined grains.

How Many Grain Foods Are Needed Daily?

The amount of grains you need to eat depends on your age, sex, and level of physical activity. Most Americans consume enough grains, but few are whole grains. **At least half of all the grains eaten should be whole grains.**

What Counts as an Ounce Equivalent of Grains?

In general, 1 slice of bread, 1 cup of ready-to-eat cereal, or ½ cup of cooked rice, cooked pasta, or cooked cereal can be considered as 1 ounce equivalent from the Grains Group.

Protein Foods

What Foods Are in the Protein Foods Group?

All foods made from meat, poultry, seafood, beans and peas, eggs, processed soy products, nuts, and seeds are considered part of the Protein Foods Group. Beans and peas are also part of the Vegetable Group.

Select a variety of protein foods to improve nutrient intake and health benefits, including at least 8 ounces of cooked seafood per week. Young children need less, depending on their age and calorie needs. The advice to consume seafood does not apply to vegetarians. Vegetarian options in the Protein Foods Group include beans and peas, processed soy products, and nuts and seeds. Meat and poultry choices should be lean or low-fat.

How Much Food from the Protein Foods Group Is Daily?

The amount of food from the Protein Foods Group you need to eat depends on age, sex, and level of physical activity. Most Americans eat enough food from this group, but need to make leaner and more varied selections of these foods.

What Counts as an Ounce-Equivalent in the Protein Foods Group?

In general, 1 ounce of meat, poultry or fish, ¼ cup cooked beans, 1 egg, 1 tablespoon of peanut butter, or ½ ounce of nuts or seeds can be considered as 1 ounce-equivalent from the Protein Foods Group.

Selection Tips

- Choose lean or low-fat meat and poultry. If higher fat choices are made, such as regular ground beef (75–80% lean) or chicken with skin, the fat counts against your maximum limit for empty calories (calories from solid fats or added sugars).

- If solid fat is added in cooking, such as frying chicken in shortening or frying eggs in butter or stick margarine, this also counts against your maximum limit for empty calories (calories from solid fats and added sugars).

- Select some seafood that is rich in omega-3 fatty acids, such as salmon, trout, sardines, anchovies, herring, Pacific oysters, and Atlantic and Pacific mackerel.

- Processed meats such as ham, sausage, frankfurters, and luncheon or deli meats have added sodium. Check the Nutrition Facts label to help limit sodium intake. Fresh chicken, turkey, and pork that have been enhanced with a salt-containing solution also have added sodium. Check the product label for statements such as "self-basting" or "contains up to __% of __", which mean that a sodium-containing solution has been added to the product.

- Choose unsalted nuts and seeds to keep sodium intake low.

Dairy

What Foods Are Included in the Dairy Group?

All fluid milk products and many foods made from milk are considered part of this food group. Most Dairy Group choices should be fat-free or low-fat. Foods made from milk that retain their calcium content are part of the group. Foods made from milk that have little to no calcium, such as cream cheese, cream, and butter, are not. Calcium-fortified soymilk (soy beverage) is also part of the Dairy Group.

How Much Food from the Dairy Group Is Needed Daily?

The amount of food from the Dairy Group you need to eat depends on age.

What Counts as a Cup in the Dairy Group?

In general, 1 cup of milk, yogurt, or soymilk (soy beverage), 1 ½ ounces of natural cheese, or 2 ounces of processed cheese can be considered as 1 cup from the Dairy Group.

Selection Tips

- Choose fat-free or low-fat milk, yogurt, and cheese. If you choose milk or yogurt that is not fat-free, or cheese that is not low-fat, the fat in the product counts against your maximum limit for "empty calories" (calories from solid fats and added sugars).

- If sweetened milk products are chosen (flavored milk, yogurt, drinkable yogurt, desserts), the added sugars also count against your maximum limit for "empty calories" (calories from solid fats and added sugars).

- For those who are lactose intolerant, smaller portions (such as 4 fluid ounces of milk) may be well tolerated. Lactose-free and lower-lactose products are available. These include lactose-reduced or lactose-free milk, yogurt, and cheese, and calcium-fortified soymilk (soy beverage). Also, enzyme preparations can be added to milk to lower the lactose content.

- Calcium choices for those who do not consume dairy products include:

    - kale leaves

    - Calcium-fortified juices, cereals, breads, rice milk, or almond milk. Calcium-fortified foods and beverages may not provide the other nutrients found in dairy products. Check the labels.

    - Canned fish (sardines, salmon with bones) soybeans and other soy products (tofu made with calcium sulfate, soy yogurt, tempeh), some other beans, and some leafy greens (collard and turnip greens, kale, bok choy). The amount of calcium that can be absorbed from these foods varies.

Oils

What Are "Oils"?

Oils are fats that are liquid at room temperature, like the vegetable oils used in cooking. Oils come from many different plants and from fish. Oils are NOT a food group, but they provide essential nutrients. Therefore, oils are included in U.S. Department of Agriculture (USDA) food patterns.

Some **commonly eaten oils** include: canola oil, corn oil, cottonseed oil, olive oil, safflower oil, soybean oil, and sunflower oil. Some oils are used mainly as **flavorings**, such as walnut oil and sesame oil. A number of foods are naturally high in oils, like nuts, olives, some fish, and avocados.

Foods that are mainly oil include mayonnaise, certain salad dressings, and soft (tub or squeeze) margarine with no trans fats. Check the Nutrition Facts label to find margarines with 0 grams of trans fat. Amounts of trans fat are required to be listed on labels.

Most oils are high in monounsaturated or polyunsaturated fats, and low in saturated fats. Oils from plant sources (vegetable and nut oils) do not contain any cholesterol. In fact, no plant foods contain cholesterol. A few plant oils, however, including coconut oil, palm oil, and palm kernel oil, are high in saturated fats and for nutritional purposes should be considered to be solid fats.

Solid fats are fats that are solid at room temperature, like butter and shortening. Solid fats come from many animal foods and can be made from vegetable oils through a process called hydrogenation. Some common fats are: butter, milk fat, beef fat (tallow, suet), chicken fat, pork fat (lard), stick margarine, shortening, and partially hydrogenated oil.

How Much Is My Allowance for Oils?

Some Americans consume enough oil in the foods they eat, such as:

- nuts
- fish

- cooking oil

- salad dressings

Others could easily consume the recommended allowance by substituting oils for some solid fats they eat. A person's allowance for oils depends on age, sex, and level of physical activity.

Section 44.3

How Much Food Should You Eat? A Guide to Portion Size

This section includes text excerpted from "Just Enough for You: About Food Portions," National Institute of Diabetes and Digestive and Kidney Diseases (NIDDK), June 2012. Reviewed March 2016.

To control your weight, you need to do more than just choose a healthy mix of foods. You should also look at the kinds of food you eat and how much you eat at a time. This section will help you understand how much you need to eat. It also will give you tips on how to control food portions so that you can eat just enough for you.

How Much Should I Eat?

To keep a healthy weight, you need to balance the calories you eat with the calories you burn. People who are more active may burn more calories. Being more active may be a good way to help you offset the calories you eat.

No set number of calories or amount of physical activity will help everyone to lose weight or keep weight off. How many calories you need to eat each day depends on your age, sex, weight, genes, and level of physical activity. For example, a 150-pound woman who burns a lot of calories through intense physical activity several times a week may need to eat more calories than a woman of similar size who is mostly inactive and only goes for a short walk once a week.

The U.S. Department of Agriculture (USDA) provides information that outlines the number of calories that a person should consider eating based on a number of factors.

What Is the Difference between a Serving and a Portion?

A serving size is the amount of food listed on a product's food label and it varies from product to product. A portion is how much food you choose to eat at one time, whether in a restaurant, from a package, or at home. Sometimes the serving size and portion size match; sometimes they do not.

For example, according to a food label, 1 cup of macaroni and cheese is one serving. But if you make yourself a large bowl of macaroni and cheese, that portion is much bigger than one serving. The same may be true if you pour yourself a large bowl of cereal for breakfast. You should be the judge of how the portion you choose to eat relates to the serving size noted on the food label.

How Can I Use the Nutrition Facts Label?

The U.S. Food and Drug Administration (FDA) Nutrition Facts label (food label) is printed on most packaged foods. The label tells you how many calories and how much fat, protein, sodium (salt), and other nutrients are in one serving of food. Most packaged foods contain more than a single serving.

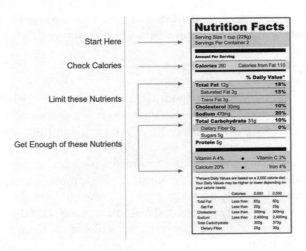

Figure 44.1. *Sample Macaroni and Cheese Label*

Keep in mind that the serving size on the food label is not a suggested amount of food to eat. It is just a quick way of letting you know the calories and nutrients in a certain amount of food. The serving size may be more or less than the amount that you should eat, depending on your age, weight, sex, and activity level.

Serving Size and Servings per Container

Take a look at the food label for a box of macaroni and cheese in Figure 44.1. To see how many servings a package has, check the "servings per container" listed on the top part of the label.

The serving size is 1 cup, but the package has 2 servings. This means that if you eat the whole package, you need to multiply the number of calories and nutrients by 2 to find out how many calories you are eating. For example, if you eat 2 servings of this product, you are eating 500 calories, as shown below:

250 calories per serving x 2 servings eaten = 500 calories eaten

Other Helpful Facts on the Label

The food label has other facts about what is in 1 serving of the chosen food. For example, as you can see in the label in Figure 44.1, 1 serving of this macaroni and cheese has 3 grams of saturated fat and 3 grams of *trans fat*, a type of fat that is unhealthy for your heart. The package includes 2 servings. If you eat the whole package, you will be eating 6 grams of saturated fat (2 servings x 3 grams per serving) and 6 grams of *trans fat* (2 servings x 3 grams per serving).

How Can I Keep Track of How Much I Am Eating?

A food diary can be a good way to keep track of how much you are eating. Write down **when**, **what**, **how much**, **where**, and **why** you eat. This action can help you be aware of how much you are eating and the times you tend to eat too much. You can keep a food diary in a notebook, on your cell phone, or on a computer.

Table 44.1 shows what 1 day of a person's food diary might look like. As shown in the diary, this person chose relatively healthy portion sizes for breakfast and lunch. At those meals, she ate to satisfy her hunger. She had a large chocolate bar in the afternoon for an emotional reason. She ate because she was bored, not because she was hungry.

By 8 p.m., this person was very hungry and ate large portions of food that were high in fat and calories. She was at a social event and

Table 44.1. An Example of a Food Diary

Time	Food	Amount	Place	Hunger/Reason	Calories
8 a.m.	Coffee, black	6 fl. oz.	Home	Slightly hungry	2
	Banana	1 medium			105
	Low-fat yogurt	1 cup			250
1 p.m.	Turkey and cheese sandwich on whole-wheat bread with mustard, tomato, low-fat cheese, and lettuce	3 oz. turkey, 1 slice low-fat cheddar cheese, 2 slices bread	Work	Hungry	363
	Potato chips, baked	1 small bag			150
	Water	16 fl. oz.			—
3 p.m.	Chocolate bar	1 bar (5 oz.)	Work	Not hungry/ Bored	760
8 p.m.	Fried potato skins with cheese and bacon	4 each	Restaurant/Out with friends	Very hungry	667
	Chicken Caesar salad	2 cups lettuce, 6 oz. chicken, 6 Tbsp. dressing, 3/4 cup croutons			633
	Breadsticks	2 large sticks			226
	Apple pie with vanilla ice cream	1/8 of a 9-inch pie, 1 cup ice cream			638
	Soft drink	12 fl. oz.			136
Total Calories =					3930

420

did not realize she was eating so much. If she had made an early evening snack of fruit and fat-free or low-fat yogurt, she might have been less hungry at 8 p.m. and eaten less. By the end of the day, she had eaten a total of 3,930 calories, which is more than most people need to eat in a day. Repeatedly eating excess calories over time can cause weight gain.

If, like the woman in the food diary, you eat even when you are not hungry, try doing something else instead of eating:

- Take a break to walk around the block.

- Read a book or magazine or listen to your favorite music.

- Try doing something with your hands, like knitting or playing cards or checkers.

- Try drinking water or herbal tea without sugar or eating a low-fat snack such as an apple if a craving hits you.

- If you are at work, grab a co-worker on the job and go for a quick walk.

Through your diary, you can become aware of the times and reasons you eat less healthy foods or more food than your body needs. This can help as you try to make different choices in the future.

How Can I Control Portions at Home?

You do not need to measure and count everything you eat for the rest of your life—just do this long enough to recognize typical serving sizes. Try the ideas below to help you control portions at home:

- Take the amount of food that is equal to one serving, according to the food label, and eat it off a plate instead of eating straight out of a large box or bag.

- Avoid eating in front of the TV or while busy with other activities. Pay attention to what you are eating, chew your food well, and fully enjoy the smell and taste of your food.

- Eat slowly so your brain can get the message when your stomach is full.

- Try using smaller dishes, bowls, and glasses. This way, when you fill up your plate or glass, you will be eating and drinking less.

- Control your intake of higher-fat, higher-calorie parts of a meal. Take seconds of vegetables and salads (watch the toppings and dressing) instead of desserts and dishes with heavy sauces.

- When cooking in large batches, freeze food that you will not serve right away. This way, you will not be tempted to finish eating the whole batch before the food goes bad. And you will have ready-made food for another day. Freeze leftovers in amounts that you can use for a single serving or for a family meal another day.

- Try to eat meals at regular times. Skipping meals or leaving large gaps of time between meals may lead you to eat larger amounts of food the next time you eat.

- When buying snacks, go for fruit or single-serving prepackaged items and foods that are lower-calorie options. If you buy larger bags or boxes of snacks, divide the items into single-serve packages right away so you won't be tempted to overeat.

- When you do have a treat like chips or ice cream, measure out only one serving as shown by the food label. Eat only ½ cup of ice cream or 1 ounce of chips, eat them slowly, and enjoy them!

How Can I Control Portions When Eating Out?

Research shows that the more often a person eats out, the more body fat he or she has. Try to prepare more meals at home. Eat out and get takeout foods less often.

Is Getting More Food for Your Money Always a Good Value?

Have you noticed that it only costs a few cents more to get larger sizes of fries or soft drinks at restaurants? Getting a larger portion of food for just a little extra money may seem like a good value, but you end up with more food and calories than you need for your body to stay healthy.

Before you buy your next "value combo," be sure you are making the best choice for your wallet and your health. If you are with someone else, share the large-size meal. If you are eating alone, skip the special deal and just order the smaller (healthier) size.

When eating out, try these tips to help you control portions:

- Check the menu for terms and icons that indicate healthy items, such as low-fat, low-calorie dishes.

- Share your meal, order a half-portion, or order an appetizer as a main meal. Examples of healthier appetizers include grilled or steamed seafood, minestrone soup, tomato or corn salsas, and vegetable salads with dressing on the side.

- Stop eating when you no longer feel hungry. It may take 15 minutes or longer for your stomach to signal to your brain that you are full. Put down your fork and focus on enjoying the setting and your friends or family for the rest of the meal.

- Avoid large beverages such as "super size" sugar-sweetened soft drinks. They have a large number of calories. Instead, try drinking water with a slice of lemon. If you want to drink soda, choose a calorie-free beverage or a small glass of regular soda. Other options are small glasses of slightly sweetened iced tea or lemonade.

On the Road Again? Tips for Traveling:

- Pack a small cooler of foods that are hard to find on the road, such as fresh fruit, sliced raw vegetables, and fat-free or low-fat yogurt.

- Include a few bottles of water instead of sugar-sweetened soda or juice.

- Bring dried fruit, nuts, and seeds to snack on. Since these foods can be high in calories, measure and pack small portions (¼ cup) in advance.

- If you stop at a restaurant, try to choose one that serves a variety of foods such as salads, grilled or steamed entrees, or vegetables.

- Consider drinking water or low-fat or fat-free milk instead of sugar-sweetened soft drinks with your meal.

- If you choose a higher-fat option like fries or pizza, order the small size. Or, you can ask for a single slice of pizza with vegetable toppings such as mushrooms or peppers.

How Can I Control Portions When Money Is Tight?

Eating better does not have to cost a lot of money. Here are some ways you can keep track of your portions without adding extra costs to your grocery bill:

- **Buy meats in bulk.** When you get home, divide the meat into single-serving packages and freeze for later use.

- **Buy fruits and vegetables when they are in season.** Buy only as much as you will use, so they will not go bad. Check out your local farmers market, as it may be less expensive than a grocery store.

- **Watch your portion sizes.** Try to stick to the serving sizes listed on the food label of prepackaged foods. Doing so can help you get the most out of the money you spend on that food. You can also better control the fat, sugar, sodium, and calories you eat.

Remember...

The amount of calories you eat affects your weight and health. In addition to selecting a healthy variety of foods, look at the size of the portions you eat. Choosing healthy foods and keeping portion sizes sensible may help you eat just enough for you.

Section 44.4

How to Read Food Labels

This section includes text excerpted from "Using the
Nutrition Facts Label: A How-To Guide for Older Adults," U.S. Food
and Drug Administration (FDA), June 1, 2015.

Why Nutrition Matters for You

Good nutrition is important throughout your life!

It can help you feel your best and stay strong. It can help reduce the risk of some diseases that are common among older adults. And, if you already have certain health issues, good nutrition can help you manage the symptoms.

Nutrition can sometimes seem complicated. But the good news is that the U.S. Food and Drug Administration (FDA) has a simple tool to help you know exactly what you're eating.

It's called the **Nutrition Facts Label**. You will find it on all packaged foods and beverages. It serves as your guide for making choices that can affect your long-term health.

Good Nutrition Can Help You Avoid or Manage These Common Diseases:

- certain cancers

- high blood pressure

- type 2 diabetes

- obesity

- heart disease

- osteoporosis

At-a-Glance: The Nutrition Facts Label

Understanding what the Nutrition Facts Label includes can help you make food choices that are best for your health.

Figure 44.2. *The Nutrition Facts Label*

1. Serving Size

2. Amount of Calories

3. Percent (%) Daily Value

4. Limit these Nutrients

5. Get Enough of these Nutrients

Three Key Areas of Importance

As you use the Nutrition Facts Label, pay particular attention to Serving Size, Percent Daily Value, and Nutrients.

1. Serving Size

The top of the Nutrition Facts Label shows the serving size and the servings per container. Serving size is the key to the rest of the information on the Nutrition Facts Label.

- The nutrition information about the food—like the calories, sodium, and fiber—is based upon one serving.

- If you eat two servings of the food, you are eating double the calories and getting twice the amount of nutrients, both good and bad.

- If you eat three servings, that means three times the calories and nutrients—and so on.

That is why knowing the serving size is important. It's how you know for sure how many calories and nutrients you are getting.

Check Serving Size!

It is very common for a food package to contain more than one serving. One bottled soft drink or a small bag of chips can actually contain two or more servings.

2. Percent Daily Value (%DV)

The %DV is a general guide to help you link nutrients in one serving of food to their contribution to your total daily diet. It can help you determine if a food is high or low in a nutrient: 5% or less is low, 20% or more is high.

You can also use the %DV to make dietary trade-offs with other foods throughout the day.

%DV: Quick Tips

You can tell if a food is high or low in a particular nutrient by taking a quick look at the %DV.

- If it has **5% percent** of the Daily Value or less, it is low in that nutrient.

This can be good or bad, depending on if it is a nutrient you want more of or less of.

- If it has **20% or more**, it is **high** in that nutrient.

This can be good for nutrients like fiber (a nutrient to get more of) but not so good for something like saturated fat (a nutrient to get less of).

Using %DV

- Once you are familiar with %DV, you can use it to compare foods and decide which is the better choice for you. Be sure to check for the particular nutrients you want more of or less of.

- Using %DV information can also help you "balance things out" for the day.

- *For example*: If you ate a favorite food at lunch that was high in sodium, a "nutrient to get less of," you would then try to choose foods for dinner that are lower in sodium.

3. Nutrients

A nutrient is an ingredient in a food that provides nourishment. Nutrients are essential for life and to keep your body functioning properly.

Nutrients to Get More Of:

There are some nutrients that are especially important for your health. You should try to get adequate amounts of these each day. They are:

- calcium
- dietary fiber
- potassium*
- vitamin A
- vitamin C

Note: The listing of potassium is optional on the Nutrition Facts Label.

Nutrients to Get Less Of:

There are other nutrients that are important, but that you should *eat in moderate amounts*. They can increase your risk of certain diseases.

They are:

- Total fat (especially saturated fat)

- Cholesterol

- Sodium

Your Guide to a Healthy Diet

The Nutrition Facts Label can help you make choices for overall health. But some nutrients can also affect certain health conditions and diseases.

Use this section as a guide for those nutrients that could impact your own health. Each nutrient section discusses:

- What the nutrient is

- What it can mean for your health

- Label-reading tips

Watch for "nutrients to get less of" (the ones that you should try to limit), and "nutrients to get more of" (the ones that are very important to be sure to get enough of). You also might want to talk to your healthcare provider about which nutrients you should track closely for your continued health. And remember—the **Nutrition Facts Label** is a tool that is available to you on every packaged food and beverage!

Nutrients and Your Needs

On the following pages, you'll find specific information about certain nutrients.

Some are **nutrients to get less of;**
others are **nutrients to get more of.**

All of them can have an impact on your **long-term health**.

In addition, here is an example of how the Nutrition Facts Label can guide you in making good decisions for long-term health and nutrition.

Example:

Heart disease is the number one cause of death in the United States today. You can use the Nutrition Facts Label to compare foods and decide which ones fit with a diet that may help reduce the risk of heart disease. Choose foods that have **fewer calories per serving** and a **lower %DV** of these "nutrients to get less of"

- Total fat
- Saturated fat
- Cholesterol
- Sodium

To lower your risk of heart disease, it is also recommended that you eat *more* fiber.

Dietary Salt / Sodium: Get less of

What It Is:

Salt is a crystal-like compound that is used to flavor and preserve food. The words "salt" and "sodium" are often used interchangeably. Salt is listed as "sodium" on the Nutrition Facts Label.

What You Should Know:

A small amount of sodium is needed to help certain organs and fluids work properly. But most people eat too much of it—and they may not even know it! That's because many packaged foods have a high amount of sodium, even when they don't taste "salty." Plus, when you add salt to food, you're adding *more* sodium.

Sodium has been linked to high blood pressure. In fact, eating less sodium can often help lower blood pressure which in turn can help reduce the risk of heart disease.

And since blood pressure normally rises with age, limiting your sodium intake becomes even more important each year.

Label Reading Tips: Salt/Sodium

- Read the label to see how much sodium is in the food you are choosing.
- 5% DV or less is *low* in sodium
- 20% DV or more is *high* in sodium
- When you are deciding between two foods, compare the amount of sodium. Look for cereals, crackers, pasta sauces, canned vegetables, and other packaged foods that are lower in sodium.

Fiber: Get more of

What It Is:

Fiber, or "dietary fiber," is sometimes called "roughage." It's the part of food that can't be broken down during digestion. So because it moves through your digestive system "undigested," it plays an important role in keeping your system moving and "in working order."

What You Should Know:

Fiber is a "nutrient to get more of." In addition to aiding in digestion, fiber has a number of other health-related benefits. These benefits are *especially* effective when you have a **high fiber diet** that is also **low in saturated fat, cholesterol, *trans* fat, added sugars, salt,** and **alcohol**.

- Eating a diet that is low in saturated fat and cholesterol and high in fruits, vegetables, and grain products that contain some types of dietary fiber, particularly soluble fiber, may help lower your cholesterol and reduce your chances of getting **heart disease**, a disease associated with many factors.

- Healthful diets that are low in fat *and* rich in fruits and vegetables that contain fiber may reduce the risk of **some types of cancer**, including colon cancer, a disease associated with many factors. In addition, such healthful diets are also associated with a reduced risk of **type 2 diabetes**.

- Fiber also aids in the regularity of bowel movements and preventing constipation. It may help reduce the risk of *diverticulosis*, a common condition in which small pouches form in the colon wall. This condition often has few or no symptoms; people who already have diverticulosis and do have symptoms often find that increased fiber consumption can reduce these symptoms. It's also important to note that if the pouches caused by diverticulosis rupture and become infected, it results in a more severe condition called **diverticulitis**.

Soluble v. Insoluble Fiber: Where To Get It, and What It Does

Fiber comes in two forms—insoluble and soluble. Most plant foods contain some of each kind.

- **Insoluble fiber** is mostly found in whole-grain products, such as wheat bran cereal, vegetables and fruit. It provides "bulk" for stool formation and helps wastes move quickly through your colon.

- **Soluble fiber** is found in peas, beans, many vegetables and fruits, oat bran, whole grains, barley, cereals, seeds, rice, and some pasta, crackers, and other bakery products. It slows the digestion of carbohydrates, and can help stabilize blood sugar if you have diabetes. In addition, it helps lower "bad cholesterol." This, in turn, reduces the risk of heart disease.

Check the **Nutrition Facts Label** to see which foods have a higher %DV of fiber.

Label Reading Tips: Fiber

- **Read food labels.** The Nutrition Facts Label tells you the amount of dietary fiber in each serving, as well as the %DV of fiber that food contains.

  When comparing the amount of fiber in food, remember:

  - 5% DV or less is *low* in fiber 20% DV or more is *high* in fiber

  The label won't indicate whether fiber is "insoluble" or "soluble," so it's best to try to get some of both.

- **Compare foods and choose the ones with higher fiber.**

Look for and compare labels on whole-grain products such as bulgur, brown rice, whole wheat couscous or kasha and whole-grain breads, cereals and pasta. In addition, compare different styles/types of canned or frozen beans and fruit.

Total Fat: Get less of

What It Is:

Fat, or "dietary fat," is a nutrient that is a major source of energy for the body. It also helps you absorb certain important vitamins. As a food ingredient, fat provides taste, consistency, and helps you feel full.

What You Should Know:

Eating too much fat can lead to a wide range of health challenges. The total amount and type of fat can contribute to and/or increase the risk of:

- heart disease
- high cholesterol
- increased risk of many cancers (including colon-rectum cancer)
- obesity
- high blood pressure
- type 2 diabetes

It is important to know that there are **different types of dietary fat**. Some have health benefits when eaten in small quantities, but others do not.

"Good" Fat: unsaturated fats (monounsaturated and polyunsaturated)

- These are healthful if eaten in moderation. In fact, small amounts can even help **lower cholesterol levels**!

- *Best Sources*: plant-based oils (sunflower, corn, soybean, cotton-seed, and safflower), olive, canola and peanut oils, nuts, and soft margarines (liquid, tub or spray).

"Undesirable" Fat: saturated and trans fats. These can raise cholesterol levels in the blood—which in turn can contribute to heart disease.

- *Common Sources*: meat, poultry, fish, butter, ice cream, cheese, coconut and palm kernel oils, solid shortenings, and hard margarines.

- Meat (including chicken and turkey) and fish supply protein, B vitamins, and iron. When selecting and preparing meat, poultry, fish and milk or milk products, choose those that are lean, low-fat, or fat-free. Doing this, along with removing the skin from fish and poultry, are good strategies for limiting "undesirable" fat from your diet. In addition, dry beans, which can be used as a meat substitute, are a good source of protein and are non-fat.

Understanding *Trans* Fat

Trans fat is one of the newest additions to the Nutrition Facts Label, so you may be hearing more about it. Here's what you need to know:

- Most *trans* fat is made when manufacturers "hydrogenize" liquid oils, turning them into solid fats, like shortening or some margarines. *Trans* fat is commonly found in crackers, cookies, snack foods, and other foods made with or fried in these solid oils.

- *Trans* fat, like saturated fat and cholesterol, raises your low-density lipoprotein (LDL) (bad) cholesterol and can increase your risk of coronary heart disease.

Trans Fat On the Label

There is no recommended total daily value for *trans* fat, so you won't find the %DV of *trans* fat on a food's Nutrition Facts Label. However, you can still use the label to see if a food contains *trans* fat and to compare two foods by checking to see if **grams** of *trans* fat are listed. If there is anything other than 0 grams listed, then the food contains *trans* fat. Because it is extremely difficult to eat a diet that is completely *trans* fat-free without decreasing other nutrient intakes, just aim to keep your intake of *trans* fat as low as possible.

Label Reading Tips: Total Fat

- When comparing foods, check the Nutrition Facts Label and choose the food with the lower %DV of total fat and saturated fat, and low or no grams of *trans* fat.

- 5% DV or less of total fat is *low*

- 20% DV or more of total fat is *high*

- When choosing foods that are labeled "fat-free" and "low-fat," be aware that *fat-free doesn't mean calorie-free*. Sometimes, to make a food tastier, extra sugars are added, which adds extra calories. Be sure to check the calories per serving.

Cholesterol: Get less of

What It Is:

Cholesterol is a crystal-like substance carried through the bloodstream by lipoproteins—the "transporters" of fat. Cholesterol is required for certain important body functions, like digesting dietary fats, making hormones, and building cell walls.

Cholesterol is found in animal-based foods, like meats and dairy products.

What You Should Know:

Too much cholesterol in the bloodstream can damage arteries, especially the ones that supply blood to the heart. It can build up in blood vessel linings. This is called **atherosclerosis**, and it can lead to heart attacks and stroke.

However, it's important to know that not all cholesterol is bad. There are **two kinds of cholesterol** found in the bloodstream. How much you have of each is what determines your risk of heart disease.

High-density lipoprotein (HDL): This **"good" cholesterol** is the form in which cholesterol *travels back to the liver*, where it can be eliminated.

- HDL helps prevent cholesterol buildup in blood vessels. A higher level of this cholesterol is better. Low HDL levels increase heart disease risk. Discuss your HDL level with your healthcare provider.

Low-density lipoprotein (LDL): This **"bad" cholesterol** is *carried into the blood*. It is the main cause of harmful fatty buildup in arteries.

- The higher the LDL cholesterol level in the blood, the greater the heart disease risk. So, a lower level of this cholesterol is better.

Label Reading Tips: Cholesterol

- Cholesterol is a "nutrient to get less of." When comparing foods, look at the Nutrition Facts Label, and choose the food with the lower %DV of cholesterol. Be sure not to go above 100% DV for the day.

- 5% DV or less of cholesterol is *low*

- 20% DV or more of cholesterol is *high*

- One of the primary ways LDL ("bad") cholesterol levels can become too high in the blood is by eating too much saturated fat and cholesterol. **Saturated fat raises LDL levels more than anything else in the diet.**

Calcium: Get more of

What It Is:

Calcium is a mineral that has a lot of uses in the body, but it is best known for its role in building healthy bones and teeth.

What You Should Know:

Lack of calcium causes **osteoporosis**, which is the primary cause of hip fractures. In fact, the word "osteoporosis" means "porous bones." It causes progressive bone loss as you age, and makes bones fragile—so that they can break easily. It's extremely important (especially for women) to get enough calcium throughout your life, especially after menopause. Women are at much higher risk for osteoporosis, but men can get it too.

It's true that many dairy products, which contain high levels of calcium, are relatively high in fat and calories. But keep in mind that **fat-free or low-fat types of milk products** are excellent calcium sources. Nutritionists recommend that you try to get most of your calcium from calcium-rich foods, rather than from calcium supplements. The Nutrition Facts Label can help you make good high-calcium choices.

Other good sources of calcium are:

- canned salmon (with bones, which are edible)

- calcium-fortified soy beverages

- tofu (soybean curd that is "calcium-processed")

- certain vegetables (for example, dark leafy greens such as collards and turnip greens)

- legumes (blackeyed peas and white beans)

- calcium-fortified grain products

- calcium-fortified juice

Label Reading: Tips Calcium

- Read the label to see how much calcium is in the food you are choosing.

- 5% DV or less is *low* in calcium

- 20% DV or more is *high* in calcium

- Select foods that are high in calcium as often as possible.

A Note About Vitamin D

For calcium to be properly absorbed by the body, you also need to get enough vitamin D. Many milk products and cereals are fortified with vitamin D; also, vitamin D is produced by the body when exposed to sunlight.

If you aren't exposed to outdoor sunlight on a regular basis, ask your healthcare provider whether you should take vitamin D supplements.

Section 44.5

Improving Your Eating Habits

This section includes text excerpted from "Improving
Your Eating Habits," Centers for Disease Control
and Prevention (CDC), May 15, 2015.

When it comes to eating, we have strong habits. Some are good ("I
always eat breakfast"), and some are not so good ("I always clean my
plate"). Although many of our eating habits were established during
childhood, it doesn't mean it's too late to change them.

Making sudden, radical changes to eating habits such as eating
nothing but cabbage soup, can lead to short term weight loss. However,
such radical changes are neither healthy nor a good idea, and won't
be successful in the long run. Permanently improving your eating
habits requires a thoughtful approach in which you Reflect, Replace,
and Reinforce.

- **REFLECT** on all of your specific eating habits, both bad and
  good; and, your common triggers for unhealthy eating.

- **REPLACE** your unhealthy eating habits with healthier ones.

- **REINFORCE** your new, healthier eating habits.

Reflect, Replace, Reinforce: A Process for Improving Your Eating Habits

1. **Create a list of your eating habits.** Keeping a food diary for
   a few days, in which you write down everything you eat and
   the time of day you ate it, will help you uncover your habits.
   For example, you might discover that you always seek a sweet
   snack to get you through the mid-afternoon energy slump. It's
   good to note how you were feeling when you decided to eat,
   especially if you were eating when not hungry. Were you tired?
   Stressed out?

2. **Highlight the habits** on your list that may be leading you to
   overeat. Common eating habits that can lead to weight gain are:

- Eating too fast
  - Always cleaning your plate
  - Eating when not hungry
  - Eating while standing up (may lead to eating mindlessly or too quickly)
  - Always eating dessert
  - Skipping meals (or maybe just breakfast)

1. **Look at the unhealthy eating habits** you've highlighted. Be sure you've identified all the triggers that cause you to engage in those habits. Identify a few you'd like to work on improving first. Don't forget to pat yourself on the back for the things you're doing right. Maybe you almost always eat fruit for dessert, or you drink low-fat or fat-free milk. These are good habits! Recognizing your successes will help encourage you to make more changes.

2. **Create a list of "cues"** by reviewing your food diary to become more aware of when and where you're "triggered" to eat for reasons other than hunger. Note how you are typically feeling at those times. Often an environmental "cue", or a particular emotional state, is what encourages eating for non-hunger reasons.

Common triggers for eating when not hungry are:

- Opening up the cabinet and seeing your favorite snack food.
  - Sitting at home watching television.
  - Before or after a stressful meeting or situation at work.
  - Coming home after work and having no idea what's for dinner.
  - Having someone offer you a dish they made "just for you!"
  - Walking past a candy dish on the counter.
  - Sitting in the break room beside the vending machine.
  - Seeing a plate of doughnuts at the morning staff meeting.
  - Swinging through your favorite drive-through every morning.

- Feeling bored or tired and thinking food might offer a pick-me-up.

1. **Circle the "cues" on your list that you face on a daily or weekly basis.** Going home for the Thanksgiving holiday may be a trigger for you to overeat, and eventually, you want to have a plan for as many eating cues as you can. But for now, focus on the ones you face more often.

2. **Ask yourself** these questions for each "cue" you've circled:

- **Is there anything I can do to avoid the cue or situation?** This option works best for cues that don't involve others. For example, could you choose a different route to work to avoid stopping at a fast food restaurant on the way? Is there another place in the break room where you can sit so you're not next to the vending machine?

  - **For things I can't avoid, can I do something differently that would be healthier?** Obviously, you can't avoid all situations that trigger your unhealthy eating habits, like staff meetings at work. In these situations, evaluate your options. Could you suggest or bring healthier snacks or beverages? Could you offer to take notes to distract your attention? Could you sit farther away from the food so it won't be as easy to grab something? Could you plan ahead and eat a healthy snack before the meeting?

1. **Replace unhealthy habits with new, healthy ones.** For example, in reflecting upon your eating habits, you may realize that you eat too fast when you eat alone. So, make a commitment to share a lunch each week with a colleague, or have a neighbor over for dinner one night a week. Other strategies might include putting your fork down between bites or minimizing other distractions (i.e., watching the news during dinner) that might keep you from paying attention to how quickly—and how much—you're eating.

Here are more ideas to help you replace unhealthy habits:

- Eat more slowly. If you eat too quickly, you may "clean your plate" instead of paying attention to whether your hunger is satisfied.

- Eat only when you're truly hungry instead of when you are tired, anxious, or feeling an emotion besides hunger. If you find yourself eating when you are experiencing an emotion besides hunger, such as boredom or anxiety, try to find a non-eating activity to do instead. You may find a quick walk or phone call with a friend helps you feel better.

- Plan meals ahead of time to ensure that you eat a healthy well-balanced meal.

2. **Reinforce your new, healthy habits and be patient with yourself.** Habits take time to develop. It doesn't happen overnight. When you do find yourself engaging in an unhealthy habit, stop as quickly as possible and ask yourself: Why do I do this? When did I start doing this? What changes do I need to make? Be careful not to berate yourself or think that one mistake "blows" a whole day's worth of healthy habits. You can do it! It just takes one day at a time!

Section 44.6

The Importance of Family Meals

This section contains text excerpted from the following sources: Text beginning with heading "The Importance of Family Meals" is excerpted from "What Is the Relationship between Frequency and Regularity of Family Meals and Measures of Weight and Obesity in U.S. Population Groups?" U.S. Department of Agriculture (USDA), February 19, 2015; Text beginning with the heading "Benefits of Family Meals" is excerpted from "Family Meal," National Heart, Lung and Blood Institute (NHLBI), November 8, 2013; Text beginning with the heading "Making Mealtime Family Time" is excerpted from "Making Mealtime Family Time," WhiteHouse.gov, November 20, 2014.

Cross-sectional studies have suggested that when families share meals, they achieve better diet quality and improved nutrient intake, and to some extent are better able to maintain appropriate body weight. Family mealtime may act as a protective factor for many nutritional health-related problems. For example, they provide an opportunity for parents to model good eating behaviors and create a positive atmosphere by providing time for social interaction and thus a sense of social support for all members.

Benefits of Family Meals:

1. Family meals influence children's eating habits.

2. Families bond during meal time.

3. Parents model good eating habits.

4. Children spend less time in front of television.

5. Children practice social and conversational skills.

Making Mealtime Family Time

With the hustle and bustle of work, school, sports and other activities, it can be tough to find quality time to share meals with your family. Try tackling mealtime as a team by including the whole family in choosing and making meals!

Check out these simple tips and resources to help with family mealtime:

Set a time for family meals. Let everyone in the family know that there is a specific mealtime so that activities can be planned around it. Prioritizing mealtime will allow the family to eat together more often. Even if it can't be every night, try cooking and sharing one more meal at home together each week.

Select the meal together. Decide what meal will be prepared as a family. Getting everyone on board for the meal is a great way to build more excitement around family mealtime. Encourage your family to try healthier versions of some of their favorite meals.

Designate kitchen helpers. Many hands make the work light! Try assigning tasks to each family member. Having everyone pitch in on ordinary mealtime activities like setting the table, prepping the vegetables, pouring the water or clearing the table are excellent ways to engage the whole family and take the pressure off one person. In addition, kids who help prepare meals are often open to trying new foods, and they will learn skills they will carry throughout their lives and build confidence in the kitchen.

Reduce meal prep time. A family-on-the-go may have less time to prepare meals at home. Check out these resources to making cooking at home easier for your family:

- *Kitchen Hacks* board on the MyPlate Pinterest page (www.pinterest.com/MyPlateRecipes/kitchen-hacks), which is filled with clever tips and tricks to preparing certain foods and meals.

- *USDA's SuperTracker* (www.supertracker.usda.gov), which can help you plan, analyze and track what you eat.

- *MyPlate* (www.choosemyplate.gov), which includes tips, videos, and recipes to help you build a healthier plate.

Make mealtime = family time. Once the meal has been prepared, try turning off the TV and removing other distractions. This is the perfect time to catch up on your family's day. Make mealtime fun by incorporating games, activities, and questions about topics your kids are interested in. Eating together has many benefits, including improving family communication. In addition, children tend to perform better in school and get along better with their peers as a result of sharing family meals together.

Mealtime spent together at home is a great way for families to begin building healthier eating habits and enjoying more quality time together. Get started by picking one meal a week that will be cooked and shared at home together, and use the tips and resources above to make the process easier and more fun for everyone!

Section 44.7

Eating Out

This section includes text excerpted from "Make Better Choices When Eating Out," U.S. Department of Agriculture (USDA), July 30, 2015.

How often do you eat out? Once a day? Once a week? Rarely? Almost every meal? People who eat out more often, particularly at fast food restaurants, are more likely to be overweight or obese. However, you can still manage your body weight when eating out by making better choices.

To eat out without blowing your calorie budget, there are three things to think about:

1. What you are eating and drinking?

2. How much you are eating and drinking?

3. How your meal is prepared?

Get Started

1. **What** are you eating and drinking?

- Check posted calorie amounts, and choose lower calorie menu options. Many restaurants post calories on menus, in pamphlets, or on their websites. Compare food and beverage options and think about how they fit within your daily calorie limit. For example, if your daily calorie limit is 1600 calories, think twice before ordering a meal with 1300 calories. Also, don't forget about the calories from drinks, dressings, dips, appetizers, and desserts. They all count!

- Choose dishes that include vegetables, fruits, whole grains, low-fat dairy products, and lean protein foods. Focusing on smart food choices from each of the 5 food groups can help you stay on track at restaurants.

- Think about what you drink. Ask for water or order fat-free or low-fat milk, unsweetened tea, or other drinks without added sugars. If you choose to drink alcoholic beverages, select options with fewer calories. For example, a frozen pina colada or margarita can have over 400 calories!

- Watch out for desserts. Some restaurants are serving small portions of desserts, which can help decrease calorie intake. However, as a good rule, eat dessert less often.

2. **How much** are you eating and drinking?

- Avoid oversized portions. A major challenge for many people when they eat out is being served large portions. Most people eat and drink more when served larger portions. To overcome this challenge, choose a smaller size option, share your meal, or take home half of your meal. For example, hamburgers can range from as few as 250 calories to 800 calories or more. Choose a smaller option with fewer calories.

- To help you eat less when eating out, order from the menu instead of heading for the all-you-can-eat buffet. Many people overeat at buffets. Getting a plate of food, instead of unlimited access to food, may help you eat less. Don't forget that you don't have to clean your plate!

3. **How** is your meal prepared?

- Order steamed, grilled, or broiled dishes instead of those that are fried or sauteéd. Avoid choosing foods with the following words: creamy, breaded, battered, or buttered. These words indicate that the food is higher in calories.

- Ask for dressings, sauces, and syrups "on the side" so you can add only as much as you want. These sides are often high in calories—so don't eat much of them.

Stumbling Blocks

Concerned about **making better choices when eating out?** Below are some common "stumbling blocks" and ideas to help you overcome these barriers.

Table 44.2. Stumbling blocks when eating out

"I feel that I have to eat everything on my plate since it is there in front of me or else I feel like I'm wasting food."	To control how much you eat, ask for a take home box with your order, and box half of the food up as soon as it arrives. This way you know that you will have saved on calories and also have a delicious lunch for the following day.
"I like to have a cocktail with dinner."	Moderate alcohol consumption can be a part of a healthy diet. Limit alcohol to no more than 1 drink per day for women and 2 drinks per day for men. Don't forget that some drinks provide a lot of calories. Many alcoholic beverages range from 100 to 400 calories each.
"I have heard that salads can be worse for you than a big meal!"	Salads can be high in calories if they have toppings like fried chicken, loads of cheese, and creamy dressing. To start a meal, choose a salad that is all vegetables, and ask for dressing on the side. For a main dish salad, choose one with topped with grilled or baked chicken, seafood, or lean beef.
"It's a tradition now to get dessert after our meals when we eat out."	Ask your friends or family to support your efforts to eat less by understanding that you won't be ordering dessert. While they eat dessert, have a cup of tea or coffee. Have one bite of someone's dessert if they offer to share. If fruit is available as a dessert option, order it without the whipped topping or sauce.

Section 44.8

Nutrition and the Health of Young People

This section includes text excerpted from "Nutrition
and the Health of Young People," Centers for Disease
Control and Prevention (CDC), August 28, 2015.

Healthy Eating

- Healthy eating helps prevent high cholesterol and high blood
  pressure and helps reduce the risk of developing chronic diseases such as cardiovascular disease, cancer, and diabetes.

- Healthy eating helps reduce one's risk for developing obesity,
  osteoporosis, iron deficiency, and dental caries (cavities).

- Healthy eating is associated with reduced risk for many diseases, including several of the leading causes of death: heart disease, cancer, stroke, and diabetes.

- Healthy eating in childhood and adolescence is important
  for proper growth and development and can prevent health
  problems such as obesity, dental caries, iron deficiency, and
  osteoporosis.

- The *Dietary Guidelines for Americans* recommend a diet rich
  in fruits and vegetables, whole grains, and fat-free and low-fat
  dairy products for persons aged 2 years and older. The guidelines
  also recommend that children, adolescents, and adults limit
  intake of solid fats (major sources of saturated and trans fatty
  acids), cholesterol, sodium, added sugars, and refined grains.
  Unfortunately, most young people are not following the recommendations set forth in the Dietary Guidelines for Americans.

- Schools are in a unique position to promote healthy eating
  and help ensure appropriate food and nutrient intake among
  students. Schools provide students with opportunities to consume an array of foods and beverages throughout the school
  day and enable students to learn about and practice healthy
  eating behaviors. For example, as a healthy alternative to

sugar-sweetened beverages, schools can provide students access to safe, free drinking water.

- Schools should ensure that only nutritious and appealing foods and beverages are provided in school cafeterias, vending machines, snack bars, school stores, and other venues that offer food and beverages to students. In addition, nutrition education should be part of a comprehensive school health education curriculum.

Benefits of Healthy Eating

- Proper nutrition promotes the optimal growth and development of children.
- Healthy eating helps prevent high cholesterol and high blood pressure and helps reduce the risk of developing chronic diseases such as cardiovascular disease, cancer, and diabetes.
- Healthy eating helps reduce one's risk for developing obesity, osteoporosis, iron deficiency, and dental caries (cavities).

Consequences of a Poor Diet

- A poor diet can lead to energy imbalance (e.g., eating more calories than one expends through physical activity) and can increase one's risk for overweight and obesity.
- A poor diet can increase the risk for lung, esophageal, stomach, colorectal, and prostate cancers.
- Individuals who eat fast food one or more times per week are at increased risk for weight gain, overweight, and obesity.
- Drinking sugar-sweetened beverages can result in weight gain, overweight, and obesity.
- Providing access to drinking water gives students a healthy alternative to sugar-sweetened beverages.
- Hunger and *food insecurity* (i.e., reduced food intake and disrupted eating patterns because a household lacks money and other resources for food) might increase the risk for lower dietary quality and undernutrition. In turn, undernutrition can negatively affect overall health, cognitive development, and school performance.

Eating Behaviors of Young People

- Most U.S. youth

- Do not meet the recommendations for eating 2½ cups to 6½ cups of fruits and vegetables each day

- Do not eat the minimum recommended amounts of whole grains (2–3 ounces each day)

- Eat more than the recommended maximum daily intake of sodium (1,500–2,300 mg each day).

- Empty calories from added sugars and solid fats contribute to 40% of daily calories for children and adolescents aged 2–18 years, affecting the overall quality of their diets. Approximately half of these empty calories come from six sources: soda, fruit drinks, dairy desserts, grain desserts, pizza, and whole milk.

- Adolescents drink more full-calorie soda per day than milk. Males aged 12–19 years drink an average of 22 ounces of full-calorie soda per day, more than twice their intake of fluid milk (10 ounces), and females drink an average of 14 ounces of full-calorie soda and only 6 ounces of fluid milk.

Diet and Academic Performance

- Eating a healthy breakfast is associated with improved cognitive function (especially memory), reduced absenteeism, and improved mood.

Chapter 45

Guidelines for Healthy Exercise

Chapter Contents

Section 45.1

Physical Activity for a Healthy Weight

This section includes text excerpted from "Physical Activity for a Healthy Weight," Centers for Disease Control and Prevention (CDC), May 15, 2015.

Why Is Physical Activity Important?

Regular physical activity is important for good health, and it's especially important if you're trying to lose weight or to maintain a healthy weight.

- When losing weight, more physical activity increases the number of calories your body uses for energy or "burns off." The burning of calories through physical activity, combined with reducing the number of calories you eat, creates a "calorie deficit" that results in weight loss.

- Most weight loss occurs because of decreased caloric intake. However, evidence shows the only way to *maintain* weight loss is to be engaged in regular physical activity.

- Most importantly, physical activity reduces risks of cardiovascular disease and diabetes beyond that produced by weight reduction alone.

Physical activity also helps to—

- Maintain weight.

- Reduce high blood pressure.

- Reduce risk for type 2 diabetes, heart attack, stroke, and several forms of cancer.

- Reduce arthritis pain and associated disability.

- Reduce risk for osteoporosis and falls.

- Reduce symptoms of depression and anxiety.

How Much Physical Activity Do I Need?

When it comes to weight management, people vary greatly in how much physical activity they need. Here are some guidelines to follow:

To maintain your weight: Work your way up to 150 minutes of moderate-intensity aerobic activity, 75 minutes of vigorous-intensity aerobic activity, or an equivalent mix of the two each week. Strong scientific evidence shows that physical activity can help you maintain your weight over time. However, the exact amount of physical activity needed to do this is not clear since it varies greatly from person to person. It's possible that you may need to do more than the equivalent of 150 minutes of moderate-intensity activity a week to maintain your weight.

To lose weight and keep it off: You will need a high amount of physical activity unless you also adjust your diet and reduce the amount of calories you're eating and drinking. Getting to and staying at a healthy weight requires both regular physical activity and a healthy eating plan.

What Do Moderate- and Vigorous-Intensity Mean?

Moderate: While performing the physical activity, if your breathing and heart rate is noticeably faster but you can still carry on a conversation—it's probably moderately intense. Examples include—

- Walking briskly (a 15-minute mile).
- Light yard work (raking/bagging leaves or using a lawn mower).
- Light snow shoveling.
- Actively playing with children.
- Biking at a casual pace.

Vigorous: Your heart rate is increased substantially and you are breathing too hard and fast to have a conversation, it's probably vigorously intense. Examples include—

- Jogging/running.
- Swimming laps.
- Rollerblading/inline skating at a brisk pace.
- Cross-country skiing.
- Most competitive sports (football, basketball, or soccer).
- Jumping rope.

How Many Calories Are Used in Typical Activities?

The following table shows calories used in common physical activities at both moderate and vigorous levels.

Table 45.1. Calories Used per Hour in Common Physical Activities

Moderate Physical Activity	Approximate Calories/30 Minutes for a 154 lb Person[1]	Approximate Calories/ Hr for a 154 lb Person[1]
Hiking	185	370
Light gardening/yard work	165	330
Dancing	165	330
Golf (walking and carrying clubs)	165	330
Bicycling (<10 mph)	145	290
Walking (3.5 mph)	140	280
Weight lifting (general light workout)	110	220
Stretching	90	180
Vigorous Physical Activity	**Approximate Calories/30 Minutes for a 154 lb Person[1]**	**Approximate Calories/ Hr for a 154 lb Person[1]**
Running/jogging (5 mph)	295	590
Bicycling (>10 mph)	295	590
Swimming (slow freestyle laps)	255	510
Aerobics	240	480
Walking (4.5 mph)	230	460
Heavy yard work (chopping wood)	220	440
Weight lifting (vigorous effort)	220	440
Basketball (vigorous)	220	440

[1] *Calories burned per hour will be higher for persons who weigh more than 154 lbs (70 kg) and lower for persons who weigh less.*

Section 45.2

Benefits of Exercise

This section contains text excerpted from the following sources:
Text beginning with the heading "The Benefits of Physical
Activity" is excerpted from "Physical Activity and Health,"
Centers for Disease Control and Prevention (CDC),
June 4, 2015; Text beginning with the heading "One of the
Healthiest Things You Can Do" is excerpted from "Health
Benefits," National Institutes of Health (NIH), January 5, 2015.

The Benefits of Physical Activity

If you're not sure about becoming active or boosting your level of physical activity because you're afraid of getting hurt, the good news is that moderate-intensity aerobic activity, like brisk walking, is generally safe for most people.

Start slowly. Cardiac events, such as a heart attack, are rare during physical activity. But the risk does go up when you suddenly become much more active than usual. For example, you can put yourself at risk if you don't usually get much physical activity and then all of a sudden do vigorous-intensity aerobic activity, like shoveling snow. That's why it's important to start slowly and gradually increase your level of activity.

If you have a chronic health condition such as arthritis, diabetes, or heart disease, talk with your doctor to find out if your condition limits, in any way, your ability to be active. Then, work with your doctor to come up with a physical activity plan that matches your abilities. If your condition stops you from meeting the minimum guidelines, try to do as much as you can. What's important is that you avoid being inactive. Even 60 minutes a week of moderate-intensity aerobic activity is good for you.

The bottom line is—the health benefits of physical activity far outweigh the risks of getting hurt.

If you want to know more about how physical activity improves your health, the section below gives more detail on what research studies have found.

Control Your Weight

Looking to get to or stay at a healthy weight? Both diet and physical activity play a critical role in controlling your weight. You gain weight when the calories you burn, including those burned during physical activity, are less than the calories you eat or drink. When it comes to weight management, people vary greatly in how much physical activity they need. You may need to be more active than others to achieve or maintain a healthy weight.

To maintain your weight: Work your way up to 150 minutes of moderate-intensity aerobic activity, 75 minutes of vigorous-intensity aerobic activity, or an equivalent mix of the two each week. Strong scientific evidence shows that physical activity can help you maintain your weight over time. However, the exact amount of physical activity needed to do this is not clear since it varies greatly from person to person. It's possible that you may need to do more than the equivalent of 150 minutes of moderate-intensity activity a week to maintain your weight.

To lose weight and keep it off: You will need a high amount of physical activity unless you also adjust your diet and reduce the amount of calories you're eating and drinking. Getting to and staying at a healthy weight requires both regular physical activity and a healthy eating plan.

Reduce Your Risk of Cardiovascular Disease

Heart disease and stroke are two of the leading causes of death in the United States. But following the Guidelines and getting at least 150 minutes a week (2 hours and 30 minutes) of moderate-intensity aerobic activity can put you at a lower risk for these diseases. You can reduce your risk even further with more physical activity. Regular physical activity can also lower your blood pressure and improve your cholesterol levels.

Reduce Your Risk of Type 2 Diabetes and Metabolic Syndrome

Regular physical activity can reduce your risk of developing type 2 diabetes and metabolic syndrome. Metabolic syndrome is a condition in which you have some combination of too much fat around the waist, high blood pressure, low High-density lipoprotein (HDL) cholesterol, high triglycerides, or high blood sugar. Research shows that lower rates of these conditions are seen with 120 to 150 minutes (2 hours to

2 hours and 30 minutes) a week of at least moderate-intensity aerobic activity. And the more physical activity you do, the lower your risk will be.

Reduce Your Risk of Some Cancers

Being physically active lowers your risk for two types of cancer: colon and breast. Research shows that:

- Physically active people have a lower risk of colon cancer than do people who are not active.

- Physically active women have a lower risk of breast cancer than do people who are not active.

Reduce your risk of endometrial and lung cancer. Although the research is not yet final, some findings suggest that your risk of endometrial cancer and lung cancer may be lower if you get regular physical activity compared to people who are not active.

Improve your quality of life. If you are a cancer survivor, research shows that getting regular physical activity not only helps give you a better quality of life, but also improves your physical fitness.

Strengthen Your Bones and Muscles

As you age, it's important to protect your bones, joints and muscles. Not only do they support your body and help you move, but keeping bones, joints and muscles healthy can help ensure that you're able to do your daily activities and be physically active. Research shows that doing aerobic, muscle-strengthening and bone-strengthening physical activity of at least a moderately-intense level can slow the loss of bone density that comes with age.

Hip fracture is a serious health condition that can have life-changing negative effects, especially if you're an older adult. But research shows that people who do 120 to 300 minutes of at least moderate-intensity aerobic activity each week have a lower risk of hip fracture.

Regular physical activity helps with arthritis and other conditions affecting the joints. If you have arthritis, research shows that doing 130 to 150 (2 hours and 10 minutes to 2 hours and 30 minutes) a week of moderate-intensity, low-impact aerobic activity can not only improve your ability to manage pain and do everyday tasks, but it can also make your quality of life better.

Build strong, healthy muscles. Muscle-strengthening activities can help you increase or maintain your muscle mass and strength. Slowly increasing the amount of weight and number of repetitions you do will give you even more benefits, no matter your age.

Improve Your Mental Health and Mood

Regular physical activity can help keep your thinking, learning, and judgment skills sharp as you age. It can also reduce your risk of depression and may help you sleep better. Research has shown that doing aerobic or a mix of aerobic and muscle-strengthening activities 3 to 5 times a week for 30 to 60 minutes can give you these mental health benefits. Some scientific evidence has also shown that even lower levels of physical activity can be beneficial.

Improve Your Ability to do Daily Activities and Prevent Falls

A functional limitation is a loss of the ability to do everyday activities such as climbing stairs, grocery shopping, or playing with your grandchildren.

How Does This Relate to Physical Activity?

If you're a physically active middle-aged or older adult, you have a lower risk of functional limitations than people who are inactive

Already Have Trouble Doing Some of Your Everyday Activities?

Aerobic and muscle-strengthening activities can help improve your ability to do these types of tasks.

Are You an Older Adult Who Is at Risk for Falls?

Research shows that doing balance and muscle-strengthening activities each week along with **moderate-intensity aerobic activity**, like brisk walking, can help reduce your risk of falling.

Increase Your Chances of Living Longer

Science shows that physical activity can reduce your risk of dying early from the leading causes of death, like heart disease and some cancers. This is remarkable in two ways:

1. Only a few lifestyle choices have as large an impact on your health as physical activity. People who are physically active

for about 7 hours a week have a 40 percent lower risk of dying early than those who are active for less than 30 minutes a week.

2. You don't have to do high amounts of activity or vigorous-intensity activity to reduce your risk of premature death. You can put yourself at lower risk of dying early by doing at least 150 minutes a week of moderate-intensity aerobic activity.

Everyone can gain the health benefits of physical activity—age, ethnicity, shape or size do not matter.

One of the Healthiest Things You Can Do

Like most people, you've probably heard that physical activity and exercise are good for you. In fact, being physically active on a regular basis is one of the healthiest things you can do for yourself. Studies have shown that exercise provides many health benefits and that older adults can gain a lot by staying physically active. Even moderate exercise and physical activity can improve the health of people who are frail or who have diseases that accompany aging.

Being physically active can also help you stay strong and fit enough to keep doing the things you like to do as you get older. Making exercise and physical activity a regular part of your life can improve your health and help you maintain your independence as you age.

Be as Active as Possible

Regular physical activity and exercise are important to the physical and mental health of almost everyone, including older adults. Staying physically active and exercising regularly can produce long-term health benefits and even improve health for some older people who already have diseases and disabilities. That's why health experts say that older adults should aim to be as active as possible.

Being Inactive Can Be Risky

Although exercise and physical activity are among the healthiest things you can do for yourself, some older adults are reluctant to exercise. Some are afraid that exercise will be too hard or that physical activity will harm them. Others might think they have to join a gym or have special equipment. Yet, studies show that "taking it easy" is risky. For the most part, when older people lose their ability to do things on their own, it doesn't happen just because they've aged. It's usually because they're not active. Lack of physical activity also can lead to more visits to the doctor, more hospitalizations, and more use of medicines for a variety of illnesses.

Prevent or Delay Disease

Scientists have found that staying physically active and exercising regularly can help prevent or delay many diseases and disabilities. In some cases, exercise is an effective treatment for many chronic conditions. For example, studies show that people with arthritis, heart disease, or diabetes benefit from regular exercise. Exercise also helps people with high blood pressure, balance problems, or difficulty walking.

Manage Stress, Improve Mood

Regular, moderate physical activity can help manage stress and improve your mood. And, being active on a regular basis may help reduce feelings of depression. Studies also suggest that exercise can improve or maintain some aspects of cognitive function, such as your ability to shift quickly between tasks, plan an activity, and ignore irrelevant information.

Some people may wonder what the difference is between physical activity and exercise. Physical activities are activities that get your body moving such as gardening, walking the dog and taking the stairs instead of the elevator. Exercise is a form of physical activity that is specifically planned, structured, and repetitive such as weight training, tai chi, or an aerobics class. Including both in your life will provide you with health benefits that can help you feel better and enjoy life more as you age.

Section 45.3

Why Exercise Is Wise

Rewards and Benefits

Experts recommend that teens get 60 minutes or more of moderate to vigorous physical activity each day. Here are some of the reasons:

- **Exercise benefits every part of the body, including the mind.** Exercising causes the body to produce endorphins, chemicals that can help a person to feel more peaceful and happy. Exercise can help some people sleep better. It can also help some people who have mild depression and low self-esteem. Plus, exercise can give people a real sense of accomplishment and pride at having achieved a certain goal—like beating an old time in the 100-meter dash.

- **Exercising can help you look better.** People who exercise burn more calories and look more toned than those who don't. In fact, exercise is one of the most important parts of keeping your body at a healthy weight.

- **Exercise helps people lose weight and lower the risk of some diseases.** Exercising to maintain a healthy weight decreases a person's risk of developing certain diseases, including type 2 diabetes and high blood pressure. These diseases, which used to be found mostly in adults, are becoming more common in teens.

- **Exercise can help a person age well.** This may not seem important now, but your body will thank you later. Women are especially prone to a condition called osteoporosis (a weakening of the bones) as they get older. Studies have found that weight-bearing exercise—like jumping, running, or brisk walking—can help girls (and guys!) keep their bones strong.

The three components to a well-balanced exercise routine are: aerobic exercise, strength training, and flexibility training.

Aerobic Exercise

Like other muscles, the heart enjoys a good workout. You can provide it with one in the form of aerobic exercise. Aerobic exercise is any type of exercise that gets the heart pumping and quickens your breathing. When you give your heart this kind of workout regularly, it will get stronger and more efficient in delivering oxygen (in the form of oxygen-carrying blood cells) to all parts of your body.

If you play team sports, you're probably meeting the recommendation for 60 minutes or more of moderate to vigorous activity on practice days. Some team sports that give you a great aerobic workout are swimming, basketball, soccer, lacrosse, hockey, and rowing.

But if you don't play team sports, don't worry—there are plenty of ways to get aerobic exercise on your own or with friends. These include biking, running, swimming, dancing, in-line skating, tennis, cross-country skiing, hiking, and walking quickly. In fact, the types of exercise that you do on your own are easier to continue when you leave high school and go on to work or college, making it easier to stay fit later in life as well.

Strength Training

The heart isn't the only muscle to benefit from regular exercise. Most of the other muscles in your body enjoy exercise, too. When you use your muscles and they become stronger, it allows you to be active for longer periods of time without getting worn out.

Strong muscles are also a plus because they actually help protect you when you exercise by supporting your joints and helping to prevent injuries. Muscle also burns more energy when a person's at rest than fat does, so building your muscles will help you burn more calories and maintain a healthy weight.

Different types of exercise strengthen different muscle groups, for example:

- For arms, try rowing or cross-country skiing. Pull-ups and push-ups, those old gym class standbys, are also good for building arm muscles.

- For strong legs, try running, biking, rowing, or skating. Squats and leg raises also work the legs.

- For shapely abs, you can't beat rowing, yoga or pilates, and crunches.

Flexibility Training

Strengthening the heart and other muscles isn't the only important goal of exercise. Exercise also helps the body stay flexible, meaning that your muscles and joints stretch and bend easily. People who are flexible can worry less about strained muscles and sprains.

Being flexible may also help improve a person's sports performance. Some activities, like dance or martial arts, obviously require great flexibility, but increased flexibility also can help people perform better at other sports, such as soccer or lacrosse.

Sports and activities that encourage flexibility are easy to find. Martial arts like karate also help a person stay flexible. Ballet, gymnastics, pilates, and yoga are other good choices. Stretching after your workout will also help you improve your flexibility.

What's Right for Me?

One of the biggest reasons people drop an exercise program is lack of interest: If what you're doing isn't fun, it's hard to keep it up. The good news is that there are tons of different sports and activities that you can try out to see which one inspires you.

When picking the right type of exercise, it can help to consider your workout personality. For example, do you like to work out alone and on your own schedule? If so, solo sports like biking or snowboarding could be for you. Or do you like the shared motivation and companionship that comes from being part of a team?

You also need to plan around practical considerations, such as whether your chosen activity is affordable and available to you. (Activities like horseback riding may be harder for people who live in cities, for example.) You'll also want to think about how much time you can set aside for your sport.

It's a good idea to talk to someone who understands the exercise, like a coach or fitness expert at a gym. He or she can get you started on a program that's right for you and your level of fitness.

Another thing to consider is whether any health conditions may affect how—and how much—you exercise. Doctors know that most people benefit from regular exercise, even those with disabilities or conditions like asthma. But if you have a health problem or other considerations (like being overweight or very out of shape), talk to your doctor before beginning an exercise plan. That way you can get information on which exercise programs are best and which to avoid.

Too Much of a Good Thing

As with all good things, it's possible to overdo exercise. Although exercising is a great way to maintain a healthy weight, exercising too much to lose weight isn't healthy. The body needs enough calories to function properly. This is especially true for teens, who are still growing.Exercising too much in an effort to burn calories and lose weight can be a sign of an eating disorder. If you ever get the feeling that your exercise is in charge of you rather than the other way around, talk with your doctor, a parent, or another adult you trust.

It's also possible to overtrain—something high school athletes need to watch out for. If you participate in one sport, experts recommend that you limit that activity to a maximum of 5 days a week, with at least 2–3 months off per year. You can still train more than that as long as it's cross-training in a different sport (such as swimming or biking if you play football).

Participating in more than one activity or sport can help athletes use different skills and avoid injury. Also, never exercise through pain. And, if you have an injury, make sure you give yourself enough time to heal. Your body—and your performance—will thank you.

Considering the benefits to the heart, muscles, joints, and mind, it's easy to see why exercise is wise. And the great thing about exercise is that it's never too late to start. Even small things can count as exercise when you're starting out—like taking a short bike ride, walking the dog, or raking leaves.

If you're already getting regular exercise now, try to keep it up after you graduate from high school. Staying fit is often one of the biggest challenges for people as they get busy with college and careers.

Section 45.4

Exercise and Bone Health for Women

This section includes text excerpted from "Exercise
and Bone Health for Women: The Skeletal Risk of
Overtraining," National Institute of Arthritis and
Musculoskeletal and Skin Diseases (NIAMS), April 2015.

Why Is Missing My Period Such a Big Deal?

Some athletes see amenorrhea (the absence of menstrual periods) as
a sign of successful training. Others see it as a great answer to a monthly
inconvenience. And some young women accept it blindly, not stopping
to think of the consequences. But missing your periods is often a sign of
decreased estrogen levels. And lower estrogen levels can lead to osteoporosis, a disease in which your bones become brittle and more likely to break.

Usually, bones don't become brittle and break until women are
much older. But some young women, especially those who exercise so
much that their periods stop, develop brittle bones, and may start to
have fractures at a very early age. Some 20-year-old female athletes
have been said to have the bones of an 80-year-old woman. Even if
bones don't break when you're young, low estrogen levels during the
peak years of bone-building, the preteen and teen years, can affect bone
density for the rest of your life. And studies show that bone growth
lost during these years may never be regained.

Broken bones don't just hurt—they can cause lasting physical mal-
formations. Have you noticed that some older women and men have
stooped postures? This is not a normal sign of aging. Fractures from
osteoporosis have left their spines permanently altered.

Overtraining can cause other problems besides missed periods. If
you don't take in enough calcium and vitamin D (among other nutrients), bone loss may result. This may lead to decreased athletic performance, decreased ability to exercise or train at desired levels of
intensity or duration, and increased risk of injury.

Who Is at Risk for These Problems?

Girls and women who engage in rigorous exercise regimens or who
try to lose weight by restricting their eating are at risk for these health

problems. They may include serious athletes, "gym rats" (who spend considerable time and energy working out), and girls and women who believe "you can never be too thin."

How Can I Tell if Someone I Know, Train With, or Coach May Be at Risk for Bone Loss, Fracture, and Other Health Problems?

Here are some signs to look for:

- missed or irregular menstrual periods

- extreme or "unhealthy-looking" thinness

- extreme or rapid weight loss

- behaviors that reflect frequent dieting, such as eating very little, not eating in front of others, trips to the bathroom following meals, preoccupation with thinness or weight, focus on low-calorie and diet foods, possible increase in the consumption of water and other no- and low-calorie foods and beverages, possible increase in gum chewing, limiting diet to one food group, or eliminating a food group

- frequent intense bouts of exercise (e.g., taking an aerobics class, then running 5 miles, then swimming for an hour, followed by weight-lifting)

- an "I can't miss a day of exercise/practice" attitude

- an overly anxious preoccupation with an injury

- exercising despite illness, inclement weather, injury, and other conditions that might lead someone else to take the day off

- an unusual amount of self-criticism or self-dissatisfaction

- indications of significant psychological or physical stress, including: depression, anxiety or nervousness, inability to concentrate, low levels of self-esteem, feeling cold all the time, problems sleeping, fatigue, injuries, and constantly talking about weight.

How Can I Make Needed Changes to Improve My Bone Health?

If you recognize some of these signs in yourself, the best thing you can do is to make your diet more healthful. That includes consuming enough calories to support your activity level. If you've missed periods, it's best to check with a doctor to make sure it's not a sign of some other problem and to get his or her help as you work toward a more healthy balance of food and exercise. Also, a doctor can help you take steps to protect your bones from further damage.

What Can I Do if I Suspect a Friend May Have Some of These Signs?

First, be supportive. Approach your friend or teammate carefully, and be sensitive. She probably won't appreciate a lecture about how she should be taking better care of herself. But maybe you could suggest that she talk to a trainer, coach, or doctor about the symptoms she's experiencing.

My Friend Drinks a Lot of Diet Sodas. She Says This Helps Keep Her Trim.

Girls and women who may be dieting often drink diet sodas rather than milk. Yet, milk and other dairy products are a good source of calcium, an essential ingredient for healthy bones. Drinking sodas instead of milk can be a problem, especially during the teen years when rapid bone growth occurs. If you (or your friend) find yourself drinking a lot of sodas, try drinking half as many sodas each day, and gradually add more milk and dairy products to your diet. A frozen yogurt shake can be an occasional low-fat, tasty treat. Or try a fruit smoothie made with frozen yogurt, fruit, or calcium-enriched orange juice.

For Fitness Instructors and Trainers

It's important for you to be aware of problems associated with bone loss in today's active young women. As an instructor or trainer, you are the one who sees, leads, and perhaps even evaluates the training sessions and performances of your clients. You may know best when something seems to be amiss. You also may be the best person to help a zealous female exerciser recognize that she is putting herself at risk for bone loss and other health problems and that she should establish new goals.

Trainers and instructors also should be aware of the implicit or explicit messages they send. Health, strength, and fitness should be emphasized, rather than thinness. Use caution when advising female clients to lose weight. And, if such a recommendation is deemed necessary, knowledgeable personnel should offer education and assistance about proper and safe weight management. As an instructor or trainer, it's best to maintain a professional rapport with your clients, so they can feel comfortable approaching you with concerns about their exercise training programs, appropriate exercise goals and time lines, body image and nutrition issues, as well as more personal problems regarding eating practices and menstruation.

My Coach and I Think I Should Lose Just a Little More Weight. I Want to Be Able to Excel at My Sport!

Years ago, it was not unusual for coaches to encourage athletes to be as thin as possible for many sports (e.g., dancing, gymnastics, figure skating, swimming, diving, and running). However, many coaches now realize that being too thin is unhealthy and can negatively affect performance. It's important to exercise and watch what you eat. However, it's also important to develop and maintain healthy bones and bodies. Without these, it will not matter how fast you can run, how thin you are, or how long you exercise each day. Balance is the key!

I'm Still Not Convinced. If My Bones Become Brittle, So What? What's the Worst Thing That Could Happen to Me?

Brittle bones may not sound as scary as a fatal or rare disease. The fact is that osteoporosis can lead to fractures. It can cause disability.

Imagine having so many spine fractures that you've lost inches in height and walk bent over. Imagine looking down at the ground everywhere you go because you can't straighten your back. Imagine not being able to find clothes that fit you. Imagine having difficulty breathing and eating because your lungs and stomach are compressed into a smaller space. Imagine having difficulty walking, let alone exercising, because of pain and misshapen bones. Imagine constantly having to be aware of what you are doing and having to do things so slowly and carefully because of a very real fear and dread of a fracture—a fracture that could lead to a drastic change in your life, including pain, loss of independence, loss of mobility, loss of freedom, and more.

Osteoporosis isn't just an "older person's" disease. Young women also experience fractures. Imagine being sidelined because of a broken bone and not being able to get those good feelings you get from regular activity.

Eating for Healthy Bones

How Much Calcium Do I Need?

It's very important to your bone health that you receive adequate daily amounts of calcium, vitamin D, phosphorus, and magnesium. These vitamins and minerals are the most influential in building bones and teeth. This table will help you decide how much calcium you need.

Table 45.2. Recommended Calcium Intakes (mg/day)

Age	Amount
9 to 13	1300
14 to 18	1300
19 to 30	1000

Source: Food and Nutrition Board, Institute of Medicine, National Academy of Sciences, 2010.

Where Can I Get Calcium and Vitamin D?

Dairy products are the primary food sources of calcium. Choose low-fat milk, yogurt, cheeses, ice cream, or products made or served with these choices to fulfill your daily requirement. Three servings of dairy products per day should give you at least 900 mg (milligrams) of calcium. Green vegetables are another source. A cup of broccoli, for example, has about 136 mg of calcium.

Milk and dairy products. Many great snack and meal items contain calcium. With a little planning and "know-how," you can make meals and snacks calcium-rich!

- Milk: Wouldn't a tall, cold glass of this refreshing thirst quencher be great right now? If you're concerned about fat and calories, choose reduced-fat or fat-free milk. You can drink it plain or with a low- or no-fat syrup or flavoring, such as chocolate syrup, vanilla extract, hazelnut flavoring, or cinnamon.

- Cheese: Again, you can choose the low- or no-fat varieties. Use all different types of cheese for sandwiches, bagels, omelets, vegetable dishes, pasta creations, or as a snack by itself!

- Pudding (prepared with milk): You can now purchase (or make from a mix) pudding in a variety of flavors with little or no fat, such as chocolate fudge, lemon, butterscotch, vanilla, and pistachio. Try them all!

- Yogurt: Add fruit. Eat it plain. Add a low- or no-fat sauce or syrup. No matter how you choose to eat this calcium-rich food, yogurt remains a quick, easy, and convenient choice. It's also available in a variety of flavors. Try mocha-fudge-peppermint-swirl if you're more adventurous at heart and vanilla if you're a more traditional yogurt snacker!

- Frozen yogurt (or fat-free ice cream): Everybody loves ice cream. And now, without the unnecessary fat, you can enjoy it more often! Mix yogurt, milk, and fruit to create a breakfast shake. Have a cone at lunchtime or as a snack. A scoop or two after dinner can be cool and refreshing.

What Are Other Sources of Calcium?

Many foods you already buy and eat may be "calcium-fortified." Try calcium-fortified orange juice or calcium-fortified cereal. Check food labels to see if some of your other favorite foods may be good sources of calcium. You also can take calcium supplements if you think you may not be getting enough from your diet.

Chapter 46

Coping with Holidays and Food-Related Challenges

Resolve to Undo Holiday Overindulgences

This Holiday Season Maintain, Don't Gain!

What comes to mind when you think of the holiday season? Spending time with family? Shopping? Playing in the snow? Eating a lot of food probably makes the list too. But that doesn't mean you have to pack on the pounds. Why not focus on balancing the calories you consume with the calories you burn to avoid weight gain this year? Here are some ways to help you eat healthier and move more this holiday season.

Continue to Think "Healthy Foods" throughout the Season

It's challenging to keep the pounds off during the holidays. The temptation to eat high-calorie food is everywhere. Here are some suggestions for cutting your calories.

- **Enjoy your holiday comfort foods, but try a lower-calorie version.** Use lower-calorie ingredients or prepare meals differently. For example, if your macaroni and cheese recipe uses

---

This chapter includes text excerpted from "Resolve to Undo Holiday Overindulgences," Centers for Disease Control and Prevention (CDC), December 8, 2014.

whole milk, butter, and full-fat cheese, try remaking it with non-fat milk, less butter, light cream cheese, and include vegetables like fresh spinach and tomatoes.

- **Fruits and Veggies: keep it simple!** Most fruits and veggies are low-calorie and will fill you up, but the way you prepare them can change that. Breading and frying, and using high-fat creams or butter with vegetables and fruit will add extra calories. Try steaming vegetables and using spices and low-fat sauces for flavor. And enjoy the natural sweetness of raw fruit.

- **Eat smaller food portions.** When eating out, save some of your meal and take it home to make another meal or split one meal between two people. At home, try putting only the amount you want to eat in a small bowl and don't go back for more. People eat more when served larger portion sizes.

- **Drink water.** Choose water instead of sugar-sweetened beverages. This tip can help with weight management. Substituting water for one 20-ounce sugar-sweetened soda will save you around 200 or more calories, depending on the drink you choose. Give your water a little pizzazz by adding a wedge of lime or lemon. This may improve the taste, and you just might drink more water than you usually do.

- **Eat breakfast every day.** When you don't eat breakfast, you are likely to make up for the calories you saved by eating more later on in the day. Many people who maintain long-term weight loss eat breakfast daily.

- **Nibble on health snacks** like whole grain crackers, fruit, or raw vegetables before the big feast. You will eat less.

- **It takes your brain some time to signal you are full.** Wait 10–15 minutes before eating seconds. This may keep you from overeating!

- **It's not rude to say no to food.** Don't be pressured to eat, if you aren't hungry.

- **Eating holiday goodies** like fudge, peanut brittle, cookies, and other baked goods is fine, but eat them in small portions.

Get Active, Healthy, and Happy

Maintain your physical activity routine. Regular physical activity is an important part of maintaining weight loss.

- Regular physical activity helps with weight control, reduces the risk for many diseases, and strengthens muscles, bones and joints.

- Maintain your physical activity during the holidays—better yet, try to get more active!

- Find fun, creative ways your friends and family can spend time being active instead of eating.

Part Seven

Additional Help and Information

Chapter 47

Glossary of Terms Related to Eating Disorders

abstinence: Not having sex of any kind.

abuse: Misuse, wrong use, especially excessive use, of anything.

added sugars: These sugars, syrups, and other caloric sweeteners are added when foods are processed or prepared. Added sugars do not include sugars that occur naturally, like fructose in fruit or lactose in milk.

addiction: An illness in which you become dependent on, or can't do without, certain physical substances or an activity. When a person is addicted to something, they cannot control or stop their urges.

adrenal gland: One of a pair of small glands, each of which sits on top of the kidneys. These glands produce hormones that help to control the body's heart rate, blood pressure, the way food gets used, and other functions. They make the hormone adrenaline, which the body releases in response to stress.

aerobic: Fat-fueled; aerobic exercise increases basal metabolic rate, reduces appetite, firms muscles, improves cardiac and respiratory function, and burns flab.

This glossary contains terms excerpted from documents produced by several-sources deemed reliable.

allergies: A sensitivity to things that are usually not harmful, such as certain foods or animals. When a person is exposed to an allergen (something she or he is allergic to), the person's immune system gives off a much bigger response than it normally would.

amenorrhea: The loss of the menstrual cycle. In terms of eating disorders this is usually the result of excessive weight loss and often accompanied by excessive exercise.

anorexia nervosa: Self-induced starvation with at least 15 percent of original body weight lost. Victims also have amenorrhea, fat phobia, and a severe distortion of body image.

antidepressant: Drugs given by your doctor to treat depression.

anxiety disorder: Serious medical illness that fills people's lives with anxiety and fear. Some anxiety disorders include panic disorder, obsessive-compulsive disorder, posttraumatic stress disorder, social phobia (or social anxiety disorder), specific phobias, and generalized anxiety disorder.

artery: Any of the thick-walled blood vessels that carry blood away from the heart to other parts of the body.

autism: A disorder in the brain that affects both verbal and nonverbal communication.

bariatric surgery: Also known as gastrointestinal surgery or weight-loss surgery, this is surgery on the stomach and/or intestines to help patients with extreme obesity lose weight.

behavior therapy: An offshoot of psychotherapy involving the use of procedures and techniques associated with research in the fields of conditioning and learning for the treatment of a variety of psychologic conditions; distinguished from psychotherapy because specific symptoms (e.g., phobia, enuresis, high blood pressure) are selected as the target for change, planned interventions or remedial steps to extinguish or modify these symptoms are then employed, and the progress of changes is continuously and quantitatively monitored.

behavioral therapy: A kind of therapy used by a psychologist or a psychiatrist that helps people to change the way they behave and act.

binge eating disorder: An eating disorder caused by a person being unable to control the need to overeat.

bipolar disorder: Medical illness that causes unusual shifts in mood, energy, and activity levels. It is also known as manic-depressive illness.

body dysmorphic disorder: A psychosomatic (somatoform) disorder characterized by preoccupation with some imagined defect in appearance in a normal-appearing person.

body image: Personal conception of one's own body as distinct from one's actual anatomic body or the conception other persons have of it.

body mass index (BMI): An anthropometric measure of body mass, defined as weight in kilograms divided by height in meters squared; a method of determining caloric nutritional status.

bone mineral density testing: A test that measures bone strength and fracture risk.

bulimia nervosa: Uncontrolled eating in the presence of a strong desire to lose weight.

calcium: A mineral that is an essential nutrient for bone health. It is also needed for the heart, muscles and nerves to function properly and for blood to clot.

calories: The energy provided by food/nutrients. On the label, calories shown are for one serving.

celiac disease: An inherited intestinal disorder in which the body cannot tolerate gluten, which is found in foods made with wheat, rye, and barley.

cholesterol: A necessary nutrient from animal-based foods that is carried in the bloodstream.

cognitive therapy: Any of a variety of techniques in psychotherapy that utilizes guided self-discovery, imaging, self-inspection, symbolic modeling, and related forms of explicitly elicited cognitions as the principal mode of treatment.

daily value: The amount of certain nutrients that most people need each day.

diabetes: A disease in which the body does not produce or properly use insulin. Insulin is a hormone that is needed to convert sugar, starches, and other food into energy.

diuretic: A chemical that stimulates the production of urine. Also known as a water pill.

dual-energy X-ray absorptiometry (DXA): A common test for measuring bone mineral density. It is painless, a bit like having an X-ray, but with much less exposure to radiation.

Eating disorder not otherwise specified (EDNOS): This is a classification for eating disorders that do not meet the criteria of anorexia nervosa or bulimia nervosa, however it involves a combination of multiple symptoms of eating disorders. It is the most common diagnosis of eating disorder among individuals seeking treatment.

eating disorders: A group of mental disorders including anorexia nervosa, bulimia nervosa, pica, and rumination disorder of infancy.

endocrinologist: A doctor who treats the endocrine system, which are the glands and hormones that help control the body's metabolic activity.

enema: The injection of a liquid into the lower bowel through the rectum to compel elimination.

flexibility: The range of motion of a muscle or group of muscles. Along with balance and strength, improving flexibility can significantly reduce the risk of falling.

fracture: Broken bone. People with osteoporosis, osteogenesis imperfecta, and Paget's disease are at greater risk for bone fracture.

gallstone: Solid material that forms in the gallbladder or common bile duct. Gallstones are made of cholesterol or other substances found in the gallbladder.

gastroesophageal reflux: The backward flow of stomach acid contents into the esophagus (the tube that connects the mouth to the stomach).

glucose: Glucose is a major source of energy for our bodies and a building block for many carbohydrates.

gynecologist: A doctor who diagnoses and treats conditions of the female reproductive system and associated disorders.

healthy weight: Healthy weight status is often based on having a body mass index (BMI) that falls in the normal (or healthy) range.

hypertension: High blood pressure.

hypogonadism: Abnormally low levels of sex hormone. Low levels of testosterone is sometimes a secondary cause of osteoporosis in men.

indigestion: Also called dyspepsia. Indigestion is a common problem that causes a vague feeling of abdominal discomfort after meals. Symptoms also can include an uncomfortable fullness, belching, bloating, and nausea.

insulin: A hormone made by the pancreas, insulin helps move glucose (sugar) from the blood to muscles and other tissues. Insulin controls blood sugar levels.

internist: A doctor trained in general internal medicine. These doctors diagnose and treat many diseases.

intervention: An action or ministration that produces an effect or that is intended to alter the course of a pathologic process.

kinase: A type of enzyme (a protein that speeds up chemical reactions in the body) that adds chemicals called phosphates to other molecules, such as sugars or proteins.

laxative: Mildly cathartic, having the action of loosening the bowels; a mild cathartic, a remedy that moves the bowels slightly without pain or violent action.

legume: A seed or pod of a certain kind of plant that is used as food. Legumes include beans, peas, lentils, and peanuts.

lupus: A chronic inflammatory disease that occurs when the body's immune system attacks its own tissues and organs. Also called systemic lupus erythematosus (SLE).

malnutrition: Faulty nutrition resulting from malabsorption, poor diet, or overeating.

menopause: The cessation of menstruation in women. Bone health in women often deteriorates after menopause due to a decrease in the female hormone estrogen.

metabolism: Metabolism refers to all of the processes in the body that make and use energy, such as digesting food and nutrients and removing waste through urine and feces.

nutrient: An ingredient in a food that provides nourishment or nutritional benefit.

nutrition: A function of living plants and animals, consisting in the taking in and metabolism of food material whereby tissue is built up and energy liberated.

nutrition facts label: The black-and-white box found on food and beverage packages.

obesity: Obesity refers to excess body fat. Because body fat is usually not measured directly, a ratio of body weight to height is often used instead. An adult who has a BMI of 30 or higher is considered obese.

obsessive-compulsive disorder (OCD): An anxiety disorder in which a person suffers from obsessive thoughts and compulsive actions, such as cleaning, checking, counting, or hoarding.

occupational therapist: A health care specialist who helps people with a disability, illness, injury, or other health issue learn or relearn how to do daily activities like eating, dressing, or bathing.

osteoporosis: Reduction in the quantity of bone or atrophy of skeletal tissue; an age-related disorder characterized by decreased bone mass and increased susceptibility to fractures.

overweight: Overweight refers to an excessive amount of body weight that includes muscle, bone, fat, and water. A person who has a body mass index (BMI) of 25 to 29.9 is considered overweight.

oxidative stress: A condition in which antioxidant levels are lower than normal. Antioxidant levels are usually measured in blood plasma.

parathyroid hormone: A form of human parathyroid hormone (PTH) is approved for the treatment of osteoporosis.

percent daily value (%DV): The percentage of a nutrient found in one serving of food, based on the established standard of 2000 calories per day.

phobia: An unrealistic fear, often with obsessional characteristics.

pica: A perverse appetite for substances not fit as food or of no nutritional value.

polyunsaturated fat: This type of fat is liquid at room temperature. There are two types of polyunsaturated fatty acids (PUFAs), omega-6 and omega-3.

portion size: The amount of a food served or eaten in one occasion. A portion is not a standard amount. The amount of food it includes may vary by person and occasion

postpartum: A depression that follows child birth in some mothers. Cases can be mild or severe enough to be labeled psychosis and require hospitalization.

posttraumatic stress disorder (PTSD): A psychological condition that can happen when a person sees or experiences something traumatic, such as rape, murder, torture, or wartime combat.

psychotherapy: Counseling or talk therapy with a qualified practitioner in which a person can explore difficult, and often painful, emotions and experiences, such as feelings of anxiety, depression, or trauma.

purging: A forced cleansing or release. In terms of eating disorders this is usually done by vomiting or laxative abuse.

recovery: A getting back or regaining; recuperation.

relapse: Return of the manifestations of a disease after an interval of improvement.

rumination: The apparently voluntary regurgitation, chewing, and reswallowing of food.

saturated fat: A type of fat that is solid at room temperature. It is usually animal-based. This type of fat is associated with certain health risks.

sodium: Dietary salt that is important in the diet. However, too much sodium can lead to high blood pressure and risk of heart disease.

solid fats: These types of fats are usually not liquid at room temperature. Solid fats are found in most animal foods but also can be made from vegetable oils through hydrogenation.

starvation: Lengthy and continuous deprivation of food.

stroke: A stroke occurs when blood flow to your brain stops. Within minutes, brain cells begin to die.

sugar-sweetened beverages: Drinks that are sweetened with added sugars often add a large number of calories. These beverages include, but are not limited to, energy and sports drinks, fruit drinks, soda, and fruit juices

total fat: The combined fats that provide energy to the body. Some types of fat are healthier than others.

trans fat: A type of fat, usually made by food manufacturers so that foods last longer on shelves or in cans. Eating trans fats increases the risk of some illnesses, like heart disease.

triglycerides: A type of fat in your blood, triglycerides can contribute to the hardening and narrowing of your arteries if levels are too high. This puts you at risk of having a heart attack or stroke.

unsaturated fat: A type of fat that is liquid at room temperature; can be plant-based or animal-based. These are usually "good fats."

very low-calorie diet (VLCD): A VLCD is a diet supervised by a health care professional that typically uses commercially prepared formulas to promote rapid weight loss in some patients who are considered to be obese. People on a VLCD consume about 800 calories a day or less.

vitamin A: A family of fat-soluble compounds that play an important role in vision, bone growth, reproduction, cell division, and cell differentiation.

vitamin D: A nutrient that the body needs to absorb calcium.

waist circumference: Excess fat around the waist and a larger waist size increase the risk of health problems linked to obesity.

weight control: This refers to achieving and maintaining a healthy weight with healthy eating and physical activity.

Chapter 48

Directory of Eating Disorder Resources

Government Organizations

***Agency for Healthcare
Research and Quality
(AHRQ)***
5600 Fishers Ln.
Rockville, MD 20857
Phone: 301-427-1364
Website: www.ahrq.gov
E-mail: info.ahrq.gov

***Centers for Disease Control
and Prevention (CDC)***
1600 Clifton Rd.
Atlanta, GA 30333-4027
Toll-Free: 800-CDC-INFO
(800-232-4636)
TTY: 888-232-6348
Website: www.
allianceforeatingdisorders.com
Email: cdcinfo@cdc.gov

girlshealth.gov
200 Independence Ave. S.W.
Rm. 712E
Washington, DC 20201
Toll-Free: 800-994-9662
Website: www.girlshealth.gov

***National Heart, Lung, and
Blood Institute (NHLBI)***
P.O. Box 30105
Bethesda, MD 20824-0105
Phone: 301-592-8573
TTY: 240-629-3255
Fax: 240-629-3246
Website: www.nhlbi.nih.gov
E-mail: nhlbiinfo@nhlbi.nih.gov

Information in this chapter was compiled from various sources deemed reliable.
All contact information was verified and updated in March 2016.

National Institute of Diabetes and Digestive and Kidney Diseases (NIDDK)
31 Center Dr., MSC 2560
Bldg. 31, Rm. 9A06
Bethesda, MD 20892-2560
Toll-Free: 888-693-NDEP
(888-693-6337)
Phone: 301-496-3583
TTY: 866-569-1162
Fax: 301-594-9358
Website: www.niddk.nih.gov
E-mail: niddkstepup@mail.nih.gov

National Institute of Mental Health (NIMH)
6001 Executive Blvd.
Rm. 8184 MSC 9663
Bethesda, MD 20892-9663
Toll-Free: 866-615-NIMH
(866-615-6464)
Phone: 301-443-4513
TTY: 301-443-8431
TTY Toll-Free: 866-415-8051
Fax: 301-443-4279
Website: www.nimh.nih.gov
E-mail: nimhinfo@nih.gov

National Institutes of Health (NIH)
9000 Rockville Pike
Bethesda, MD 20892
Toll-Free: 800-222-2225
Phone Number: 301-496-4000
TTY: 301-402-9612
Fax: 301-496-4000
Website: www.nih.gov
E-mail: NIHinfo@od.nih.gov

The National Institutes of Health Osteoporosis and Related Bone Diseases
National Resource Center
2 AMS Cir.
Bethesda, MD 20892-3676
Toll-Free: 877-22-NIAMS
(877-226-4267)
Phone: 301-495-4484
TTY: 301-565-2966
Fax: 301-718-6366
Website: www.niams.nih.gov
E-mail: NIHBoneInfo@mail.nih.gov

National Women's Health Information Center (NWHIC)
Toll-free: 800-994-9662
TDD: 888-220-5446
Website: www.womenshealth.gov
E-mail: womenshealth@hhs.gov

Office on Women's Health (OWH)
U.S. Department of Health and Human Services
200 Independence Ave. S.W.
Washington, DC,20201
Toll-Free: 800-994-9662
TTY: 888-220-5446
Website: www.womenshealth.gov
E-mail: womenshealth@hhs.gov

President's Council on Fitness, Sports & Nutrition
1101 Wootton Pkwy
Ste. 560
Rockville, MD 20852
Phone: 240-276-9567
Fax: 240-276-9860
Website: www.fitness.gov
E-mail: fitness@hhs.gov

United States Department of Agriculture (USDA)
1400 Independence Ave. S.W.
Washington, DC 20250
Toll-Free: 866-536-7593
Phone: 202-720-2791
Website: www.usda.gov
E-mail: Outreach@usda.gov

U.S. Department of Veterans Affairs (VA)
810 Vermont Ave. N.W.
Washington, DC 20420
Toll-Free: 800-273-TALK
(800-273-8255)
Website: www.va.gov
E-mail: vaoighotline@va.gov

U.S. Food and Drug Administration (FDA)
10903 New Hampshire Ave.
Silver Spring, MD 20993
Toll-Free: 888-INFO-FDA
(888-463-6332)
Website: www.fda.gov
E-mail: DRUGINFO@fda.hhs.gov

Weight-control Information Network (WIN)
1 WIN Way
Bethesda, MD 20892–3665
Toll-Free: 877-946-4627
Phone: 202-828–1025
Fax: 202-828-1028
Website: www.win.niddk.nih.gov
E-mail: win@info.niddk.nih.gov

Private Organizations

The Academy for Eating Disorders (AED)
12100 Sunset Hills Rd., Ste. 130
Reston, VA 20190
Toll-Free: 888-236-2427
Phone: 703-234-4079
Fax: 703-435-4390
Website: www.aedweb.org
E-mail: info@aedweb.org

The Alliance for Eating Disorders Awareness ("The Alliance")
1649 Forum Pl., Ste. 2
West Palm Beach, FL 33401
Toll-Free: 866-662-1235
Phone: 561-841-0900
Website: www.
allianceforeatingdisorders.com
E-mail: info@
allianceforeatingdisorders.com

American Dietetic Association
120 S. Riverside Plaza
Ste. 2000
Chicago, IL 60606-6995
Toll-Free: 800-877-1600
Phone: 312-899-0040
Website: www.eatright.org
E-mail: affiliate@eatright.org

Association For Size Diversity and Health (ASDAH)
P.O. Box 3093
Redwood City, CA 94064
Toll-Free: 877-576-1102
Website: www.
SizeDiversityandHealth.org
E-mail: contact@
sizediversityandhealth.org

The Binge Eating Disorder Association (BEDA)
637 Emerson Pl.
Severna Park, MD 21146
Toll-Free: 855-855-BEDA
(855-855-2332)
Phone: 410-741-3037
Website: bedaonline.com
E-mail: lizabeth@bedaonline.com.

Body Positive
P.O. Box 7801
Berkeley, CA 94707
Phone: 510-528-0101
Fax: 510-558-0979
Website: www.thebodypositive.org
E-mail: info@thebodypositive.org

The British Columbia Eating Disorders Association (BCEDA)
526 Michigan St.
Victoria 1S2
Canada
Phone: 250-383-2755
Website: webhome.idirect.com/~bceda
E-mail: bceda@direct.ca

Bulimia Anorexia Nervosa Association (BANA)
1500 Ouellette Ave.
Ste. 100
Windsor, ON N8X 1K7
Canada
Toll-Free: 855-969-5530
Phone: 519-969-2112
Fax: 519-969-0227
Website: www.bana.ca
E-mail: info@bana.ca

Bulimia Nervosa Resource Guide
5200 Butler Pike
Plymouth Meeting, PA 19462
Phone: 610-825-6000
Fax: 610-834-1275
Website: www.bulimiaguide.org
E-mail: dzenzel@ecri.org

Caring Online
Website: www.caringonline.com
E-mail: AmAnBu@aol.com

Casa Palmera
14750 El Camino Real
Del Mar, CA 92014
Toll-Free: 888-206-6814
Phone: 866-768-6719 or
858-481-4411
Website: www.casapalmera.com
E-mail: info@casapalmera.com

Center for Eating Disorders (CED)
111 N. First St.
Ste. 2
Ann Arbor, MI 48104
Phone: 734-668-8585
Fax: 734-668-2645
Website: www.center4ed.org
E-mail: info@center4ed.org

Diabulimia Helpline
Phone: 425-985-3635
Website: www.diabulimiahelpline.org
E-mail: info@diabulimiahelpline.org

*The Eating Disorder
Foundation*
1901 E. 20th Ave.
Denver, CO 80205
Phone: 303-322-3373
Fax: 303-322-3364
Website:
eatingdisorderfoundation.org
E-mail: info@
eatingdisorderfoundation.org

Eating Disorder Hope
8520 Golden Pheasant Ct.
Redmond, OR 97756
Toll-Free: 800-986-4160
Website: www.
eatingdisorderhope.com
E-mail: info@eatingdisorderhope.
com

*Eating Disorder Referral
and Information Center*
Website: www.edreferral.com

*Eating Disorder Support
Network of Alberta (EDSNA)*
Website: www.eatingdisorder
supportnetworkofalberta.com
E-mail: info@EDSNA.ca

Eating Disorders Coalition
720 7th St. N.W.
Ste. 300
Washington, DC 20001
Phone: 202-543-9570
Website: www.
eatingdisorderscoalition.org
E-mail: manager@
eatingdisorderscoalition.org

*Eating Disorders Foundation
of Canada (EDF)*
100 Collip Cir., Research Park,
Western University
Ste. 230A
London, ON N6G 4X8
Canada
Phone: 519-858-5111
Fax: 519-858-5086
Website: www.edfofcanada.com
E-mail: info@edfofcanada.com

*Eating Disorders Foundation
of Victoria*
Level 2, Collingwood Football
Club Community Centre, cnr
Lulie and Abbot St.
Abbotsford, VIC 3067
Australia
Phone: 1300-550-236
Website: www.eatingdisorders.
org.au
E-mail: webmaster@
eatingdisorders.org.au

*Eating Disorders Recovery
Center*
232 Vance Rd.
Ste. 206
St. Louis, MO 63088
Phone: 636-225-3700

*Families Empowered and
Supporting Treatment of
Eating Disorders (FEAST)*
P.O. Box 11608
Milwaukee, WI 53211
Toll-Free: 855-503-3278
Website: www.feast-ed.org
E-mail: info@feast-ed.org

Female Athlete Triad Coalition
Website: www.
femaleathletetriad.org
E-mail: president@
femaleathletetriad.org

Harris Center for Education and Advocacy in Eating Disorders
2 Longfellow Place
Ste. 200
Boston, MA 2114
Phone: 617-726-8470
Website: www2.massgeneral.org/
harriscenter/index.asp

Hopewell
Heartwood House 404 McArthur
Ave Ottawa, ON K1K 1G8
Canada
Phone: 613-241-3428
Website: www.hopewell.ca
E-mail: info@hopewell.ca

The Joy Project
PO Box 16488
St Paul, MN 55116
Phone: 310-825-9822
Website: joyproject.org
E-mail: volunteercoordinator@
joyproject.org

KidsHealth
The Nemours Foundation
1600 Rockland Rd.
Wilmington, DE 19803
Phone: 302-651-4046
Website: www.kidshealth.org
E-mail: info@KidsHealth.org

The Krevoy Institute For Eating Disorders
9454 Wilshire Blvd.
Beverly Hills, CA 90212
Phone: 310-550-1776
Website: www.drkrevoy.com
E-mail: info@drkrevoy.com

The Kyla Fox Centre
174 Bedford Rd.
Toronto, ON M5R 2K9
Canada
Phone: 416-518-0440
Fax: 888-398-5952
Website: kylafoxcentre.com

Looking Glass Foundation
4116 Angus Dr.
Vancouver, BC V6J 4H9
Canada
Toll-Free: 888-980-5874
Phone: 604-314-0548
Fax: 604-829-2586
Website: www.lookingglassbc.
com
E-mail: info@lookingglassbc.com

Monte Nindo & Affiliates
Toll-Free: 888-228-1253
Phone: 310-457-9958
TTY: 310-457-8442
Website: www.montenido.com
E-mail: info@montenido.com

Multi-Service Eating Disorders Association, Inc. (MEDA)
288 Walnut St.
Ste. 130
Newton, MA 02460
Phone: 617-558-1881
Website: www.medainc.org
E-mail: info@medainc.org

National Association of Anorexia Nervosa and Associated Disorders (ANAD)
750 E Diehl Rd.
Ste. 127
Naperville, IL 60563
Phone: 630-577-1330
Website: www.anad.org
E-mail: anadhelp@anad.org

The National Association for Males with Eating Disorders (NAMED)
164 Palm Dr.
Ste. 2
Naples, FL 34112
Website: namedinc.org
E-mail: info@findacurepanel.com

National Center for Overcoming Overeating
Website: www.overcoming
overeating.com
E-mail: webmaster@
overcomingovereating.com

The National Eating Disorder Information Centre (NEDIC)
ES 7-421, 200 Elizabeth St.
Toronto, ON M5G 2C4
Canada
Toll-Free: 866-NEDIC-20
(866-633-4220)
Phone: 416-340-4156
Fax: 416-340-4736
Website: nedic.ca
E-mail: nedic@uhn.ca

National Eating Disorders Association (NEDA)
165 W. 46th St.
Ste. 402
New York, NY 10036
Toll-Free: 800-931-2237
Phone: 212-575-6200
Fax: 212-575-1650
Website: www.
nationaleatingdisorders.org
E-mail: info@
NationalEatingDisorders.org

National Initiative for Eating Disorders (NIED)
Phone: 647-347-2393
Website: nied.ca
E-mail: info@nied.ca

New Directions Eating Disorders Center
4419 Van Nuys Blvd.
Ste. 410
Sherman Oaks, CA 91403
Phone: 818-377-4442
Website:
newdirectionseatingdisorders.
com
Email: info@
newdirectionseatingdisorders.
com

Oklahoma Eating Disorders Association (OEDA)
6003 N. Robinson Ave.
Ste. 112
OKC, OK 73118
Phone: 405-418-4448

Ophelia's Place
407 Tulip St.
Liverpool, NY 13078
Phone: 315-451-5544
Website: www.opheliasplace.org
E-mail: director@opheliasplace.
org

Overeaters Anonymous
P.O. Box 44020
Rio Rancho, NM 87174-4020
Phone: 505-891-2664
Fax: 505-891-4320
Website: www.oa.org
E-mail: conventioninfo@oa.org

Project Heal
38-18 West Dr.
Douglaston, NY 11363
Phone: 718 709 7787
Website: theprojectheal.org
Email: Recoveryis@
theprojectheal.org

Rader Programs
Toll-Free: 877-632-4293
Website: www.raderprograms.
com

**The Renfrew Center
Foundation**
475 Spring Ln.
Philadelphia, PA 19128
Toll-Free: 800-RENFREW
(800-736-3739)
Fax: 215-482-2695
Website: renfrewcenter.com
Email: conorati@renfrewcenter.
com

Sheena's Place
87 Spadina Rd.
Toronto, ON M5R 2T1
Canada
Phone: 416-927-8900
Fax: 416-927-8844
Website: sheenasplace.org
E-mail: info@sheenasplace.org

**The Something Fishy
Website on Eating Disorders**
P.O. Box 837
Holbrook, NY 11741
Toll-Free: 866-418-1207
Website: www.something-fishy.
org
E-mail: admin@something-fishy.
org

**Upstate New York Eating
Disorder Service**
1003 Walnut St.
Elmira, NY 14901
Toll-Free: 877-765-7866
Phone: 607-732-5646
Fax: 607-732-0373
Website: unyed.com
E-mail: enc1003@aol.com

Valenta Inc.
9479 Haven Ave.
Rancho Cucamonga, CA 91730
Phone: 909-771-8023
Website: www.valentaonline.com

We Are Diabetes (WAD)
P.O. Box 16263
Minneapolis, MN 55416
Website: www.wearediabetes.org
E-mail: contact@wearediabetes.
org

Index

Index